Origins and development of authoritarian and single-party states

Michael Lynch

HODDER
EDUCATION
AN HACHETTE UK COMPANY

For Elizabeth Suzanne Clare

The material in this title has been developed independently of the International Baccalaureate®, which in no way endorses it.

The Publishers would like to thank the following for permission to reproduce copyright material:

Photo credits
p.33 Bettmann/Corbis; **p.41** © David King Collection; **p.48** *t* © Fotosearch/Getty Images, *b* © Michael Nicholson/Corbis; **p.89** © Photos 12/Alamy; **p.93** © 2000 Topham Picturepoint/TopFoto; **p.97** © Mary Evans Picture Library/Weimar Archive; **p.112** © Cody Images; **p.123** © Bettmann/Corbis; **p.182** © 2003 Topham Picturepoint/TopFoto; **p.210** © OFF/AFP/Getty Images; **p.224** © Picture Alliance/Photoshot; **p.245** © AP/Press Association Images; **p.257** Poster courtesy of the Museum für Gestaltung Zürich, Plakatsammlung, © ZHdK; **p.272** © AP/Press Association Images; **p.295** © TopFoto; **p.312** © Roger-Viollet/TopFoto.

Acknowledgements
Guy Arnold: from *Africa: A Modern History* (Atlantic Books, 2005); **IndexMundi**: Tables: Infant mortality rates in different countries and regions; Life expectancy in different countries and regions; Literacy rates in different countries and regions, from www.indexmundi.com; **Guido Indij**: 'The Twenty Truths', quoted in *Perón Meidante*, translated by Mitchell Abidor (La Manca Editora, 2006); **Robert Service**: from *Stalin: A Biography* (Macmillan, 2004); World Bank: Table showing World Development Indicators for Tanzania, from *Bank/Tanzania Relations*, 1990. PFPs, IMF RED (1999).

Every effort has been made to trace all copyright holders, but if any have been inadvertently overlooked the Publishers will be pleased to make the necessary arrangements at the first opportunity.

Although every effort has been made to ensure that website addresses are correct at time of going to press, Hodder Education cannot be held responsible for the content of any website mentioned in this book. It is sometimes possible to find a relocated web page by typing in the address of the home page for a website in the URL window of your browser.

Hachette UK's policy is to use papers that are natural, renewable and recyclable products and made from wood grown in sustainable forests. The logging and manufacturing processes are expected to conform to the environmental regulations of the country of origin.

Orders: please contact Bookpoint Ltd, 130 Milton Park, Abingdon, Oxon OX14 4SB. Telephone: +44 (0)1235 827720. Fax: +44 (0)1235 400454. Lines are open 9.00a.m.–5.00p.m., Monday to Saturday, with a 24-hour message answering service. Visit our website at www.hoddereducation.co.uk

© Michael Lynch 2013

First published in 2013 by
Hodder Education,
An Hachette UK Company
338 Euston Road
London NW1 3BH

Impression number	10 9 8 7 6 5 4 3 2 1
Year	2017 2016 2015 2014 2013

Cover photo: poster depicting Joseph Stalin (1879–1953) and Mao Tse-tung (1893–1976) shaking hands, *c.*1950 (colour litho), Russian School, (20th century)/Bibliotheque Nationale, Paris, France/Archives Charmet/The Bridgeman Art Library
Illustrations by Barking Dog Art
Typeset in 10/13pt Palatino and produced by Integra Software Services Pvt. Ltd., Pondicherry, India
Printed in Italy

A catalogue record for this title is available from the British Library

ISBN 978 14441 56447

Contents

Dedication

Keith Randell (1943–2002)

The original *Access to History* series was conceived and developed by Keith, who created a series to 'cater for students as they are, not as we might wish them to be'. He leaves a living legacy of a series that for over 20 years has provided a trusted, stimulating and well-loved accompaniment to post-16 study. Our aim with these new editions for the IB is to continue to offer students the best possible support for their studies.

Introduction

This book has been written to support your study of Topic 3: Origins and development of authoritarian and single-party states of the IB History Diploma Route 2.

This introduction gives you an overview of:

✪ the content you could study for Topic 3: Origins and development of authoritarian and single-party states and how you will be assessed for Paper 2

✪ the different features of this book and how these will aid your learning.

What you will study

The twentieth century has seen the rise and rule of various authoritarian, single-party states. This book covers the regimes of Stalin in the Soviet Union, Hitler in Germany, Mao in the People's Republic of China, Nasser in Egypt, Castro in Cuba, Perón in Argentina and Nyerere in Tanzania.

You will need to study regimes from at least two of these different regions:

- Africa
- Asia and Oceania
- Americas
- Europe and the Middle East.

How you will be assessed

Paper 2

The IB History Diploma can be studied either to Standard or Higher Level. It has three papers in total: Papers 1 and 2 for Standard Level and a further Paper 3 for Higher Level. It also has an internal assessment which all students must do.

- For Paper 1 you need to answer four source-based questions on a prescribed subject. This counts for 20 per cent of your overall marks at Higher Level, or 30 per cent of your overall marks at Standard Level.
- For Paper 2 you need to answer two essay questions on two different topics. This counts for 25 per cent of your overall marks at Higher Level, or 45 per cent of your overall marks at Standard Level.
- For Paper 3 you need to answer three essay questions on two or three sections. This counts for 35 per cent of your overall marks at Higher Level.

For the Internal Assessment you need to carry out a historical investigation. This counts for 20 per cent of your overall marks at Higher Level, or 25 per cent of your overall marks at Standard Level.

Topic 3: Origins and development of authoritarian and single-party states is assessed through Paper 2. There are five topics on Paper 2 and you will answer two questions in total, one each from a different topic. Questions for Topic 3 may ask you to discuss the rise and rule of a specific leader of an authoritarian regime, the role of education in maintaining a leader or various leaders in power, to compare and contrast two leaders each from the same governing philosophy or perhaps from two different regions, to assess the importance of an authoritarian regime on women, and so forth.

Examination questions

You should answer only one question out of the six questions you will find on Topic 3: Origins and development of authoritarian and single-party states. Your answer will take the form of an essay. These questions are not in any particular order. There will be questions that your teacher has prepared you to answer, but others that you will not be able to address. This is normal and expected. Topic 3 has many authoritarian regimes that may be studied and your teacher has selected various states, covering different regions. This book prepares you to answer questions on Stalin of the Soviet Union, Hitler of Germany, Mao of the People's Republic of China, Nasser of Egypt, Castro of Cuba, Perón of Argentina and Nyerere of Tanzania.

There are different types of questions, as described below.

Questions about a single-party state leader

Your examination will contain questions regarding a single leader. This leader may be named, or the question may allow you to choose one to address.

Example 1
Assess the significance of Stalin's purges in maintaining his authority in the Soviet Union.

Example 2
How did one Left-wing single-party state leader affect education in his country?

Example 3
For what reasons, and with what results, did Mao's policies change the lives of women in the People's Republic of China?

Example 4
Discuss the importance of the military during Perón's rule in Argentina.

Questions about more than one authoritarian leader

Your examination will contain questions regarding more than one leader. Some questions will name the two leaders to be covered, while others allow you to choose the leaders you wish to use to address the question.

Example 1
To what extent did both Stalin and Mao successfully employ nationalism in maintaining their authority in their respective countries?

Example 2
Compare and contrast the economic policies of two leaders of different single-party states, each from a different region.

Example 3
Discuss the importance of the military for both Mao and Nasser.

Example 4
Assess the importance of opposition for two leaders of single-party states.

The appearance of the examination paper

Cover
The cover of the examination paper states the date of the examination and the length of time you have to complete it: 1 hour and 30 minutes. Please note that there are two routes in history. Make sure your paper says Route 2 on it. Instructions are limited and simply state that you:

- should not open it until told to do so
- should answer only two questions, each from a different topic
- should make sure that you understand what the paper means by regions. A map indicates the regions for you.

Topics
Once you are allowed to open your examination paper, you will note that there are five topics, each numbered and titled. Topic 3 obviously comes third and six questions are below this title. Again, the questions are in no particular order, so a question on a more recent authoritarian leader may precede that of a much earlier one.

Questions
You are required to answer only one of the six questions. Make sure you have read through all the questions before starting, selecting the question you know the most about and feel the most comfortable with. It is important to understand that you need to answer the question fully in an essay format. We will discuss more about answering questions at the end of each chapter.

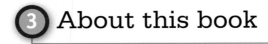 About this book

Coverage of course content
This book addresses the key areas listed in the IB History Guide for Route 2: Twentieth-century world history Topic 3: Origins and development of authoritarian and single-party states. It has chapters on:

- Stalin's USSR
- Hitler's Nazi Germany

- Mao's China
- Nasser's Egypt
- Castro's Cuba
- Perón's Argentina
- Nyerere's Tanzania.

These chapters start with an introduction outlining the key questions they address. They are then divided into a series of sections and topics covering the course content. Throughout the chapters you will find the following features to aid your study of the course content.

Key and leading questions

Each section heading in the chapter has a related key question which gives a focus to your reading and understanding of the section. These are also listed in the chapter introduction. You should be able to answer the questions after completing the relevant section.

Topics within the sections have leading questions which are designed to help you focus on the key points within a topic and give you more practice in answering questions.

Key terms

Key terms are the important terms you need to know to gain an understanding of the period. These are emboldened in the text and are defined in the margin the first time they appear in a chapter. They also appear in the glossary at the end of the book.

Sources

Throughout the book are several written and visual sources. Historical sources are important in understanding more fully why specific decisions were taken or on what contemporary writers and politicians based their actions. The sources are accompanied by questions to help you understand them better and which are similar to questions found on Paper 1 examinations.

Key debates

Historians often disagree on historical events and this historical debate is referred to as historiography. Knowledge of historiography is helpful in reaching the upper mark bands when you take your IB History examinations. There are a number of debates throughout the book to develop your understanding of historiography, some of which quote important historians that you may wish to refer to in your examination.

Theory of Knowledge (TOK) questions

It is important to understand that there are strong links between IB History and Theory of Knowledge (TOK) issues. Chapters 2–9 have Theory of Knowledge questions that make this link.

Summary diagrams

At the end of most sections is a summary diagram which gives a visual summary of the content of the section. It is intended as an aid for revision.

Chapter summary

At the end of each of the topic chapters is a short summary of the content of that chapter. This is intended to help you revise and consolidate your knowledge and understanding of the content.

Skills development

At the end of each chapter, there are examination-style questions to practice and suggestions for activities to extend your learning. These activities will include ideas for debate, essays, displays and research.

Chapter 10 gives guidance on how to answer different question types, accompanied by a sample answer and commentary designed to help you focus on specific details.

End of the book

The book concludes with the following sections.

Glossary

All key terms in the book are defined in the glossary.

Further reading

This contains a list of books and websites which may help you with further independent research and presentations. It may also be helpful when further information is required for internal assessments and extended essays in history. You may wish to share the contents of this section with your school or local librarian.

Internal assessment

All IB History diploma students are required to write a historical investigation which is internally assessed. The investigation is an opportunity for you to dig more deeply into a subject that interests you. This gives you a list of possible areas for research.

CHAPTER 1

Authoritarian and single-party states

Throughout the text a number of political terms are frequently used in analysing the character of the regimes and states under consideration. This opening chapter defines those terms and places them in their historical context in relation to the development of the authoritarian and totalitarian regimes of the twentieth century.

You need to consider the following questions throughout this chapter:

✪ What shades of meaning do political terms have?

✪ What factors explain the development of authoritarian regimes in the twentieth century?

1 Political terms

▶ *Key question: What shades of meaning do political terms have?*

It is notoriously difficult to attach a precise meaning to political terms. The context in which they are used and the movements to which they are ascribed often differ considerably. The definitions that follow, therefore, are not accurate in any absolute sense. However, they do offer a guide to general meaning and common usage.

> **What distinctions can be drawn between Left and Right?**

Left and Right

The terms Right and Left are not exact political descriptions, but are useful, broad distinctions between movements characterized by conservative or **reactionary** attitudes (Right) and those whose predominant features include a desire for **radical** or revolutionary change (Left). Both 'wings' believe in the power of the central government as the main agency of state action. As political reference points, the terms Left and Right had their origin in the French Revolution of the late eighteenth century when, in the **Estates-General**, revolutionaries sat on the left side of the chamber and conservatives on the right. This helped establish the idea of politics as a Left–Right spectrum.

Despite the lack of exact definition, a number of key differences between Left and Right can be identified (see table on page 8).

 **KEY TERM**

Reactionary Fiercely resistant to change.

Radical Change at the very roots.

Estates-General A French Assembly made up of 'the three orders' – aristocracy, clergy and commons – which gathered in 1789. The assertion by the commons that they alone were the sovereign authority was a critical stage in the development of the French Revolution.

Left typical attitudes	Right typical attitudes
Progressive outlook	Reactionary outlook
Essentially optimistic view of human nature	Essentially pessimistic view of human nature
Belief in equality as a social imperative	Belief that equality is an impossible goal and its pursuit socially disruptive
Rejection of the past	Respect for the past
Belief in the future	Lack of confidence about the future
Belief that history is predetermined	Belief that history is contingent upon the play of events
Sense of alienation from existing society	Sense that existing society represents accumulated, lasting values
Belief that change is essential	Belief that change is destructive
Belief in the perfectibility of society through revolution	Belief that human beings are incapable of social perfectibility
Inspired by ideology	Suspicious of ideology
Lack of realism	Strong sense of realism
Socialist in outlook	Conservative in outlook
Holding a conviction that compromise betrays weakness	Ready to compromise to preserve social stability

Limitations to categorization

One could, of course, challenge such a listing, pointing out, for example, that the regimes of Left and Right have often shared attitudes, and that, in their extreme forms, their methods have been indistinguishable. Interestingly, the extreme Right and Left movements of the twentieth century are now commonly seen by modern scholars as having many overlapping features. Indeed, the more extreme the Right and Left were, the more they resembled each other. This theme is taken up in later chapters.

How imprecise the division between Left and Right is evident in the use of such a key term as **socialism**. Usually thought of as descriptive of Left-wing movements, it has to be remembered that **Nazism**, commonly regarded as the most extreme of Right-wing regimes, was itself a socialist movement. Indeed, the term Nazism is an abbreviation derived from National *Socialism*. Similarly, **nationalism**, often regarded as a characteristic of Right-wing movements, is a feature of all the regimes that you will study. In supposedly Left-wing movements, such as those in the People's Republic of China and the **USSR**, intense nationalism was as much a driving force as it was in Germany in the era of Nazism. Indeed, Stalin and Mao used socialism and **communism** as mechanisms for achieving nationalistic ends.

It is also very unlikely that committed members of the political Left and Right would accept that all, if any, of the tabled categories (see above) applied to

them. Furthermore, it should be acknowledged that many scholars regard the traditional way of referring to the Left and the Right as a dated practice that causes more problems than it solves, their argument being that the labels tend to obscure rather than clarify the movements to which they are ascribed. The terms create an assumption that what is being described falls into one of a set of opposing categories, whereas the emphasis in modern research is on the similarities between movements such as **fascism** and communism.

Yet, notwithstanding these reservations and accepting that the categories do not pretend to be precise, the list offers a workable set of broad definitions and can be used in the following chapters as a check list when examining the features of the regimes under study.

Democracy

In ideal terms, democracy is a representative system in which ultimate authority lies not with the government but with the governed, who express their judgement in regular free elections. Democracy was given its modern definition in Abraham Lincoln's timeless words: 'government of the people, by the people, and for the people'. The paradox is that nearly all regimes across the extremes of Left and Right have described themselves as democratic, asserting that their form of government truly represented the will of the people.

Abraham Lincoln

US President at the time of the American Civil War (1861–65). His words were part of his celebrated address at Gettysburg in which he paid tribute to the honoured dead of both sides, Union and Confederacy, who had fallen in a great battle there.

Nationalism

Nationalism is an intense belief that the nation-state is the highest form of political organization and that it is as members of the nation that individuals derive their true identity and worth. It was the dynamic force of the nineteenth and twentieth centuries, but it seldom expressed itself in democratic forms. The achievement of statehood by Germany and Italy in the second half of the nineteenth century had been a triumph not of democracy, but of authoritarian, centralized power. Otto von Bismarck, one of the founders of the modern German state in 1871, declared in 1862: 'It is not through speeches and majority decisions that the great questions of the day are decided. It is by iron and blood.'

Otto von Bismarck

As President of Prussia, the strongest of the separate German states, Bismarck conducted a series of aggressive wars which, backed by adroit diplomacy, led to the creation of the state of Germany in 1871.

🔑 KEY TERM

Fascism The ultra-nationalist movement that operated in Italy under Mussolini between 1922 and 1943. The term came generally to be used to describe extreme Right-wing regimes and ideas.

← **What are the main characteristics of democracy?**

← **What are the main characteristics of nationalism?**

Liberalism

What are the main characteristics of liberalism?

Liberalism, a product of the **Enlightenment**, was an influential movement that developed in many countries in Europe in the nineteenth century. It argued for greater freedom of the individual from government control. As a term, it is frequently linked to **liberal-democracy**. Nationalist movements often adopted liberal arguments in support of their claims. However, many of the authoritarian states analysed in this book were a rejection of liberalism. The extreme wings of both the Left and Right condemned liberal-democracy as effete and inefficient. The Left tended to stress economic class as the principal dynamic that shaped history, while the Right regarded the nation as the agency through which society achieved its ultimate destiny. In both cases, the individual was regarded as secondary to the group.

Authoritarianism

What are the main characteristics of authoritarianism?

Authoritarianism refers to a governmental system in a given country or region in which the levers of power are exclusively in the hands of a group or an individual whose decisions are not subject to control from below. Although an authoritarian government is not directly answerable to its people, this does not necessarily mean it is unpopular; its authoritarian measures may be approved of by the population, albeit the government does not depend on such approval.

Totalitarianism

What are the main characteristics of totalitarianism?

Totalitarianism is an extension and intensifying of authoritarianism. A totalitarian system is necessarily authoritarian, but it goes much further. What distinguishes a system as totalitarian is how it uses its monopoly of power.

- In a totalitarian state, individuals are subordinate to the state and personal autonomy is not tolerated.
- Such a regime seeks to control not simply political life, but society in all its features: institutional, economic, moral and personal.
- Its power is exercised pervasively, affecting every person.
- The lives of the population, collectively and as individuals, are subject to the direction of the state which demands complete obedience from its citizens on pain of the direst punishments for those who do not conform.
- Totalitarian systems base their right to absolute control by reference to a basic ideology, which both explains why they hold power and justifies its exercise.
- In their extreme forms, totalitarian systems of both Left and Right regard history as predetermined. Their belief is that societies develop in accordance with iron laws of progress that follow a set pattern to an unavoidable conclusion.

🔑 KEY TERM

Enlightenment A flowering in the eighteenth century of new political, philosophical and social ideas about the nature of society and the individual. Key elements were the promotion of the rights of the individual and emphasis on the power of applied reason to solve society's problems.

Liberal-democracy Descriptive of states which function according to the principles of individual freedom and equality and operate systems under which governments can be removed at elections.

Characteristics of the totalitarian state

The following list is neither a definitive nor an exclusive one, but it does indicate some of the main features evident in most totalitarian regimes:

1 Only one political party is allowed to exist.
2 Power is exercised by the party leader who controls the party.
3 The leader's authority is underpinned by a dominant ideology.
4 The leader claims that his authority derives from the immutable laws of historical development.
5 The state maintains social and political control through terror.
6 The state crushes opposition through control of the media.
7 The state exercises central control of the economy.
8 The regime uses the armed forces and law enforcement bodies to operate a police state.
9 The state uses censorship and propaganda to promote the idea of a faultless leader.
10 Religion is either outlawed and persecuted as an affront to state ideology or exploited as another means of controlling the people.
11 Independent institutions, such as religious organizations and trade unions, are suppressed.
12 The legal system is politicized so that it becomes an instrument of state control.
13 The state seeks to reshape culture so that it conforms to state ideology.
14 Internal opponents are identified and persecuted.
15 An aggressive stance is adopted towards external ideological enemies.

In the two outstanding examples of European totalitarianism, Soviet communism and Nazism, each was inspired by a passionate commitment to an ideology. In the Soviet case, it was Stalin's class concepts that motivated his policies. He saw his prime purpose to be the destruction of all those he deemed to be the class enemies of the Soviet state. In the German case, it was Hitler's notion of race that shaped his policies; he saw it as his destiny to rid Germany of all those he deemed to be racial inferiors.

Problems in analysis

Cultural and linguistic

In analysing authoritarian and single-party systems, what has to be allowed for is the wide difference between cultures. This is particularly important where concepts are concerned. Some words do not easily translate and political concepts sometimes shift their meaning or emphasis. An obvious example is 'democracy'. In a Western liberal sense the word relates to the rights of the individual. In a Russian or Chinese context it refers to the rights of the group. That was why Mao and Stalin could use the word democracy unblushingly to describe the unchallengeable control of their single-party systems. In Western terms a single-party democracy is a contradiction in terms whereas for Julius Nyerere, the Tanzanian leader, the single-party system was the best means of achieving democracy (see pages 295–296).

> **What difficulties may arise when analysing differing authoritarian regimes?**

Preconceptions

A major problem for liberal historians, particularly those in the West, is that they tend to see democracy as the basic form of responsible representative government. Any system that does not accord with that notion is regarded as falling short of an ideal. However, thinkers and leaders from other cultures dismiss this as an example of Western presumption. Western values are not definitive and should not, therefore, be regarded as prescriptive. As Nyerere was concerned to point out, democracy was not an end but a means and there was no absolute value attaching to it. Context and practical considerations, not an abstract notion, should determine what the ideal system was for a particular region. Nyerere, indeed, claimed that the two-party system as it operated in Britain and other Western countries was a barrier to, not a guarantee of, genuinely representative government.

Although all the systems in this book claimed to be revolutionary, not all were so in practice, or in effect. Later chapters will show that a number of them looked back as much as forward:

- Nazism was essentially an appeal to the past, an attempt to restore the traditional *volkisch* values and virtues of German history (see Chapter 3).
- Nyerere declared that the socialism he was adopting as the way forward for the new Tanzanian nation was drawn directly from the collective values of Africa's tribal past (see Chapter 9).
- Castro's personalized form of communism was an expression of his desire to rid Cuba of its colonial inheritance and return his people to a pre-colonial form of national purity (see Chapter 7).
- Nasser worked under the banner of socialism, but his primary aim was to assert the independence of Egypt and lead his nation in a resurgent Arab and African world (see Chapter 6).
- Péron took a similar line in Argentina. His wish was to see his country modernize by basing its growth on the traditional virtues and skills of the Argentinian people (see Chapter 8).

The development of authoritarianism and totalitarianism

▶ *Key question: What factors explain the development of authoritarian regimes in the twentieth century?*

This section explains the historical context in which the authoritarian and totalitarian regimes of the twentieth century developed.

The impact of the First World War, 1914–18

Historians suggest that it was no accident that the twentieth century saw a spate of authoritarian and totalitarian regimes. The phenomenon was in large part a reaction to the destructive impact of the **First World War** that ended in 1918. Prior to that war, liberalism, a political movement which contained a central belief in human progress, had made considerable strides in Europe. There was a common conviction that the improvement in social conditions and the spread of education, which had followed the recognition by European governments of the need to tackle physical and intellectual deprivation, heralded a time of improvement for the world's peoples. The 1914–18 conflict shattered such dreams. In the face of the appalling devastation of the war, liberals found it difficult to sustain their concept of ordered human progress. For some persuasive radical thinkers, it was a short step from this to a conviction that discipline and control from above were more likely to create order and national well-being than was cumbersome democracy.

Adding weight to this view was the plentiful evidence of the benefits of state authority. Every nation in the First World War had undergone a large and rapid extension of centralized control over politics, society and the economy. It was arguable that without this centralization, no European nation would have survived. The lessons for national regeneration post-war were obvious. In times of crisis, democratic procedures were too inefficient to meet the needs of the state.

Significant groups, who were to become influential, concluded that social and political ideals were impossible to achieve by moderate, evolutionary means. Progress did not occur spontaneously, ran the argument; it had to be imposed. Strong governments had to be prepared to make the sweeping, even violent, changes that were needed.

Such views were particularly strongly held among certain sections in the relatively new states of Germany and Italy where democratic traditions were weak or non-existent. Scorning what they regarded as the ineffectual methods of democracy, certain groups of nationalists in those countries

What was the effect of the First World War in the development of authoritarian regimes?

🔑 **KEY TERM**

First World War (1914–18) Fought mainly between the Central Powers (Germany and Austria–Hungary) and the Entente Powers (France, Britain and Russia).

How did the economic situation in the inter-war years contribute to the development of authoritarian regimes?

developed an extreme form of anti-democratic politics, believing that only by such means could their nation achieve its destiny. Nowhere was this more evident than in Germany where a significant number of the population had a searing sense of bitterness at their defeat in the First World War in 1918. It was such bitterness that the National Socialists, or Nazis, relied upon, directing their attack at the German government, which, they asserted, had cravenly accepted a humiliating, dictated peace.

The triumph of democracy?

What sometimes confuses the analysis is that the First World War was still regarded by some as a triumph of democracy since this is what the victorious **Allies** claimed they represented. But that was a late development. At the start of the war in 1914, democracy had not been one of the Allies' declared aims; their only certain objective had been to defeat the enemy, the **Central Powers**. Moreover, the idea of one of the Allies, **Tsarist Russia**, as a champion of democracy defied common sense. It is true that as the war dragged on Britain and France claimed to be fighting for civilized values against German decadence, but what eventually gave the Allies their democratic image was the entry of the USA into the war in 1917 with the express purpose, as stated by its President Woodrow Wilson, 'to make the world safe for democracy'. It was this that enabled the Allies to claim retrospectively that that had been their purpose all along.

Self-determination

The peace settlement that followed the military collapse of the Central Powers was supposedly based on the principle of **self-determination**. Yet, powerful though self-determination was as an idea, it did not always imply democracy since it was applied in a very selective way. Although it was meant to recognize legitimate national aspirations, the principle was not extended to the defeated nations. Indeed, it was used as a justification for dismembering the German, Austro-Hungarian and Ottoman Empires and creating new states out of the remnants, a process that left Germany, and other parts of Europe, with a deep sense of grievance. Self-determination was also regarded with grave suspicion by the **imperial powers** that survived the war, Britain and France: they saw the principle as a threat to their continued hold over their colonies.

The impact of economic crises

Anti-democratic arguments might have had less influence had there been a general recovery from the economic effects of the First World War, but, apart from occasional, short-lived economic booms in the 1920s, the post-war trend was unremittingly grim, reaching its nadir in the **Great Depression** of the 1930s. In the atmosphere of despair and recrimination that the economic hardships created, fragile democratic structures collapsed. Nor should it be thought that the dictatorships of the period were always imposed on an unwilling people. The success of Italian fascism starting in the 1920s and

German Nazism in the 1930s in taking over the state was related to the genuine popularity of their regimes. The conversion of the middle classes, the traditional supporters of **constitutionalism**, to the support of the extreme Right was a clear sign that those seeking order and security no longer believed that these could be guaranteed by the processes of democracy.

Inter-war dictatorships

Between 1919 and 1939, when the **Second World War** began in Europe, many states came under the control of regimes which abandoned any pretensions to liberal-democracy. Russia (the Soviet Union after 1922), Italy, Turkey, Germany, Spain and Portugal, as well as many central and eastern European states, adopted dictatorships or became increasingly authoritarian and placed crippling limits on democratic institutions.

- In Russia, the **Bolshevik** (Communist) Party, led by Vladimir Lenin, had seized power in 1917 and imposed what it called the dictatorship of the **proletariat** (see page 18).
- In Italy, Benito Mussolini led his **Fascist** Party to power in 1922 and ruled as dictator until being overthrown in 1943.
- In Turkey, Mustafa Kemal Atatürk (1881–1938), although intent on avoiding the extremes of fascism and communism, attempted to turn his country into a modern **secular state** and resorted to increasingly dictatorial methods of control to do so.
- In Germany, Adolf Hitler's National Socialist German Workers' Party came to power in 1933.
- In Spain, Francisco Franco, having led his ultra-nationalist Falangist Party to victory in a civil war that ended in 1939, ruled as a Right-wing dictator until his death in 1975.
- In Portugal, António Salazar, as prime minister and then president, led his New State Party in a Right-wing dictatorship from 1932 to 1974.

Even where democracy appeared to operate, for example in some western European nations, it was arguable that appearance belied reality. That, indeed, was the charge that Lenin made. He defined liberal-democracy as a charade used by the propertied classes, who held power in such countries as Britain and France, to justify and perpetuate their rule over the people. He dismissed the supposedly free elections in those countries as shams which left the **bourgeois** power structure untouched.

Outside Europe during the same period, it was a very similar story of growing authoritarianism.

- The tendency towards dictatorship was clearly evident in Central and South America whose constitutional traditions were even weaker than in Europe.
- The areas of Africa sufficiently free of colonial control to shape their own systems exhibited a similar trend. Tribal traditions and cultures were essentially authoritarian.

Which countries became dictatorships in the inter-war years?

🔑 KEY TERM

Constitutionalism The belief that ordered progress is best achieved by keeping to established laws and precedents.

Second World War, 1939–45 Fought between the Allies (principally Britain, China, USSR and the USA) and the Axis powers (principally Germany, Italy and Japan).

Bolshevik The dominant branch of Russian communism, led by V.I. Lenin, which claimed to be the true interpreter of Marxism and which took power in Russia in the October Revolution of 1917.

Proletariat The revolutionary working class destined, in Marxist revolutionary theory, to achieve ultimate triumph in the class war.

Fascist In strict terms, the word applies specifically to Italy's ultra-nationalist Fascist Party whose symbol was a bundle of rods (*fasces* in Latin), representing power and authority, but the term became used generally to describe Right-wing regimes of the twentieth century.

- Imperialist Japan developed along authoritarian lines matching those of fascist Europe. **Emperor Hirohito** came under the controlling influence of an aggressive war party intent on shaping Japan into a military power capable of colonizing Asia by force.
- In China, the Guomindang (**GMD**) government was democratic in theory, but authoritarian in practice. **Sun Yatsen** declared 'On no account must we give more liberty to the individual. Let us secure liberty instead for the nation.' Under his successor Chiang Kai-shek, the Guomindang government became markedly authoritarian.
- There were even critics in the USA who argued that Roosevelt's **New Deal** was undemocratic since the state-directed methods it used smacked of either socialism or fascism.

The impact of the Second World War, 1939–45

At the end of the Second World War, there was an understandable sympathy for the idea of the **collective state**. It had been through collective, even regimented, effort that the Allies had emerged victorious. In response to the national crisis that war brought, many countries resorted to authoritarian methods. Indeed, even in the supposedly liberal democracies, some form of authoritarianism had been the norm for all the states involved in the Second World War. Britain had introduced restrictions such as internment and **DORA**. The USA had also interned those of its citizens, such as Japanese-Americans, whom it regarded as a potential threat to the war effort. The great majority of the population accepted these restrictions as the price to be paid for national security and perhaps survival. These were not totalitarian states, since the measures were meant to be temporary, not permanent. Popular support is not required for a state to be authoritarian since central government can impose itself on the popular will, but it is possible for a state to be popular and authoritarian.

The acceptance of authoritarianism extended in some instances into the acceptance of totalitarianism. It was evident that one of the Allies, Stalin's USSR, did not conform to liberal-democratic standards, but such was the desire of the other Allies to win the war that this was ignored. The prodigious effort made by the Soviet people in defeating Germany was so impressive that many admirers in the Western countries concluded that without the totalitarian methods used by Stalin to direct the war effort, the USSR would have been defeated.

The Second World War also had a pronounced influence outside Europe in promoting centralized control:

- North Korea, freed from Japan's control in 1945, adopted a particularly extreme form of communism under its leader Kim Il-Sung.
- In China, in 1949, Mao Zedong and the Chinese Communist Party defeated their Nationalist (Guomindang) opponents and began to create a communist People's Republic of China under his leadership.

- Although the colonial powers in south-east Asia, principally France, Britain and the Netherlands, had eventually won the war against Japan, the struggle had exposed their military weakness and encouraged the growth of strong nationalist movements which demanded independence. The movements were invariably authoritarian in outlook and methods. A notable example was Indonesia where Sukarno led his independence movement to power in 1949 and for the next seventeen years governed the country according to the principle of 'Guided Democracy', a euphemism for dictatorial control which involved the destruction of all forms of opposition.

KEY TERM

DORA The British Defence of the Realm Act, which restricted civil freedoms by suspending traditional legal procedures and granted the government a range of powers over its citizens, including direction of labour.

Conclusion

← **Why did dictatorships flourish in the twentieth century?**

The history of the twentieth century suggests that the military, social and economic uncertainties of the period were judged at critical times to require an all-powerful state to combat them. Internal and external enemies could be overcome only through effective government. Dictatorship, aided by modern technology, flourished in such an atmosphere. The absence or weakness of the traditions of democracy, the damaging of the liberal ethic by the two world wars, the mutual fears of Right and Left, the collapse of economic security, the ideal of the nation state: these factors combined to prepare or consolidate the ground for authoritarian regimes.

Of the seven authoritarian or totalitarian states examined in this book, the first chronologically were European states: the Soviet Union and Germany. Although the regimes that developed elsewhere did not directly copy them, they did, in a sense, create models for the development of modern dictatorships. They certainly provide the observer with a valuable set of reference points. Of particular note is that the two regimes theoretically represented the opposite ends of the Left–Right political spectrum. When the regimes studied or referred to in this text are placed on that spectrum, the following pattern emerges.

Extreme	Left	vs.	Right	Extreme
Stalin's USSR				Hitler's Germany
	Castro's Cuba			
	Nasser's Egypt			
				Hirohito's Japan
				Mussolini's Italy
				Franco's Spain
Mao's China			Salazar's Portugal	
Kim Il Sung's North Korea			Perón's Argentina	
	Nyerere's Tanzania		Atatürk's Turkey	

As a visual illustration, it suffers from the weakness of suggesting fixed placement, but it does provide a set of references which can then be debated as to their accuracy once you have studied your chosen regimes from the following chapters.

CHAPTER 2

The USSR under Joseph Stalin, 1924–53

Joseph Stalin emerged victorious from the power struggle that followed the death in 1924 of Lenin, the creator of the USSR. Having taken control by the late 1920s, Stalin, over the next quarter century, used the most ruthless means to impose himself on all aspects of Soviet life. He revolutionized the economy by enforced policies of collectivization and industrialization, and destroyed political opposition with a series of ferocious purges. Such was the extent of his authority that, by the time of his death in 1953, Soviet communism had become Stalinism. This chapter examines the following key questions:

✪ What circumstances favoured the rise of Stalin?
✪ How did Stalin impose his authority on the Soviet Union?
✪ What impact did Stalinism have on the lives of the Soviet people?
✪ How far did Stalin achieve a totalitarian state?

 Stalin's rise to power, 1924–29

▶ *Key question: What circumstances favoured the rise of Stalin?*

> **Why had revolutionary Russia become a one-party state by 1924?**

 **KEY TERM**

October Revolution The seizure by the Bolsheviks of power in October 1917 from the interim Provisional Government that had led Russia since the abdication of the monarchy in February 1917.

Bolshevik Party The Russian Communist Party which had taken power in 1917.

The one-party state in the USSR

Having taken power in the **October Revolution** in 1917, Lenin had led his **Bolshevik Party** in laying the foundations of the world's first **Marxist** state. The Bolsheviks claimed that their triumph gave them an absolute right to govern Russia. There was a powerful ideology underlying this assumption. As Marxists, the Bolsheviks believed that they truly represented the will of the Russian proletariat who now ruled, in accordance with the scientific laws of **the dialectic**.

Bolshevik consolidation of power

By the time of Lenin's death in 1924, the Bolsheviks had overcome all the major challenges to their authority and had transformed Russia into the USSR. This involved their fighting and winning a desperate civil war, successfully resisting a series of foreign interventions, and surviving a series of severe economic crises.

The consolidation of Bolshevik power was a remarkable achievement, but it was gained only by using the most violent means. Lenin had allowed no opposition to his government. Political enemies had been crushed and critics within the party had been suppressed. Lenin's years in power left the Soviet Union with a tradition of authoritarian rule and terror. There were also serious economic problems that had still to be solved if the USSR was to survive as a nation.

Governmental structures

By 1924 the governmental structure of the Soviet Union had developed two main features: the Council of Peoples' Commissars, and the Secretariat. Both these bodies and the various committees they established were staffed and controlled by the Bolshevik (Communist) Party under Lenin. It has to be stressed that the vital characteristic of this governmental system was that the Party ruled. This, in effect, meant Lenin ruled, since his moral authority and standing in the Party were so strong that he was unchallengeable. In practical terms, the key organization was the **Politburo**. By 1922, the Soviet Union was a one-party, Leninist state. Membership of that one party was essential for all who held government posts at whatever level.

Democratic centralism

A central feature of Lenin's control of the Communist Party was the principle of '**democratic centralism**'. This was the notion, as developed by Lenin, that true democracy in the Bolshevik Party lay in the obedience of the members to the authority and instructions of the leaders. The justification for this was that while, as representatives of the workers, all Bolsheviks were genuine revolutionaries, only the leaders were sufficiently educated in the science of revolution to understand what needed to be done. In practice, democratic centralism meant the Bolsheviks doing what Lenin told them to do. It was the principle which Stalin was to inherit and exploit in his own leadership of the Soviet Union.

Authoritarian rule

Lenin created an authoritarian system which returned Russia to the **absolutism** that it had known under the **tsars**. The basic apparatus of oppression for which Stalin later became notorious for using was in place at Lenin's death. The main features of Lenin's authoritarian rule between 1917 and 1924 were:

- The one-party state – all parties other than the Communist Party of the Soviet Union (**CPSU**) were outlawed.
- The bureaucratic state – central power increased under Lenin and the number of government departments and officials grew.
- The police state – the *Cheka* was the first of a series of secret police organizations in the Soviet Union whose task was to impose government control over the people.

KEY TERM

Marxist Relating to the ideas of Karl Marx, a German revolutionary, who had advanced the notion that human society developed historically as a continuous series of class struggles between those who possessed economic and political power and those who did not. He taught that the culmination of this dialectical process would be the crushing victory of the proletariat over the bourgeoisie.

The dialectic The dynamic force that drives history along a predestined path.

Politburo An inner core of some twenty leading members of the Communist Party.

Democratic centralism The notion, first advanced by Lenin, that true democracy lies in party members' obedience to enlightened leadership.

Absolutism A governmental system in which the levers of power are exclusively in the hands of a group or an individual.

Tsars The traditional absolute rulers of imperial Russia.

CPSU Communist Party of the Soviet Union.

Cheka The All-Russian Extraordinary Commission for Combating Counter-Revolution, later known by such acronyms as OGPU and KGB.

SOURCE A

Map of the Republics of the USSR.

Study Source A. What geographical evidence is there for judging Russia to have been the dominant Republic in the USSR?

🔑 **KEY TERM**

Factionalism Open criticism within the CPSU of central orders.

Purges A system of terror used by Lenin and Stalin in the USSR and Mao in China for removing anyone regarded as a threat to their authority.

Show trials Special public court hearings, meant as propaganda exercises, in which the accused were paraded as enemies of the people.

SRs Socialist Revolutionaries, the largest of the revolutionary parties in Russia until outlawed by the Bolsheviks after 1917.

- The ban on **factionalism** – Lenin prohibited criticism of the leadership within the party, which was, in effect, a ban on free speech.
- The destruction of the trade unions – Leon Trotsky, Commissar for War under Lenin, destroyed the independence of the trade unions.
- The politicizing of the law – under Lenin the law was not a means of protecting society but an extension of political control.
- The system of **purges** and **show trials** – outstanding examples of these were the public trials in 1922 of the Moscow clergy and of the **SRs**.
- Concentration camps – at the time of Lenin's death there were over 300 such camps. They held rebel peasants and 'anti-Bolsheviks'.
- Prohibition of public worship – the Orthodox Christian churches were looted and then closed; atheism was adopted as a replacement for religious belief.
- Nationalization – Lenin's government took over private companies and banks.
- Imposed economic policies – faced with famine, Lenin had tried a series of experiments ranging from fierce repression of the peasants under 'War Communism' (see page 24) to the more lenient approach of **NEP**. Lenin claimed that NEP was a temporary measure but it was still in operation at his death.
- Cultural revolution – the Bolsheviks claimed that in revolutionary Russia the people were now ready to be moulded into a new species: 'Man can be made whatever we want him to be'. Culture was to be shaped by the power of the state.
- International isolation – Lenin had originally expected the Russian revolution to be the prelude to a worldwide proletarian uprising. That was

the reason for creating the **Comintern**. When no such international rising occurred, he had to adjust to a situation in which the Soviet Union became an isolated Marxist, revolutionary state, beset by external enemies.

Stalin's emergence as leading contender for power

In the uncertain political atmosphere that followed Lenin's death in January 1924, a number of fortunate developments helped Stalin promote his claims.

Stalin's positions

A critical factor was that Lenin had left no clear instructions as to what form of government should be adopted after him. This meant that the power was there for the taking; it was in this regard that Stalin found himself particularly well placed. That he had worked closely with Lenin and had held important administrative positions in the Party put him in a position of prominence that no rival could match. Here, the pragmatic way in which the Bolsheviks had first governed proved very important. Certain posts, which initially had not been considered especially significant, began to provide their holders with a controlling influence. Stalin's previous appointments to key posts in both government and Party now proved crucial. These had been:

- **People's Commissar for Nationalities (1917):** Stalin was in charge of the officials in the many regions and republics that made up the USSR. Lenin judged that Stalin, as a Georgian, had a special understanding of the national minorities.
- **Liaison Officer between the Politburo and Orgburo (1919):** Stalin was in a unique position to monitor both the Party's policy and the Party's personnel.
- **Head of the Workers' and Peasants' Inspectorate (1919):** Stalin oversaw the work of all government departments.
- **General Secretary of the Communist Party (1922):** Stalin recorded and conveyed Party policy. This enabled him to build up dossiers on all the members of the Party. Nothing of note happened that Stalin did not know about.

Stalin became the indispensable link in the chain of command in the Communist Party and the Soviet government. Above all, what these posts gave him was the power of **patronage**. He used this authority to place his own supporters in key positions. Since they then owed their place to him, Stalin could count on their support in the voting in the various committees which made up the organization of the Party and the government.

Such were the advantages held by Stalin during the Party in-fighting over the succession to Lenin that no other contender came near to matching him in his hold on the Party machine. Whatever the ability of the individuals or groups who opposed him, he could always out-vote and out-manoeuvre them.

← **What positions of influence did Stalin hold by 1924?**

 **KEY TERM**

NEP The New Economic Policy, which permitted the peasants to return to farming for private profit.

Comintern The Communist International, formed in 1919 in Moscow to organize worldwide revolution. The Comintern took a particular interest in China, believing that it could impose itself on the young CCP.

Orgburo The Soviet Organizational Bureau of the Secretariat responsible for turning the government's executive decisions and policies into practice.

Patronage Providing government approval and support and extending privileges to selected individuals and groups.

22

? How does Source B indicate the influence Stalin had gained in the USSR by 1924?

SOURCE B

The governmental structure in 1924.

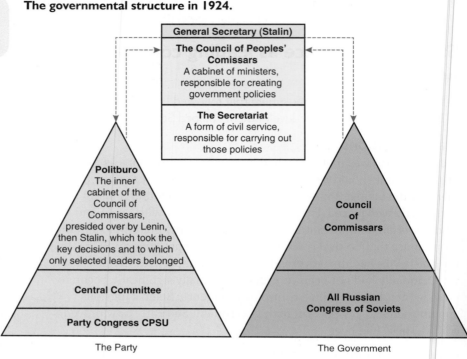

General Secretary (Stalin)

The Council of Peoples' Comissars
A cabinet of ministers, responsible for creating government policies

The Secretariat
A form of civil service, responsible for carrying out those policies

Politburo
The inner cabinet of the Council of Commissars, presided over by Lenin, then Stalin, which took the key decisions and to which only selected leaders belonged

Central Committee

Party Congress CPSU

The Party

Council of Commissars

All Russian Congress of Soviets

The Government

The Lenin enrolment

Stalin had also gained considerably from recent changes in the structure of the Communist Party. Between 1923 and 1925, the Party had set out to increase the number of workers in its ranks. This was known as 'the Lenin enrolment'. It resulted in the membership of the CPSU rising from 340,000 in 1922 to 600,000 by 1925.

The new members were fully aware that the many privileges which came with Party membership depended on their being loyal to those who had first invited them into the Bolshevik ranks. In every case it was members of the Secretariat, working directly under Stalin as General Secretary, who had issued the invitations. The result was the expansion of the Party, which added to Stalin's growing power of patronage. It provided him with a reliable body of votes in the various Party committees at local and central level.

How did Stalin exploit the situation following Lenin's death?

→ ## Stalin's bid for power

Lenin's funeral

Immediately after Lenin's death, the Politburo publicly proclaimed their intention to continue as a collective leadership, but behind the scenes the competition for individual authority had already begun. In the manoeuvring, Stalin gained an advantage by being the one to deliver the oration at Lenin's funeral. The sight of Stalin as leading mourner suggested a continuity between him and Lenin, an impression heightened by the contents of his speech in which, in the name of the Party, he dedicated himself to following in the tradition of the departed leader (see Source C).

SOURCE C

Excerpt from Stalin's speech reported in *Pravda*, January 1924, quoted in *Stalin: A Biography* by Robert Service, published by Macmillan, UK, 2004, p. 220.

In leaving us, Comrade Lenin commanded us to keep the unity of our Party. We swear to thee, Comrade Lenin, to honour thy command. In leaving us, Comrade Lenin ordered us to maintain and strengthen the dictatorship of the proletariat. We swear to thee, Comrade Lenin, to exert our full strength in honouring thy command. In leaving us, Comrade Lenin ordered us to strengthen with all our might the union of workers and peasants. We swear to thee, Comrade Lenin, to honour thy command.

According to Stalin in Source C, what obligations had Lenin left the Soviet Union? **?**

Since Stalin's speech was the first crucial move to promote himself as Lenin's successor, it was to be expected that Leon Trotsky, his chief rival, would try to counter it in some way. Trotsky was a prominent figure in the Party. He had played a key role in the 1917 October Revolution and had been the brilliant organizer of the **Red Army**, which had won the civil war against **the Whites**. Yet Trotsky was not even present at the funeral. His excuse was that Stalin had given him the wrong date. Whatever the truth of this, Trotsky's behaviour hardly appeared to be that of a dedicated Leninist.

 **KEY TERM**

Red Army The Bolshevik defence forces; the title was also adopted by the Chinese Communist forces.

The Whites Tsarists and anti-Bolsheviks.

Suppression of Lenin's Testament

Although Stalin had been totally loyal to Lenin, there had been times when he had offended his leader. One such occasion occurred in 1922 when Lenin learned from his wife, Krupskaya, that Stalin had verbally abused her during a telephone conversation. In an angry response, Lenin added a severe criticism of Stalin to a document he had been dictating. Later known as Lenin's Testament, this was a set of observations on the strengths and weaknesses of the Party's leading members. Lenin had been especially critical of Stalin's hunger for 'boundless power' and urged the comrades to consider ways of removing him as Secretary, but this was not done. Lenin was too ill during the last year of his life to be politically active. At his death in January 1924, he had still not taken any formal steps to remove Stalin, and the 'Testament' had not been made public.

If it were now to be published, Stalin would be gravely damaged by its contents. However, here again fortune favoured him. Since the Testament contained Lenin's criticism not simply of Stalin, but of all the members of the Politburo, they all had reason for suppressing it, which they formally did in May 1924. Since Trotsky had been criticized in the Testament for his 'excessive self-confidence', he went along with the decision, but in doing so he lost an opportunity to challenge Stalin. In fact it was Trotsky, not Stalin, whom the Politburo regarded as the greater danger.

→ Trotsky's opposition to Stalin

Lev Kamenev and Grigory Zinoviev, who had been leading players in the 1917 Revolution, joined Stalin in an unofficial **triumvirate** within the Politburo. Their aim was to isolate Trotsky by exploiting his unpopularity with large sections of the Party.

Trotsky's handicaps

- Trotsky was a Jew and very conscious of the fact that this constituted a political handicap. Anti-Semitism was an ingrained feature of Russian society and continued under communist rule. In 1917 he had declined Lenin's offer to be a commissar on the grounds that his appointment would be an embarrassment to Lenin and the government; he said it would 'give enemies grounds for claiming that the country was ruled by a Jew'.
- His intellectualism, coupled with an aloof style and manner, gave him the appearance of an outsider who was not fully committed to the CPSU. This deprived him of a significant following in the Party.
- CPSU members tended to regard Trotsky as dangerously ambitious and his rival Stalin as reliably self-effacing. This was because Trotsky was flamboyant and brilliant, while his rival was unspectacular and methodical.
- Trotsky had not become a Bolshevik until 1917, which raised doubts about how committed he was to the Party.

The New Economic Policy (NEP)

Trotsky's reputation was further damaged by the issue of the New Economic Policy. Soon after taking power Lenin had implemented a policy known as 'War Communism'. This was a series of harshly restrictive economic measures intended to help the Bolsheviks win the civil war of 1918–20. These measures:

- brought agriculture and industry under central control
- used government requisition squads to seize grain stocks from the peasants
- prohibited farming for profit.

However, War Communism did not produce the expected results. The interference with the peasants' traditional ways caused disruption and resentment. Hunger did not lessen; it intensified. Despite the government's terror tactics there were many instances of serious resistance. Always flexible in his approach, Lenin decided on a U-turn. He judged that, if the peasants could not be forced, they must be persuaded. At a Party Congress in 1921 he told members that it made no sense for Bolsheviks to pretend that they could pursue an economic policy which took no account of the real situation. He then announced that War Communism was to be replaced with a New Economic Policy, the main features of which were:

- central economic control to be relaxed
- grain requisitioning to be abandoned
- the peasants to be allowed to keep their food surpluses and sell them for a profit.

NEP clearly marked a retreat from the principle of state control of the economy. It restored a mixed economy in which certain features of capitalism existed alongside socialism. It was this that troubled the members of the Party, including Trotsky, who had welcomed the repressive measures of War Communism. To their mind, squeezing the peasants was exactly what the Bolsheviks should be doing since it advanced the revolution. It disturbed them that the peasants were being cosseted and that capitalist ways were being tolerated.

Leftists and rightists

When introducing NEP in 1921, Lenin had admitted that it was a relaxing of strict socialism, but had emphasized that it was a temporary measure. However, at the time of his death in 1924 the question was already being asked as to how long in fact NEP was meant to last. The Party members who were unhappy with it saw its continuation as a betrayal of revolutionary principles. A serious division had developed in the Party between **leftists** and **rightists**. Initially the disagreement was simply about timing: how long was the NEP to continue? However, in the power struggle of the 1920s these minor differences deepened into questions of political correctness and Party loyalty. A rival's attitude towards the NEP might be a weakness to be exploited.

Stalin did precisely this. He used Trotsky's attitude towards NEP as a way of undermining him. Trotsky, in 1923, had openly declared that to continue with NEP was to put the interests of the **Nepmen** above those of the Revolution and to undermine the gains made from War Communism. Stalin was quick to suggest to Party members that Trotsky was an unacceptably disruptive force. The interesting point here is that Stalin's own view of NEP was far from clear at this stage. He had loyally supported Lenin's introduction of it in 1921, but had given little indication as to whether, or how long, it should be retained after Lenin's death. He preferred to keep his own views to himself and play on the differences among party members.

The Left–Right division over modernization

The ideological argument over NEP merged with another demanding question. How should the Soviet Union plan for the future? The USSR was a poor country. To modernize and overcome its poverty it would have to **industrialize**. The quarrel in the Party was not whether the USSR should industrialize, but over how and at what speed.

The country was rich in natural resources, but these had yet to be effectively exploited, and it certainly did not possess large amounts of capital. Nor could it easily borrow any since the Bolsheviks after taking power had rejected **capitalist methods of finance** and caused international outrage by refusing to honour any of the debts incurred by the Tsarist state. Few countries after 1917 were willing to risk investing in revolutionary Russia.

The only usable resource, therefore, was the Soviet people themselves, 80 per cent of whom were peasants. To achieve industrialization, it was necessary that the peasants produce a food surplus which could then be sold abroad to

🔑 KEY TERM

Leftists Bolshevik Party members who wanted NEP abandoned.

Rightists Bolshevik Party and CCP members who argued for a slower, less violent development of revolution and for the continuation of the NEP.

Nepmen A derisive term for the profiteers who had supposedly exploited the commercial freedoms allowed under NEP in order to enrich themselves.

Industrialization The process of creating a factory-based manufacturing economy.

Capitalist methods of finance The system in which the owners of private capital (money) increase their wealth by making loans on which they later receive interest.

raise capital for industrial investment. Both Left and Right agreed that this was the only solution, but, whereas the Right were content to rely on persuading the peasants to co-operate, the Left demanded that the peasantry be forced to conform.

It was Trotsky who most clearly represented the view of the Left on this. He wanted the peasants to be coerced. However, for him the industrialization debate was secondary to the far more demanding question of the Soviet Union's role as the organizer of international revolution. His views on this created a wide divergence between him and Stalin, expressed in terms of a clash between the opposed notions of 'Permanent Revolution' and 'Socialism in One Country'.

Ideological conflict between Trotsky and Stalin

Trotsky was an international Marxist. His central political belief at this time was in 'Permanent Revolution', a concept made up of three essential ideas:

- Revolution was not a single event but a permanent (continuous) process in which risings took place from country to country.
- The events in Russia since 1917 were simply a first step towards a worldwide revolution of the proletariat.
- The USSR could not survive alone in a hostile world. It needed to 'export revolution'. Unless there was international revolution, the Soviet Union would not survive.

Stalin countered Trotsky's notion of 'Permanent Revolution' with his own concept of 'Socialism in One Country'. He meant by this that the nation's first task was to consolidate Lenin's Revolution by turning the USSR into a modern state, capable of defending itself against its internal and external enemies. The Soviet Union's task, therefore, was to:

- overcome its present agricultural and industrial problems by its own unaided efforts
- proceed to build a modern state, the equal of any nation in the world
- make the survival of the Soviet Union an absolute priority, even if this meant suspending efforts to create international revolution.

Stalin used the contrast between his programme and Trotsky's to portray his rival as an enemy of the Soviet Union. He condemned Trotsky's ideas as a threat to the security of the USSR. Trotsky's position was further weakened by the fact that throughout the 1920s the Soviet Union had a constant fear of invasion by the combined capitalist nations. Although this fear was ill-founded, the tense atmosphere it created made Trotsky's notion of the USSR's engaging in foreign revolutionary wars appear irresponsible.

Why was Stalin able to overcome the challenge from the Left?

→ # The defeat of Trotsky and the Left

Trotsky's failure in the propaganda war of the 1920s meant that he was in no position to persuade either the Politburo or the Central Committee to support his proposals. Following a vote against him in the 1925 Party

Congress, Trotsky was removed from his position as Commissar for War. Kamenev and Zinoviev, the respective Chairmen of the Moscow and Leningrad **Soviets**, played a key part in this. They used their influence over the local Party organizations to ensure that it was a pro-Stalin, anti-Trotsky Congress that gathered.

The New Opposition

With Trotsky weakened, Stalin turned to the problem of how to deal with the two key figures he now saw as potential rivals, Kamenev and Zinoviev. In the event, they created a trap for themselves. In 1925, worried by the USSR's slow economic growth, the two men called for the NEP to be abandoned, concessions to the peasants withdrawn, and industrialization enforced. Their viewpoint formed the basis of what was termed the 'New Opposition', but there was little to distinguish it from old Trotskyism. It was no surprise, therefore, when Trotsky joined his former opponents in 1926 to form a 'Trotskyite-Kamenevite-Zinovievite' opposition bloc.

Again, Stalin's control of the Party machine proved decisive. The Party Congress declined to be influenced by pressure from the 'New Opposition'. The Right Communists backed Stalin and outvoted the Left bloc. Kamenev and Zinoviev were dismissed from their posts as Soviet chairmen, to be replaced by two of Stalin's staunchest allies: Vyacheslav Molotov in Moscow and Sergei Kirov in Leningrad. It was little surprise that, soon after, Trotsky was expelled from both the Politburo and the Central Committee.

Bureaucratization

Trotsky attempted to fight back. The issue he chose was bureaucratization. He defined this as the abandonment of genuine discussion within the Party and the growth in power of the Secretariat, which was able to make decisions and operate policies without reference to ordinary Party members. Trotsky called for greater Party democracy to fight this growth. But his campaign was misjudged. In trying to expose the growing bureaucracy in the Communist Party, Trotsky overlooked the essential fact that Bolshevik rule since 1917 had always been bureaucratic. Indeed, it was because the Soviet state functioned as a bureaucracy that Party members received privileges in political and public life. Trotsky gained little support from Party members who had a vested interest in maintaining the Party's bureaucratic ways. His censure of bureaucracy left Stalin unscathed.

Trotsky's expulsion

Trotsky still did not admit defeat. In 1927, on the tenth anniversary of the Bolshevik rising, he tried to rally support in a direct challenge to Stalin's authority. He was again heavily outvoted. His complete failure led to Congress accepting Stalin's proposal that Trotsky be expelled from the Party altogether. An internal exile order against him in 1927 was followed two years later by deportation from the USSR itself. That Trotsky was not executed at this point suggests that Stalin did not yet regard himself as being in full political control.

KEY TERM

Soviet Bolshevik/ Communist-dominated worker–soldier local councils. In China, the term described a communist community dedicated to the practical application of Marxist egalitarian principles.

Why were the Right
unable to mount an
effective challenge to
Stalin?

The defeat of the Right opposition

Having defeated the Left, Stalin turned on the Right opposition whose major representatives were Alexei Rykov, Mikhail Tomsky and Nicholai Bukharin, three men who had loyally served Stalin in his outflanking of Trotsky and the Left. Politically, the Right were by no means as challenging to Stalin as the Trotskyite bloc had been. What made Stalin move against them was that they stood in the way of the industrial and agricultural schemes that he began to implement in 1928. His attack on the Right was, therefore, an aspect of his massive transformation of the Soviet economy.

It is uncertain when Stalin finally decided that the answer to the Soviet Union's growth problem was **collectivization** and industrialization (see pages 31–37). The likelihood is that it was probably another piece of opportunism; having defeated the Left politically, he felt free to adopt their economic policies.

KEY TERM

Collectivization Depriving the peasants of their land and requiring them to live and work in communes.

State procurements Enforced collections of grain from the peasants.

The attitude of the Right opposition

Bukharin and the Right argued that it would be less disruptive to let Soviet industry develop its own momentum. The state should assist, but it should not direct. Similarly, the peasants should not be oppressed as this would make them resentful and less productive. The Right agreed that it was from the land that the means of financing industrialization would have to come, but they stressed that, by offering the peasants the chance to become prosperous, far more grain would be produced for sale abroad.

Bukharin declared in the Politburo and at the Party Congress in 1928 that Stalin's aggressive policy of **state procurements** was counter-productive. He was prepared to state openly what everybody knew, but was afraid to admit: that Stalin's programme was little different to the one that Trotsky had previously advocated.

Weakness of the Right opposition

The Right suffered from a number of weaknesses, which Stalin was able to exploit. These related to their ideas, their organization and their support.

Ideas

A notable skill that Stalin employed throughout his career after 1924 was his ability to play upon the fears of his colleagues and compatriots. He consistently claimed that the USSR was under threat from internal and external enemies within and without. This seldom accorded with reality but his constant exaggerations were believed by a Party which became convinced that only through vigilance and ruthless treatment of enemies could the regime be safeguarded from the reactionaries who wished to overthrow it. Typical of Stalin's statements was his listing of the USSR's

internal enemies to show the danger in which the Revolution stood
(see Source D).

SOURCE D

Excerpt from a speech by Stalin in 1933, quoted in *Stalin: Triumph and Tragedy*, by Dmitri Volkogonov, published by Weidenfeld & Nicolson, UK, 1991, p. 211.

The remnants of the dying classes – industrialists and their servants, private traders and their stooges, former nobles and priests, kulaks and their henchman – they have all wormed their way into our factories, our institutions. What have they brought with them? Of course, they have brought their hatred of the Soviet regime, their feeling of hostility to the new forms of the economy, way of life, culture.

According to Source D, who are the internal enemies of the Soviet state and what threat do they pose?

Stalin used the fears for the Revolution felt by the Party to undermine the Right. Scorning Bukharin for underestimating the difficulties the Soviet Union faced, he asserted that the dangerous times required not concessions to the peasants, but a tough policy towards them. In taking this line, Stalin showed a shrewd understanding of the mentality of Party members. The majority were far more likely to respond to the call for a return to a rigorous policy on the land than they were to risk the Revolution itself by untimely concessions to reactionary peasants.

Organization

The Right experienced the same difficulty that the Left had. How could they impress their ideas upon the Party while Stalin remained master of the Party machine? Bukharin and his colleagues wanted to remain faithful Party members and it was this sense of loyalty that weakened them in their attempts to oppose Stalin. Fearful of recreating the 'factionalism' condemned by Lenin, they hoped that they could win the Party over by persuasion. Their basic approach was conciliatory. All this played into Stalin's hands. Since it was largely his supporters who were responsible for drafting and distributing Party information, it was not difficult for Stalin to belittle the Right as a weak and irresponsible clique.

Lack of support

The Right's only substantial support lay in the trade unions, whose Central Council was chaired by Tomsky, and in the CPSU's Moscow branch where Nicolai Uglanov, an admirer and supporter of Bukharin, was the Party Secretary. When Stalin realized that these might be a source of opposition, he acted quickly and decisively. He sent Lazar Kaganovich, a ruthlessly ambitious young Politburo member from Ukraine, to arrest the suspect trade unionists. The Right were overwhelmed by this political assault. Molotov was dispatched to Moscow where he enlisted the support of the pro-Stalin members to terrify local Party officials into line.

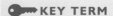

KEY TERM

Premier Soviet Chairman of the Council of Commissars.

Vozhd Russian for a supreme leader, equivalent to the *Führer* in German.

Collapse of the Right

By early 1929, the Right were beyond recovery. Tomsky was no longer the national trade union leader; Rykov had been superseded as **premier** by Molotov; and Bukharin had lost his place in the Politburo. This trio of 'Right Opportunists' were allowed to remain in the Party but only after publicly admitting the error of their ways. Stalin's triumph over both Left and Right was complete. He was now in a position to exercise power as the new *Vozhd*, having become, in effect, a communist tsar. The defeat of the Right marks the end of any serious challenge to limit his power. From the late 1920s to his death in 1953, Stalin would become increasingly dictatorial.

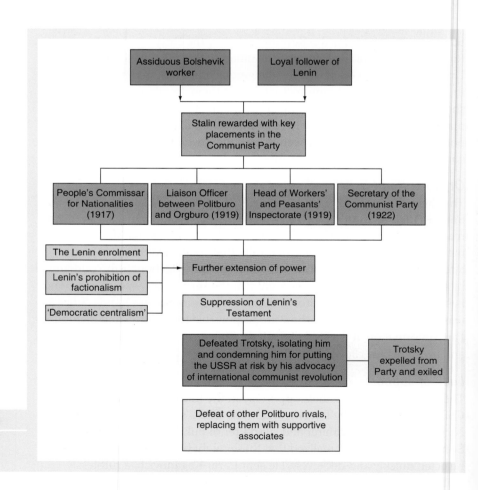

SUMMARY DIAGRAM

Stalin's rise to power, 1924–29

Stalin's establishment of an authoritarian state

> ▶ **Key question:** *How did Stalin impose his authority on the Soviet Union?*

Stalin's imposition of a dictatorial control over the Soviet Union was achieved by the manner in which he developed his domestic policies. These are examined in this section under two headings: economic policy and the purges.

Economic policy

Stalin had decided by 1928 that the USSR could not survive unless it rapidly modernized its economy. To this end, he set about completely reshaping Soviet agriculture and industry. The pretext for this had been provided in 1926 by a critical resolution of the Party Congress: 'To transform our country from an agrarian into an industrial one, capable by its own efforts of producing the necessary means'. Stalin planned to turn that resolution into reality. There were three main aspects to this, which were:

- economic aims
- the collectivization of the peasantry
- industrialization.

Economic aims

Stalin's economic policy had one essential aim, the **modernization** of the Soviet economy. This was to be achieved by two essential methods, collectivization and industrialization. So socially disruptive was this programme, involving as it did the greatest land transfer in Russian history and the redirection of people's lives, that it could be achieved only by Stalin's government taking complete control of the Soviet people.

Revolution from above

From 1928 onwards, the Soviet state took over the running of the nation's economy. In theory, 1917 had been a revolution from below. The Bolshevik-led proletariat had begun the construction of a state in which the workers ruled. Bukharin and the Right had used this notion to argue that, since the USSR was now a proletarian society, the economy should be left to develop at its own pace, without interference from the government. Stalin's economic programme ended such thinking. The state would now command the economy from above. Stalin called this momentous decision 'the second revolution' to indicate that it was as important a stage in Soviet history as the original 1917 Revolution. This comparison was obviously intended to enhance his own status as a revolutionary leader following in the footsteps of Lenin.

← **How did Stalin use his economic policies to impose his authority over the Soviet Union?**

 **KEY TERM**

Modernization The movement of a nation from a rural, agricultural society to an urban, industrial one.

Modernization

Stalin believed that the survival of the Soviet Union depended on the nation's ability to turn itself into a modern industrial society within the shortest possible time. He expressed this with particular force in 1931 (see Source E).

? According to Source E, what must the Soviet Union do to avoid being crushed?

SOURCE E

Excerpt from a speech by Stalin, February 1931, reported in *Pravda*, quoted in *Stalin: A Biography* by Robert Service, published by Macmillan, UK, 2004, pp. 272–73.

It is sometimes asked whether it is not possible to slow down the tempo somewhat, to put a check on the movement. No, comrades, it is not possible! The tempo must not be reduced! To slacken the tempo would mean falling behind. And those who fall behind get beaten. But we do not want to be beaten. We are fifty or a hundred years behind the advanced countries. We must make good this distance in ten years. Either we do it, or we shall be crushed. This is what our obligations to the workers and peasants of the USSR dictate to us.

This passionate appeal to Russian history subordinated everything to the driving need for national survival. Stalin used this appeal as the pretext for the severity that accompanied collectivization and industrialization.

Collectivization

Stalin adopted collectivization for two reasons – to bring the peasants under control and to raise capital. Stalin worked to a simple formula:

- The USSR needed industrial investment and manpower.
- The land could provide both.
- Surplus grain would be sold abroad to raise investment funds for industry.
- Surplus peasants would become factory workers.

As a revolutionary, Stalin had little sympathy for the peasants. Communist theory taught that the days of the peasantry as a revolutionary social force had passed. October 1917 had been the first stage in the triumph of the industrial proletariat. Therefore, it was perfectly fitting that the peasantry should bow to the demands of industrialization.

 **KEY TERM**

Collective farms Farms run as co-operatives in which the peasants shared the labour and the wages.

Stalin defined collectivization as 'the setting up of **collective farms** in order to squeeze out all capitalist elements from the land'. The state would now own the land. The peasants would no longer farm the land for their own individual profit. The plan was to group between 50 and 100 peasant holdings into one unit. It was believed that large farms would be more efficient and would encourage the effective use of agricultural machinery.

The Kulaks

When introducing collectivization in 1928, Stalin claimed that it was 'voluntary', but in truth it was forced on a very reluctant peasantry. In a major propaganda offensive, Stalin identified a class of 'Kulaks', rich peasants who were holding back the workers' revolution by hoarding their produce and keeping food prices high, thus making themselves wealthy at the expense of the workers and poorer peasants. They had to be broken as a class; thus, 'de-Kulakization' became a state-enforced campaign.

The concept of a Kulak class was a Stalinist myth. The so-called Kulaks were really only those hard-working peasants who had proved more efficient farmers than their neighbours. In no sense did they constitute the class of exploiting landowners described in Stalinist propaganda. Nonetheless, given the tradition of landlord oppression going back to Tsarist times, the notion of a Kulak class proved a very powerful one and provided the grounds for the coercion of the peasantry as a whole – middle and poor peasants, as well as Kulaks.

De-Kulakization

In some regions the poorer peasants undertook 'de-Kulakization' with enthusiasm, since it provided them with an excuse to settle old scores and to give vent to local jealousies. Land and property were seized from the minority of better-off peasants, and they and their families were physically attacked. Such treatment was often the prelude to arrest and deportation by **OGPU** anti-Kulak squads.

The renewal of terror also served as a warning to the mass of the peasantry of the likely consequences of resisting the state reorganization of Soviet agriculture. The destruction of the Kulaks was thus an integral part of the whole collectivization process. As a Soviet official later admitted: 'most Party officers thought that the whole point of de-Kulakization was its value as an administrative measure, speeding up tempos of collectivization'.

SOURCE F

An anti-Kulak demonstration on a collective farm in 1930. The banner reads 'Liquidate the Kulaks as a class'.

🔑 KEY TERM

OGPU Succeeded the *Cheka* as the Soviet state security force. In turn it became the NKVD and then the KGB.

Who was likely to have organized the demonstration shown in Source F? Why would peasants be willing to join such a demonstration?

Resistance to collectivization

In the period between December 1929 and March 1930, nearly a quarter of the peasant farms in the USSR were collectivized. Yet peasants in their millions resisted. What amounted to civil war broke out in the countryside. The following details indicate the scale of the disturbances as recorded in official figures:

- During 1929–30, there were 30,000 arson attacks.
- The number of organized rural mass disturbances increased from 172 for the first half of 1929 to 229 for the second half.

However, peasant resistance, no matter how valiant and desperate, stood no chance of stopping collectivization. By the end of the 1930s, virtually the whole of the peasantry had been collectivized (see Source G).

? What does Source G suggest about the resolution with which Stalin pursued collectivization?

SOURCE G

Graph showing cumulative percentage of peasant holdings collectivized in the USSR, 1930–41.

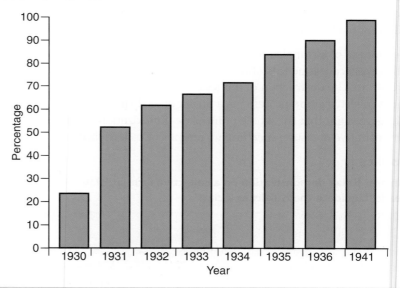

SOURCE H

Annual food consumption (in kilograms per head).

Year	Bread	Potatoes	Meat and lard	Butter
1928	250.4	141.1	24.8	1.35
1932	214.6	125.0	11.2	0.7

SOURCE I

Number of livestock (in millions).

Year	Horses	Cattle	Pigs	Sheep and goats
1928	33	70	26	146
1932	15	34	9	42

What trends are evident in the tables in Sources H and I? What are the possible explanations for the trends shown?

The consequences of collectivization

- Collectivization created a massive social upheaval. Bewildered and confused, the peasants became disorientated by the deliberate destruction of their traditional way of life. The consequences were increasingly tragic. The majority of peasants ate their seed corn and slaughtered their livestock. There were no crops left to reap or animals to rear.
- Starvation, which in many parts of the Soviet Union persisted throughout the 1930s, was at its worst in the years 1932–33, when a national famine occurred. Estimates suggest that 6 to 8 million people died, with the population of Ukraine and Kazakhstan suffering particularly severely.
- Desperate peasants moved to the towns in huge numbers. So great was the migration that a system of internal passports had to be introduced in an effort to control the flow.
- Despite overwhelming evidence of the tragedy that had overtaken the USSR, there were only two oblique references to it in the state press. As well as serving to protect the image of Stalin the great planner, this conspiracy of silence effectively prevented the introduction of measures to ease the distress.
- Leaving aside questions of human suffering, the enforced migration under Stalin had one positive economic result: it relieved the pressure on the land and provided the workforce that enabled the industrialization programme to be started.

Industrialization

Stalin described his industrialization plans for the USSR as an attempt to establish a war economy. He declared that he was making war on the failings of Russia's past and on the class enemies within the nation. He also claimed that he was preparing the USSR for war against its capitalist foes abroad. This was not simply martial imagery; Stalin regarded iron, steel and oil as the sinews of war. Their successful production would guarantee the strength and readiness of the nation to face its enemies.

Soviet industrialization under Stalin took the form of a series of Five-Year Plans (FYPs). *Gosplan* was required by Stalin to draw up a list of quotas of production ranging across the whole of Soviet industry. The process began in 1928 and, except for the war years 1941–45, lasted until Stalin's death in 1953. In all, there were five separate plans:

- First FYP: October 1928 to December 1932
- Second FYP: January 1933 to December 1937
- Third FYP: January 1938 to June 1941

🔑 KEY TERM

Gosplan The Soviet state economic planning agency.

- Fourth FYP: January 1946 to December 1950
- Fifth FYP: January 1951 to December 1955.

The First Five-Year Plan, 1928–32

The term 'plan' is misleading. The First FYP laid down what was to be achieved, but did not say how it was to be done. It simply assumed the quotas would be met. What the First FYP represented, therefore, was a set of targets rather than a plan. As had happened with collectivization, local officials and managers falsified their production figures to give the impression they had met their targets when, in fact, they had fallen short. For this reason, precise statistics for the First FYP are difficult to determine. A further complication is that three quite distinct versions of the First FYP eventually appeared.

Impressed by the apparent progress of the Plan in its early stages, Stalin encouraged the formulation of an 'optimal' plan which reassessed targets upwards. These new quotas were hopelessly unrealistic and stood no chance of being reached. Nonetheless, on the basis of the supposed achievements of this 'optimal' plan, the figures were revised still higher. Western analysts suggest the figures in Source J are the closest approximation to the real figures.

? How is the difference between the four categories in Source J – First Plan, Optimal, Revised and Actual – to be explained?

SOURCE J

Industrial output in million tons of the First Five-Year Plan.

Product	1927–28 First Plan	1929–31 Optimal	1932 Revised	1932 Actual
Coal	35.0	75.0	95–105	64.0
Oil	11.7	21.7	40–55	21.4
Iron ore	6.7	20.2	24–32	12.1
Pig iron	3.2	10.0	15–16	6.2

The importance of these figures should not be exaggerated. At the time it was the grand design, not the detail, that mattered. The Plan was a huge propaganda project which aimed at convincing the Soviet people that they were personally engaged in a vast industrial enterprise. Nor was it all a matter of state enforcement. Among the young especially, there was an enthusiasm and a commitment that suggested that many Soviet citizens believed they were genuinely building a new and better world.

To show how successful they were, officials often exaggerated the production figures. Nevertheless, the First FYP was an extraordinary achievement overall. Coal, iron, and generation of electricity all increased in huge proportions. The production of steel and chemicals was less impressive, while the output of finished textiles actually declined.

The Second and Third Five-Year Plans

Although the Second and Third FYPs were modelled on the pattern of the First, the targets set for them were more realistic. Nevertheless, they still revealed the same lack of co-ordination that had characterized the First. Over-production occurred in some parts of the economy and under-production in others, which frequently led to whole branches of industry being held up for lack of vital supplies. As a result there was hoarding of resources and a lack of co-operation between the various parts of the industrial system. Complaints about poor standards, carefully veiled so as not to appear critical of Stalin and the Plan, were frequent. What successes there were occurred again in heavy industry where the Second FYP began to reap the benefit of the creation of large-scale plants under the First Plan.

Stalin's industrial record

The four key products coal, steel, oil and electricity provided the basis for the war economy which enabled the USSR not only to survive four years of German occupation (1941–45) but eventually to win a great victory over Germany in May 1945.

SOURCE K

Industrial output during the first three Five-Year Plans.

Product	1927	1930	1932	1935	1937	1940
Coal (million tons)	35	60	64	100	128	150
Steel (million tons)	3	5	6	13	18	18
Oil (million tons)	12	17	21	24	26	26
Electricity (million kWh)	18	22	20	45	80	90

> What trends are discernible in Source K in regard to the production of coal, steel, oil and electricity? **?**

- Stalin's industrial programme succeeded in the areas of heavy industry. The building of large projects such as factories, bridges, refineries and canals were impressive achievements.
- However, the Soviet economy itself remained unbalanced. Little attention was given to **light engineering**, which the advanced industrial nations were successfully developing. Stalin's love of what he called 'the Grand Projects of Communism' meant too little attention was paid to producing quality goods that could then be profitably sold abroad.
- Stalin's schemes failed to raise the living standards of the Soviet workers. Indeed, such measures as direction of labour and the imposition of severe penalties for slacking and absenteeism created harsher conditions for the workforce. In 1941, when the German invasion effectively destroyed the Third FYP, the living conditions of the Soviet industrial workers were lower than in 1928.

> **KEY TERM**
>
> **Light engineering** Skilled, specialized activities such as precision tool-making.

The early purges

Having become the *Vozhd* of the Soviet Union by 1929, Stalin spent the rest of his life consolidating and extending his authority. The purges were his principal weapon for achieving this. They became the chief mechanism for removing anyone he regarded as a threat to his authority. The Stalinist purges, which began in 1932, were not unprecedented. Public show trials had been held during the early stages of the First Five-Year Plan as a way of exposing 'saboteurs' who were accused of damaging the USSR's industrial programme.

> ← **How were the early purges used to suppress opposition?**

Party card The official CPSU warrant granting membership and privileges to the holder. It was a prized possession in the Soviet Union.

Ryutin affair In 1932, the followers of M. N. Ryutin, a Right communist, published an attack on Stalin, describing him as 'the evil genius who had brought the Revolution to the verge of destruction'. The Ryutinites were put on public trial and expelled from the Party.

? According to Source L, how intensely did Stalin bear grudges?

At the beginning, Party purges were generally not as violent as they later became. The usual procedure was to oblige members to hand in their **party card** for checking, at which point any suspect individuals would not have their cards returned to them. This amounted to expulsion since, without cards, members were denied access to all Party activities. Under such a system, it became progressively difficult to mount effective opposition. Despite this, efforts were made in the early 1930s to criticize Stalin, as the **Ryutin affair** in 1932 illustrates. Yet, although the Ryutinites had clearly failed, their attempted challenge convinced Stalin that organized resistance to him was still possible.

In analysing Stalin's rule, historians generally accept that they are dealing with behaviour that sometimes went beyond reason and logic. Stalin was deeply suspicious by nature and suffered from increasing paranoia as he grew older, as the letter below from his daughter, Svetlana, attests (see Source L).

SOURCE L

Excerpt from *Twenty Letters to a Friend* by Svetlana Allilueva, 1967, quoted in *Stalin: A Biography* by Robert Service, published by Macmillan, UK, 2004, p. 285.

If he cast out of his heart someone who had been known to him for a long time and if in his soul he had already translated that person into the ranks of 'enemies', it was impossible to hold a conversation with him about that person.

Stalin's methods of control

In the years 1933–34, as an accompaniment to the purges, Stalin centralized all the major law enforcement agencies:

- the civilian police
- **labour camp** commandants and guards
- border and security guards.

All these bodies were put under the authority of the **NKVD**, a body which was directly answerable to Stalin.

The post-Kirov purges, 1934–36

In Leningrad on 1 December 1934, Kirov, the secretary of the Leningrad Soviet, was shot and killed in his office. It is possible Stalin was implicated. What is certain is that the murder worked directly to his advantage. Kirov had been a highly popular figure in the Party and had been elected to the Politburo. He was known to be unhappy with the speed of Stalin's industrialization drive and also with the growing number of purges. If organized opposition to Stalin were to form within the Party, Kirov was the most likely individual around whom dissatisfied members might have rallied. That danger to Stalin had now been removed.

Stalin was quick to exploit the situation. Within two hours of learning of Kirov's murder he had signed a '**Decree Against Terrorist Acts**'. On the

Labour camps Prisons and detention centres in which the inmates are required to perform heavy work.

NKVD The People's Commissariat of Internal Affairs, the Soviet secret police.

Decree Against Terrorist Acts An order giving the NKVD limitless powers in pursuing the enemies of the Soviet state and the Communist Party.

pretext of hunting down the killers, a fresh purge of the Party was begun, led by Genrikh Yagoda, head of the NKVD. Three thousand suspected conspirators were rounded up and then imprisoned or executed and tens of thousands of other people were deported from Leningrad. Stalin then filled the vacant positions with his own nominees:

- In 1935, Kirov's key post as Party boss in Leningrad was filled by Andrei Zhdanov, a dedicated Stalinist.
- The equivalent post in Moscow was taken by Nikita Khrushchev, another ardent Stalin supporter.
- In recognition of his successful courtroom bullying of 'oppositionists' in the earlier purge trials, Andrei Vyshinsky was appointed State Prosecutor.
- Stalin's fellow Georgian, Lavrenti Beria, was entrusted with overseeing state security in the national minority areas of the USSR.
- Stalin's personal secretary, Alexander Poskrebyshev, was put in charge of the Secretariat.

As a result of these placements, there remained no significant area of Soviet bureaucracy which Stalin did not control.

The outstanding feature of the post-Kirov purge was the status of many of its victims. Prominent among those arrested were Kamenev and Zinoviev. Their arrest sent out a clear message: no Party members, whatever their status, were safe. Arbitrary arrest and summary execution became the norm, as the fate of the representatives at the Party Congress of 1934 suggests:

- Of the 1,996 delegates who attended, 1,108 were executed during the next three years.
- In addition, out of the 139 Central Committee members elected at that gathering, all but 41 of them were executed during the purges.

Historian Leonard Shapiro, in a celebrated study of the CPSU, described these events as 'Stalin's victory over the Party'. From this point on, the Soviet Communist Party was entirely under his control. It ceased, in effect, to have a separate existence. Stalin had become the Party.

The Stalin Enrolment, 1931–34

Stalin's successful purge was made easier by a recent shift in the make-up of the Party, known as 'the Stalin Enrolment'. Between 1931 and 1934, the CPSU had recruited a higher proportion of skilled workers and industrial managers than at any time since 1917. Stalin encouraged this as a means of tightening the links between the Party and those actually operating the First Five-Year Plan, but it also had the effect of bringing in a large number of members who joined the Party primarily to advance their careers. Acutely aware that they owed their privileged position directly to Stalin's patronage, the new members eagerly supported the elimination of the anti-Stalinist elements in the Party – it improved their chances of promotion. The competition for good jobs in the Soviet Union was invariably fierce and purges always left positions to be filled. As the chief dispenser of positions, Stalin knew that the self-interest of these new Party members would keep them loyal to him.

Why was Stalin able to extend the purges on such a huge scale?

'The Great Terror', 1936–39

It might be expected that the purges would stop once Stalin's complete mastery over the Party had been established, but they did not; in fact, they increased in intensity. Repeating his constant assertion that the Soviet Union was in a state of siege, Stalin called for still greater vigilance against the enemies within who were in league with the Soviet Union's foreign enemies. Between 1936 and 1939, a progressive terrorizing of the Soviet Union occurred affecting the whole population. Its scale merited the title, given to it by historians, of 'the Great Terror', which took its most dramatic form in the public show trials of Stalin's former Bolshevik colleagues (see page 41). The one-time heroes of the 1917 Revolution were imprisoned or executed as enemies of the state.

The descriptions applied to the accused during the purges bore little relation to political reality. 'Right', 'Left' and 'Centre' opposition blocs were identified and the groupings invariably had the catch-all term 'Trotskyite' tagged on to them, but such words were convenient prosecution labels rather than definitions of a genuine political opposition. They were intended to isolate those in the CPSU and the Soviet state whom Stalin wished to destroy.

Stalin's 'Great Terror' programme breaks down conveniently into three sections, which are:

- the purge of the Party
- the purge of the armed services
- the purge of the people.

The purge of the Party

Stalin's destruction of those in the Party he regarded as a major threat was achieved by the holding of three major show trials:

- In 1936, Kamenev and Zinoviev and fourteen other leading Bolsheviks were tried and executed.
- In 1937, seventeen Bolsheviks were denounced collectively as the 'Anti-Soviet Trotskyist Centre', and were charged with spying for Germany. All but three of them were executed.
- In 1938, Bukharin, Rykov, Tomsky and twenty others, branded 'Trotskyite-rightists', were publicly tried on a variety of counts, including sabotage, spying and conspiracy to murder Stalin: all were found guilty. Bukharin and Rykov were executed; Tomsky committed suicide.

Remarkably, the great majority went to their death after confessing their guilt. An obvious question arises. Why did they confess? After all, these men were tough Bolsheviks. Physical and mental tortures, including threats to their families, were used, but arguably more important was their sense of demoralization at having been accused and disgraced by the Party to which they had dedicated their lives. In a curious sense, their admission of guilt was a last act of loyalty to the Party. In his final speech in court, Bukharin accepted the infallibility of the Party and of Stalin, referring to him as 'the hope of the world'.

Whatever their reasons, that the leading Bolsheviks did confess made it extremely difficult for other victims to plead their own innocence. The psychological impact of the public confessions of such figures as Kamenev and Zinoviev was profound. It created an atmosphere in which innocent victims submitted in open court to false charges, and went to their death begging the Party's forgiveness.

The legality of the purges

Stalin's insistence on a policy of show trials illustrated his astuteness. There is little doubt that he had the power to conduct the purges without using legal proceedings. However, by making the victims deliver humiliating confessions in open court, Stalin was able to suggest the scale of the conspiracy against him and thus to prove the need for the purges to continue.

SOURCE M

This montage, composed by Trotsky's supporters, illustrates the remarkable fact that of the original 1917 Central Committee of the Bolshevik Party only Stalin was still alive in 1940; the majority of the other 23 members had, of course, been destroyed in the purges.

Why did those who were purged by Stalin, shown in Source M, offer so little resistance?

The purge of the armed forces

A particularly significant development in the purges occurred in 1937 when the Soviet military came under threat. Stalin's control of the Soviet Union would not have been complete if the armed services had continued as an independent force. It was essential that they be kept subservient. Stalin also had a lingering fear that the army, which had been Trotsky's creation (see page 23), might still have sympathy for their old leader. In May 1937, Vyshinksy, Stalin's chief prosecutor, announced that 'a gigantic conspiracy' had been uncovered in the Red Army. Marshal Mikhail Tukhachevsky, who had been one of the founders of that army, was arrested along with seven other generals. On the pretext that speed was essential to prevent a military coup, a trial was held immediately, this time in secret. Tukhachevsky was charged with having spied for Germany and Japan.

The outcome was predetermined. In June 1937, after their ritual confession and condemnation, Tukhachevsky and his fellow generals were shot. To prevent any chance of a military reaction, a wholesale destruction of the Red Army establishment was undertaken. During the following eighteen months:

(see page 23)

- All eleven **War Commissars** were removed from office.
- Three of the five **Marshals of the Soviet Union** were dismissed.
- Ninety-one of the 101-man Supreme Military Council were arrested, of whom 80 were executed.
- Fourteen of the sixteen army commanders, and nearly two-thirds of the 280 divisional commanders were removed.
- Up to 35,000 commissioned officers were either imprisoned or shot.
- The Soviet Union's Navy did not escape: between 1937 and 1939 all the serving admirals of the fleet were shot and thousands of naval officers were sent to labour camps.
- The Soviet Union's Air Force was similarly purged during that period: only one of its senior commanders survived.

The result was that all three services were left seriously undermanned and staffed by inexperienced or incompetent replacements. Given the defence needs of the USSR, the deliberate crippling of the Soviet military is the aspect of the purges that appears to be the most irrational.

The purge of the people

Stalin's gaining of total dominance over Party, government and military did not mean the end of the purges. The apparatus of terror was retained and the search for enemies continued. Purges were used to achieve the goals of the FYPs; charges of industrial sabotage were made against managers and workers in the factories. The purges were also a way of forcing the regions and nationalities into total subordination to Stalin. To accommodate the great numbers of prisoners created by the purges, the *Gulag*, a network of prison and labour camps, was established across the USSR.

The show trials that had taken place in Moscow and Leningrad, with their catalogue of accusations, confessions and death sentences, were repeated in all the republics of the USSR. For example, between 1937 and 1939 in Stalin's home state of Georgia:

- two state prime ministers were removed
- four-fifths of the regional Party secretaries were dismissed
- thousands of lesser officials lost their posts.

SOURCE N

The Gulag, 1937–57. **By 1941, as a result of the purges, there were an estimated 8 million prisoners in the *Gulag*. The average sentence was ten years, which, given the conditions in the camps, was equivalent to a death sentence. As an example of state-organized repression, Stalin's *Gulag* stands alongside Hitler's concentration camps (see page 76) and Mao Zedong's *laogai* (see page 136).**

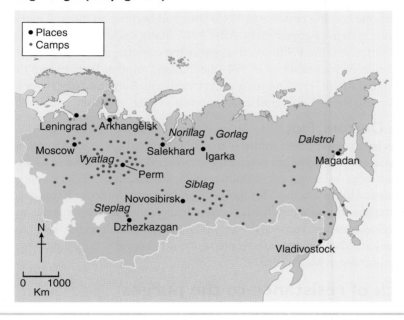

What does Source N indicate about the extent of Stalin's repression?

Mass repression

No area of Soviet life entirely escaped the purges. The constant fear that the purges created conditioned the way the Soviet people lived their lives. Their greatest impact was on the middle and lower ranks of Soviet society:

- One person in every eight of the population was arrested during Stalin's purges.
- Almost every family in the USSR suffered the loss of at least one of its members as a victim of the terror.

In the years 1937–38, mass repression was imposed. Known as the 'Yezhovschina', after its chief organizer, Nicolai Yezhov, head of the NKVD in 1937, this purge was typified by the practice in which NKVD squads entered selected localities and removed hundreds of inhabitants for execution. The number of victims to be arrested was specified in set quotas, as if they were industrial production targets. There was no appeal against sentences and the death warrant invariably required that the execution 'be carried our immediately'. The shootings took place in specially designated zones. One notorious example of this was Butovo, a village outside Moscow, which became one of the NKVD's killing fields. Excavations have revealed mass graves there containing over 20,000 bodies dating back to the late 1930s and indicating that nightly, over many months, victims had been taken to Butovo and shot in batches of a hundred.

Insofar as the terrorizing of ordinary people had a specific purpose, it was to frighten the USSR's national minorities into abandoning any remaining thoughts of challenging Moscow's control and to force them into a full acceptance of Stalin's enforced industrialization programme.

Later purges, 1941–53

Why did Stalin persist with the purges in his later years?

The purges did not end with the onset of **the Great Fatherland War** in 1941 or with the coming of peace in 1945. They had become an integral part of the Stalinist system of government. After 1947, Stalin dispensed with the Central Committee and the Politburo, thus removing even the semblance of a restriction on his authority. In 1949, he initiated another Party purge, 'the Leningrad Affair'. Leading party and city officials were tried on charges of attempting to use Leningrad as an opposition base, and shot.

KEY TERM

The Great Fatherland War The term adopted in the Soviet Union to describe the ferocious struggle that began with the German invasion of the USSR in 1941 and concluded with Soviet forces smashing their way into Germany in 1945.

The Doctors' Plot

Soviet Jews were the next section of the population to be selected for organized persecution. Anti-Semitism was a long-established aspect of Russian society and it was a factor in the last purge Stalin contemplated. Early in 1953 it was officially announced that a 'Doctors' Plot' had been uncovered in Moscow; it was asserted that the Jewish-dominated medical centre had planned to murder Stalin and the other Soviet leaders. Preparations began for a major assault on the Soviet medical profession. What prevented those preparations being put into operation was the death of Stalin in March 1953.

Lack of resistance to the purges

Why did the victims of the purges offer such little resistance?

Robert Service, a celebrated biographer of Stalin, says of him: 'Nowadays, virtually all writers accept that he initiated the Great Terror.' Stalin exploited the Russian autocratic tradition that he inherited to rid himself of real or imagined enemies. Yet Service, along with all the leading experts in the field, is careful to acknowledge that, while Stalin was undoubtedly the architect of the terror, the responsibility for implementing it goes beyond him:

- Stalinism was not as monolithic a system of government as has been often assumed. The disorganized state of much of Soviet bureaucracy, particularly at local level, allowed officials to use their own initiative in applying the terror.
- How the purges were actually carried out largely depended on the local party organization. Many officials welcomed the purges as an opportunity to increase their local power.
- Revolutionary idealism was swamped by self-interest as Party members saw the purges as a way of advancing themselves by filling the jobs vacated by the victims. This relates to an argument advanced by some historians that the purges came as much from below as from above. The suggestion is that the purges were sustained in their ferocity by the lower rank officials in government and Party who wanted to replace their superiors, whom they regarded as a conservative elite.

- The purges were popular with those in the Soviet Union who believed their country could survive only by being powerfully and ruthlessly led. Such people judged that Stalin's unrelenting methods were precisely what the nation needed.
- The disruption of Soviet society, caused by upheavals of collectivization and industrialization, destroyed social cohesion and so encouraged Party and government officials to resort to the most extreme measures.

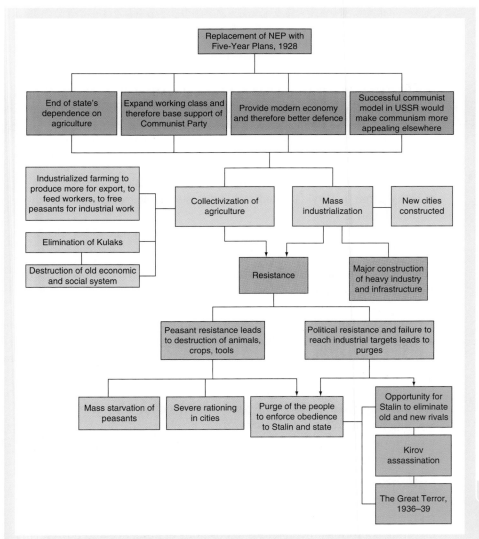

SUMMARY DIAGRAM

Stalin's establishment of an authoritarian state

Stalin's domestic policies and their impact, 1929–53

> ► **Key question:** *What impact did Stalinism have on the lives of the Soviet people?*

Arts and the media

How was Soviet culture manipulated to strengthen Stalin's power?

🔑 **KEY TERM**

Social realism
Representational work which related directly to the lives of the people.

Soviet Union of Writers
The body which had authority over all published writers and had the right to ban any work of which it disapproved.

Literature

In 1932, Stalin declared to a gathering of Soviet writers that they were 'engineers of the human soul'. Their task was essentially a social not an artistic one. They had to reshape the thinking and behaviour of the Soviet people. The goal of the artist had to be **social realism**. It is not surprising, therefore, that when the **Soviet Union of Writers** was formed in 1934 it declared that its first objective was to convince all its members of the need to struggle for socialist realism in their works. This could be best achieved by conforming to a set of guidelines. Writers were to make sure that their work:

● was acceptable to the Party in theme and presentation
● was written in a style immediately understandable to the workers who would read it
● contained characters whom the readers could recognize as socialist role models or examples of class enemies.

These rules applied to creative writing in all its forms: novels, plays, poems and film scripts. It was not easy for genuine writers to continue working within these restrictions, but conformity was the price of acceptance, of survival even. Surveillance, scrutiny and denunciations intensified throughout the 1930s. In such an intimidating atmosphere, suicides became common. Historian Robert Service notes in his biography of Stalin that 'more great intellectuals perished in the 1930s than survived'. In 1934, Osip Mandelstam, a leading literary figure, recited a mocking poem about Stalin at a private gathering of writers, which contained the lines 'Around him, fawning half-men for him to play with, as he prates and points a finger'. He was informed on and died four years later in the *Gulag*. He once remarked, 'Only in Russia is poetry taken seriously, so seriously men are killed for it.'

Stalin took a close personal interest in new artistic works. One word of criticism from him was enough to destroy a writer. The atmosphere of repression and the restrictions on genuine creativity had the effect of elevating conformist mediocrities to positions of influence and power. This was a common characteristic of totalitarian regimes in the twentieth century.

Pasternak and Solzhenitsyn

Among the most prominent of the writers persecuted under Stalin were Boris Pasternak and Alexander Solzhenitsyn. Pasternak's works were regarded by the authorities as implicitly critical of the Soviet system and therefore unacceptable. His *Dr Zhivago*, a novel that later became greatly admired in the West, was refused publication in the USSR during his lifetime. Solzhenitsyn, a deeply spiritual man, was regarded by the authorities as a subversive and spent many years in the *Gulag* for falling foul of Stalin's censors. His documentary novels, such as *One Day in the Life of Ivan Denisovich* and *The Gulag Archipelago*, which was published after Stalin's death, described the horrific conditions in the labour camps.

Theatre and film

The Union of Writers set the tone for all other organizations in the arts. Film-making, opera and ballet, all had to respond to the Stalinist demand for socialist realism. Abstract forms were frowned upon because they broke the rules that works should be immediately accessible to the public. An idea of the repression that operated can be gained from the following figures:

- In the years 1936–37, 68 films out of 150 had to be withdrawn mid-production and another 30 taken out of circulation.
- In the same period, ten out of nineteen plays and ballets were ordered to be withdrawn.
- In the 1937–38 theatre season, 60 plays were banned from performance and 10 theatres closed in Moscow and another 10 in Leningrad.

Vsevolod Meyerhold

A prominent victim was the director, Vsevolod Meyerhold, whose concept of **total theatre** had a major influence on European drama. Despite his wish to bring theatre closer to the people, his appeal for artistic liberty – 'The theatre is a living creative thing. We must have freedom, yes, freedom' – led to a campaign being mounted against him by Stalin's sycophantic supporters. He was arrested in 1938. After a two-year imprisonment during which he was regularly beaten until he fainted, he was shot. His name was one on a list of 346 death sentences that Stalin signed on one day – 16 January 1940.

Sergei Eisenstein

Even the internationally-acclaimed director, Sergei Eisenstein, whose films *Battleship Potemkin* and *October*, celebrating the revolutionary Russian proletariat, had done so much to advance the communist cause, was heavily censured. This was because a later work of his, *Ivan the Terrible*, was judged to be an unflattering portrait of a great Russian leader and, therefore, by implication, disrespectful of Stalin.

Painting and sculpture

Painters and sculptors were left in no doubt as to what was required of them. Their duty to conform to socialist realism in their style and at the same time

KEY TERM

Total theatre An approach which sought to break down the barriers between actors and audience by novel use of lighting, sound and stage settings.

honour their great leader was captured in an article in the art magazine *Iskusstvo* describing a prize painting of Stalin in 1948: 'The image of Comrade Stalin is the symbol of the Soviet people's glory, calling for new heroic exploits for the benefit of our great motherland.'

SOURCE O

In what ways do the posters in Source O illustrate the artistic notion of socialist realism?

Posters from the 1930s, typical of the propaganda of the time, showing Stalin as the leader of his adoring people. Poster art was a very effective way for the Stalinist authorities to spread their propaganda.

'Under the leadership of the great Stalin, forward to Communism!'

Music

Since music is an essentially abstract art form, it was more difficult to make composers respond to Stalin's notions of social realism. Nevertheless, it was the art form which most interested Stalin, who regarded himself as an expert in the field. He claimed to be able to recognize socialist music and to know what type of song would inspire the people. He tried to impose his judgement on the Soviet Union's leading composer, Dmitri Shostakovich, some of whose works were banned for being 'bourgeois and formalistic'. However, the Great Fatherland War gave Shostakovich the opportunity to express his deep patriotism. His powerful orchestral works depicted in sound the courageous struggle and final victory of the Soviet people. At the end of the war, in return for being reinstated, he promised to bring his music closer to 'the folk art of the people'.

Stalin's cult of personality

One of the strongest charges made against Stalin after his death was that he had indulged in the **cult of personality**. He had certainly dominated every aspect of Soviet life, becoming not simply a leader but the embodiment of the nation itself. From the 1930s on, his picture appeared everywhere. Every newspaper, book and film, no matter what its theme, carried a reference to Stalin's greatness. Biographies poured off the press, each one trying to outbid the other in its veneration of the leader. Every achievement of the USSR was credited to Stalin. Such was his all-pervasive presence that Soviet communism became identified with him as a person.

The cult of personality was not a spontaneous response of the people. It was imposed from above. The image of Stalin as hero and saviour of the Soviet people was manufactured. It was a product of the Communist Party machine which controlled all the main forms of information – newspapers, cinema and radio, as Roy Medvedev, a Soviet historian who lived through Stalinism, later explained (see Source P).

> **How was propaganda used to promote the idea of Stalin as an all-powerful leader?**

> **🔑 KEY TERM**
>
> **Cult of personality** A consistent use of mass propaganda to promote the idea of the leader as an ideal, heroic figure, elevated above ordinary people and politics.

SOURCE P

Excerpt from *Let History Judge* by Roy Medvedev, published by OUP, UK, 1989, p. 588.

Everywhere he put up monuments to himself – thousands upon thousands of factories and firms named [after] Stalin, and many cities: Stalinsk, Stalino, Stalingrad … more than can be counted. When Stalin was encouraging the cult of his personality he and his cohorts shamelessly falsified party history, twisting and suppressing many facts and producing a flood of books, articles and pamphlets filled with distortions.

> According to Source P, how did Stalin promote the cult of personality? **?**

The Stakhanovite movement

A fascinating example of distortion was the Stakhanovite movement. In August 1935, it was claimed that a coal miner, Alexei Stakhanov, had hewn fourteen times his required quota of coal in one shift. The story was wholly fabricated, but the authorities exploited it so effectively that Stakhanov's purported achievement became an inspiring example of what heights could be reached by selfless workers responding to the call of their great leader, Stalin.

Stalin in print

Stalin's wisdom and brilliance was extolled daily in the official Soviet newspapers. Hardly an article appeared in any journal that did not include the obligatory reference to his greatness. Children learned from their earliest moments to venerate Stalin as the provider of all good things. There were no textbooks in any subject that did not laud the virtues of Stalin the master builder of the Soviet nation and inspiration to his people.

Konsomol

A particularly useful instrument for the spread of Stalinist propaganda was **Konsomol**, a youth movement which had begun in Lenin's time but was created as a formal body in 1926 under the direct control of the CPSU. Among its main features were the following:

- It was open to those ages between 14 and 28, with a Young Pioneer movement for those under 14.
- It pledged itself totally to Stalin and the Party. (In this regard it paralleled the Hitler Youth in Germany – see page 93.)
- Membership was not compulsory but its attraction for young people was that it offered them the chance of eventual full membership of the CPSU.
- It grew from 2 million members in 1927 to 10 million in 1940.

Konsomol members were among the most enthusiastic supporters of the Five-Year Plans, as they proved by going off in their thousands to help build the new industrial cities. It was Konsomol which provided the flag-wavers and the cheerleaders, and organized the huge gymnastic displays that were the centrepieces of the massive parades on **May Day** and Stalin's birthday.

How did Stalin deal with the minority peoples within the Soviet Union?

Treatment of national minorities

Although as a Georgian, Stalin belonged to one of the USSR's minority peoples, his concern was always with promoting the dominance of Russia within the Soviet state. He feared that to allow minority rights would encourage challenges to his central authority. One of his motives in implementing the purges was to suppress any signs of national independence by removing potential leaders of breakaway movements. A basic method he employed to suppress possible opposition was to deport whole peoples from their homeland to a distant region of the USSR. Outstanding examples of this were:

- In 1940, the takeover of the Baltic states (Lithuania, Estonia and Latvia), and of Bukovina and Bessarabia resulted in 2 million being deported, the majority of whom died.

KEY TERM

Konsomol The Soviet Communist Union of Youth.

May Day Or 'Labour Day' – 1 May, traditionally regarded as a special day for honouring the workers and the achievements of socialism.

- In 1941, after the outbreak of war, Stalin, anxious to prevent the peoples of the western region of the USSR from actively supporting the invading German armies, ordered the deportation to Siberia of various national groups, including Kalmyks, Ukrainians, Chechens, Crimean Tatars and Volga Germans; the deportations led to the deaths of one-third of the 4 million involved.
- By 1945, some 20 million Soviet people had been uprooted.

SOURCE Q

Map of Stalin's deportations of minority peoples.

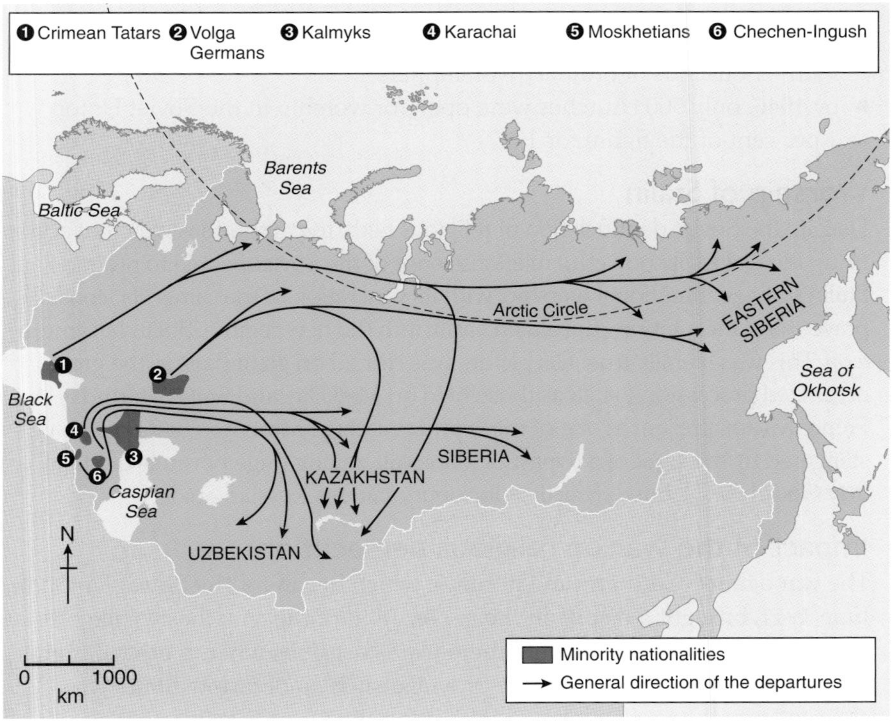

1 Crimean Tatars 2 Volga Germans 3 Kalmyks 4 Karachai 5 Moskhetians 6 Chechen-Ingush
Barents Sea
Baltic Sea
Arctic Circle
EASTERN SIBERIA
Sea of Okhotsk
Black Sea
SIBERIA
KAZAKHSTAN
Caspian Sea
UZBEKISTAN
N
0 1000 km
Minority nationalities
General direction of the departures

What does Source Q indicate regarding the extent of Stalin's deportation policies?

Religion

Why was religion persecuted under Stalin?

Religious persecution

Stalin shared Lenin's notion that religious faith had no place in a communist society. Religion, with its other-worldly values, was seen as an affront to the collective needs of the nation. In 1928, a campaign to close the churches was begun. The Russian Orthodox Christian Church was the main target but all religions and denominations were at risk. Clerics who refused to co-operate were arrested; thousands in Moscow and Leningrad were sent into exile.

The suppression of religion in the urban areas proved a fairly straightforward affair. It was a different story in the countryside. The destruction of the rural churches and the confiscation of the relics and **icons** that most peasants had in their homes led to revolts in many areas. The authorities had failed to

KEY TERM

Icons Paintings of Christ and the saints; icons were one of the great achievements of Russian culture.

understand that what to their secular mind were merely superstitions were to the peasants a precious part of their traditions. The result was widespread resistance across the rural provinces of the USSR. The response of the authorities was to declare that those who opposed the restrictions on religion were really doing so in order to resist collectivization. This allowed the requisition squads to brand the religious protesters as Kulaks and to seize their property.

Such was the bitterness these methods created that Stalin instructed his officials to call a halt. But this was only temporary. In the late 1930s, as part of the Great Terror, the assault on religion was renewed:

- 800 higher clergy and 4,000 ordinary priests were imprisoned, along with many thousands of ordinary worshippers
- by 1940, only 500 churches were open for worship in the Soviet Union – 1 per cent of the figure for 1917.

Worship of Stalin

Despite the Soviet denunciation of religious faith, the authorities were not above using the residually powerful religious sense of the Soviet people to promote Stalin's image. Traditional worship, with its veneration of the saints, its icons, prayers and incantations translated easily into the new regime. Stalin became an icon. This was literally true. His picture was carried on giant flags in the great organized processions, such as those held on May Day and Stalin's birthday. A French visitor, present at one of these processions in Moscow's Red Square, was staggered by the sight of a flypast of planes all trailing huge portraits of Stalin. 'My God!' he exclaimed. 'Exactly, Monsieur', said his Russian guide.

Impact of the war on religious persecution

The war against Germany and its allies, which began for the Soviet Union in June 1941, brought a respite in the persecution of the churches. While official policy was to denigrate religion, there were occasions when it proved highly useful to the authorities. Wartime provided such an occasion. Stalin was shrewd enough to enlist religion in fighting the Great Fatherland War. The churches were re-opened, the clergy released and the people encouraged to celebrate the uplifting Orthodox Church ceremonies. For the period of the war, the Soviet authorities under Stalin played down politics and emphasized nationalism. Talk of the proletarian struggle gave way to an appeal to defend holy Russia against the godless invaders.

The Church leaders responded as Stalin had intended. The clergy turned their services into patriotic gatherings, which expressed passionate defiance of the Germans. They urged their congregations to rally behind their great leader, Stalin, in a supreme war effort. The reward for the Church's co-operation was a lifting of the anti-religious persecution.

Post-war suppression

The improved Church-state relations continued after the war. By the time of Stalin's death in 1953, 25,000 churches had re-opened along with a number of monasteries and **seminaries**. However, this did not represent any real freedom for the Orthodox Church. The price for being allowed to exist openly was its total subservience to the regime. In 1946, Stalin required that all the Christian denominations in the Soviet Union come under the authority of the Orthodox Church which was made responsible for ensuring that organized religion did not become a source of political opposition. The Church became, in effect, an arm of government.

Education

Stalin believed that a first step in modernizing the USSR was to spread literacy. To this end, formal education was made a priority, with these key features:

- ten years of compulsory schooling for all children aged five to fifteen
- core curriculum specified reading and writing, maths, science, history, geography, Russian language and Marxist theory
- state-prescribed textbooks to be used
- homework to be a regular requirement
- state-organized tests and examinations
- school uniforms made compulsory
- fees to be charged for the last three years (ages fifteen to eighteen) of non-compulsory secondary schooling.

Development of an elite

The emphasis on regulation was not accidental. The intention was to create a disciplined generation of young people ready to join the workforce which was engaged through the Five-Year Plans in constructing the new communist society. The last feature, regarding the payment of fees, may appear to challenge the notion of an egalitarian education system. The official justification for it was that the Soviet Union needed a specially trained section of the community to serve the people in expert ways; doctors and scientists were obvious examples. Those who stayed on at school after the age of fifteen were obviously young people of marked ability who would eventually enter university to become the specialists of the future. This was undeniably a selection process, but the argument was that it was selection by ability, not by class.

That was the official line. However, although there was an undoubted rise in overall standards, the system also created an educated elite. Those who continued their education after the age of fifteen were mainly the children of government officials and Party members who could afford the fees. Private tuition and private education became normal for them. As a consequence, as university education expanded, it was Party members or their children who had the first claim on the best places. As graduates, they then had access to the three key areas of Soviet administration – industry, the civil service and the armed services.

The nomenklatura

The promotional process had an important political consequence. It enhanced Stalin's power by creating a **nomenklatura** that had every motive for

KEY TERM

Seminaries Training colleges for priests.

What role did education play in consolidating Stalin's authority?

KEY TERM

Nomenklatura The Soviet 'establishment' – privileged officials who ran the Party and government.

supporting him. The poet, Osip Mandelstam, described this precisely: 'A thin layer of privileged people gradually came into being with "**packets**". Those who had been granted a share of the cake eagerly did everything asked of them.'

The status of women

How did the status of women in the Soviet Union change under Stalin?

Marriage

In keeping with their Marxist rejection of marriage as a bourgeois institution, Lenin's Bolsheviks had made divorce easier and had attempted to liberate women from the bondage of children and family. However, after only a brief period of experiment, Lenin's government had come to question its earlier enthusiasm for sweeping change in this area. Stalin shared their doubts. Indeed, he was convinced the earlier Bolshevik social experiment had failed. By the end of the 1930s, the Soviet divorce rate was the highest in Europe – one divorce for every two marriages. This led him to embark on what has been called 'the great retreat'. Stalin began to stress the value of the family as a stabilizing influence in society. He let it be known that he did not approve of the sexual freedoms that had followed the 1917 Revolution. He argued that a good communist was a socially responsible one: 'a poor husband and father, a poor wife and mother, cannot be good citizens'.

Stalin, aware of the social upheavals collectivization and industrialization were causing, was trying to create some form of balance by emphasizing the traditional social values attaching to the role of women as home-makers and child-raisers. He was also greatly exercised by the number of orphaned children living on the streets of the urban areas. Left to fend for themselves, the children had formed themselves into feral gangs of scavengers and violent thieves. Disorder of this kind further convinced Stalin of the need to re-establish family structures.

Changes in social policy

His first major move came in June 1936 with a decree that reversed much of earlier Bolshevik social policy:

- Unregistered marriages were no longer recognized.
- Divorce was made more difficult.
- The right to abortion was severely restricted.
- The family was declared to be the basis of Soviet society.
- Homosexuality was outlawed.

Conscious of both the falling birth rate and of how many people were dying in the Great Fatherland War, the authorities introduced measures in July 1944 re-affirming the importance of the family in the USSR and giving incentives to women to have large numbers of children:

- Restrictions on divorce were further tightened.
- Abortion was totally outlawed.
- Mothers with more than two children were declared to be 'heroines of the Soviet Union'.

- Heavier taxes were imposed on parents with fewer than two children.
- The right to inherit family property was re-established.

Women and equality

One group that certainly felt they had lost out were the female members of the Party and the **intelligentsia**, who had welcomed the Russian Revolution as the beginning of female liberation. However, the strictures on sexual freedom under Stalin, and the emphasis on family and motherhood, allowed little room for the notion of the independent female.

Soviet propaganda spoke of the equality of women, but there was no great advance towards this in practical terms. A 'Housewives' Movement' was created in 1936 under Stalin's patronage. Composed largely of the wives of high-ranking industrialists and managers, it set itself the task of 'civilizing' the tastes and improving the conditions of the workers. However, the reality was that few resources were allocated and little attention was paid to organizations such as this. Stalin spoke continually of the nation being under siege and of the need to build a war economy. This made any movement not directly concerned with industrial production or defence seem largely irrelevant. Most women's organizations fell into this category.

Impact of war on women's status

There were individual cases of women gaining in status and income in Stalin's time. However, these were in a small minority and were invariably unmarried or childless women. Married women with children carried a double burden. The great demand for labour that accompanied Stalin's industrialization drive required that women join the workforce. They now had to fulfil two roles: as mothers raising the young and as workers contributing to the modernization of the Soviet Union. This imposed great strains upon them, markedly so during the war of 1941–45. The loss of men at the front and the desperate need to keep the armaments factories running meant that women became indispensable. In 1936 there had been 9 million women in the industrial workforce. By 1945, the number had risen to 15 million.

Equally striking figures, such as those in Source R (page 56), show that during the war over half a million women fought in the Soviet armed forces and that, by 1945, half of all Soviet workers were female. Without their effort the USSR could not have survived. Yet women received no comparable reward. Despite their contribution to the Five-Year Plans and to the war effort, women's pay rates in real terms dropped between 1930 and 1945.

The clear conclusion is that, for all the Soviet talk of women's progress under Stalinism, the evidence suggests that they were increasingly exploited. It is hard to dispute the conclusion of the distinguished scholar, Geoffrey Hosking, that 'the fruits of female emancipation became building blocks of the Stalinist **neopatriarchal** social system'.

KEY TERM

Intelligentsia Persons of influence in the intellectual world; for example, academics and writers.

Neopatriarchal A new form of male domination.

SOURCE R

Number of women in the Soviet industrial workforce.

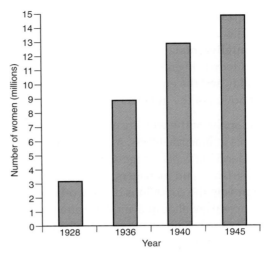

SUMMARY DIAGRAM

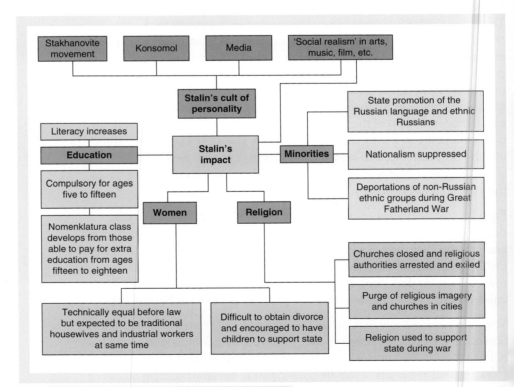

Stalin's domestic policies and their impact, 1929–53

4 Key debate

> ▶ **Key question:** *How far did Stalin achieve a totalitarian state?*

There will probably never be total agreement as to what Stalinism actually was, but the following list suggests some of the principal features of the system which operated during the quarter of a century during which Stalin had mastery over the USSR:

- Stalin ran the USSR by a bureaucratic system of government.
- He fulfilled the work begun by Lenin of turning revolutionary Russia into a one-party state.
- Political and social control was maintained by a terror system whose main instruments were regular purges and show trials directed against the Party, the armed services and the people.
- Stalin created a command economy with agriculture and industry under central direction.
- Stalin's highly individual rule developed into a 'cult of personality' which led to his becoming absolute in authority since he was regarded as the embodiment of the Communist Party and the nation.
- He created a siege mentality in the USSR, insisting that even in peace time the Soviet people had to be on permanent guard from enemies within and hostile nations outside.
- He imposed his concept of 'socialism in one country', a policy which subordinated everything to the interests of the Soviet Union as a nation.
- Stalin's rule meant the suppression of any form of genuine democracy, since he operated on the principle, laid down by Lenin, of democratic centralism (see pages 19–20), which obliged members of the CPSU to accept uncritically and obey all orders and instructions handed down by the Party leaders.
- The USSR recognized only one correct and acceptable ideology: Marxism-Leninism-Stalinism. All other belief systems were prohibited.
- Strict censorship was imposed as a means of enforcing cultural conformity in accordance with Stalin's notion of socialist realism.

Character of the Soviet state

Such details present a strong argument for defining Stalin's regime as totalitarian. However, some historians are reluctant to use that particular adjective to describe Stalin's domination of the USSR. They suggest that he was not all-powerful – no one individual in a nation can be – and that his power depended on the willingness of thousands of underlings to carry out his orders and policies. While not disputing the huge impact that Stalin had upon his country, such writers point to other areas of significant development that occurred which did not depend on Stalin. This school of thought concentrates not so much on what Stalin did during the era he dominated the USSR, but on the character of Soviet communism itself.

← **What were the main features of the Soviet state under Stalin?**

Intrinsic violence of Soviet communism

Richard Overy draws attention to the violence that was intrinsic to Soviet communism. He quotes Stalin's assertion that violence was an 'inevitable law of the revolutionary movement' and links it to Lenin's declaration that the task of Bolshevism was 'the ruthless destruction of the enemy'. The Stalinist purges, therefore, were a logical historical progression.

Lack of a tradition of civil rights

In this connection, other scholars have laid weight on how undeveloped the concepts of individual or civil rights were in Russia. Tsardom had been an autocracy in which the first duty of the people had been to obey. The Communists had not changed that. Indeed, they had re-emphasized the necessity of obedience to central authority.

Self-interest of the nomenklatura

It was certainly true Stalin had no difficulty in finding eager subordinates to organize the purges. The common characteristic of those who led Stalin's campaigns was their unswerving personal loyalty to him, a loyalty that overcame any doubts they might have had regarding the nature of their work. They formed the new class of officials that Stalin created to replace the old Bolsheviks, whom he had decimated in the purges. One prominent historian, M. Agursky, has stressed this development as the basic explanation of why terror became so embedded in the Stalinist system. Dedicated to Stalin on whom their positions depended, the nomenklatura enjoyed rights and privileges denied to the rest of the population. Including their families, they numbered around 600,000 (1.2 per cent of the population) by the late 1930s. Such persons once in post were unlikely to question Stalin's orders. The more potential rivals they exterminated the safer their jobs were.

Fear of Stalin

In a major study, Simon Sebag Montefiore has added an interesting slant by illustrating the eagerness with which Stalin's top ministers carried out his campaigns of terror and persecution. Though they were terrified of him, they did not simply obey him out of fear. People like Beria and Molotov derived the same vindictive satisfaction from their work as their master. Like him, they appeared to have no moral scruples.

Revolution from above

Yet the hard fact remains that, notwithstanding the attitudes of ordinary Soviet people, of the nomenklatura, and of government ministers, it was Stalin who gave the USSR its essential shape. Whatever the motives of those who carried out Stalin's policies, he was the great motivator. Little of importance took place in the USSR of which he did not approve. That is why some prominent historians, such as Robert Tucker, still speak of Stalinism as 'revolution from above', meaning that the changes that occurred under Stalin were directed by him from the top down. This is one definition of Stalin's totalitarianism that is likely to stand.

Chapter summary

The USSR under Joseph Stalin, 1924–53

Following Lenin's death in 1924, Stalin proved victorious in a power struggle with both the Left and the Right of the Soviet Communist Party. With the defeat of his main rival, Trotsky, in 1929, Stalin was free to shape the USSR according to his own design. Under the slogan 'Socialism in One Country', he planned to modernize the USSR so that it would not be at the mercy of its external enemies. To achieve this, he launched a 'second revolution': the Soviet economy was to be revolutionized through collectivization and industrialization, policies which involved a huge social upheaval.

It was to quell the protests caused by the turmoil that Stalin resorted to the purges, a system of oppression that lasted from the early 1930s until his death in 1953. The purges were used to remove all real and imagined opposition to him: the Communist Party, the armed services, and ordinary citizens were all targeted as Stalin, driven as much by paranoia as rational judgement, imposed his authority. He was backed in this by officials and administrators who were eager to fill the positions that the purges made vacant.

In building his power, Stalin developed a 'cult of personality'. Soviet propaganda extolled him as the supremely wise leader of the nation, whose inspired understanding covered all areas of political, economic and social life. Strength was given to this image by Stalin's successful guidance of his people through the Great Fatherland War against Germany between 1941 and 1945. Victory in the war also appeared to vindicate the harsh measures he had previously adopted in enforcing industrialization at breathless speed.

Stalin's all-pervading influence extended into culture. It was at his insistence that all creative artists conform to his notion of 'social realism'. He also made improvement in education a priority, successfully encouraging the raising of literacy levels among the people. A social conservative by nature, Stalin was unhappy at some of the progressive developments that had occurred since 1917. He insisted that the family and the role of women as mothers and homemakers must remain central to Soviet society.

Examination practice

Below are a number of different questions for you to practise. For guidance on how to answer exam-style questions, see Chapter 10.

1 Explain Stalin's rise to power by 1928.

2 Discuss the role of propaganda in maintaining Stalin as the Soviet Union's leader.

3 Analyse the importance of ideology in Stalin's rise and maintenance of power until his death.

4 To what extent were Stalin's economic plans successful?

5 How did Stalin view the role of women in Soviet society?

6 What was the importance of the purges for Stalin?

7 How did Stalin's rule impact upon religion and minority groups?

8 Discuss the impact of Stalin's rule on the arts.

9 To what extent was Stalin successful in achieving his political and economic aims by 1941?

10 Analyse the impact of Stalin's rule on peasants and industrial workers by 1941.

 # Activities

I Create a timeline of Stalin's rise to, and consolidation of, power (1917–53). You could expand this to include visual images, biographies and historiography.

2 Consider the following points with reference to history and TOK in a class discussion:
   a) Stalin's rule destroyed the lives of many people, but this was acceptable since the majority of the Soviet Union's citizens benefited.
   b) The goal of a totally equal society is a moral obligation for the world's citizens.
   c) Social and economic equality is unobtainable and should therefore not be attempted.

3 Research the views of Trotsky in regards to communism. Compare and contrast these views with Stalin's. Make a judgement as to which of these two visions of communism was:
   a) more practical
   b) more in line with Marxism
   c) more likely to succeed.

CHAPTER 3

Germany under Adolf Hitler, 1933–45

In the years 1933–45, Adolf Hitler created the Third Reich, a German state based on the ideas that he had promoted as leader of the Nazi Party since the 1920s. Using authoritarian methods, the Nazi Party and government under Hitler sought to develop Germany as an economically self-sufficient nation, free of all Jewish influences and intent on restoring the pride lost by its defeat in the First World War of 1914–18. This chapter examines the following key questions:

✪ What circumstances favoured the rise of Hitler?
✪ How did Hitler impose his authority on Germany?
✪ What impact did the Nazi regime have on the lives of the German people?
✪ How far did Hitler achieve a totalitarian state?

① Hitler's rise to power, 1919–33

What were conditions and methods that allowed Nazis to come to power

> ▶ *Key question: What circumstances favoured the rise of Hitler?*

Germany after 1918

> **What problems did its defeat in 1918 leave Germany?**

Germany emerged from the First World War a defeated and embittered nation. For many Germans, the humiliation they felt at having lost the war was intensified by the anger they felt towards their political leaders who had allowed it to happen. Most Germans had enthusiastically welcomed the outbreak of war in 1914 as an opportunity for them to prove the strength of their young nation by a great victory over their European rivals. Tragically for them, no such victory occurred. After four years of exhausting struggle, an impoverished Germany was forced to admit defeat in 1918. The losses and suffering of four long years of war had been in vain. The anger this created was intensified by the terms imposed on Germany by the victors under the Treaty of Versailles signed in June 1919.

The main terms of the Treaty of Versailles, 1919

- Loss of territories in Europe to France and Poland, depriving Germany of 4 million people.
- Loss of Germany's overseas colonies.
- German army limited to 100,000.

- Germany obliged to pay heavy financial reparations for war damage.
- Germany had to accept a war-guilt clause, declaring it responsible for starting the war.

Map of Germany after the Versailles settlement, 1919.

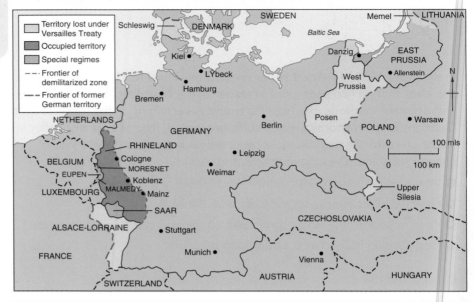

Study Source A. What territories in Europe did Germany lose in the Treaty of Versailles?

What the Germans also resented was that the Versailles Treaty was a *diktat*. The German delegation was not allowed to discuss the terms; it was simply told to agree to them or suffer continued occupation and a renewal of the war.

Factors creating post-war instability

Resentment at the imposed peace settlement, combined with the shock of military defeat and the conviction that the nation had been betrayed from within by corrupt and craven politicians, created post-war political instability in Germany. The situation was made worse by economic problems created by crippling war debts, the burden of having to pay reparations, and high unemployment.

Such factors made post-war Germany a volatile place. Resentment was widespread and deeply felt. Violence was a constant presence as parties of the Right and Left struggled to exploit the situation. Street fights between contending factions became commonplace. In such an atmosphere revolution seemed increasingly likely.

The Weimar Republic

Germany's defeat in war destroyed the Second **Reich**. The Kaiser (emperor) abdicated and the imperial government resigned, to be replaced by the **Weimar** republic which in 1919 adopted a new constitution with:

- a President as head of state, to be elected every seven years, given power to rule by decree in a time of national emergency

---

🔑 KEY TERM

Diktat An imposed settlement.

Reich The German word for 'empire'. There were three Germanic empires, the First (962–1806), the Second (1871–1918) and the Third (1933–45).

Weimar A country town chosen as the new capital and seat of government of Germany in 1919 instead of troubled Berlin.

- a Chancellor, appointed by the President, to be head of government
- an elected Reichstag in which seats would be allocated to parties by **PR**.

Despite its democratic appearance, the constitution proved to have two serious weaknesses:

- The right of the President to rule by decree in times of crisis gave him potentially dictatorial powers.
- The spreading of seats across as many parties as possible through PR had the effect of making it very difficult for a single party to form a majority government. Unstable coalitions became the norm.

Consequently, from its beginning, the Weimar government lacked the confidence of the German people. This was clear from the series of violent challenges to it from both Left and Right. German communists, inspired by the Russian Revolution of 1917 (see page 18), tried to achieve a similar revolution in Germany, only to be crushed by the *freikorps*, a loose organization of soldiers returning from the war who held strong nationalist feelings and who were sharply opposed to the communists.

The emergence of Adolf Hitler

Before 1918, Adolf Hitler, an Austrian by birth, had displayed no particular political gifts. Having gone to Vienna in 1907 at the age of eighteen with the aim of training as an artist, he had failed the art college entrance exam. For the next seven years he did little. He became a drifter, staying in cheap hostels and living off a small inherited income. Hitler later claimed that it was during his Vienna years that he developed the political ideas that became the basis of his subsequent politics. In *Mein Kampf* ('My Struggle'), an autobiographical account written in 1924, he defined these as German nationalism and hatred of Jews. However, research has shown that *Mein Kampf* is unreliable. It is true that he had developed a genuine attachment to Germany, but there is no evidence that Hitler had strong anti-Semitic ideas in Vienna. Moreover, during the 1914–18 war, as a serving soldier in a German regiment, he had raised no objections to serving with Jewish comrades or being commanded by Jewish officers.

Hitler's political ideas

Hitler's thoughts did not turn towards active politics until Germany's defeat in 1918. The picture that emerges from the evidence is of a Hitler made bitterly angry by Germany's capitulation, but uncertain how to respond. His uncertainty made him susceptible to extremist ideas. He was willing to contemplate revolution as a way of achieving German recovery but not sure whether the revolution should come from the Left or Right. His initial decision was to support the communists when they seized power in Munich in April 1919 and established a revolutionary **Soviet**.

However, when, after a few weeks, the Soviet was bloodily suppressed, Hitler quickly switched from Left- to Right-wing socialism. Pushing him in

KEY TERM

PR Proportional representation, the allocation of seats according to the number of votes cast for each party.

Freikorps German paramilitary units of demobbed soldiers.

Soviet An attempted recreation of the type of workers' council which Lenin's communists had established in Russia.

Why did Hitler become an extreme nationalist?

White *émigrés* Tsarist
supporters who had fled to
Germany from Russia after
the Russian Revolution.

NSDAP National Socialist
German Workers' Party
(Nazi Party).

Volk The nation as a
community of racially pure
Germans.

SA *Sturmabteilung* ('storm
troopers'): Hitler's
paramilitary force.

this direction were the contacts he made in 1919 with influential nationalist
groups in Munich. The nationalists had acted as hosts to a number of **White
*émigrés*** who had settled in Munich. Rabidly anti-Semitic, the *émigrés* drew
on their first-hand knowledge of Lenin's regime (see page 20) to explain
Germany's current crisis in simple terms. It was, they argued, the product of
a Jewish–Bolshevik plot to undermine German culture and society. The
argument appealed to the nationalists' sense of victimhood. Hitler found it
convincing and swiftly adopted it as an expression of his political thinking.

Hitler's targets

To advance his views, Hitler began to make speeches to political gatherings
in Munich and southern Germany. Favourite venues were beer halls and
bars where raucous political debate was a traditional activity. Hitler excelled
in such surroundings. He discovered in himself a particular talent for public
speaking. He played on the prejudices of his audience by denouncing those
Germans who had betrayed Germany at the end of the First World War.
Developing the notions to which the White *émigrés* had introduced him, he
identified particular targets:

- the politicians who had accepted Germany's defeat in 1918
- communists
- Jews who, in league with communists, were engaged in a worldwide
  conspiracy to destroy international finance as a first step to Jewish global
  domination.

What were the aims
of the Nazi Party
under Hitler?

The Nazi Party

Given Hitler's views, it was unsurprising that he found himself attracted to
the Munich-based German Workers' Party (DAP) whose ultra-nationalism
matched the ideas he had begun to develop. Having joined the young party,
which renamed itself the Nazi Party in 1920, Hitler very quickly rose to
become its leader a year later.

National Socialism (Nazism)

The change of the party's name from DAP to National Socialist German
Workers' Party (**NSDAP** or Nazi) was accompanied by the issuing of a new
party programme, which Hitler helped to draft. The extreme nationalist
character of the programme was evident in its key demands, which were:

- the union of all Germans in a greater Germany
- the revocation of the Treaty of Versailles
- the gaining of territories to accommodate German's surplus population
- the restriction of state citizenship to those of German blood
- Jews to be denied membership of the *Volk*.

The SA

In the tough world of the German streets in the 1920s, it was essential for a
party to have physical force at its disposal. To meet this need, Hitler
established the **SA** as his strong-arm guards. Under the leadership of Ernst

Röhm, the SA recruited its members from the large number of rootless, unemployed young men who were to be found in most of Germany's cities in the 1920s. Wearing brown shirt uniforms, the SA members felt a keen sense of brotherhood as they were directed by their leaders to attack communists and Jews. Their aggressive marches, their singing and their torchlight processions terrified opponents into silence and advertised Nazism to the German people.

The Munich *Putsch*, 1923

In November 1923, Hitler believed that the Nazis were strong enough to seize power. He took his cue from the **hyper-inflation** that had begun earlier in the year as a consequence of the French occupation of the Ruhr, which denied Germany access to its most economically productive region. Between January and October 1923, the value of the German mark fell from 7,590 per US dollar to 4,200,000,000,000. Attempting to exploit the unrest this upheaval created, Hitler and General Ludendorff, a former head of the German army in the First World War and now a leading Nazi Party member, attempted to seize power in Munich in an armed rising. However, when the Nazis marched on the government offices, the Bavarian police fired on the marchers, who scattered in disorder. Hitler was arrested, tried for treason and sentenced to five years' imprisonment.

The authorities, embarrassed by rumours that a number of officials had been implicated in the ***putsch*** and sympathetic towards Hitler's basic nationalism, decided not to treat him too severely, as his release after less than a year made clear. Hitler had behaved arrogantly during the trial, an indication that he did not regard the *putsch* as a failure: it had provided the opportunity to spread Nazi propaganda and he vowed that his time would come again. The *putsch* quickly became a piece of Nazi lore, celebrated annually as 'Martyrs' Day' in honour of the sixteen marchers who had been killed in the rising.

Mein Kampf

Hitler used his time in prison to write *Mein Kampf*, a mixture of autobiography and ideology. The book was not so much a plan of action as an emotional appeal to the German people to identify their enemies and then follow the Nazis in destroying them. The text expressed his main political ideas, including:

- the conviction that politics was dialectical – a bitter struggle between irreconcilable opposites
- unshakable belief in Germany's destiny as a great **Aryan** nation to destroy Jewry and seize the Slav lands of the east
- a passionate hatred of communism
- belief in the power of the state as the central social organization
- the conviction that women were subordinate to men and should not engage in politics.

 **KEY TERM**

Hyper-inflation Very rapid and destructive fall in the purchasing value of money, causing a rapid drop in the value of the currency and a sharp rise in prices.

Putsch An armed rising.

Aryan A person of Caucasian race; as understood by Hitler, the ideal racial type that was superior to all others.

According to Source B, what were the main features of National Socialism as defined by Hitler?

SOURCE B

Excerpt from *Hitler* by Michael Lynch, published by Routledge, UK, 2013, p. 62.

Many historians have come to regard it [Mein Kampf] as the nearest we have to a definitive analysis of National Socialism whose essential features were: an unshakable belief in Germany's role as a great Aryan nation destined to save itself and the world, the rejection of the crippling Versailles Treaty that had been imposed on Germany, and a burning hatred of Jews and Communists, who were joined in an enterprise to destroy German identity and culture.

Hitler's change of strategy

When Hitler came out of prison in 1924 he was resolved upon a new strategy. While still relying on violent tactics in the streets to silence opposition, he would present the Nazi movement to the voters as a constitutional party, bent on winning power democratically. Although he despised democracy as a feeble process, he was prepared for expedient reasons to use Weimar's electoral system.

According to Hitler in Source C, what new strategy had he decided to adopt?

SOURCE C

A comment by Hitler to one of the Nazi Party's financial backers in 1924, quoted in *I Knew Hitler* by Kurt Lüdecke, published by Jarrolds Publishers Ltd, UK, 1938, p. 234.

Instead of working to achieve power by an armed coup we shall have to hold our noses and enter the Reichstag against the Catholic and Marxist deputies. If out-voting them takes longer than outshooting them, at least the results will be guaranteed by their own constitution! Any lawful process is slow. Sooner or later we will have a majority, and after that – Germany.

Hitler's power struggle within the party, 1925–30

Hitler's change of approach upset those in the Nazi Party who wanted to continue with the previous uncompromisingly tough methods. Factions developed and Hitler found himself involved in a power struggle within the Nazi Party. His major opponents were the brothers, Otto and Gregor Strasser, who led a minority group who believed that Nazism should be much more socialist in its approach and should openly oppose capitalism. The Strassers attacked the big German industrialists and argued that the Nazis should develop closer relations with the anti-capitalist Soviet Union. Hitler, however, was anxious to enlist the support of the leading industrialists in Germany and believed that the Strassers' ideas would undermine the NSDAP.

The leadership question

A series of fierce disputes followed. Beneath the disagreements about policy, there was a more fundamental issue: Hitler's leadership. Otto Strasser criticized Hitler for attempting to make himself more important than the Nazi Party itself: 'A leader must serve the Idea. To this alone can we devote ourselves entirely, since it is eternal whereas the Leader passes and makes mistakes.' Hitler responded by asserting that the leader defined the movement. He spoke bitterly of Strasser's 'revolting democracy', explaining: 'For us the Leader is the Idea, and each party member has to obey only the Leader.'

In July 1930, Otto Strasser attempted to split the NSDAP and weaken Hitler by resigning from the party and establishing his own organization, the Union of Revolutionary Socialists. However, only 25 other Nazis joined him and these did not even include his brother, Gregor, who remained loyal to Hitler. Otto Strasser's desperate move had failed and he left Germany. He continued to attack Hitler from afar, but his influence rapidly decreased and what little support he had had dwindled.

What Strasser had unwittingly done by his challenge to Hitler was to hand him a victory within the Nazi Party that put his leadership of it beyond doubt. Hitler now personified the Nazi Party. Nazism was Hitlerism.

The influence of the Great Depression

Remarkable though Hitler's personal powers were, he and his party would have made little progress in attracting popular support had not Germany in the late 1920s entered a period of economic crisis. During the 1920s the German economy recovered well from its post-war difficulties; having survived the hyper-inflation of 1923, its industrial output grew considerably and the number of unemployed workers fell. In the improved economic climate, the Nazis had made little progress. A German commentator remarked: 'If the sun shines once more on the German economy, Hitler's voters will melt away like snow.'

However, by 1930, Germany had begun to feel the full effects of the Great Depression. Workers were laid off, shops and businesses closed, and banks collapsed. The Weimar government had no answer. Indeed, the protective policies it adopted, such as restricting foreign imports, led to retaliation by other countries and produced higher unemployment in Germany.

It was this harsh reality that gave the Nazis a new relevance and saved them from being an impotent, fringe party. As Source E (page 68) shows, the Nazi Party's early record in the elections to the Reichstag was unimpressive. It was not until 1930 that its percentage of the vote reached double figures. The reason for that increase in support was that, by that date, the Nazis were able to exploit the economic difficulties that had begun to threaten Germany's stability.

? Study Source D. What information does it provide regarding unemployment in Germany between 1926 and 1933?

SOURCE D

Graph showing German unemployment figures, 1926–33.

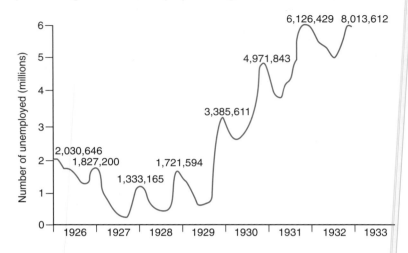

? In what ways do the data in Source D help to explain the performance of the Nazis as recorded in Source E?

SOURCE E

The Reichstag election results, 1924–32, showing the relative performance of three main parties: NSDAP, Communists (KPD) and Socialists (SPD).

Elections	May 1924	Dec 1924	May 1928	Sep 1930	Jul 1932	Nov 1932
Seats						
NSDAP	32	14	12	107	230	196
KPD	62	45	54	77	89	100
SPD	100	131	153	143	133	121
% of vote						
NSDAP	6.6	3.0	2.6	18.3	37.4	33.1
KPD	12.6	9.0	10.6	13.1	14.6	16.9
SPD	20.5	26.0	29.8	24.5	21.6	20.4

🔑 KEY TERM

Lower middle class
Shopkeepers, traders, professional people, etc.

Support for Hitler and the Nazis

It was the **lower middle class**, traditionally regarded as the respectable, dependable element in German society, who felt most threatened by the economic collapse. Believing that their security and livelihood were at risk, they turned away from the ineffectual Weimar system with its weak political parties and towards the Nazis. This class provided the backbone of Nazi support.

A number of other factors came together in the early 1930s to make the Nazis the most appealing of the parties to the German electorate:

- The Weimar Republic was increasingly judged to be incapable of dealing with Germany's political and economic problems.

- Defectors from the ineffectual moderate parties turned to the extremist parties.
- The intense nationalism of the Nazi Party proved of greater attraction than the pro-Soviet bias of the **KPD**.
- The other political parties represented sectional interests and lacked the wide appeal of the Nazis who claimed to be a genuinely national party.
- Many patriotic Germans turned towards Nazism as the great protector of the nation against the menace of communism.
- Younger voters were drawn to Hitler's populist image as someone who understood their needs.
- The unemployed saw hope in the Nazi promises of salvation. A typical unemployed labourer remarked, 'I had lost all I possessed through bad economic conditions. And so, early in 1930, I joined the Nazi Party.'
- The *Landbund*, representing the landowner class, pledged its support for the Nazis in 1931 after Hitler's promise that he would protect them from the land-grabbing communists.
- German industrialists, disillusioned with Weimar's economic failures, dropped their earlier objections to the Nazi movement.
- Hitler's passionate support for the millions of Germans who, under the Treaty of Versailles, had been placed under foreign governments appealed to all those Germans who felt that the Weimar Republic had failed to defend German interests abroad.

KEY TERM

KPD *Kommunistische Partei Deutschlands* (German Communist Party).

Hitler's path to the Chancellorship

← By what steps did Hitler attain the Chancellorship in 1933?

Between 1930 and 1933 the political situation worked greatly to Hitler's advantage. Party politics ceased to function in any meaningful sense. Since none of the parties had a majority in the Reichstag, governments were necessarily coalitions incapable of exercising real authority. This made them reliant on President Hindenburg to put their policies into effect by issuing emergency decrees.

The coalitions, 1930–33

Between 1930 and 1933 Germany was led by three successive coalition governments:

- March 1930 – May 1932 led by Heinrich Brüning
- May 1932 – December 1932 led by Franz von Papen
- December 1932 – January 1933 led by Kurt von Schleicher.

Brüning and von Papen both belonged to the Catholic Centre Party and their cabinets were made up largely of members of Right-wing and nationalist parties. Hitler was invited to join the coalitions in a minor role but he preferred to bide his time. Hitler was also under pressure from within his own party. Some Nazis, led by Gregor Strasser, the most prominent socialist-minded member in the party, grew impatient and urged Hitler to exploit the unstable political situation by directing the SA to overthrow the government and take power by force.

Hitler rejected the notion. He believed that if he waited upon events they would eventually unfold in his favour legally. He judged that as leader of the largest party he could not be ignored. And so it proved. The conservative Hindenburg, who disliked Hitler only slightly less than he did the Communist Party, reluctantly asked him to serve as Vice-Chancellor under von Papen. Again Hitler refused. He wanted the Chancellorship and calculated that as leader of the largest single party that prize could not long be denied him.

The presidential elections, 1932

Hitler considerably strengthened his hand in 1932 by standing against Hindenburg in the presidential election of that year. He did not expect victory; his aim was to measure his popularity. Since the first election did not give Hindenburg outright victory, a second election was held. The results were highly satisfying for Hitler. Rounded to the nearest thousand they were:

	Hindenburg	Hitler
March 1932	18,000,000	11,000,000
April 1932	19,000,000	13,000,000

Reichstag elections, 1932

Further encouragement came in the Reichstag election of July 1932: the Nazis doubled their previous vote and won twice as many seats. However, just how closely tied Nazi support was to the economic situation was revealed by the election returns of November 1932, when an improvement in conditions saw a swing of over 4 per cent away from the NSDAP and a loss of 34 seats.

Hitler becomes Chancellor

Yet this proved only a minor setback; the fact remained that the Nazis were still the largest party. When General von Schleicher, frustrated by his failure to form a workable coalition, asked Hindenburg to give him the authority to impose military rule on Germany, the President refused. Eventually at the end of January 1933, after being assured by Franz von Papen, the acting Chancellor, that Hitler would be far less dangerous in office than out, Hindenburg formally appointed Hitler as Chancellor. Hitler's combination of patience and opportunism had outmanoeuvred a set of conservative politicians who had mistakenly thought they could render him harmless by inviting him into office.

Explaining Hitler's success

- One of the extraordinary aspects of Hitler's success in gaining the Chancellorship was how ill-defined his stated objectives had been: Nazi propaganda (see page 89) had been directed towards attacking political opponents, rather than developing a clearly defined Nazi programme.
- Hitler calculated that for the electorate it was more important that it knew what the Nazis were against than what they were for. Exploiting people's fears of communists and Jews brought more votes than presenting a detailed set of measured Nazi policies.
- There was no contemporary German politician capable of matching Hitler's determination and political ability.
- Hitler was the beneficiary of what would now be called a protest vote: Richard J. Evans, a celebrated historian of the Nazi movement, uses the term 'protest vote' as a way of explaining why the German electorate were attracted by Hitler and the Nazis.

SOURCE F

Excerpt from *The Coming of the Third Reich* by Richard J. Evans, published by Allen Lane, UK, 2003, p. 448.

[T]he Nazi vote was above all a protest vote; and, after 1928, Hitler … and the Party leadership recognized this implicitly by removing most of their specific policies, in so far as they had any, from the limelight, and concentrating on a vague, emotional appeal that emphasized little more than the Party's youth and dynamism, its determination to destroy the Weimar Republic, the Communist Party and the Social Democrats, and its belief that only through the unity of all social classes could Germany be reborn.

According to Source F, what were the key aspects of the Nazi protest vote?

Another remarkable aspect of Hitler's success was that he somehow looked upon himself as above the politics in which he was engaged. He appeared to be waiting upon events as if he knew that it was his destiny to take power. One of his Nazi associates, Ernst Hanfstaengl, commenting on Hitler's attitude, observed:

SOURCE G

Excerpt from *Hitler: The Missing Years* by Ernst Hanfstaengl, published by Arcade Publishing, USA, 1994 edition (first published 1957), p. 81.

He did not concern himself with the day-to-day kaleidoscope of the political scene. He was not looking for alliances or coalitions or temporary tactical advantage. He wanted power, supreme and complete, and was convinced that if he talked often enough and aroused the masses sufficiently, he must in due course be swept into office.

According to Source G, why was Hitler so confident of eventually gaining power?

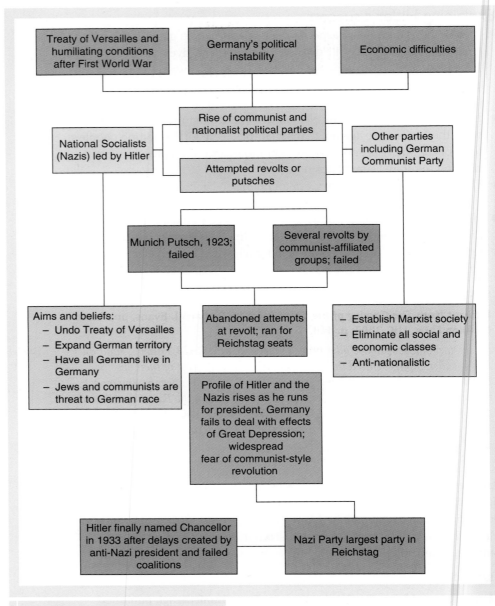

SUMMARY DIAGRAM

Hitler's rise to power, 1919–33

2 Hitler's establishment of an authoritarian state

▶ *Key question:* How did Hitler impose his authority on Germany?

Von Papen's boast that Hitler as Chancellor would effectively be under the control of the other parties in the government proved hopelessly ill-judged. Within two months of becoming Chancellor, Hitler had largely removed the constitutional limits to his authority. Two connected events formed the prelude to this: the burning of the Reichstag building and Nazi success in what was to prove the last Reichstag election.

Hitler was concerned to consolidate his authority by apparently constitutional means. He wanted the Reichstag to pass an **Enabling Bill** giving him personal power. To that end, he persuaded Hindenburg to call an election in March. Piers Brendon, a modern scholar, aptly notes: 'To consolidate his position as Chancellor Hitler insisted on holding a democratic election to end democracy.'

The structuring of Hitler's power, 1933–34

The Reichstag fire, February 1933

In February 1933, a Dutch communist set fire to the Reichstag building in Berlin. It was a lone action but the Nazis immediately denounced it as part of a large-scale communist plot. Watching the fire on the night of 27 February, Hitler exclaimed: 'It is the work of the Reds [communists]. We must crush these murderous pests with an iron fist.' Joseph Goebbels, the Nazi Propaganda Minister, and his team immediately picked up the *Führer*'s cue. Skilfully using the charged atmosphere that the fire had created in the run-up to the Reichstag elections in March, they mounted an aggressive campaign, asserting that only a strong Nazi government led by Hitler could save Germany from communist revolution. On the streets, the SA terrorized the other parties into virtual silence. The principal target was the KPD, whose leaders were arrested, whose personnel were physically and openly attacked, and whose offices were vandalized.

The Reichstag election, March 1933

Since, under the Weimar constitution, a two-thirds majority in the Reichstag was necessary for the Enabling Bill to be passed, it was essential that the elections return a Reichstag dominated by the NSDAP. Hitler needed to prevent KPD and SPD deputies being returned to the new Reichstag in anything like their previous numbers. The persuasive and aggressive election campaign proved highly successful. The NSDAP's share of the vote increased from 33 per cent to 44 per cent and its number of seats rose from 196 to 288. The Nazis now had far more popular support than any other party.

KEY TERM

Enabling Bill A measure which granted the German Chancellor the power to govern by personal decree without reference to the Reichstag.

Führer The 'leader', used informally from 1924 to refer to Hitler and adopted in 1934 as his formal title.

By what steps did Hitler create his power base?

Review the data in Source H.
What do they suggest about
the importance of the centre
parties, Zentrum and DNVP?

SOURCE H

Reichstag election results, March 1933.

Party	Number of votes	% of vote	Seats
NSDAP (Nazis)	17.3 million	43.9	288
Socialists (SPD)	7.5 million	18.3	120
Communists (KDP)	4.8 million	12.3	81
Catholic Centre Party (Zentrum)	4.4 million	11.2	74
National People's Party (DNVP)	3.1 million	8	52
Bavarian People's Party	1.1 million	2.7	18
Others	1.2 million	3	14

Negotiations

However, since the Nazis did not have an overall majority, the question now was whether the Reichstag would give Hitler the two-thirds majority required to push through an Enabling Bill. The centre parties were crucial: he still needed Zentrum and the DNVP to vote with the Nazis. In discussions with the respective leaders of these parties, Ludwig Kaas and Alfred Hugenberg, Hitler adopted a conciliatory approach, expressing regret at the violence surrounding the elections and suggesting that it had occurred against his wishes. He assured Kaas that Catholic interests would be protected in Nazi-ruled Germany. His assurances convinced the leaders. When the Enabling Bill was presented in the Reichstag, the Zentrum and DNVP deputies voted in its favour. It was passed by 441 votes to 94.

The Enabling Act, March 1933

The Enabling Act allowed Hitler to govern as Chancellor without reference to the Reichstag. In effect, the Reichstag had voted away its power. There was now no constitutional restriction on his personal authority or that of the party he led. In *Mein Kampf*, Hitler had insisted that 'one person must have absolute authority and bear all responsibility'. It was, he said, a basic principle of Nazism. He was now free to turn principle into practice.

Gleichschaltung, 1933–34

Within a year Hitler had used the powers that the Enabling Act granted him to implement a programme which turned Germany into a one-party state. In a process known as *Gleichschaltung* he had:

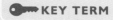

KEY TERM

Gleichschaltung
Consolidation of authority.

- brought the parliaments in all the individual German states under total Nazi control
- outlawed all political parties other than the NSDAP
- destroyed the trade unions as an independent force
- subordinated the legal system to Nazi control
- begun the process of removing Jews from all public offices
- coerced the Churches into accepting the Nazi regime.

Crushing opposition – the Night of the Long Knives, June 1934

To forestall any challenge to *Gleichschaltung* from within his own party, Hitler launched a violent purge in the summer of 1934. In what was later called 'the Night of the Long Knives', he had Ernst Röhm, the leader of the SA, arrested and shot. Thousands of others were rounded up and executed. Hitler claimed that Röhm was preparing a *putsch* against him. Röhm's real intentions are unclear, but rather than wait for him to act, a group of army generals concocted a fake order, which made it appear he had instructed his SA forces to prepare for a strike against Hitler and the army. The army's behaviour was significant. In the new Germany, the military was eager to assert its authority over its chief rivals, the SA, by backing Hitler.

The SA had played a key role in the rise of Nazism, but Hitler now had no more use for it. Röhm had been a socialist revolutionary. He wanted the workers and soldiers to run society and he thought that Hitler shared his desire to break the old German privileged society by force. But Hitler, having come to power by legal means, wished to consolidate his position by winning over, not destroying, the traditional ruling classes in Germany. The SA was not immediately disbanded, but its place was usurped by a more powerful body, the **SS**.

Hitler becomes President, August 1934

In August 1934, following the death of Hindenburg, Hitler added the presidency to his Chancellorship. His supreme power was recognized in his adoption of the title *Führer* (leader), which from then on was the formal way he was addressed. Two weeks later, in a plebiscite asking the people whether they approved Hitler's extension of power, 30 million Germans – 92 per cent of the electorate – voted yes.

The main instruments of Nazi control

In order to consolidate Hitler's grip upon Germany a number of key organizations were either created or modified in such a way as to make them instruments of Nazi control. Chief among these were the SS, the army and the *gauleiters*.

The SS

The SS began as Hitler's personal bodyguard in Munich in 1924. He encouraged the setting up of similar protective squads to guard Nazi officials elsewhere. In 1929 Heinrich Himmler took over the co-ordinating of these squads. He saw them as a means of developing a powerful control system within the Nazi Party and eventually within Germany itself. The destruction of Röhm and the SA opened the way for the SS to become an elite body answerable only to Adolf Hitler. It was basically a civilian police network run on military lines, enforcing the law while itself operating outside the law. Himmler's success in this merits the description of the Third Reich as an 'SS state'.

KEY TERM

SS Nazi *Schutzstaffeln* (protective squads).

Gauleiters Local Nazi Party secretaries who played a vital role in enforcing Nazi rule in the regions.

← **What organizations enabled the Nazis to exercise authority under Hitler?**

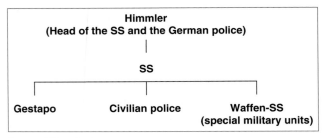

KEY TERM

Concentration camps
Originally detention centres where anti-Nazis were held, they developed into a widespread prison network which became notorious for the barbarity with which inmates were treated.

Death's Head Division
A unit which took its name from the skull and crossbones emblem its members wore on their caps.

Gestapo *Geheime Staatspolizei*, special state police in Germany and German-occupied Europe.

Wehrmacht (previously the *Reichswehr*) The German armed services, comprising the army, navy and air force, though the term was often used simply to describe the army.

One of the first tasks the SS undertook was the running of the **concentration camps**. A centralized system was created which enforced a standard pattern of brutality in accordance with the guiding principle, 'tolerance is weakness'. A special SS **Death's Head Division** was set up to guard the camps.

SS ideology

By 1936, Himmler had succeeded in bringing the police forces of all the German states under SS authority (see diagram). He declared that there were four fundamental principles to which the SS was committed, which were:

- the protection of Germany from racial corruption
- the cultivation of a fighting spirit among its members
- loyalty to the German state
- absolute obedience to the orders of the *Führer*.

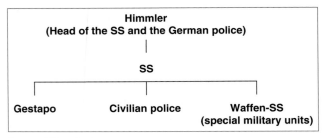

Himmler
(Head of the SS and the German police)

SS

| Gestapo | Civilian police | Waffen-SS (special military units) |

Extent of SS authority

The Gestapo

The **Gestapo**, which was a special arm of the SS, developed into a nationwide organization dedicated to exposing and removing 'enemies of the state'. The civilian police force was subject to its authority, and there was no legal restriction on its powers of arrest or its methods of interrogation. This meant it could detain anyone on suspicion. Torture became standard practice. Since it operated outside the ordinary court system, it had no obligation to apply the normal rules of evidence.

Given its unlimited powers of arrest and interrogation, the Gestapo was arguably the most fearful aspect of the Nazi regime for ordinary Germans. Yet the remarkable fact was that the Gestapo depended on the support of the people at large. It simply was not big enough to have imposed itself without the co-operation of the German public. It acquired much of its knowledge not from its own investigation but from information provided by ordinary citizens who were prepared to inform on their neighbours and workmates.

The army

It is essential for any authoritarian regime, whether of the Left or Right, to have the support of the army. Without this, its power is fragile. Given German history with its strong military tradition and Hitler's notion that the army had been betrayed by the politicians at the end of the First World War, it was to be expected that he would lay stress on the role of the *Wehrmacht* in the creation of the Third Reich.

The army oath

Hitler regarded military strength as an expression of German greatness, which was why he had been appalled by the betrayal of the army by the politicians in accepting the **armistice** in 1918. He wanted a powerful army in Nazi Germany, but he did not want it to be an independent organization capable of challenging his authority. One of his shrewdest moves soon after coming to power was to make the army feel that it had a special relationship with him as leader of the nation. He did this by making the oath that the officers and men took a declaration of 'unconditional loyalty to the person of the *Führer*'. From now on the loyalty of the military was to Hitler personally, not simply to him as head of state. The army welcomed this because, although it was now tied to Hitler, it had also made itself independent of the Nazi Party. General Werner von Blomberg pledged the army to Hitler's service in these words: 'The *Wehrmacht*, as the sole armed force of the entire nation, while remaining apart from the conflicts of internal politics, will express its gratitude by its devotion and fidelity.'

Army scandals

Despite such avowals, Hitler was concerned that as long as the army remained politically independent it represented a source of potential opposition. Conscious that the army leaders, who came mainly from the Prussian aristocracy, tended to regard him as an Austrian upstart who had never risen above the rank of private, he was eager to achieve complete control of the military. His opportunity came in 1938 in the form of two separate sex scandals.

The first involved Blomberg, recently appointed Hitler's first Field Marshal, whose newly-married wife was rumoured to be a former prostitute. The second involved Verner von Fritsch, Commander-in-Chief of the German army, who was accused of consorting with a male prostitute. Eager to assert the primacy of the Nazi Party and the SS over the army, Himmler and **Hermann Goering** exploited the scandals to suggest that the *Wehrmacht* was corrupt at the very top and could no longer be trusted. Hitler dismissed both Blomberg and Fritsch and took the title of Commander-in-Chief for himself. Nor was it merely a courtesy title: from now on Hitler was the active commander of Germany's armed forces. It consolidated and increased the power he held.

The structure and organization of government

In theory, the structure of the Third Reich was a balance between the German state and the Nazi Party. However, the theory did not fit the practice. In reality, all the key posts in the state organizations were held by Nazis. Thus the lines between state and party power were blurred.

🔑 KEY TERM

Armistice An agreement between the warring sides to cease fighting in order to prepare the way for a formal peace treaty.

Hermann Goering A member of the Nazi Party since its earliest days, he was one of Hitler's most important ministers. At the time of the army scandals in 1938, Goering was chief of the *Luftwaffe* (German air force) and responsible for the Third Reich's economic programme.

← **How did the structure of the Third Reich enhance Hitler's personal authority?**

Party organizations	State organizations
SS	Government ministries
Gestapo	Chancellery (civil service)
Gauleiters	Regional governments
	Courts

Nazi Party and state organizations

Organizations and institutions overlapped, which resulted in confusion and rivalry. Odd though it may seem, Hitler welcomed the confusion since it meant that he became the one fixed point in the system. It emphasized the personal nature of Nazi rule. It was he, Adolf Hitler, who gave definition and purpose to it all. Otto Dietrich, Hitler's press officer, described the rivalry which Hitler encouraged (see Source I).

SOURCE I

Excerpt from *The Hitler I Knew* by Otto Dietrich, published by Methuen, London, 1957, p. 117.

*In the sphere of culture Goebbels and **Rosenberg** quarrelled incessantly; in art Goering and Goebbels were rivals ... In the party organization **Ley** and **Bormann** had the same radius of activities; in Party education Rosenberg and Ley were in competition. In the armed forces the interests of army, Waffen-SS (SS-in-arms) and air force field divisions were inextricably set up for these organizations side by side.*

In this way Hitler had at his disposal two or three 'chiefs' in every field, each with an extensive apparatus. He could ensure the execution of his plans by playing one man off against another ... His method systematically disorganized the objective authority of the higher departments of government – so that he could push the authority of his own will to the point of despotic tyranny.

?

According to Source I, why did Hitler allow rivalry to operate between various organizations?

KEY TERM

Alfred Rosenberg The Nazi Party's leading race theorist.

Robert Ley Director of the German Labour Front.

Martin Bormann Nazi Party Secretary.

'Working towards the *Führer*'

It is significant that after coming to power Hitler did not set about creating a whole new governmental and legal system. Provided they expressed loyalty and were not Jewish, most institutions and the civil servants who ran them were left in place. When he wanted something particular doing, he would set up agencies or bodies with special powers and give them the right to act on their own jurisdiction. An expression came into common use among administrators in Nazi Germany: 'working towards the *Führer*'. It referred to the practice of ministers and senior officials making a judgement from Hitler's statements as to what policies he wanted them to follow and then producing practical ways of implementing them.

As for the actual business of government, it was not something that especially interested Hitler. With the exception of his management of the Second World War, he certainly did not engage in it on a daily basis. He preferred to leave the work to the ministers he appointed. This gave them considerable personal power and room for initiative which often led to fierce rivalry between them, rivalry that he actually encouraged since it prevented opposition factions being formed.

Opposition to Hitler

There was no consistent, organized resistance movement in Hitler's Germany. It had been possible to oppose the Nazis before they came to power; it was not so after. When moves were made against Hitler, they were invariably desperate, doomed affairs. The isolated cases of individual or group resistance that did occur usually coincided with times of uncertainty, as in 1939 when a number of Germans doubted the wisdom of going to war, and in the period 1942–45 when Germany began to suffer serious military reverses. However, it is noticeable that between 1939 and 1942, when Hitler was making Germany master of Europe, opposition became dormant. What all this suggests is that opposition was rarely a matter of moral objection to Nazism. It was at its weakest when Germany was doing well under Hitler and at its strongest when his foreign wars appeared to be putting Germany at risk.

Of the different forms of resistance that can be measured, the three main types that stand out are:

- the Left, made up of communists and socialists
- the Right, made up of traditionalists and conservatives
- the young.

Interestingly, the main opposition to Hitler in Germany came from the political Right rather than the Left.

> **Why was opposition to Hitler so unsuccessful?**

The key moments and main phases of the Second World War, 1939–45

1939 German seizure of Poland	**1943** Beginning of Battle of Stalingrad
Britain and France declare war on Germany	Allied victory at El Alamein
1940 German invasion of Denmark and Norway	German surrender at Stalingrad
German seizure of Holland and Belgium	German defeat at Kursk
Fall of France	Mussolini overthrown; Italy switches to the Allied side
Italy enters war as ally of Germany	
German aerial attack on Britain	**1944** Allied landings at Normandy open a second front in western Europe
North Africa campaigns	Failure of July Bomb Plot to kill Hitler
1941 German invasion of USSR	Battle of the Bulge
USA declares war on Japan	**1945** Soviet forces take Berlin
Germany declares war on USA	Hitler prefers to see the Third Reich destroyed rather than surrender
1942 War in Western Desert	Hitler commits suicide
	Germany signs unconditional surrender

Opposition from the Left

The socialists and communists in Germany did not try to organize a broad resistance to Nazism, something that can be explained by the severity with which they were suppressed. Hitler was as savage in his hatred of communists as he was of Jews. Beginning in 1933, some 1,000 SDP members and 150,000 KPD members were held in concentration camps. By 1935, what remained of the Communist Party had been driven underground.

The signing of the **Nazi–Soviet Pact** in August 1939 saw some easing of the persecution. But after the war with the Soviet Union began in June 1941, German communists again became targets. Those who were not arrested remained quiet, intent simply on surviving. A complaint made after the war was that the German working classes had been reluctant to confront Nazism. But this overlooked just how restricted the workers had been. The trade unions had been destroyed in the *Gleichschaltung* and their place taken by the Labour Front (see page 95). Over 2,000 workers were executed for belonging to illegal labour organizations and another 52,000 imprisoned.

🔑 **KEY TERM**

Nazi–Soviet Pact A ten-year non-aggression agreement between the Third Reich and the USSR.

Schwartz Kapelle The 'Black Organization', a Gestapo designation for those on the political Right who were suspected of being anti-Hitler.

Opposition from the Right (*Schwartz Kapelle*)

The *Schwartz Kapelle* was never a specific body. Indeed, it was only in the loosest sense an organization at all. The one point linking those included under the title was their dislike of Hitler's leadership. Among them were aristocratic Germans whose distaste for Hitler as a vulgar upstart deepened into hatred as his war policies appeared to be taking Germany towards destruction. Prominent among this type were General Beck, a Prussian officer, who resigned as Chief of the General Staff in protest against Germany's seizure of Czechoslovakia in 1939, and Helmut von Moltke, a landed aristocrat.

It was Moltke who founded the Kreisau Circle, a gathering of those concerned at the direction Germany was heading under Nazism. The Circle was not an organized conspiracy since its members could not agree on what action should be taken. Ethical qualms prevented the majority of them from contemplating Hitler's assassination. However, by 1944, there were Germans who considered that the killing of Hitler was the only option left to them if their country was to be saved morally and militarily. One such was Colonel Claus von Stauffenberg, the organizer of the July Bomb Plot in 1944.

The July Bomb Plot, 1944

After 1939 there were some fifteen attempts to kill Hitler. Most of these were individual actions by people who never got close enough to their target to be a real danger. The more serious attempts always came from within the army. This was because it was among the military that the greatest dissatisfaction with Hitler was to be found, especially after the war began to go against Germany. There was also the simple fact that military personnel had closer access to the *Führer* than any other group of Germans. It was this that gave Stauffenberg, who as a colonel personally attended the *Führer*'s regular strategy meetings at his headquarters in East Prussia, the hope that he could blow up Hitler with a planted bomb. The aim was then to establish a government of generals and leading civilians ready to make peace with the Allies. The plan came near to succeeding. The bomb exploded but, despite being injured, Hitler survived. Survival strengthened Hitler's belief that **providence** was on his side. The plot fell apart. The ring leaders, including Stauffenberg, were quickly rounded up and executed after a series of **show trials**. There was no further attempt from within the military to remove Hitler.

Opposition from the young

The White Rose Group

In 1942, five students and one staff member at Munich University were drawn together by their disgust at the increasing brutality of the Nazi regime in Germany and **occupied Europe**. The key players were a brother and sister, Hans and Sophie Scholl, who enlisted the help of a professor known to be critical of the Nazi regime. They secretly produced and distributed a set of leaflets, entitled the **White Rose**, which called attention to the inhuman acts being committed in Germany's name.

They managed to avoid detection for over a year, but they were always at risk. In 1943, two weeks after the German defeat at the **Battle of Stalingrad**, the White Rose distributed leaflets which bitterly condemned Hitler for 'senselessly and irresponsibly' sending Germany's young men to their death. It proved to be the group's last protest. A university porter exposed them to the authorities. Within five weeks, all six had been arrested, tried and guillotined. The university staff and students joined in praising the porter for his patriotic action.

The fate of the White Rose illustrates the main weakness of all the opposition groups. Short of assassinating the Nazi leaders, which was so desperate a notion that it was usually rejected on practical, if not moral, grounds, there was little that could be done to organize effective opposition.

Edelweiss

One set of German resisters with strong Catholic associations was the group of young people who took the Edelweiss flower as their badge. The flower, which grows in profusion in Bavaria in southern Germany, symbolized the group's wish to promote lasting German values in the face of the amoral doctrines of Nazism. As an organization, Edelweiss spread to many parts of Germany. Reacting against this, the Gestapo, which claimed that some sections of the Hitler Youth (see page 93) had been infiltrated by the movement, was ferocious in hunting down Edelweiss members. In Cologne in 1944, twelve youngsters known to belong to Edelweiss were hanged in public. As with all the resistance movements, Edelweiss is remembered for the heroism of its members rather than for any great influence it had on the German people.

🔑 KEY TERM

Providence The notion that fate is predetermined by the force of history.

Show trial Special public court hearings, meant as propaganda exercises, in which the accused were paraded as enemies of the people.

Occupied Europe The areas overrun by German forces between 1939 and 1942 which were then placed under German administration and control.

White Rose A group opposed to the Nazis, named after the flower as a symbol of peace.

Battle of Stalingrad A savage six-month battle on the Eastern Front in the winter of 1942–43, which ended with a humiliating defeat for the German armies at the hands of the Soviet forces.

Swingjugend (swinging youth)

A group that deserves mention in the list of those who declined to accept Nazism is the *Swingjugend*. These were young people with a passion for American jazz. They were never formally a resistance movement and, indeed, made a point of being non-political, but they were social non-conformists. Their behaviour and appearance did not fit the Nazi image of responsible and serious German youth. Their long hair, unconventional clothes, and taste for loud music led to their being described as 'deviants'. They were constantly harried by the authorities. A 'swing festival' in Hamburg in 1940, attended by hundreds of young people, was broken up by the police. The organizers were arrested; one of the charges against them was that they had encouraged 'jitterbugging'. The light-hearted non-conformity of *Swingjugend* stood in marked contrast to the dour and deadly seriousness of Nazism.

Why resistance failed

The failure of all the movements against Hitler indicates the near-impossibility of destroying a totalitarian system from inside. Hitler's genuine popularity with the people lasted at least until 1942, and, even after the war started to go badly, those who began to lose faith in the *Führer* rarely turned against him openly. His shrewd decision to take power by legal means had profound repercussions. Any challenge to him was illegal; conspirators against him always had to act outside the law. This made them appear traitors in the eyes of the German people. Bound by their oath of loyalty to Hitler personally, the army generals were reduced to impotence. Unless they were prepared to break their code of honour, and few of them were, they could not move against their leader.

What attitude did the Churches take towards Nazi Germany?

Religious opposition

Individual responses

It would be reasonable to expect that, since Nazism in theory and practice raised so many moral questions, the Christian Churches would have been foremost in resisting it. There were certainly many individual churchmen who questioned Nazi policies. Outstanding examples include the following:

- Dietrich Bonhoeffer, a Protestant pastor, attacked the Nazi cult of violence and intimidation. His opposition to Hitler eventually led to his arrest after the July Bomb Plot, although as a pacifist he had avoided involvement in the planned assassination. He was executed four weeks before the close of the war.
- Clemens von Galen, the Catholic Archbishop of Münster, was a constant thorn in Hitler's side. In sermons and writings, he condemned the Third Reich's racial laws, and denounced the sterilization programme as contrary to the will of God (see page 100). Hitler feared that removing him might provoke a major Catholic reaction – an interesting example of his awareness of German sensitivities. However, in the aftermath of the July Bomb Plot, von Galen was sent to a concentration camp.
- Martin Niemöller was a Protestant theologian who defied the Nazis by setting up the **Confessional Church**. On Hitler's personal orders, Niemöller was arrested in 1938 and spent seven years in concentration camps.

KEY TERM

Confessional Church
Established by Martin Niemöller in 1934 as a protest against the Nazi takeover of the Lutheran Church.

- Bernhard Lichtenberg, a Jesuit priest, took up the cause of the Jews and denounced their persecution. He also condemned the euthanasia programme (see page 98). He was arrested in 1941 and died in prison in Berlin in 1943.

There were hundreds of other lesser known clergy who risked their freedom to speak out against Nazism. In **Dachau**, a special block was built for clergy who had opposed the regime. In its time it held over 400 Catholic priests and 40 Protestant pastors.

Attitude of the Churches

In contrast to the actions of such individual clerics, neither the Catholic nor the Protestant Churches, apart from Niemöller's Confessional Church, formally challenged or resisted the Nazi regime. One reason is that, on certain major issues, Church and State were in accord: for example, the desirability of an ordered society and the need to fight what the Catholic Church called 'godless communism'. This is a controversial area. It has been suggested that the Churches' apparent reticence was a subtle form of resistance. By appearing to co-operate with the regime, the Churches were able to maintain an influence on Nazi policies that led on many occasions to their being modified or withdrawn, an example being Hitler's abandonment of the T4 euthanasia programme (see page 98). Had the Churches chosen to condemn Nazism, it would have polarized the situation and made things impossible for those who were both believers and loyal Germans.

However, it should also be noted that Church dignitaries often showed an eagerness to support the Nazi regime which went beyond mere diplomatic courtesy. When, for example, Hitler drove triumphantly into Austria in March 1938 to celebrate the **Anschluss**, the Catholic bishops of Austria praised the Nazi takeover, thanking God that 'through the actions of the National Socialist Movement the danger of godless Bolshevism would be fended off'.

Support for Nazism

Nazi propaganda played an important role in promoting the image of Adolf Hitler as a great German leader. But indoctrination was only one part of the story. Many Germans protected their position in society by joining or supporting the Nazi Party. They saw that their chances of preferment or promotion would be greatly enhanced by backing the Nazi Party. It was bureaucrats acting out of self-interest who allowed Nazism to flourish.

This extended into the classroom and the lecture hall; teachers and academics were quick to join the Nazi side. In the first year of Hitler's Chancellorship, the Nazi Party grew from some 2.5 million to over 4 million. Nazism became all-embracing – even apparently non-political groups like gardening clubs, choral societies and sports organizations chose to affiliate to the Nazi Party. This was not coercion from the top; it was done willingly by ordinary, respectable Germans. A striking fact is that most of those who might be regarded as the natural leaders of society – teachers, doctors, professors, priests and pastors – were among the strongest supporters of Hitler's Nazi regime. It was not surprising that where they led, most Germans followed.

KEY TERM

Dachau Germany's first concentration camp, opened in 1933.

Anschluss The re-incorporation of Austria into the Third Reich in 1938.

← **Why were so many Germans prepared to support Hitler and the Nazis?**

Many Germans regarded Hitler as a saviour. As one German journalist put it: 'Adolf Hitler – the living incarnation of the nation's yearning.' His great conquests as a war leader between 1939 and 1942 raised his prestige in Germany to unprecedented heights. The British historian, A.J.P. Taylor, remarked that Hitler was the most popular leader of any European country in modern Europe and that it was 'silly to claim otherwise'. Resistance to the Nazis in power was minimal. It was only from 1942 onwards, after things began to go badly militarily, that opposition became at all significant. Nazism answered to the aspirations and needs of the great majority of German people. They took pride in a leader and a regime that elevated their nation's standing. It must be stressed that when Nazi Germany did finally collapse it was not because its people rose up and rejected the regime. Nazism was broken by force of Allied arms, not by internal resistance.

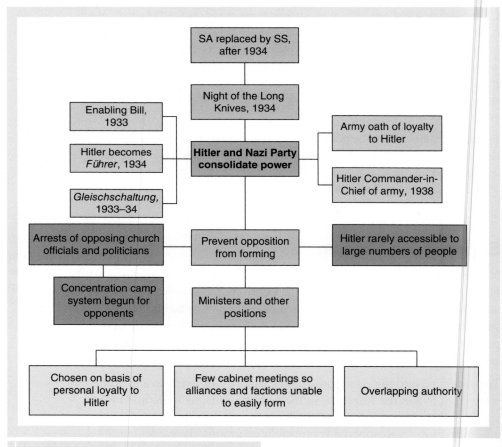

SUMMARY DIAGRAM

Hitler's establishment of an authoritarian state

Hitler's domestic policies and their impact, 1933–45

> ▶ **Key question:** *What impact did the Nazi regime have on the lives of the German people?*

Until the war intervened, the Third Reich's economic policies undoubtedly proved beneficial for most Germans. This was particularly true in regard to the fall in unemployment. However, with the coming of the war in 1939, economic and social polices had to be adjusted, with the consequence that hardship and restrictions spread.

Hitler's economic policies

What were Hitler's main economic aims?

The 1930s were a period of international recovery from economic depression, and Germany shared in that recovery. This gave Hitler a reputation for having created a powerful industry, which had ended unemployment and restored Germany's pride in itself. But while it is true that Germany did perform well down to 1939, Hitler's aim was not economic growth for its own sake. He was less concerned with improving the living standards of the people than with creating a strong industrial economy that would provide the sinews of war.

Hitler was not an economic planner. He left that to his economics ministers. However, he did demand that they prepare Germany for rearmament. The development of the German economy under Hitler, therefore, is a story of a series of strategies followed by a succession of ministers, trying in often quite different ways to meet Hitler's wishes. There was no single, consistent Nazi economic programme or master plan.

The policies of Hjalmar Schacht (1934–37)

In 1934, Hitler appointed Hjalmar Schacht as his Economics Minister. Schacht had shown great skill as a financier during the Weimar Republic, one of his major achievements having been the stabilizing of the German currency and the ending of the catastrophic inflation that had struck Germany in 1923. He never became a Nazi Party member but he admired Hitler who, he believed, could make Germany powerful again. Schacht remarked, 'I desire a great and strong Germany and to achieve it I would enter an alliance with the devil.' That was why Schacht had urged major industrial companies, such as Krupp Steel and I.G. Farben (the chemical giant), to support the Nazis in the elections of the early 1930s. He had also urged Hindenburg to appoint Hitler Chancellor.

His programme for the recovery of the Germany economy was complex in detail but simple in its basic aim – financial and economic growth.

- Using his many contacts among the big bankers and industrialists, Schacht established the 'Organization of Industry'. This was a body made up of business guilds, employers' associations and finance houses.

- So successful was the Organization in promoting trade and industry that a number of countries began to advance loans to Germany. This was a remarkable achievement for a country which since 1918 had struggled desperately to raise capital for itself.
- Schacht also approved of taxation as a way of increasing state funds. However, he insisted on two things: tax should be fairly assessed so that it would not be a burden and disincentive to private industry, and the revenue that it raised should be reinvested by the government in productive ways.

The New Plan, 1934

With the aim of ending the high unemployment that had blighted Germany during the Great Depression, Schacht introduced 'the New Plan'. This was a programme which built on some of the measures introduced under the Weimar government. Among the Plan's proposal were:

- schemes for creating employment through public works projects, such as road repairs, forest clearing and planting, and the building of new hospitals and schools
- young men aged 18–25 were required to join the National Labour Service for six months, during which time they would be trained in basic skills and directed to work where it was most needed.

Rearmament

Since Hitler's main objective was the expansion of Germany's military strength, Schacht knew that he would have to provide funds for rearmament. But he did not want spending on arms to drain away vital funds and thus undermine economic recovery. He therefore proposed that rearmament be introduced in stages as the economy strengthened. His proposal had begun to work. By 1935 funding was becoming available for rearmament. However, this was too slow for Hitler. A *Führer* **memorandum** of August 1936 asserted: 'If we do not succeed in bringing the German army as rapidly as possible to the rank of the premier army in the world then Germany will be lost.' Schacht was not dismissed but he was bypassed in favour of Hermann Goering, who was given the task of pushing Germany towards rapid militarization.

Goering's Four-Year Plan, 1936–39

Goering's first move was to introduce a Four-Year Plan in October 1936, the chief aim of which was to make Germany an **autarky**. To achieve this, a number of targets were set, including:

- the bringing of Germany's labour force under tighter control so that it could directed into vital areas such as arms production
- increased use of import controls to protect German manufactures
- the production of synthetic substitutes for rubber and oil to avoid these essentials having to be imported.

Economic historians suggest that in the twentieth century autarky was an impossible goal for advanced industrial states like Germany. Their commerce was too interlinked internationally and no country had all the vital resources

to be self-sufficient. In 1939 German industry was still importing a third of the raw materials it needed. Nevertheless, although autarky had not been achieved by that date, Germany had made significant economic advances.

SOURCE J

The growth in German manufacturing (calculated to an index of 100 in 1936).

	Consumer goods	Industrial goods
1933	80	56
1934	91	81
1936	100	114
1938	116	144

SOURCE K

The limited post–recession recovery in the average wage rates of German industrial workers (calculated to an index of 100 in 1936).

1928	125
1933	88
1934	94
1936	100
1938	106

In what way does Source K indicate that German workers had experienced only limited recovery in their wage rates between 1933 and 1938?

SOURCE L

Graph showing the fall in unemployment in Germany, 1932–39.

How far do the Sources J, K and L complement each other in showing the development of the German economy in the 1930s?

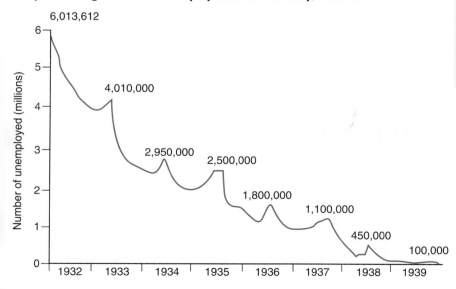

The most striking aspect of Germany's economic performance was the sustained fall in unemployment, which added greatly to Hitler's popularity. Encouraged by the figures of industrial growth, he announced major spending programmes for all three armed services that would make Germany ready for war. But when war came in the autumn of 1939, there were fears among a number of Hitler's generals that Germany was not yet ready for a major European conflict.

The wartime economy

A remarkable feature of the Germany economy was that there was no ministry or body with overall responsibility for organizing the war effort. This encouraged rivalry between government departments and the armed services and made a concerted effort difficult. Communication between departments was seldom smooth which meant that decisions and instructions were not always clear. It is a further reminder that Nazi Germany was never the monolithic super-efficient state that its own propaganda suggested and popular imagination believed.

Albert Speer

It was to tackle the problem of liaison and co-ordination that Hitler in 1942 appointed Albert Speer as Minister of Armaments and War Production. As with Schacht earlier, Speer was given a very large measure of freedom to develop policies as he saw fit. He used it skilfully and effectively. Transport and freight movement were streamlined so that bottlenecks were avoided and materials reached the plants on schedule. Despite mounting pressure from Allied bombing raids over Germany, Speer actually doubled German armaments production overall. To quote one example: when he took over as Armaments Minister in 1942, German factories had turned out 4,500 tanks since 1939; by 1944, Speer had raised that figure to 17,300.

How well industry responded to Speer's leadership can be seen in Source M, which indicates that he managed to sustain high output right through to 1944, even though for most of that time Allied attacks on Germany were causing severe damage to factories and plants.

SOURCE M

German industrial output, 1941–44.

	1941	1942	1943	1944
Steel (millions of tons)	31.8	32.1	34.6	28.5
Coal (millions of tons)	248.3	264.2	268.9	249.0
Synthetic oil (millions of tons)	4.1	4.95	5.7	3.8
Synthetic rubber (thousands of tons)	69.0	98.0	117.0	104.0
Aluminium (thousands of tons)	233.6	263.9	250.0	245.3

? Study Source M. What trends do the figures indicate regarding Germany's wartime production of vital resources?

Speer used slave labour. By 1944, a quarter of Germany's workforce of 40 million was composed of foreigners. Some of these were voluntary workers from the nations allied with Germany but the vast majority were forced labourers, deported to Germany and made to work in appalling conditions. In the pressure of war, Speer paid scant attention to their plight. Circumstances required that he regard them not as people but as economic units.

Propaganda and the media

As soon as the Nazis took power in 1933, Goebbels, as Propaganda Minister, began to promote the idea of the German nation unified under the direction of the Nazi Party and its inspired leader, Adolf Hitler. Goebbels worked from the premise that repetition is the key to inculcating ideas: the repeated slogan or phrase, the recurring image. All the media of the day were used: radio, film, the gramophone, display boards and posters. Hitler's name and image and the swastika appeared everywhere.

←
How was propaganda used to consolidate Hitler's authority?

SOURCE N

A 1936 poster, *Der Bannertrager* (the Bearer of the Banner).

What image of Hitler is being projected in the poster in Source N? **?**

A spectacular element of the propaganda campaign was the great Nazi Party rallies, often held at night by torchlight. Nuremberg was the major centre for these. The gifted film-maker, Leni Riefenstahl, brilliantly captured the essence of these displays in her documentary *The Triumph of the Will*. Her sweeping panoramas conveyed Hitler as the man of destiny creating a Third Reich that expressed the will of the nation he had transformed. She captured the powerful religious impulse to Nazism: Hitler was the new Messiah.

A Berlin professor declared that 'tomorrow has become today – the end of the world mood has been transformed to an awakening. The leader, yearned for and prophesised, has appeared'.

Nazi propaganda under Goebbels was a giant public relations exercise. His aim was nothing less than the transformation of German culture. His Propaganda Ministry set itself these essential tasks, which were to:

- promote the German nation as the supreme form of social and cultural organization
- oblige the media always to present the *Führer* and the Nazi Party in the most positive light
- develop **the *Führer* principle**
- rid the nation of all Jewish influences
- encourage pride in the Aryan race as the highest form of human development
- develop German–Aryan arts free from corruption and decadence.

The Berlin Olympics, 1936

Sport was effectively used as a propaganda tool, the outstanding example being the Berlin Olympics which were held in 1936. The specially-built athletics stadium held 110,000 spectators and was filled every day of the Games. Hitler also attended every day; his appearances occasioned massive outbursts of affection both in the stadium and along the crowd-thronged route. It was also a great sporting success for Germany, whose athletes won more medals than those from any other country.

The press

There had been an abundance of German newspapers before 1933. Determined to prevent an independent press becoming a possible source of opposition to the Nazi regime, Goebbels systematically brought newspapers under control:

- *Eher Verlag*, the NSDAP's own publishing firm, used its financial resources to negotiate the purchase of a wide range of newspapers and journals. By 1939, only a third of German newspapers remained independent and these, for survival reasons, were reluctant to take an anti-Nazi line.
- Control was further strengthened by bringing all the news agencies on which the newspapers depended for their information into one organization, the Nazi-dominated **DNB**. Newspapers now had to rely solely on Nazi-approved sources
- Under the terms of the 'Editors Law', first passed in 1933 and regularly renewed, editors were made personally responsible for what appeared in their papers. This provided an easy means for Goebbels to control the contents, since fearful editors became, in effect, their own censors.

The result of such measures was that Goebbels soon acquired a tame co-operative press, which provided a highly influential weapon for the inculcation of Nazi ideas in the general public.

The arts

Goebbels' constant theme as Propaganda Minister was the need to guard against what he described as Jewish corruption. In laying such stress on destroying Jewish influences Goebbels was defining culture by what it was against, rather than what it was for. This inhibited genuine cultural growth. Nazism was an attempt to force people to think along prescribed lines. It stifled creativity. The arts did not flourish; they became unadventurous and predictable.

Censorship ensured that painting and sculpture glorified the myths of the German past and emphasized manly, heroic deeds. Abstract works were unacceptable. Jazz was rejected as the product of a decadent African-American sub-culture. Art had to be formal and figurative. Directors of opera or ballet, as with theatre producers and playwrights, had to be careful that the story line did not offend Nazi values. The music of the composer Richard Wagner (1813–83) was reverentially referred to as an expression of the German soul.

Most Germans who had a career in the arts chose to co-operate with the Nazis' demands for cultural conformity, evidence that the majority of German writers, performers and artists, without being avid supporters of Hitler's Reich, were quite prepared to make the necessary compromises in order to be able to continue to work.

Prominent examples were the celebrated conductors Wilhelm Furtwangler and Herbert Von Karajan, and the renowned composer, Richard Strauss. Furtwangler later justified his behaviour by saying that since music transcended politics he felt no guilt. Critics responded by asking why, if music was transcendental, had he not protested against the Nazi ban on performing the works of the Jewish composers Mahler, Schoenberg, Mendelssohn and Hindemith.

Perhaps the outstanding example of intellectual betrayal was that of the philosopher Martin Heidegger, who called upon his colleagues and students to reject such notions as freedom of speech and instead place themselves with entire obedience in the service of the new German Reich. It should be added that, rather than put up with political control, some 2,500 artists and scientists went into voluntary exile. If they were Jewish, of course, their motive was not simply artistic freedom but sheer survival.

Radio

Goebbels was swift to exploit radio broadcasting. By 1933 he had established the Reich Radio Company (RRC) whose sole purpose was the spread of Nazi propaganda. A vital development was a campaign to provide as many Germans as possible with radios. Between 1932 and 1937 the number of Germans with access to broadcasting rose from 22 to 70 per cent of the population. A sinister development was the ban on listening to foreign broadcasts, a prohibition which was enforced especially severely during wartime.

How was education
used to inculcate Nazi
ideas?

Education

Under the Nazis, education became a major means of promoting National
Socialist ideas. The school system was brought under the control of a
centralized Ministry of Education, headed by Bernhard Rust, one of whose
projects was the creation of 'National Political Educational Institutions'
(Napolas). Although part of the state education system, the Napolas were
intended as training academies for young Nazis. It was this that brought
Rust into conflict with Baldur von Schirach, head of the Hitler Youth (see
page 93), who regarded such training as the province of his organization. In
retaliation, von Schirach insisted that the Hitler Youth set up its own special
'Adolf Hitler Schools'. He claimed that in doing so he was responding to a
direct instruction from the *Führer*. Whether this was the case is unclear, since
Hitler declined to take sides in the dispute. He seemed to draw satisfaction
from observing the enthusiasm with which Nazi administrators sought to
show their commitment to him.

The curriculum

The inculcation of Nazi thought was to be achieved by heavy emphasis in
the curriculum on race and ideology. The traditional subjects, like German
language and history, were also modified to reflect Nazi notions of Germanic
superiority. As the textbooks indicated, the race theories the pupils studied
were of a simple, repetitive 'Aryans good – Jews bad' kind. History was
presented as a study of Jews trying to undermine the great achievements of
the Germans. This was backed up in biology classes by models which
showed that, as in nature, harmful germs could corrupt the whole body, so in
society the Jews could damage the whole people. A typical morning's
timetable in a secondary school read:

8.50	9.40	10.25	11.00	12.10	1.00
German	History	Biology	Mathematics	**Eugenics**	Ideology

Progressively throughout the 1930s, in keeping with the anti-Semitic tenor
of the curriculum, Jews were demoted or dismissed from teaching positions
in schools and universities, and Jewish pupils and students were barred
entry. There seems to have been little sustained protest over this from fellow
teachers. A career could be blighted, perhaps ended, if a teacher spoke out.

Dispute with the Churches

The Nazi administrators' pointed exclusion of religious instruction from the
curriculum in the new schools angered the Churches, who were by tradition
the main providers of school education in Germany. The Catholic Church in
particular feared that the Nazis were intent on undermining religious
schools by imposing an atheist curriculum. Catholic spokesmen claimed this
would be in breach of the **Concordat** of 1933, which had guaranteed the
right of the Catholic Church to administer its own schools independently of
the state. It is significant that when Hitler learned of the over-zealous way in

Eugenics The science of
breeding human beings for
their fitness and intelligence.

Concordat An agreement
between the Papacy and the
Nazi government, signed in
July 1933.

which Nazi officials in some areas were threatening the Catholic schools he instructed them to desist. There was to be no organized Nazi anti-Catholic campaign. Hitler wished to avoid the confrontation which might well follow if the interests of the Catholic Church, whose adherents comprised a major section of the German population, were unnecessarily threatened.

The Hitler Youth and the BDM

The Nazis deliberately set out to give young people a particular sense of belonging in the new society that National Socialism was building. The mechanism for this was the Hitler Youth, an organization run by Baldur von Schirach with the aim of training young men in National Socialist values: patriotism, loyalty and a readiness to put the *Führer* and the nation before thoughts of self. But it was not all politics. The Hitler Youth laid great emphasis on physical activities and the outdoor life. In those respects it could be enjoyed in the same way that scouting legitimately was in other countries.

How did the Nazis develop their propaganda to appeal to the young?

SOURCE O

This 1940 poster reads 'Youth Serves the *Führer*. Every ten-year old into the HJ' (HJ is the *Hitler Jugend* – i.e. the Hitler Youth).

Study Source O. What image of Hitler and the young is the poster attempting to convey?

The League of German Maidens (BDM in its German initials) was the sister movement to the boys' Hitler Youth. Both organizations aimed at providing an outdoor life that would keep the young people healthy at the same time as developing their understanding of National Socialism and making them feel truly part of the *Volk*, the community of Germans. The BDM's essential purpose was described by Jutta Rudinger, one the BDM's national leaders. She spoke of the movement developing in the girls' character and the ability to perform, not useless knowledge, but an all-round education, and an exemplary bearing'.

The obvious aim of the Nazi bosses in creating a youth movement was to produce political conformity in the young so that they would go on as adults to have unquestioning loyalty to National Socialism. But it is also important to appreciate that, for all its politics, the BDM did give young women a sense of pride and self-worth. It also introduced them to people of their own age from other classes and regions of Germany, whom they would never have met but for BDM.

Membership

At first, membership of both the Hitler Youth and the BDM was voluntary but there was strong peer pressure on the young to join. This may in part explain the movements' popularity in the 1930s. Taken together, they showed an increase in membership from 108,000 in 1932 to 7.3 million in 1940. These numbers included the 10–14 year olds who belonged to the DJ and the JM, younger versions of the Hitler Youth and BDM. In 1939, that membership was made compulsory, an indication both of the success of the movement and the tightening of central control in the Third Reich.

? Study the graph in Source P. What trends are observable in the growth of the youth movements between 1933 and 1940?

SOURCE P

Graph showing membership of the various Hitler Youth movements.

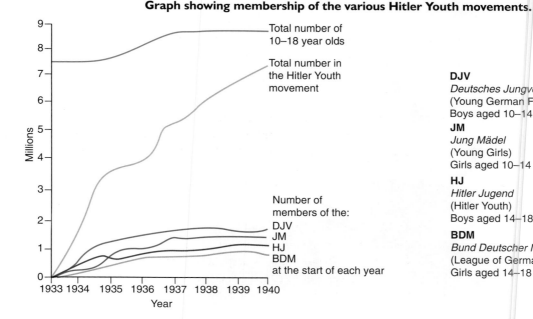

DJV
Deutsches Jungvolk
(Young German Folk)
Boys aged 10–14

JM
Jung Mädel
(Young Girls)
Girls aged 10–14

HJ
Hitler Jugend
(Hitler Youth)
Boys aged 14–18

BDM
Bund Deutscher Mädel
(League of German Girls
Girls aged 14–18

German workers

In the world of work, the single largest organization that affected the German people was the German Labour Front (*Deutsche Arbeitsfront*). This began in 1933 under the direction of Robert Ley, who threw himself into the job with great energy. His aim as Director of the Front was to regulate the German workforce along military lines. He expressed this purpose in his motto: 'Every worker must regard himself as a soldier of the economy'. His first step towards this was to destroy the trade unions. Under the pretext of giving them a greater role in the economic life of the nation, he made them part of the Front. This meant effectively that they came under state control and lost their independence. No longer were they entitled to take strike action or withdraw their labour. Wage rates and conditions were not negotiable; they were dictated by Ley from the top.

During the twelve years of the Third Reich, the Labour Front came to control 25 million workers. Ley presented the Front as the summit of Nazi ideals. He spoke of ending all class conflict in Germany by creating 'social peace'. Workers and people would come together in the *Volk*, a word much used by Hitler to denote the sense of unity and purpose of the German people. They would work together for the good of Germany, willingly subordinating themselves as individuals to the collective will of the nation. To heighten the sense of solidarity, workers were encouraged to wear identical blue uniforms.

Behind the idealistic description, the reality was that the Labour Front required the workers to do what they were told. It was the Front's officials who decided who was to be employed, promoted or dismissed, and what they were to be paid. This control increased after Germany went to war.

Yet it would be wrong to regard the Labour Front simply as a mechanism of oppression. Its military-style discipline did not rule out a strong commitment to workers' welfare. Insurance schemes covering sickness, injury and bereavement were made available to deserving workers. Schooling was provided for the workers' children and adult education was available to the workers themselves.

Kraft durch Freude

Recreational needs were catered for by the Labour Front's sponsoring of one of the most remarkable social experiments in Nazi Germany, the **Kraft durch Freude (KDF)** movement. The KDF was organized leisure for the masses. It covered everything: theatre, concerts, opera, musicals, lectures, dancing, and sports of every kind. Ley spoke of its offering: 'the best of the best in food for the soul, the mind, and body'.

An especially successful scheme was the provision of holidays for the workers and their families. Special hotels and campsites, invariably of a very high order of comfort, were set up; one consequence was a great boom in tourism within Germany in the 1930s. In all, some 10 million Germans, over one in seven of the population, were involved in KDF activities at some point between 1933 and 1943.

> **How did the conditions for German workers change under Nazism?**

 **KEY TERM**

Kraft durch Freude **(KDF)**
The Nazi 'Strength through Joy' movement.

Impact of war

In purely material terms, leaving aside questions of enforced conformity, there is no doubt that in the years up to 1942 the conditions for German workers had markedly improved. After that, things changed. To sustain its demanding war effort, Germany required a huge labour force. To meet this need, a massive labour conscription programme was introduced in April 1942. The good days were over. During the next three years the grimness of the wartime conditions in Germany with its very high civilian casualty rate destroyed the KDF and made the Labour Front increasingly dictatorial.

How far did the status of women change in the Nazi period?

The status of women

Hitler's plans for a new Germany certainly did not include the advancement of women, whom he did not accept as equals to men. He defined female emancipation as a Jewish idea deliberately designed to weaken society. Although some local Nazi women's organizations were formed, they were not allowed to join the main Party. In 1931, Hitler had ordered that all the separate women's groups be brought into one body, the National Socialist Womanhood (NSF), whose purpose was to keep Nazi women under the control of the exclusively male party.

Motherhood

One of Hitler's particular concerns was that the birth rate was dropping in Germany; he wanted women to embrace motherhood as an ideal. A motherhood campaign was introduced to encourage women to give up work, return to the home and become mothers for the greater good of the nation. The NSF backed the government's measures introduced as part of the campaign. As a result of the restrictions imposed:

- fewer women were allocated university places
- the professions, such as the law and higher education, provided fewer positions for women
- the civil service no longer accepted women entrants.

Campaigns of this kind continued for most of the 1930s. Birth control clinics were obliged to close and abortion was made illegal. In a mixture of puritanism and racism, the authorities strongly discouraged women, particularly if they were mothers, from wearing make-up; it was described as a Jewish habit that good German women should shun. Smoking, too, was held to be unsuitable. The NSF did its part by impressing upon women that what the beloved *Führer* admired in German women was their 'feminine grace and female charm'.

Impact of war

The coming of the war meant an abrupt change in Nazi policy towards women. Their prime duty now was to assist the war effort:

- In September 1939, the month that the war started, a Land Year programme was introduced, a form of obligatory national service requiring unattached females to spend a year working on farms. It was no easy life. The farm camps were usually military-style barracks and the work could be unremittingly hard.
- The pressure of war also obliged the Nazis to drop their opposition to women in the industrial workforce. In 1942 they began to encourage, even to demand, that women go into the factories. By the last full year of the war over half the industrial workers in Germany were women.

In what ways does Source Q present an idealized concept of Nazi womanhood?

SOURCE Q

Nazi propaganda poster *Mutter und Kind* (Mother and Child).

The war proved a great destroyer of social convention in Germany. The huge gaps that appeared in manpower as the lists of war dead lengthened could be filled in only one way: German women would have to produce children in such numbers that Germany's future could be secured. But the absence and death of so many husbands meant there were no longer enough married couples to fulfil this task. Himmler's answer was to appeal to women to make themselves pregnant outside the normal confines of marriage. He spoke of this as a 'sublime task'. The Ministry of Justice backed him by ruling in 1944 that the leaders of Germany's youth movements were acting wholly legally in urging the girls to have unmarried sex in order to 'donate a child to the *Führer*'.

The reality was that the war had changed everything. The Nazis found it impossible to sustain their traditional policies towards women in the face of a war that ultimately destroyed German society.

How were Germany's minorities treated under Nazism?

Treatment of minorities

Nazi racial theory held that 'undesirables', a term which covered the seriously handicapped and racial inferiors, were expendable.

Sterilization programme

As early as July 1933 Hitler had approved the introduction of a 'Law for the Prevention of Hereditarily Diseased Offspring', which required that those suffering from specified diseases, such as epilepsy, deafness and blindness, undergo sterilization. By 1939, some 350,000 sterilizations had taken place; for example, 17,000 deaf people were sterilized.

Euthanasia programme

In September 1939, on one of the rare occasions when he issued a written order, Hitler gave instructions that a programme of 'mercy killing' was to be implemented. An organization, code-named T4, was commissioned to oversee the elimination of **defectives**. Necessarily relying on the co-operation of the medical profession to run the programme, T4 set up seven killing centres at various places in Germany. The centres, which presented themselves as hospitals or clinics, were responsible for 70,000 deaths during the period of the Third Reich.

At one of the centres, Hadamar, the technique employed was to group patients in a specially-constructed, air-tight chamber and then pump in carbon monoxide. All the bodies, except those kept back for dissection, were then carried on trolleys to the crematorium to be incinerated. The mental asylums were the obvious places around which to construct the programme. The usual method was to tell the selected patients that they were being taken in buses from the asylum for special treatment. Since those selected never returned, it soon became whispered knowledge among the inmates

KEY TERM

Defectives The Nazi term for those regarded as suffering from incapacitating physical or mental disorders.

that to be selected was to be marked for death. On occasion, this led to scenes of panic and resistance when the buses arrived. Force had to be used to restrain the desperate victims and force them aboard.

The practice among the medical staff was to inform the relatives of those who had been killed that the patient had regrettably died from 'breathing problems'. What such a euphemism indicated was that the authorities knew that if the true nature of their programme of death was made public it would be impossible to continue with it. The result was a conspiracy of silence among a large part of the medical profession. Death certificates were completed in such a way that they hid the real causes of death. The T4 administrators issued doctors with a set of 60 suggested formulae from which to choose according to the age and previous condition of the deceased. Those given in Source R were typical.

SOURCE R

Excerpt from an undated document among the medical records for the town of Wiesbaden, quoted in *The Third Reich: A New History* by Michael Burleigh, published by Macmillan, UK, 2000, p. 394.

Pneumonia is an ideal cause of death because the population at large always regard it as a critical illness.

Strokes. This cause of death is especially suitable in the case of older people; in the case of young people it is so rare that one should not use it.

> According to Source R why are certain diseases considered 'ideal' causes of death?

Resistance to the programme

Some doctors did protest by refusing to participate in the programme. Dr Friedrich Hölzel turned down the post offered him of 'Head of Children's Euthanasia' in Eglfing-Haar Asylum with these words: 'It is repugnant to me to carry this out as a systematic policy after cold-blooded deliberation and according to objective scientific principles, and without any feeling towards the patient.' Others, without openly disobeying the authorities, found ways of saving some of their patients. One trick was to claim that listed inmates were so important as maintenance workers or assistants to the staff that the asylum could not afford to lose them. Most doctors and nurses, however, remained silent and participated in the programme.

There were many examples of relatives demanding that the deaths of members of their family be fully explained. The standard response from the authorities was initially to commiserate with the family and then use threats if they persisted with their questions. One father who could not understand why his schizophrenic son could have been so healthy one day but suddenly die the next pressed for a proper explanation. He was finally brow-beaten into silence by a menacing letter (see Source S, page 100).

In what ways do Sources R (page 99) and S illustrate the official attitude of the T4 authorities towards euthanasia?

SOURCE S

Excerpt from a letter written in 1941 by Dr Waltar Schmidt of the Eichberg Asylum to the father of a schizophrenic patient, quoted in *The Third Reich: A New History* by Michael Burleigh, published by Macmillan, UK, 2000, p. 397.

In the course of the year we repeatedly detect the ingratitude of relatives of hereditarily ill mental patients … The nature and tone of your letter gives me cause to view you in a psychiatric light. I cannot refrain from notifying you that in the event you do not cease burdening us with letters, I will be compelled to have you examined by the public health doctor … You are dealing with a public authority, which you cannot assail when you feel like it.

Strong-arm tactics were also used to silence the inhabitants of areas near the extermination centres who asked what was going on. The crematorium chimneys attached to one such centre at Hartheim gave off an oily, black smoke which filled the air with strands of human hair and produced such a stench that locals vomited. When they gathered in the town to protest they were visited by one of the T4 administrators who told them that if they continued to complain they would be imprisoned.

Religious protests

When information about the sterilization and euthanasia programme did leak out, there were a number of spirited protests. A number of Protestant and Catholic clergy spoke out against it from the pulpit. Gerhard Braune, a Pastor of the Lutheran Church in Gallneukirchen, having heard rumours of a secret euthanasia programme being run at the local asylum, discovered that in the space of two months over 2,000 inmates had inexplicably died. Appalled, Braune wrote an open letter to Hitler himself, quoting this horrific figure. It is doubtful that the letter ever reached the *Führer*. What is certain is that within days of sending it, Braune was arrested and sent to prison for three months.

Bernhard Lichtenberg, a Catholic priest, condemned the euthanasia programme and asked that the Reich's physician-in-chief should be charged with the murder of the mentally disabled. The Protestant Bishop of Württemberg warned that to treat mental defectives 'merely from the point of view of transient utility' could lead to the justifying of 'brutal extermination'. He asked whether Hitler knew of what was happening in his name. 'Has he approved it?'

Von Galen

The most resounding voice of protest was that of Clemens von Galen, the Bishop of Münster, who, on learning that asylums within his own diocese were included in the euthanasia programme, angrily denounced it (see Source T).

His denunciations became a campaign against state-directed euthanasia. He warned that if the programme continued Germany would sink into 'moral depravity'. Many Nazis wanted von Galen forcibly removed, but Hitler decided otherwise. Taking into account the residual sense of decency of most Germans and aware of the moral authority that the Bishop possessed among Catholics, Hitler considered it more prudent to withdraw. In August 1941, he issued an order suspending the operation of T4 and thereby ended the euthanasia programme.

SOURCE T

Excerpt from a sermon by Bishop von Galen, August 1941, quoted in *Nazism 1919–1945*, edited by Jeremy Noakes and Geoffrey Pridham, published by University of Exeter, UK, 1998, vol. 3, p. 1038.

We are not dealing with machines, horses and cows whose only function is to serve mankind. No, we are dealing with human beings, our fellow human beings, our brothers and sisters, with poor people, with sick people, with unproductive people. But have they for that reason forfeited the right to life? Have you, have I, the right to live only so long as we are productive, so long as we are recognized by others as productive?

> According to Source T, on what grounds does von Galen attack the euthanasia programme?

The persecution of the Jews

Although the Jews made up scarcely 1 per cent of the German population, they were subject to systematic persecution from 1933 onwards. The twelve years of Nazi rule are a story of applied hatred, climaxing in an attempt to destroy all the Jews in Europe. However, there is no evidence that the physical annihilation of the Jews was planned from the beginning. Rather it was a cumulative process with persecution increasing stage by stage until, with the coming of the war, all restraints on Nazi behaviour were removed. Claiming that the Jews represented a mortal threat in Germany's time of crisis, the Nazis embarked on what they called the '**Final Solution**'.

> ← **By what stages did Nazi Germany move towards the annihilation of the Jews?**

 **KEY TERM**

Final Solution The Nazi euphemism for the extermination of the Jews.

Cumulative radicalization

There is no record of Hitler's ordering the Final Solution. An obvious but vital point is that he could not have carried it out on his own. His hatred intensified the German detestation of the Jews and, therefore, he must bear the ultimate responsibility for what happened. But of equal importance was the process described now by historians as 'cumulative radicalization'. By this they mean the system under which officials, eager 'to work towards the *Führer*' (see page 78), turned his vague ideas into deadly policies.

The major stages in the persecution
1933
- Goebbels began to organize open violence against the Jews.
- Jews were barred from positions in the civil service and the professions.

1935
The Nuremberg Race Laws created a systematic programme for depriving Jews of legal and civil rights:

- Marriage and sexual relations between Jews and Germans were forbidden.
- Full Jews were deprived of German citizenship.

- Full Jews were defined as those having three or four Jewish grandparents.

1938
- Jewish doctors were debarred from medical practice.
- Jewish businesses were forbidden to operate.
- Jewish students were dismissed from state schools and universities.
- A strict curfew was imposed on Jews living in towns and cities.
- 18,000 Polish Jews resident in Germany were forcibly expelled.

It is clear that by 1938 Hitler wanted the Jews removed from Germany and considered mass migration as a possibility. In April 1938 Goebbels recorded: 'The *Führer* wants gradually to push them all out. Negotiate with Poland and Romania. Madagascar would be the most suitable for them.' However, questions of international law and the coming of war in 1939 meant that such a policy was never implemented.

Kristallnacht

The expulsion of Polish Jews was the prelude to the Nazis' most openly violent anti-Jewish action yet. In protest at the expulsions, a young Jewish man assassinated a German diplomat in Paris. Exploiting this as a pretext for retaliation, the Nazis unleashed what became known as '***Kristallnacht***'. On the night of the 9–10 November 1938, over 100 Jews were killed in a series of violent attacks. Houses were smashed, shops looted and synagogues desecrated. The Jews themselves were blamed and 20,000 were arrested, with the majority being sent to concentration camps.

1939

The outbreak of war in 1939 had the effect of intensifying the anti-Jewish persecution which had been building since 1933. In preparing the German people for the likelihood of war, Hitler had insisted that if conflict came it would be the Jews who had caused it. This gave him the excuse to claim that war would offer the German people the chance to exact revenge for the Jews' leading the nation to defeat in 1918. In January 1939, he prophesied in the Reichstag what form that vengeance would take: 'the annihilation of the Jewish race in Europe'.

1939–42

The occupation of eastern Europe by German armies between 1939 and 1942 provided the opportunity for annihilation. Deportations and killings became more organized and more widespread. Special SS units followed the German forces as they marched into Poland and Russia and killed thousands of Jews.

1942: The 'Final Solution'

In January 1942, some of the most prominent of the Nazi leaders gathered in conference at Wannsee, a suburb of Berlin. They met to consider plans for the 'Final Solution'. The chief spokesmen were Reinhard Heydrich and Adolf Eichmann. Heydrich defined the Nazi objectives: Europe from east to west was to be 'cleansed' of its 11 million Jews. In a planned operation they were to be transported to eastern Europe where they would be made to work unti they dropped dead from exhaustion and hunger. Any Jews who survived this would be systematically exterminated.

All those present at Wannsee agreed in principle and none raised serious moral objections to this 'Final Solution'. Furthermore, none doubted that in implementing the plan they were carrying out Hitler's wishes even though he had not issued a specific written order. The only disagreements were over the timing and pace of this vast logistical enterprise. Robert Ley, director of the Labour Front, publicly declared in May 1942, 'It is not enough to isolate the Jewish enemy; the Jews have got to be exterminated.'

1942–45: The Holocaust

Within months of the Wannsee Conference, special concentration camps were established to carry out methodical mass extermination. Bureaucrats sat in offices calculating how they could most efficiently destroy a whole race of people. The extermination programme came as near to achievement as the circumstances of war permitted. By the end of the war some 6 million Jews had been murdered in the camps.

Persecution of other minorities

Attention has rightly been paid to the **Holocaust** as the most destructive of Hitler's race polices, but racial discrimination and persecution were directed towards all those he regarded as racial inferiors or 'asocial degenerates'. This explains the treatment of:

- The Roma gypsies – of the 900,000 Roma estimated to have been living in Europe before the war, some 23 per cent were killed in the Nazi extermination campaign.
- Homosexuals – following the murder of Röhm in 1934 (see page 75), scandalous reports came out about what were described as his 'perversions'. This led to police hunts and prosecutions under the laws against homosexual practices. During the Nazi period, 50,000 men were convicted of 'indecency'; of these some 15,000 were put in concentration camps where part of their degradation was to be made to wear a pink triangle. Homosexuals who did not 'come out' were usually not hunted down. Although female homosexuality was unlawful, there is no recorded case of a woman being prosecuted for this.
- **Jehovah's Witnesses** – 2,000 were murdered under the Nazi regime, 250 specifically for refusing to be conscripted. Those Witnesses who were prepared to sign allegiance to the regime were left untouched.
- 'Rhineland bastards' – this was Hitler's term for the mixed-race children, the offspring of either **black Germans** or of German women and French colonial troops who had been stationed in the Rhineland area after its occupation by France in 1919, including Algerian Arabs. For expedient reasons, since he looked for support from anti-British Arab leaders, Hitler publicly played down his distaste for Arabs. Yet since they, like Jews, were a Semitic people, his anti-Semitism included them as well. Among the first victims of the Nazi sterilization programme were the mixed-race Rhineland children.

← **How were other minorities treated under Nazism?**

 **KEY TERM**

Holocaust The systematic killing by Nazi Germany of 6 million European Jews between 1942 and 1945.

Jehovah's Witnesses A Christian religious sect whose beliefs included the notion that, since the secular state was corrupt, its laws did not need to be obeyed, a view that offended the authorities.

Black Germans There were some 25,000 people of African origin living in the Third Reich, descendants of those whose who had come from the German colonies before 1918.

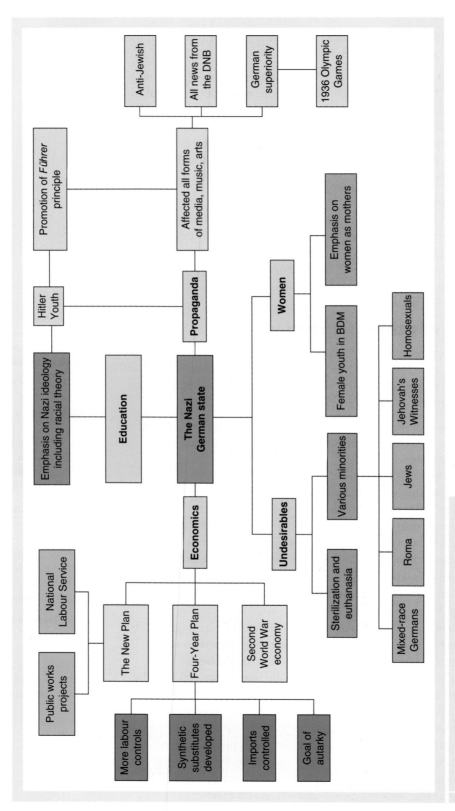

SUMMARY DIAGRAM

Hitler's domestic policies and their impact, 1933–45

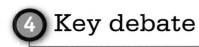

Key debate

▶ **Key question:** *How far did Hitler achieve a totalitarian state?*

A question that underlies all assessments of Nazi totalitarianism, and which divides historians, is whether Hitler was a 'weak' or a 'strong' leader. Those who support the weak argument, most notably the German scholars, Hans Mommsen and Martin Broszat, suggest that, despite appearing to exercise totalitarian authority over the state, Hitler was not all-powerful. Three main reasons are offered:

- Hitler was often indecisive.
- His instructions were not always carried out.
- The political and administrative system of Nazi Germany prevented him from dictating policy.

However, the majority of historians in this field maintain that Hitler was a 'strong' leader. Writers such as Alan Bullock and Richard Evans accept that Hitler delegated the duties of government but suggest that this did not diminish his power. Indeed, his policy of encouraging rivalry among ministers and institutions increased his power according to the divide and rule principle. The main points in the 'strong' argument are:

- The Enabling Act and *Gleichshaltung* left Hitler 'the supreme judge of the nation'.
- There was no open defiance of him among ministers and officials.
- Only one political party was permitted, Hitler's own Nazi Party.
- Opposition was treasonable.
- The trade unions had been abolished.
- The armed services swore an oath of loyalty to Hitler personally. From 1938 Hitler was Commander-in-Chief.
- The legal system operated in Hitler's name; judges swore allegiance to him.
- The Churches were either supportive or quiescent.
- The German press was wholly pro-Hitler.
- The **Reichsbank** was subservient.
- The Reichstag became an exclusively Nazi body, existing only to confirm Hitler's decisions.
- The Cabinet existed only at Hitler's pleasure and ceased to meet at all after 1937.

The weak versus strong argument has become merged with the intentionalist versus structuralist dispute:

- Intentionalists regard Hitler's policies as having been the result of his deliberate planning.
- Structuralists see Hitler as having been subject to pressures that obliged him to adopt policies not of his own choosing.

KEY TERM

Reichsbank The German state bank.

Hitler's authority

The limitation of the structuralist case is that, while Hitler may well not have initiated policies, the basic fact remained that such was his political dominance that no policy could proceed unless it met with his approval. Although Nazi Germany was not a clearly defined integrated political structure, everything of note had ultimately to pass the scrutiny of the *Führer*. The vital thing for any minister was to keep the confidence of the *Führer*. Those he trusted could approach him and ask for support for their proposals; as Chancellor any instructions he issued had priority over all other orders. That made the policies he backed unchallengeable.

Everything that was done in Germany after 1933 was done in Hitler's name. It is difficult to accept that anything of which he really disapproved would have been pursued. The intentionalist viewpoint is strengthened by a comment of Hitler's in 1939 to the effect that his polices were a compound of planning and the right circumstances. Opportunism, he said, was always the key: 'The actual timing could naturally not be foreseen at the beginning.'

It was in wartime that Hitler's authority showed itself in an absolute form. As Commander-in-Chief of the army, Hitler made himself so central to the strategic planning of the war that everything had to go through him. He ran the war, a situation which left his generals frustrated. They knew he was making major errors yet, short of assassinating him, they felt they could not stop him.

An important observation is one made by Sir Ian Kershaw. He suggests that the weak/strong, intentionalist/structuralist terms are as much complementary as they are contradictory. They are not exclusive. There is no need for an either/or approach. Strengths and weaknesses can exist side by side. It is also too easy to be misled by terms. 'Weakness' conveys the notion of absence of power, whereas Hitler often chose to let others use power in his name, which is not weakness but a delegation of authority. In Hitler's case, it was a style of government.

T
O
K

Historians continue to debate the role of Hitler in his government's decisions. To what extent is history essentially unknowable? (History, Language, Reason)

Chapter summary

Germany under Adolf Hitler, 1933–45

Embittered by Germany's humiliating defeat in 1918, Adolf Hitler found an outlet for his bitterness in the Nazi Party whose leader he became. Failing to take power in a *putsch* in 1923, he cynically resolved to gain office by legal means. Possessed of a deep hatred of Jews and communists, whom he blamed for Germany's ills, he exploited the troubled economic times to develop the Nazi Party to a position in 1932 where it gained a third of the popular vote. Using guile and skilful propaganda he then outmanoeuvred the politicians of the Weimar Republic to become Chancellor in 1933.

Once in office Hitler adopted *Gleichshaltung*, a programme that destroyed all opposition within the Nazi movement and the country at large. By 1934, he held supreme power as *Führer*. He then stepped back from the domestic scene, leaving day-to-day government to his ministers and officials, of whom he made two demands: they were to rearm the Third Reich and also make it a racial state. This second demand meant that the persecution of the Jews became the outstanding feature of Nazi Germany, culminating in the Holocaust.

Hitler's political pre-occupation was with foreign affairs. His aim was to restore to Germany the territories and peoples taken from it in 1919. Between 1933 and 1939, when his policies tipped into war, he opportunistically used bluff and threats to get his way. In 1939 he went too far and became involved in a war with France and Britain. Two years later his over-ambition resulted in war with the Soviet Union and the USA. Having won all their major campaigns down to 1942, the German forces then found themselves overstretched in a multi-front struggle and by 1945 they had been defeated.

Until war came, Hitler was hugely popular with the German people who admired him for ending unemployment and raising their living, working and educational levels. Understandably, however, the achievements of the Third Reich in such areas have been overshadowed by the horrors to which he ultimately subjected the peoples of Germany and Europe.

Examination practice

Below are a number of different questions for you to practise. For guidance on how to answer exam-style questions, see Chapter 10.

1   Analyse the factors that allowed Hitler to become Germany's Chancellor by 1933.

2   To what extent had Hitler consolidated his power by the end of 1934?

3   What was the role of propaganda in maintaining Hitler's government?

4   Discuss the impact of Hitler's rule on women by 1939.

5   To what extent did Hitler's government impact upon the arts?

6   Discuss the importance of *Gleischaltung* for Hitler's rule.

7   Why was there little effective opposition to Hitler's rule?

8   How did Nazi political and racial ideology impact upon German society?

9   Explain the importance of economic success during Hitler's rule in Germany.

10   Analyse the significance of the army in Germany during Hitler's rule 1933 to 1939.

 Activities

I   Most historians acknowledge that Hitler's government benefited most Germans, primarily economically. Discuss the following question, perhaps with reference to TOK: At what point is majority rule not defensible as a governing philosophy?

2   Research the political views of Ernst Röhm. Compare and contrast these views with what Hitler's government implemented in Germany.

3   Research the Nuremberg Laws of 1935, the Jim Crow laws in the United States, and the apartheid system of South Africa. Compare and contrast these three systems in a table or chart. Extend this activity by finding other examples of legal discrimination by various states against their racial, ethnic, religious and sexual minorities and add these to an expanded chart.

CHAPTER 4

China under Mao Zedong, 1949–76

Mao Zedong led the Chinese Communist Party (CCP) to power in 1949. Over the next quarter century before his death in 1976, he was leader of the People's Republic of China (PRC). During that time, he used the most authoritarian means to shape the new nation in accordance with his particular brand of Chinese communism. He adopted policies that revolutionized the political, economic and social structure of China. These policies were accompanied by constant purges, climaxing with the Cultural Revolution of 1966–76. Such was the extent of his authority that, by the time of his death, Chinese communism had become Maoism. This chapter examines the following key questions:

✪ What circumstances favoured the rise of Mao Zedong?
✪ How did Mao impose his authority on China?
✪ What impact did Mao's rule have on the lives of the Chinese people?
✪ How far did Mao achieve a totalitarian state?

1 ⃝ Mao's rise to power, 1911–49

▶ *Key question: What circumstances favoured the rise of Mao Zedong?*

Revolutionary China

The China into which Mao Zedong was born in 1893 was a deeply troubled land. For centuries it had believed itself to be superior to all other states. But by the end of the nineteenth century its self-belief had been shattered. Ruled by the increasingly incapable imperial Qing dynasty, China was facing insurmountable problems:

- Since the 1840s, a number of Western nations, principally Britain, Germany, France and the USA, had forced the Chinese to enter into a series of 'unequal treaties' which obliged them to surrender sovereign territory and accept trade on Western terms.
- China's bitterness at such humiliating foreign domination was deepened by military defeat in 1895 by its neighbour and traditional enemy, Japan.
- The Chinese economy was backward, particularly compared to Japan's. Its industry and commerce was largely under foreign control and it was heavily in debt to foreign banks.
- China's population had doubled in the nineteenth century from a quarter of a billion to half a billion. Chinese agriculture had been unable to

Why were conditions so unstable in China in Mao's formative years?

produce the extra food needed by these growing numbers and widespread famines were frequent.

- It was clear that the ruling Qing (Manchu) dynasty was no longer capable of protecting China.
- A major weakness of the Qing dynasty was that it was not truly Chinese. This was evident from its alternative name in the West, Manchu, which denoted that it had come originally from Manchuria, a northern region outside China. Having invaded China and seized the imperial throne in 1644, its emperors had governed China from then on. The underlying resentment among many Chinese towards rule by the 'foreign' Qing dynasty intensified as China's problems mounted.

Sun Yatsen

A revolutionary movement developed whose most prominent figure was **Sun Yatsen**, the founder of the **GMD**. Sun adopted a radical programme based on the notion that China had to develop along the same lines as Japan, which had achieved modernization in the nineteenth century by adopting progressive Western military and economic ways. Sun wanted China to embrace 'a revolution against the world to join the world'. The first step in this programme had to be the removal of the Qing imperial system.

Republican China

Sun Yatsen's ideas undoubtedly helped prepare the way for the Chinese Revolution of 1911 when the Qing, unable to control mutinies in the imperial army and, faced with growing hostility, chose to abdicate. Yet the fall of the Qing did not bring the results for which the revolutionaries had hoped. Sun Yatsen was outmanoeuvred by Yuan Shikai, a military commander and conservative politician, who became president of the Republic, established in 1912. Yuan survived until 1916 but only by borrowing heavily from abroad and giving in to Japanese demands for control of parts of China. It was clear that the new Republic was no more capable of defending China's interests than the Qing had been.

The warlords

The weakness of the central Republican government provided the opportunity for a number of provincial military leaders to impose themselves as individual rulers in their own areas. Possessing their own private armies and imposing their own laws, these warlords, as they became known, ruthlessly imposed their authority on particular regions. For over a decade after 1916, they defied government attempts to bring them under control.

The May Fourth movement, 1919

Chinese resentment at the failure of the Republic and the onset of warlordism intensified when it was learned that China had been further humiliated by the victorious Allied powers at the **Paris Peace Conference**. In May 1919, China was dismissively informed that it would not be recovering the territories previously taken from it by Germany. They were being handed instead to Japan. The outrage this caused among the Chinese led to the May Fourth movement – a series of anti-government, anti-foreigner protests and demonstrations that began on 4 May 1919 and convulsed China for a number of days.

Mao Zedong

It was in this atmosphere that Mao Zedong, a peasant from Hunan province, arrived in Beijing where he became caught up in the fever of the May Fourth protests, which excited him as a spontaneous reaction of the people against foreign oppression. Intensely patriotic and embittered by China's failings, he had been greatly impressed by Sun Yatsen's revolutionary ideas. Between 1912 and 1919, Mao had witnessed scenes of great violence as rival Republican factions fought for supremacy in his home province of Hunan. He recorded that the experience deeply affected him and led him to conclude that to gain success politically or militarily required total commitment and a willingness to use extreme methods. This provides an early clue as to why throughout his career he was so ready to use the toughest means to crush political opponents. One of his most revealing sayings was that 'all power grows out of the barrel of a gun'.

In Beijing he became attracted to **Marxist** ideas and developed the conviction that if China was to regain its greatness it would have to undergo a profound social and political revolution. To further this aim, Mao, in 1921, became one of the founder members of the Chinese Communist Party (CCP). He went on to play a key role in organizing the alliance between the GMD (Nationalists) and the Communists that overcame the warlords between 1924 and 1927. However, the alliance came to an end in 1927 when the Nationalist leader, **Chiang Kaishek**, turned on his Communist allies, whom he now regarded as rivals, and tried to destroy them in an extermination campaign. Mao managed to survive by removing his CCP forces to the remote mountains of Jiangxi province where he led the Autumn Harvest Rising, an organized **guerrilla** resistance.

It was in Jiangxi, between 1927 and 1934, that Mao first endeavoured to build a Chinese soviet. It was also during the Jiangxi period that Mao again revealed the ruthlessness that characterized his whole career. In the 'Futian incident' in 1930, he ordered the torture and execution of some 4,000 Red Army troops whom he accused of plotting against him. His written instruction read: 'do not kill the important leaders too quickly, but squeeze out of them the maximum information'.

The Long March, 1934–35

Continually attacked by Chiang's army, the Communists were forced to abandon Jiangxi in 1934 and flee on what became known as the Long March, a desperate year-long journey during which Mao emerged as an increasingly important organizer. There was much dispute among the march leaders as to which route to take. Mao's insistence that the marchers head north into Shaanxi province rather than go west towards the Soviet Union

KEY TERM

Marxist Relating to the ideas of Karl Marx, a German revolutionary, who had advanced the notion that human society developed historically as a continuous series of class struggles between those who possessed economic and political power and those who did not. He taught that the culmination of this dialectical process would be the crushing victory of the proletariat over the bourgeoisie.

Chiang Kaishek Became leader of the Nationalists on Sun Yatsen's death in 1925; throughout his career Chiang remained resolutely anti-communist.

Guerrilla A style of warfare in which mobile troops, who live off the land, harass the enemy with surprise attacks while avoiding pitched battles.

ultimately proved the correct one and enhanced his reputation and authority. The marchers survived to reach the relative safety of Yanan in Shaanxi in 1935.

Why was the Yanan period so significant in Mao's rise?

Yanan, 1935–45

Once established in Yanan in 1935, Mao claimed the leadership of the CCP and over the next decade turned the base into a Communist soviet. Yanan was both a protective base and a haven to which Communist sympathizers flocked. Cave dwelling became a standard practice. The caves, which were dug into the **loess** hillside, provided shelter from the weather and from the frequent GMD air raids. Some caves were so large that they housed theatres, hospitals and a CCP university at which Mao regularly lectured.

SOURCE A

A typical cave dwelling in Yanan.

Examine Source A. How might the cave dwellings depicted in the source have increased the sense of community at Yanan?

Mao's peasant policy

It was at Yanan that Mao, building on what he had begun at Jiangxi, gave practical form to his concept of revolution by sending out Red Army units to occupy neighbouring regions. Mao's tactics for imposing CCP control in the countryside were essentially simple. Once the Reds had infiltrated or seized a village or region, the landowners were driven out or shot, and the area was declared to be '**liberated**'. This done, the land was immediately reallocated to the peasants, with the intention of thereby making them supporters of the Communist soviet that was then established.

This was all part of Mao's plan to win over the peasants. He urged the soldiers to regard themselves as ambassadors carrying the Communist message to the people. Before the Yanan period, Chinese armies had invariably terrorized the civilian population; both the imperial and warlord forces had ravaged and

🔑 **KEY TERM**

Loess A type of soil that can be dug into easily and shaped but still remains firm.

Liberated The CCP's term for the areas brought under their control and from which they drove out the landlords.

plundered. But the Red Army was instructed to behave differently. Its duty was to aid and comfort the people. Mao laid down a code of conduct for his troops, which included such instructions as in Source B.

SOURCE B

Excerpt from Mao's instruction to the Red Army, 1937, quoted in *Mao Tse-tung*, edited by Anne Freemantle, published by Mentor Books, Ireland, 1962, p. xii.

Be courteous and help out when you can.
Return all borrowed articles.
Replace all damaged articles.
Be honest in all transactions with the peasants.
Pay for all articles purchased.
Be sanitary and establish latrines at a distance from people's houses.
Don't take liberties with women.
Don't kill prisoners of war.

According to Source B, what message is being conveyed to the troops?

These instructions provided a simple guide which, when followed, endeared the Red Army to a rural population whose previous experience of marching armies had been unremittingly bitter. To win further support from the peasants in the liberated areas, the Red Army introduced a number of schemes. These included:

- the seizure of land from the landlords and its reallocation to the peasants
- the creation of local peasant associations, which were invited to work with the CCP in improving their own conditions
- a programme for ending **usury**, which had so often blighted the lives of the peasants
- literacy and education programmes
- the provision of basic medical services.

KEY TERM

Usury Charging exorbitant interest on money loans.

This evident sensitivity to the wants of the peasants was the most popular of the CCP's land policies and played its part in the growth of the party from 40,000 in 1937 to 1 million by 1945. It was from this expanding membership that the volunteers for the Red Army came. However, it was not all harmony; there was a darker side to Communist land policy.

Repression on the land

Mao was prepared to be moderate at times, but all the moves that the CCP made under him had the essential purpose of strengthening Communist control. The removal of the landlords in the areas where the Red Army held sway was often a brutal process. Moreover, despite its feeling for the peasants and its genuine popularity with many of them, the Yanan regime was fiercely authoritarian. In the liberated areas, villages that would not conform to the CCP's demands were subject to harsh penalties, such as having all their crops and livestock confiscated and ruinous taxes imposed on them.

Moreover, the idea of the local community controlling its own affairs was undermined by the way in which the Communists structured the peasant

KEY TERM

Comintern The Communist International, formed in 1919 in Moscow to organize worldwide revolution. The Comintern took a particular interest in China, believing that it could impose itself on the young CCP.

Marxism–Leninism The revolutionary theories of class war as advanced by Karl Marx and later developed by Lenin.

The dialectic The dynamic force that drives history along a predestined path.

Bourgeois stage The period of history when the middle class, having undermined the previous feudal system (see page 138), dominate society until the working-class revolution occurs.

associations. Despite the CCP's boast that the local peasants enjoyed political representation through the village committees that were set up, the fact was that every committee had to have on it a CCP member with the power to veto decisions and direct policy.

Mao's ideology

It was at Yanan that Mao formalized his revolutionary ideas in the face of opposition from within the CCP and from the **Comintern**. It is important to stress that it was because he was an ardent nationalist that Mao had adopted communism. He saw in **Marxism–Leninism** a set of principles that he could turn into a practical programme as a means of restoring China to its original greatness. Mao never became a slave to Marxist theory; he interpreted the theory to suit his purposes for China. The persistent theme in his actions and his writings was that Chinese considerations always had primacy.

Mao's central belief was that China's revolution must come from the peasants. This was heresy in the eyes of the Comintern theorists. They asserted that:

- Mao was ignoring the essential stages in **the dialectic**
- peasant revolution was not an end in itself; it was merely the precursor of the final proletarian revolution
- China lacked an urban proletariat and was, therefore, incapable of achieving a genuinely proletarian revolution
- the best that the CCP could accomplish would be to help bring about the **bourgeois stage** of revolution by merging with the Nationalists.

SOURCE C

Diagram illustrating the pattern of the dialectic.

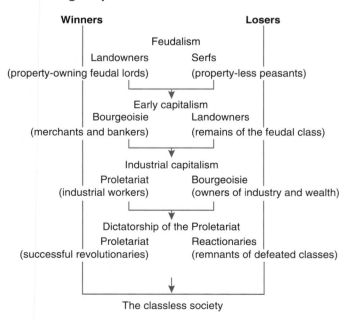

?

According to Source C, what are the principal stages in class conflict?

Mao rejected this analysis and stressed that Marxist theory had to be interpreted in the light of the actual conditions in China. He dismissed the idea that revolution could be achieved only by workers in the urban areas and asserted his own convictions.

- In China, urban industrial workers accounted for less than 4 per cent of the population, whereas the rural peasants made up over 80 per cent. It followed that a popular revolution would have to be the work of the peasantry.
- In China, therefore, a peasant revolution would be sufficient to fulfil the demands of the dialectic.
- Mao redefined the term proletarian to mean not so much a social class as an attitude. Those who were genuinely committed to revolution were *ipso facto* members of the proletariat. Anyone who had suffered oppression at the hands of class enemies could be counted a member of the proletariat.
- There was, therefore, no necessity to wait for the growth of an industrial proletariat in China. Genuine revolution would be achieved by the peasants: 'no power, however strong, can restrain them'. He told his followers that it was their task to unleash the huge potential of the peasantry: 'The peasants are the sea; we are the fish. We live in the sea.'

In a series of reflections, which were published in 1940 under the title *On New Democracy*, Mao defined the revolution which the Chinese Communists were leading not as a class movement but as a national one. Faced with the Japanese occupation of China after 1937 (see page 116), Mao declared the aim of his party to be 'long-term co-operation with all those classes, strata, political groups and individuals who were willing to fight Japan to the end'. He appealed to all Chinese who loved their country to unite against its enemies.

CCP opposition to Mao

Mao's particular interpretation of the dialectic put him at variance with the orthodox communists, such as Li Lisan, a Moscow-trained Marxist, who continued to follow the Comintern line by insisting that the Chinese communists concentrate their revolutionary activities in the urban areas. Throughout the 1930s Mao was involved in a battle to assert his authority within the Party. His major opponent was Wang Ming, leader of a faction known as '**the 28 Bolsheviks**', who followed Li Lisan in criticizing Mao for ignoring Comintern instructions and acting independently. Mao was accused of 'reckless adventurism' for assuming that the stages of proletarian revolution could be skipped at will. Mao survived such criticism thanks largely to four key factors:

1. His selection in 1934 of the correct northern route to follow on the Long March had given him a moral superiority over the pro-Moscow faction, who had argued for a different western route.
2. As a result of his own background and field researches, Mao had an unrivalled knowledge of the Chinese peasantry, which meant he dominated any discussion of the Party's peasant policy.

3. His intense self-belief and determination allowed him to silence opponents and bring doubters into line.
4. He was indispensable as a military planner.

The 'Rectification of Conduct' campaign, 1942–44

Mao's ideological victory over his Party opponents enabled him to tighten his control of the Party overall. The communism that Mao developed at Yanan was fundamentally oppressive. Discipline and obedience were required of all those living under it. Mao advanced the notion of **revolutionary correctness**, asserting that, unless the Party maintained a constant struggle against wrong thinking, it would be betrayed from within. To prevent this he launched a 'rectification of conduct' campaign which lasted from 1942 to 1944. Party members were to engage in public self-criticism. To assist them in their search for revolutionary truth, they were obliged to study prescribed texts, among which Mao's own writings figured prominently. On the grounds that they had become infected by **revisionist** ideas, over a thousand Party members were imprisoned and tortured to extract confessions.

Sixty Communist Party officials committed suicide rather than undergo public humiliation. Mao dismissed suggestions that the campaign was too harsh. In 1942, he wrote: 'Some comrades see only the interests of the part and not the whole. They do not understand the Party's system of **democratic centralism**; they do not understand that the Party's interests are above personal or sectional interests.'

Consequences

The Rectification Movement enhanced Mao's authority over the CCP:

- He had rid himself of opposition and consolidated his position as leader.
- He had finally triumphed over the pro-Moscow wing of the Party.
- He had begun to move towards **cult status** in Yanan.
- Chinese communism was now so closely identified with him personally that it had become **Maoism**.
- Mao's election as Chairman of the Central Committee of the CCP in 1943 was a formal recognition of his dominance over the Party.
- By 1945, when the Japanese war came to an end, Mao was being regularly referred to as '**the great helmsman**'.

The Japanese occupation, 1931–45

It was at Yanan that Mao, in the ongoing struggle for survival against continuing attacks from Chiang's Nationalists, developed his military skills as a strategist and tactician. That Mao was able to do so was largely explained by a factor that dominated the Chinese situation until 1945 – the occupation of China by Japan.

In 1931, as a first step towards a massive expansion into Asia, Japan had seized the northern region of Manchuria which was renamed Manchuguo. From this base the Japanese forces began to spread out into other parts of China. In 1937, the occupation became a full-scale **Sino**-Japanese war which continued until Japan's defeat in 1945.

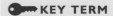

KEY TERM

Revolutionary correctness The idea that Chinese communism (Maoism) was a body of political, social and economic truth, as defined by Mao, which all CCP members had to accept.

Revisionist Reactionary, anti-Party thinking.

Democratic centralism The notion, first advanced by Lenin, that true democracy lies in party members' obedience to enlightened leadership.

Cult status A position that entitles the holder to a special veneration among the people and puts him or her beyond criticism.

Maoism The identification of Chinese communism with Mao personally.

The great helmsman A reference to Mao's wisdom in guiding the ship of state.

Sino A prefix meaning Chinese.

Chiang Kaishek was slow to respond to the Japanese action. The CCP exploited this by asserting that they, not the Nationalists, were the true defenders of China against the Japanese. The Communists both exaggerated their own contribution to China's anti-Japanese struggle and understated that of the Nationalists, who did the bulk of the fighting. Nevertheless, since Chiang's primary aim throughout was to crush the Communists, it appeared that he was not fully committed in his resistance to Japan. Ironically, as Mao later admitted, the Japanese occupation was the saving of the Chinese Communists. The Japanese, by diverting Chiang away from his main objective of destroying the CCP's bases, unwittingly enabled the Communists to survive.

The Chinese Civil War, 1945–49

The defeat of Japan at the end of the Second World War in 1945 was followed by the renewal of open hostilities between Mao's CCP and Chiang's GMD. Over the next four years a bitter civil war was fought, involving the death of 6 million soldiers. How effectively the Red Army had developed as a fighting force under Mao was revealed by its ultimate victory. The Nationalists, after some seemingly impressive successes in the first year of the war when they attempted to drive the Communists from their northern bases, were unable to achieve a single major victory between 1947 and 1949. By that later date, their grip on northern, central and southern China had been broken in a series of victorious **PLA** campaigns.

Late in 1949, Chiang fled with the remnants of his forces to the island of Taiwan (Formosa) where he began to establish a separate Chinese state. In October 1949, in the restored capital, Beijing, Mao Zedong claimed that a new nation had been created, the People's Republic of China (PRC).

A set of specific Nationalist weaknesses and Communist strengths explain Mao's success.

Nationalist weaknesses

It was Chiang Kaishek himself who in the last months of the war listed five basic reasons why his forces had lost:

- Lack of skill and judgement of his military commanders, who fought 'muddle-headed battles'. They planned poorly and issued orders irresponsibly.
- Lack of training of the rank-and-file soldiers, who were incompetently led by their officers.
- Low Nationalist morale. This was a result of the complacency among the high-level officers, many of whom were concerned solely with their own self-interest. (It should be added that the Nationalist recruitment methods were so harsh that the conscript Nationalist armies lacked spirit and purpose.)

← **Why did the Communists win the Civil War?**

 **KEY TERM**

PLA China's People's Liberation Army, formerly the Red Army.

Map of the final stages of the Chinese Civil War, 1946–49.

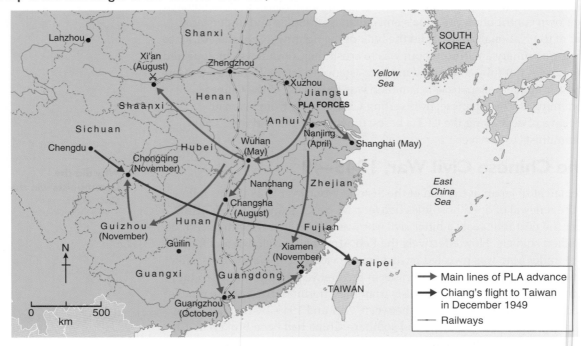

?

Study Source D. What information does it contain regarding the last stages of the Civil War?

- The GMD was unable to inspire the forces in the field because as an organization it lacked discipline and effective propaganda, attributes in which Mao and the Communists excelled.
- The Nationalists' failure to make effective use of the arms and resources with which they were provided by the USA. Too often the weapons fell into Communist hands.

To Chiang's list could be added the Nationalists' general unpopularity among ordinary Chinese people, which made it difficult for Chiang's forces to control regions except by severe repression, which was invariably counter-productive.

Communist strengths

The Communists' success was attributable to a number of reasons:

- Mao's mixture of determination and opportunism served the Communists well. When the war began Mao's main aim was simply to avoid defeat by preserving his northern bases but when he realized that the Nationalists could be beaten he adopted an attacking strategy which eventually forced Chiang out of mainland China.
- Historians now suggest that, of all the factors accounting for the CCP's ultimate victory, Mao's military leadership was the most significant. It was under him that the Communist forces who were essentially rural guerrilla fighters in 1945 had by 1949 become an effective modern army.

- A key element was Mao's self-confidence and power of command in pressing on with three decisive campaigns in the winter of 1948–49, even when his generals doubted that they could be fought successfully.
- The Red Army's ability to live off the land and obtain support, food and information from people in the localities was a huge advantage.
- Although Stalin gave some military support to the Communists, he did not want a strong united China as a neighbour, and attempted to pressure Mao into making a compromise peace with Chiang which would have left China partitioned. Mao, intent on complete victory, successfully resisted such interference.

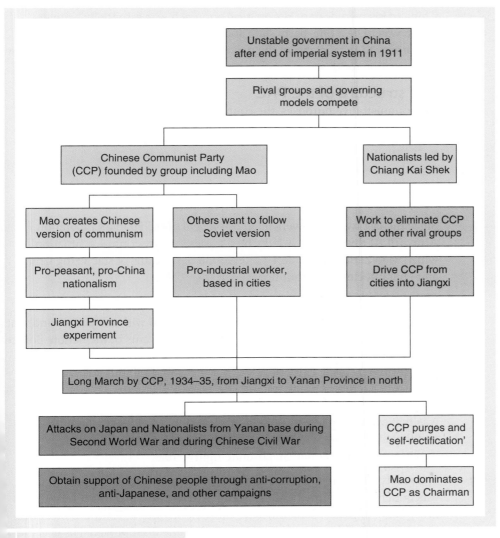

SUMMARY DIAGRAM

Mao's rise to power, 1911–49

Mao's establishment of an authoritarian state

▶ Key question: How did Mao impose his authority on China?

By what means did Mao consolidate his hold upon China?

The creation of the People's Republic of China

In Beijing, on 1 October 1949, Mao formally declared the People's Republic of China (PRC) to have come into being. He was now in a position to shape China to his own design. His political approach was essentially simple: China was to be a one-party state and the people were to act in total conformity to the dictates of the new government. The Yanan years had been a preparation for this.

The structure of the PRC

For administrative purposes, the country was divided into six regions, each governed by a bureau of four major officials:

- chairman
- party secretary
- military commander
- political commissar.

Since the last two posts were filled by officers of the People's Liberation Army (PLA) this effectively left China under military control, a situation which Mao Zedong considered offered the best means of stabilizing China and guaranteeing the continued rule of the CCP.

The structure of government

The Communist Party claimed that all power rested with the people and that the party officials and the government acted as servants of the nation. Source E shows a model of how the government supposedly operated. It was the workers and peasants who exercised authority through the various connected and overlapping bodies. The Chinese Communists made much of the claim that all party officials were elected. What was not emphasized was that only one party could stand for election, all others being outlawed, and that even those who stood as independents had to acknowledge publicly that the CCP had an absolute right to rule.

 **KEY TERM**

Politburo An inner core of some twenty leading members of the Communist Party.

The reality was that government was carried out by the **Politburo**, which was under the authority of Mao Zedong. This did not mean that he initiated every detail of policy; sometimes he chose not to attend Politburo meetings. Nevertheless, nothing could be done of which he disapproved. His was the ultimate authority.

SOURCE E

The structure of Chinese Communist Party rule.

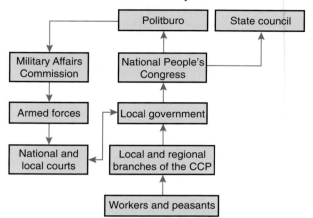

Examine Source E. How was power supposedly distributed within the CCP?

Review Source F. How was power delegated regionally within the PRC?

SOURCE F

The administrative regions of the PRC.

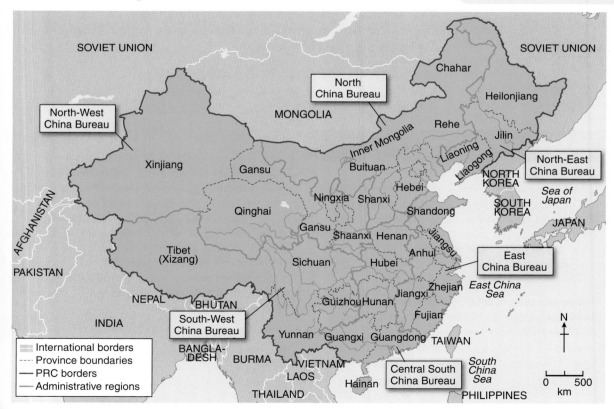

The imposition of military control

A clear sign of how dominant the new government intended to be was evident in the way it enforced its control over the outlying areas of China. In 1950, in a series of **'reunification' campaigns** three separate PLA armies were despatched west and south. Officially they were sent in order to help improve local conditions and it is true that troops did contribute to such schemes as road building. But their main purpose was to impose martial law and repress any sign of an independence movement:

- One army was sent into Tibet (Xizang).
- A second went into Xinjiang (Sinkiang).
- A third went into the southern province of Guangdong (Kwantung).

The anti-movements

The government deliberately created an atmosphere of fear and uncertainty by a series of **'anti-movements'**, launched against 'the remnants of the bourgeois class', those whom the CCP regarded as socially or politically suspect. The Chinese people were encouraged to inform on anyone they knew who was unwilling to accept the new regime. A special government department drew up a *dangan*, a dossier, on every suspected Chinese person. If an individual's dossier was dubious, he stood little chance of obtaining work or housing. The restrictive atmosphere this created was intensified by Mao's decision to enter the Korean War in 1950 in support of the North Koreans. This struggle provided further reasons for Mao to demand solidarity and loyalty from the Chinese people.

KEY TERM

'Reunification' campaigns The Chinese government's euphemism for forcibly bringing the invaded provinces into line in 1950.

Anti-movements The targeting of those accused of such crimes as waste, corruption and tax evasion.

United Nations The organization that superseded the League of Nations in 1945, committed to maintaining international security and promoting human rights. It began with 51 member states and was initially dominated by the USA upon whose financial support it depended.

The Korean War (1950–53)

The war began with communist North Korea's invasion of US-backed South Korea. The USA responded by sending its forces, under the banner of the **United Nations**, to defend South Korea. Stalin then persuaded Mao to join the struggle on the North Korean side by suggesting that China would be at grave risk if it did nothing in the face of 'American aggression'.

There was some opposition within Mao's government to China's entering the Korean War. Lin Bao, Mao's deputy, and some of the generals argued that the young PRC's primary task was to use its limited resources to crush its internal enemies, not to fight in Korea. Mao's counter-argument, based on Stalin's analysis, was that the PRC could not run the risk of staying out: if the US were to take Korea it would possess a stepping stone to China itself. His argument won the support of the Politburo which fully backed his decision in favour of war. Opposition was not entirely quelled but Mao suffered no serious challenge and remained in full control.

Anti-landlord campaign

A particularly fierce anti-movement was the anti-landlord campaign. The property of landlords was confiscated and redistributed among their former tenants. Some landlords were allowed to keep a portion of their land provided they became peasants, but the great majority were put on public trial and denounced as enemies of the people. The evidence that later came to light revealed that as many as 1 million landlords were killed during the PRC's land campaign of the early 1950s.

Study Source G. What information does it provide regarding the way trials were conducted in the people's courts?

SOURCE G

A landlord on trial in 1953.

Purges A system of terror used by Lenin and Stalin in the USSR and Mao in China for removing anyone regarded as a threat to their authority.

Rightists Those who argued for a slower, less violent development of revolution.

The '100 Flowers' campaign, 1957

Mao's **purges** extended to the Communist Party itself. Members suspected of not being fully supportive of Mao and the new China were referred to in such derogatory terms as '**rightists**', 'revisionists' and 'capitalist roaders'. A variant on, and seeming contradiction of, this hard line was Mao's invitation to CCP members to criticize government and party policies. In 1957, using the slogan 'Let a hundred flowers bloom; let a hundred schools of thought contend', Mao called on members to debate the great issues facing China. Although wary at first of responding, members eventually began to voice their feelings. Initially, only mild suggestions for improving things were expressed, but these were soon overtaken by increasingly bitter denunciations of individuals and government policies. There were even attacks on Mao; a university professor referred to the 'arbitrary and reckless' character of the Chairman's authority. Declaring himself appalled by the outpouring of disloyalty from 'rightists', Mao ordered an immediate ending of the Hundred Flowers campaign. Those who had spoken out too strongly were condemned as 'anti-socialists' who had abused the campaign in an attempt to undermine the CCP and the nation. Thousands of such 'rightists' were arrested and imprisoned.

What were Mao's motives in launching the 100 Flowers campaign?

Key debate

Was the campaign simply a ruse?

Many historians have discussed the question of why Mao introduced the 100 Flowers campaign. The reason for concentrating on this particular theme is that it is seen as illustrating the essential nature of Mao's approach to the governing of China. Some writers, most notably Jung Chang in her 2005 biography of Mao, argue that the speed with which he reversed his policy was proof that the campaign had been a trick on his part from the beginning. She suggests that, far from being intended as a liberalizing measure, it was a deliberate manoeuvre by Mao to bring his critics into the open so that they could be easily exposed, identified and removed (see Source H).

According to Source H, who were Mao's targets in the 100 Flowers campaign?

SOURCE H

An excerpt from *Mao: The Unknown Story* by Jung Chang and Jon Halliday, published Jonathan Cape, London, 2005, p. 435.

Few guessed that Mao was setting a trap, and that he was inviting people to speak out so that he could use what they said as an excuse to victimise them. Mao's targets were intellectuals and the educated, the people most likely to speak up.

As Jung Chang sees it, the 100 Flowers campaign was part of the movement towards a controlled society in which all expression of opinion had to meet the criteria of political correctness as defined by Mao. The way in which 'the anti-rightist' campaign purged the government and Party of his critics was of a scale and ruthlessness that anticipated the upheavals of the Cultural Revolution a decade later (see page 130). This is a strongly put case, but it needs to be pointed out that Jung Chang has become renowned, not to say notorious, for her personal hatred of Mao, an animus that other writers have suggested distorts her judgement. In *Was Mao Really a Monster?* (a 2010 book edited by Gregor Benton and Lin Chun), fourteen scholars offered a powerful rebuttal of Jung Chang's claims by pointing to her suspect methodology and lack of balance.

Was Mao genuinely seeking criticism?

Prior to Jung Chang's biography appearing, Lee Feigon, an American scholar, had published a revisionist argument in which he contended that Mao had been genuine in his original appeal for ideas to be expressed. This was not to say Mao was being tolerant. His intention was to undermine the bureaucrats in the government who in the short time that the PRC had been in existence had come to have too big an influence in the running of affairs. Feigon puts it in these terms:

SOURCE I

An excerpt from *Mao: A Reinterpretation* by Lee Feigon, published by Ivor R. Dee, Chicago USA, 2002, p. 112.

By giving scientists and engineers the freedom to express their ideas, Mao sought to prevent party bureaucrats from interfering with technical decisions. He wanted intellectuals to expose and attack corruption and bureaucracy. He also wanted peasants, students and workers to speak out and even demonstrate to prevent government bureaucrats from running roughshod over their rights.

According to Source I, what means did Mao use to restrict the influence of party bureaucrats?

Was the campaign part of a structured process?

Interpreting the motives behind the campaign as sinister, Yves Chevrier, a French scholar, suggests that the 100 Flowers campaign was a stage in an unfolding process by which Mao set out to reassert his authority and destroy all vestiges of opposition (see Source J).

SOURCE J

Excerpt from *Mao and the Chinese Revolution* by Yves Chevrier, translated by David Stryker, Interlink Books, Northampton, Massachusetts, USA, 2004, p. 123.

The 100 Flowers turned out to be the eye of the cyclone that would bring the Great Leap, itself a precursor of the Cultural Revolution. This moment of open debate, when contradictions were openly discussed for the first time in years, was like a carnivorous flower, ready to close upon its prey ... it enabled his [Mao's] political comeback within the Party leadership.

According to Source J, how is the 100 Flowers campaign linked with the Great Leap Forward and the Cultural Revolution?

Did the 100 Days Campaign result simply from a muddled dispute within the CCP?

Jonathan Spence, widely acknowledged by his fellow historians as the leading authority on Mao's China, dismisses the idea that the 100 Flowers campaign was a ruse by Mao to bring his enemies into the open. Spence sees the affair as the confused result of contradictory thinking among the CCP leaders (see Source K, page 126).

SOURCE K

An excerpt from *The Search for Modern China* by Jonathan Spence, published by Norton, New York, USA, 1990, p. 574.

It was rather, a muddled and inconclusive movement that grew out of conflicting attitudes within the CCP leadership. At its core was an argument about the pace and development that was best for China, a debate about the nature of the First Five-year Plan and the promise for further growth. From that debate and the political tensions that accompanied it sprang the Great Leap Forward.

Further points in the debate

There is also the possibility that Mao was influenced by events in the USSR: 1956 was the year that the new Soviet leader, Nikita Khrushchev, shook the communist world by launching an extraordinary attack on the reputation of his predecessor, Joseph Stalin, who had died three years earlier. Khrushchev denounced Stalin for his 'cult of personality' (see page 49). Mao could see how easily this charge could be made against him in China. His apparent encouragement of criticism from within the Party was, therefore, a way of taking the sting out of such a suggestion and preventing the comparison being made between him and Stalin. However, if Mao had indeed launched the 100 Flowers out of a fear of being compared with Stalin, the fear greatly lessened from late 1956. In November of that year Khrushchev sent Soviet tanks into Budapest to crush the **Hungarian Uprising**. That was the Soviet leader's way of making it clear that de-Stalinization did not mean the lessening of the grip of the Communist Party over the USSR or the weakening of Soviet control over the **Eastern bloc**.

Mao fully approved of the Soviet action for two reasons. In the first place, he believed it was the kind of tough line that communist governments should take in order to maintain their authority. In the second, he was relieved by the knowledge that the Soviet Union had merely been flirting with liberal ideas. This meant that he did not need to compete with Khrushchev in the defence of hardline communism. Neither leader had any intention of relaxing his political control over the people.

It might be wondered why Mao was so sensitive to happenings in the USSR. The answer is that, at this early stage of its development, the PRC still regarded itself as being dependent on the economic and diplomatic support of the Soviet Union. It would not be until later that Mao and the Chinese Communists would feel strong enough to throw off Soviet dominance and challenge the USSR for the leadership of international communism.

Conclusion

In the event, what most scholars agree on is that whatever Mao's motives may have been, it was the scale of the criticism that the 100 Flowers unleashed that took him aback. He had not realised the extent of the dissatisfaction with the Party which the campaign had revealed. In practical terms there was little difference as to whether he intended from the beginning to flush out opponents or whether he decided to do this once he had discovered the extent of the opposition. The outcome was the same: Mao crushed those he thought were opposed to him.

Economic policies

Nothing illustrates Mao's concept of the PRC as a collective nation more clearly than his economic programme. Although he had led a great peasant movement to victory in 1949, his basic aim was to develop China as an industrial power. However, despite attempting initially to establish the economy through a **Five-Year Plan**, introduced in 1952, the PRC had lacked the available resources and had had to rely on aid from the USSR. Mao had never been happy with this since the Soviet Union charged heavily for the loans and material it provided.

'The Great Leap Forward', 1958–62

By 1958, Mao had become resolved to break the Soviet grip. He had convinced himself that rapid industrial growth could be achieved by a huge communal endeavour of the Chinese people, which would create the resources needed. The centrepiece of this strategy was a Five-Year Plan introduced by Mao in 1958 as 'the Great Leap Forward'. It was based on two principal assumptions:

- The peasants would produce a surplus of food to be sold abroad to raise money for the expansion of Chinese industry.
- The workers, largely through the mass production of steel, would create a modern industrial economy, powerful enough to compete with the Soviet Union and the capitalist West.

Mao used the word 'leap' to suggest that China could bypass the stages through which the advanced nations had gone, and go straight from being a rural, agricultural economy to becoming an urban, industrial one. He called on the people from the youngest to the oldest in every town and village to work together in this great project.

With extraordinary enthusiasm the mass of the Chinese people tried to meet the production quotas laid down in the plan. Throughout China, the sky glowed red at night as families everywhere endeavoured to produce steel in homemade kilns. But goodwill alone cannot produce good steel. By rejecting modern technology in favour of mass effort Mao had made the targets unattainable. What was catastrophically worse than the economic failure of 'the Great Leap Forward' was the widespread famine that directly resulted from it.

China's great famine

The first step in 'the Great Leap Forward' had been a mass **collectivization** programme, under which:

- China's half a billion peasants were obliged to live and work in **communes**
- 70,000 of these were now created across China

What did Mao's economic policies aim to achieve?

 **KEY TERM**

Five-Year Plan A programme for industrial development based on a set of production quotas.

Collectivization Depriving the peasants of their land and requiring them to live and work in communes.

Communes Collective farms.

- individual peasants or families would no longer be allowed to farm for themselves or make a profit
- any surpluses became the property of the state, to be invested in industrial growth.

Mao had believed that collectivization would lead to a great increase in food production. The opposite happened. Disorientated by the disruption to their way of life, the peasants were unable to adapt to the new system imposed on them; they had no understanding of how to farm on a large communal scale. Crop yields fell sharply and hunger became widespread.

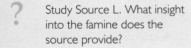
Study Source L. What insight into the famine does the source provide?

SOURCE L

China's agricultural record, 1956–62.

Year	Grain production (million tons)	Meat production (million tons)	Index of gross output value of agriculture
1956	192.8	3.4	120.5
1957	195.1	4.0	124.8
1958	200.0	4.3	127.8
1959	170.0	2.6	110.4
1960	143.5	1.3	96.4
1961	147.5	1.2	94.1
1962	160.0	1.9	99.9

The death toll

Blaming the reported shortfalls on poor local management and grain hoarding by rich peasants, Mao pressed ahead with collectivization. He claimed that it was the peasant masses who were demanding to be collectivized. Production figures were rigged to show how plentiful the harvests had become. The party launched a propaganda campaign detailing the benefits of collectivization. Newspapers carried images of beaming peasants gathering giant mounds of grain and rice. It was all untrue, but officials who expressed doubts were replaced, while peasants who protested were put into **labour camps**. Between 1958 and 1962, some 40 million Chinese starved to death. By his adherence to collectivization, Mao had turned China's rural provinces into killing fields. The death toll in the worst hit areas was:

- Shandong – 7.5 million
- Anhui – 8 million
- Henan – 7.8 million
- Sichuan – 9 million
- Qinghai – 1 million
- Tibet – 1 million.

Lack of opposition to collectivization

If there was any moment in Mao's rule of China when his opponents could have taken up the attack, the onset of the famine would seem to have

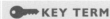**KEY TERM**

Labour camps Prisons and detention centres in which the inmates are required to perform heavy work.

Map showing the worst hit areas in the Great Famine.

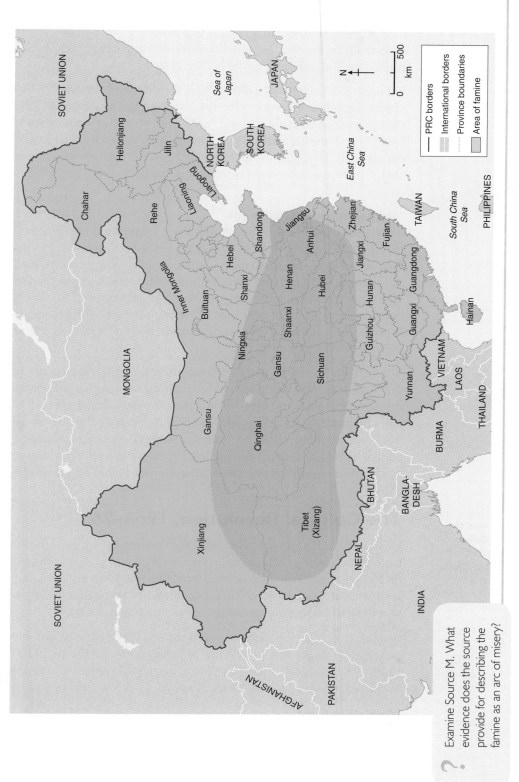

Examine Source M. What evidence does the source provide for describing the famine as an arc of misery?

provided it. At a Party gathering in Lushan in 1959, Peng Dehuai, the PRC's Minister of Defence, recounted the horrors of the famine he had seen in his own province of Anhui and begged that action be taken to alleviate the suffering. This was the moment for the other Party delegates to back him by confirming the truth of what he had described.

But none did. Unwilling to offend Mao, the delegates persisted in their obedience to him by denouncing Peng's account as a fabrication. They then proceeded to make speeches noting the advances made under the Great Leap Forward and praising Mao for his inspired leadership. The particular irony of this was that Mao had gone to Lushan expecting trouble. He feared that some members would use the occasion to attack his economic policies.

Mao's suppression of dissent

In the event, there was no attack. Whatever original intentions some members might have had before coming to Lushan, once there they allowed themselves to be overawed into submission. In an angry speech, Mao ridiculed Peng Dehuai and told the delegates that he was prepared to use the PLA against anyone in the Party who tried 'to lead the peasants to overthrow the government'. Faced with Mao's determination, the Party members, with the memories of the '100 Flowers' campaign fresh in their minds, dropped all thought of serious opposition.

What all this illustrated was that, while there doubtless were critics of Mao in the Party, such was his status and reputation as leader that they dared not risk openly challenging him. Nevertheless, having instructed two prominent party figures, Deng Xiaoping and Liu Shaoqi, to tackle the task of restoring food supplies, Mao judged it prudent to withdraw into the political background following the conference. This was not a relinquishing of power as such; he resigned no official position. He was free to return whenever he chose.

In what ways was the Cultural Revolution intended to make Mao's control of China permanent?

The Cultural Revolution, 1966–76

Deng and Liu had considerable success in ending the worst of the famine, largely because they abandoned collectivization and allowed the peasants to return to private farming. Mao, however, saw this as an undermining of the socialist principles on which China's communist revolution rested. He worried that he was losing control of the situation in China.

In 1966, Mao returned, determined to reassert his dominance in Chinese politics. The means that he adopted to achieve this was the Great Proletarian Cultural Revolution, a massive purge of party, government and people, aimed at removing all possible elements of opposition, real or imagined.

Mao's motives

A variety of intentions and motives can be adduced to explain Mao's implementation of the Cultural Revolution.

Fear of opposition from within the CCP

Mao never lost his belief that his colleagues, even those who professed the greatest personal loyalty, were ready to remove him from power if the opportunity came. He also considered that his absence from the forefront of the political scene had enabled factions to develop.

Age

In 1966 Mao was 73 and, although he was to survive for another ten years, he had begun to sense his mortality. His fear was that the revolution he had created would be betrayed after he had gone; hence his determination that before he died he would leave China so permanently marked that it could never be changed.

Paranoia

There was a marked element of paranoia in Mao. The more powerful he became, the more he feared that opposition to him was growing. He was convinced that factions in the Party were preparing to overthrow him. The fact that they did not openly challenge him made the position worse since their silence made it difficult to expose them. His answer, therefore, was to mount a massive purge of the Party to rid it of the betrayers and revisionists.

Resentment

Although Mao had acknowledged no guilt for the failure of the Great Leap Forward and the fearful famine it had produced, he knew his reputation had been damaged. That was why he had kept in the background since 1959, leaving Liu Shaoqi and Deng Xiaoping with the task of bringing the famine to an end. But the prestige they had gained from successfully doing this had made him resentful. Liu and Deng were now marked men. The Cultural Revolution would be a pretext for attacking them.

Ideology

The Cultural Revolution also fitted in with the dialectical ideas that Mao had promoted since his earliest days as a communist. He had always argued that revolution was not a single event; rather it was an unfolding process involving constant struggle.

Bureaucracy

Mao judged that the officials in the CCP and the government had become complacent and had lost their revolutionary fervour. What was needed, therefore, was a major purge which would get rid of the time-servers and restore to the Communist Party the purpose which had carried it to power in 1949. To do this, he planned to bypass the Party bureaucracy and enlist the Chinese people in a nationwide campaign that would destroy the reactionaries and save the revolution. The campaign would be deliberately disruptive. Mao spoke of 'great disorder across the land leading to great order'.

 **KEY TERM**

Reactionaries CCP members who had lost faith in the revolution.

International rivalry

Mao was also determined not to allow China to go the way of its great rival, the Soviet Union. In his eyes, the reformers who had ruled the USSR after Stalin's death in 1953 had betrayed communism by being too liberal at home and too willing, for the sake of avoiding war, to come to terms with the capitalist nations of the West. Mao extended the term 'revisionism' to include Soviet policy.

Nationalism

Mao's thinking had always been strongly nationalistic. He wanted to throw off any foreign influence that had crept in whether Western or Soviet. Whatever the cost, Mao wanted China to follow its own path.

Propaganda: the cult of Mao

Mao could not have embarked on such a gigantic enterprise as the Cultural Revolution had not the ground already been well prepared. Despite his temporary withdrawal from politics, Mao, by the mid-1960s, had become little less than a god to the great mass of the Chinese people. This was the result of a massive propaganda exercise organized by Lin Biao, head of the PLA, and the man nominated by Mao as his successor. Lin had skilfully projected the image of Mao as the saviour of the nation, the great benefactor of the people, and the voice of truth. Mao's picture was everywhere and his words were quoted constantly in the media.

'The Little Red Book'

Lin's most effective piece of propaganda was to produce what became known as 'the Little Red Book', which first appeared in 1964. Formally entitled *Quotations of Chairman Mao Zedong*, its bright red plastic covers, which contained selections from Mao's speeches and writings, made it the most instantly recognizable book in the world. Its opening exhortation indicated its purpose: 'Study Chairman Mao's writings, follow his teachings and act according to his instructions.' In its first four years, sales of the Little Red Book reached 750 million. Everyone carried a copy; it fitted into schoolchildren's satchels and workers' lunch boxes. Readings from it settled every dispute and preceded every organized public event.

The attack on revisionism

The immediate prelude to the Cultural Revolution was an official announcement in April 1966 that the Chinese Communist Party had been infected by 'revisionism'. Within the CCP's ranks had been discovered 'a sinister anti-Party line diametrically opposed to Chairman Mao's thought'. To stifle this before it could wreak irreparable harm, the PLA had been instructed to lead China in rooting out the 'anti-socialist weeds'. The Party called on the people of China to join in the attack on all those who were daring to endanger the revolution by 'taking the capitalist road'. Panic set in as officials rushed to declare their absolute loyalty to Mao. Many were too late. By the high summer of 1966, all those in the party and government whom Mao suspected of being opposed to him had been removed or demoted. The way was now open for an intensive terror campaign.

KEY TERM

Revisionism Departure from true communism, a blanket term applied to any idea of which Mao disapproved.

The August rally, 1966

The Cultural Revolution first came to the full attention of the Chinese people and to international observers on 18 August 1966. On that date Tiananmen Square in Beijing filled with a million young people, most in their teens and twenties, who over the course of the day shouted ecstatically whenever Mao appeared on a balcony of the Forbidden City overlooking the Square. He did not himself address the crowds that day; Lin Biao was the principal speaker. Lin described Mao Zedong as an incomparable genius who was 'remoulding the souls of the people'. Acting on Mao's bidding, Lin appealed to the throng to destroy revisionism by attacking the 'Four Olds', i.e.:

- old thoughts
- old habits
- old culture
- old customs.

The response of the young

Mao had selected the young to be the instruments of the Cultural Revolution. He invited them to band together in the systematic destruction of those people and values that he now deemed obsolete. The young who rushed to answer Mao's call had good reason to follow him. They readily accepted that it was the incompetence of self-interested revisionist officials in the Party and government that was denying them the career prospects and advancement to which they were entitled. The young demonstrators made a distinction between Mao and his government. The officials who should have served him had let him down and in doing so had let down the young. That was why young people were so ready to join the attack on the Four Olds. Now was the time to reform China by ridding it of bureaucrats and revisionists.

In venerating Mao, the young were reverting to a powerful Chinese tradition – worship of the emperor and obedience to his authority. This was another reminder that traditional Confucian values had survived in communist China. Yet the extraordinary paradox was that **Confucianism** was condemned as belonging to the Four Olds. Indeed, the name Confucius was tagged on to anyone or anything the Maoists wanted to condemn, as in 'Confucian capitalist revisionism'.

The Red Guards

Many of the young responded to Mao's appeals by enlisting as **Red Guards**. Wearing distinctive armbands, units of Red Guards were to be found in every major area. Taking as their watchword Mao's slogan, 'It is right to rebel', they set about destroying the Four Olds. Unhindered by the police, the Red Guards were free to attack people at will and destroy property:

- Their first target was the education system. Teachers and lecturers were dragged from classrooms and lecture halls and denounced as reactionaries for perpetuating the myths and superstitions of the past.
- They commandeered public transport and took over radio and television stations.

🔑 **KEY TERM**

Confucianism A system of ethics, based on the teachings of Confucius (551–479BC), which emphasized the need for people to be obedient to higher authority in order to preserve social harmony.

Red Guards Units of young people, specially trained by Kang Sheng, the head of Mao's secret police, to act as terror squads.

- They broke into houses to hunt down anyone showing signs of 'decadent tendencies', such as the wearing of Western clothes or make-up, and the possession of 'non-revolutionary' books.
- The discovery of private altars or religious shrines was enough to prove that the householders were enemies of the people; they and their neighbours were forced to watch as their homes were ransacked.
- Temples, libraries and museums were vandalized.
- A group that the Red Guards took particular pleasure in terrorizing were the **'intellectuals'**. Writers and artists were branded as 'bad elements' or 'class enemies'. With their crimes written on pieces of cardboard hung about their necks, they were publicly paraded and forced to confess that they had abused their positions of privilege.

The removal of Liu Shaoqi and Deng Xiaoping

As the pro-Mao demonstrations in Beijing grew more intense and the Red Guards increased their levels of terror, Mao turned directly against Liu Shaoqi and Deng Xiaoping. Both men were removed from their government positions for having taken 'a bourgeois reactionary line' and for supporting 'Soviet revisionism'. Wall posters appeared accusing them of 'betraying Maoist thought'. Liu was subjected to a series of brutal **'struggle sessions'** before being imprisoned. When he eventually died in 1973, he had been reduced to a skeletal figure, deprived of the drugs he needed for his diabetes. Deng Xiaoping escaped with his life, but only after being forced to stand in public while 3,000 Red Guards screamed abuse at him. He was then sent to perform **corrective labour** in Jiangxi province in 1969.

The CCRG

Once the Cultural Revolution had begun, Mao withdrew from Beijing, leaving things to be run by Lin Biao and the Central Cultural Revolution Group (**CCRG**). This body, which included the **Gang of Four**, provided the Red Guards with the names and whereabouts of suspect officials and Party members. The government compound off Tiananmen Square, which housed the offices and apartments of ministers and officials, was put under siege. Day and night the Red Guards, armed with loudhailers and amplifiers, maintained a non-stop assault on the ears of those trapped inside. 'Show yourselves, you dirty rightists and revisionists! Do not try to hide.' Searchlights were beamed onto the apartments at night, making sleep impossible for the inhabitants. Those who tried to leave the compound were easy targets for the besiegers who formed terrifying gauntlets through which the officials and their families had to push.

Controlling the Red Guards

After its first two years, 1966–67, the revolution which Mao had unleashed appeared to have gone too far. The widespread disruption had brought industrial production to a halt and had led to the schools and universities being closed. More immediately disturbing, a series of local civil wars raged in China. Regional Red Guard groups clashed with one another and with factory workers who had formed their own units. This convinced the authorities that matters had gone far enough. Orders were given that the work of the Red Guards should be taken over by the PLA.

The 'up to the mountains and down to the villages' campaign, 1967–72

The ultimate control that the government had over China's rebellious youngsters was evident in the ease with which it carried out its decision to redirect the energy and idealism of those who had made up the Red Guard movement. To rid the urban areas of troublesome young people whom the Revolution no longer needed, another great campaign was announced which called on the youngsters to 'go up to the mountains and down to the villages'. They were urged to go into the countryside and live among the peasants; in this way they would both learn what life was like for 80 per cent of the Chinese people and deepen their understanding of revolution.

This was an extension of Mao's policy for making city intellectuals experience the tough realities of life that were the common lot of the ordinary Chinese. The notion that people of privilege should learn 'the dignity of labour' was one of Mao's constant refrains. Between 1967 and 1972 over 12 million young people moved from the towns into the countryside. Most were wholly unprepared for the harsh conditions they encountered. Intense homesickness and near-starvation were the common lot of the youngsters. Many of them said later it was this experience that first made them question the truth of Maoist propaganda.

The 'cleansing the class ranks' campaign, 1968–71

The dispersal of the Red Guards did not mean a weakening of the movement against the anti-Maoists. Indeed, the PLA squads who replaced the Red Guards were even more vicious in their persecution of 'counter-revolutionaries'. The Central Cultural Revolution Group, with Jiang Qing's Gang of Four playing the most prominent role, developed a new campaign known as '**cleansing the class ranks**'. Committees were established in all the major regions of China and given the task of 'eradicating once and for all any signs of capitalism'. The result was an orgy of killing and destruction as grim as anything perpetrated by the Red Guards:

- In Inner Mongolia 22,900 were killed and 120,000 maimed.
- In Hebei province 84,000 were arrested, 2,955 of whom then died after being tortured.
- In Yunnan 15,000 people were 'cleansed'; of these 6,979 died from their injuries.
- In Beijing 3,731 people were killed; these cases were officially classified as 'suicide'.
- In Zhejiang 100,000 were arrested and 'struggled against'; of these 9,198 died from their treatment.
- In Binyang county in Guangxi province, 3,681 were killed in a mass execution over a ten-day period.

 **KEY TERM**

Cleansing the class ranks
A terror campaign to exterminate all those whose social background made them potential enemies of Mao and the communist state.

The Cultural Revolution – the final phase

The Cultural Revolution did not fully end until Mao's death in 1976, but by the early 1970s it had begun to lose some of its momentum. In part this was because serious concerns about it had crept in among some Chinese. These were not openly stated since open criticism of Mao was still not possible, but behind the scenes doubts were growing. These were stimulated by the strange fate that befell Lin Biao. In 1971, Lin was killed when his plane crashed in Mongolia while he was trying to flee from China, having been implicated in a plot to assassinate Mao. Since Lin had been Chief of the PLA, the Minister of Defence and Mao's nominated successor, his disgrace created doubts. A village elder remarked: 'When Liu Shaoqi was dragged down we'd been very supportive. Mao Zedong was the red sun and what not. But the Lin Biao affair made us see that the leaders up there could say today that something is round; tomorrow, that it's flat. We lost faith in the system.'

How was the *laogai* used to consolidate Mao's power?

The *laogai*

In order to enforce conformity and obedience in China, Mao created a vast network of labour camps in which those who opposed him or were suspected of opposing him were imprisoned. As the title ***laogai*** suggested, the official theory was that the camps were not places of punishment but re-education, where dissidents could be retrained and enlightened. The camps were also economically important since they provided a constant supply of slave labour. Many of the mass workforce used in the Great Leap Forward on hazardous projects, such as clearing malarial swamps and mining in dangerous areas, were camp prisoners.

Conditions in the camps

The camps were to be found throughout China, but many of the worst were deliberately built in the most inhospitable parts of the country where the bitter cold of winter or the searing heat of summer made life a torment for the prisoners. To obtain even the bare minimum ration of food, prisoners had to make a full confession of their crimes. Those who persisted in claiming that they were innocent were interrogated, deprived of sleep, held in solitary confinement and beaten and starved until they broke down and conformed.

The figures relating to the *laogai* indicate the scale of the prison-camp system:

- The average number of prisoners held in the camps each year during Mao's time was 10 million.
- Over 25 million prisoners died during that period, the number being comprised of those who were officially executed, those who died from hunger and ill treatment, and those who committed suicide. Even in death prisoners were treated with contempt. The term used by the prison authorities to describe those who took their own lives was 'alienating themselves from the Party and the people'.
- By the time of Mao's death in 1976 there were more than 1,000 labour camps spread across China.

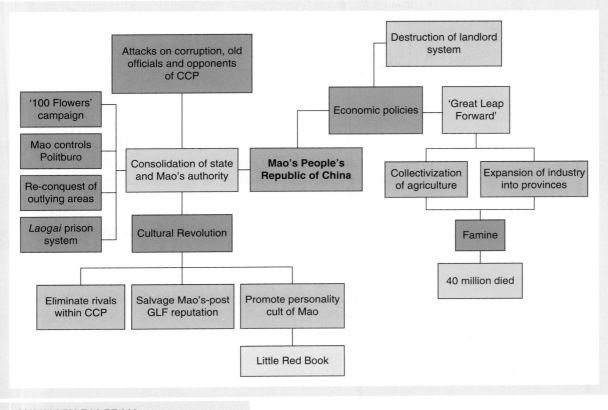

Mao's establishment of an authoritarian state

③ Life in China under Mao, 1949–76

> ▶ **Key question:** *What impact did Mao's rule have on the lives of the Chinese people?*

Mao's attempt to create and sustain a continuous revolution after 1949 fundamentally changed the lives of the Chinese people.

The reshaping of Chinese culture under Mao

It is important to understand how Mao interpreted culture. For him, it was never a separate, detached aspect of society. From the 1930s on he had taught that:

- culture was central not peripheral; a nation's culture defined its character
- culture was not a matter of refined tastes; it was about the life of the people

> ← Why was Mao determined to destroy Chinese traditional culture?

- throughout history, the culture of every society was the direct product of the values laid down by the ruling class and was the means by which rulers imposed their control over the people
- just as in the time of the **feudal** emperors, Chinese culture had been feudal, so, now that China was a proletarian society, the culture had to be proletarian
- all traces of bourgeois and feudal culture had to be eradicated. This could not be done gently or by persuasion. No ruling class ever gives up its power willingly; it has to be swept aside by force.

Given these views, it followed that after taking power Mao would be ruthless in replacing what he judged to be China's dated culture with a new proletarian one. He declared characteristically: 'A revolution is not a dinner party. A revolution is an insurrection, an act of violence by which one class overthrows another.' Mao demanded that all creative artists – writers, painters, musicians, filmmakers, etc. – must accept that their first duty was to serve the people. Their works must further the cause of revolution. Mao had no time for artistic self-expression for its own sake. He asserted that there was 'no such thing as art for art's sake, art that is detached from or independent of politics. Proletarian literature and art are part of the whole revolutionary cause'.

The role of Jiang Qing

In a remarkable move, Mao decided that his wife, Jiang Qing, was to be the creator-in-chief of the new Chinese culture he desired. He gave her the responsibility of turning his general denunciation of China's 'Four Olds' (see page 133) into a definitive programme for the suppression of traditional Chinese society. Mao instructed her to become the 'cultural purifier of the nation'. Believing that her former career as an actress was an ideal qualification, Jiang applied herself to the task with fanatical zeal. Mao once said, only half jokingly, that she was more Maoist than he was.

- Jiang imposed a rigid system of censorship which denied a public showing or performance to any work which did not meet her criteria of revolutionary purity.
- Only those writings, art works, broadcast programmes and films which had directly relevant contemporary Chinese themes were permitted.
- Western music, classical and pop, was banned.
- Traditional Chinese opera was replaced by a repertoire of specially commissioned contemporary works.

The works which Jiang commissioned were a set of opera-ballets, all concerned in the most naive fashion with the triumph of the proletariat over its class enemies. They were an exact expression of Mao's demand that Chinese culture must be relevant and meaningful to the people by having as their only theme the struggle of the heroic masses. Grindingly tedious though they were, the opera-ballets were loudly applauded by the privileged audiences of Party members and their families who dared not reveal their true feelings.

Jiang's demand for conformity

Jiang Qing's rejection of all non-proletarian culture was a destructive process that aimed at undermining all sense of tradition. In accordance with Mao's saying 'the more brutal, the more revolutionary', children were urged to knock the heads off flowers in order to show their rejection of bourgeois concepts of beauty. Zhou Guanqun, a professor of music, recalled how Jiang's edicts against bourgeois culture terrorized the staff at the Beijing **Conservatoire** into silence.

KEY TERM

Conservatoire A specialist music college.

SOURCE N

An excerpt from a taped interview with Zhou Guanqun, broadcast in a BBC radio programme, 'The Cultural Revolution', July 1998.

No music sounded anymore. The Conservatoire was silent. Everybody was just learning and doing self-criticism or accepting criticism from students. So we had to come every day, every morning at the time of office hours and sit there and read books and then do criticism. We had to analyse our mistakes in our work, our teaching or performing, because we performed a lot of classical or Chinese traditional music. We thought that we popularised the bad things to the young generation.

According to Source N, what pressure was put upon artists during the Cultural Revolution?

By the early 1970s, Jiang Qing's assault on traditional culture had begun to destroy all forms of creative artistic expression. Musicians, painters and writers who showed reluctance to embrace the new rigidities were denounced and sent to 're-educational' labour camps where they were brutally treated. One example was the denial of tools to the musicians who were sent to work in the fields; pianists and string players were made to scratch at the ground with their hands so that they would lose the sensitivity in their fingers that their playing required.

Lack of resistance to Jiang's orders

There were rare attempts to question Jiang Qing's suffocating policies. On one occasion Deng Xiaoping dared to suggest that culture was about entertainment as well as indoctrination. He remarked caustically: 'After a hard week's work people want to go to the theatre to relax, but they go there and watch Jiang Qing's pieces and find they are on a bleeding battle field.'

However, Deng apart, none of the leading politicians was prepared to challenge Jiang. They, like the majority of artists, opted publicly to approve her great cultural experiment while privately hoping that her power would be broken once the rapidly ageing Mao had died. One of the most distressing features of Mao's China was the failure of the intellectuals and natural leaders of communities to protest against the crimes of the regime. A mixture of moral cowardice and an understandable fear of what might be done to them and their families led them to accept the unacceptable without complaint.

Consequences of Jiang Qing's policies

Jiang's stranglehold on the arts lasted for the whole of the decade between 1966 and Mao's death ten years later. By then it was clear that the result of this artistic persecution had not been the creation of a new culture but merely the paralysis of the old one. Writers and artists had been frightened either into inaction or into producing politically correct dross that would not fall foul of the censors. Describing the profound damage done to China by the artistic destruction, Yan Yen, a poet, commented: 'As a result of the Cultural Revolution you could say the cultural trademark of my generation is that we have no culture.'

Religion in the PRC

Why did Mao and the CCP regard religion as a threat?

KEY TERM

Missionaries Usually religious orders of priests and nuns who sought to spread their Christian message by founding and running schools and hospitals.

Agit-prop 'Agitation propaganda', the inculcating of political ideas through entertainment.

As a Marxist movement, Chinese communism considered religious belief and worship to be superstitions deliberately cultivated by the exploiting classes to suppress the people. Mao Zedong expressed his strong personal antipathy towards religion by describing it as poison and comparing the Christian **missionaries** in China to the Nazis in Europe. It was little surprise, therefore, that in 1950 a major campaign against religion was begun. The official justification was that, now that the workers were in power, religion had no purpose since the people no longer needed such escapism. Religious worship had now to be replaced by loyalty to the Communist Party and the state. The traditional Chinese beliefs, Buddhism and Confucianism, were forbidden to be openly practised as were the major foreign religions, Christianity and Islam. Priests, monks and nuns were prohibited from wearing their distinctive dress; disobedience led to arrest and imprisonment. Churches and mosques were closed, their property seized and their clergy physically abused. Foreign clergy were expelled from China.

Wall posters, the traditional way by which Chinese governments spread their propaganda, and loudspeakers at every corner kept up a running condemnation of religion. Slogans proclaiming the virtues of the new Maoist China were to be seen everywhere. China became a slogan-ridden society. The slogans were more than simply a way of exhorting the comrades to ever greater efforts; they were a means of enforcing solidarity and conformity.

Attacks on Chinese customs and traditions

It was not merely the formal expressions of belief that were outlawed. The customs and rituals that had helped shape the life of the peasants were proscribed. These included:

- the songs and dances performed at weddings and festivals
- the chants that had accompanied work in the fields
- the sagas with which the wandering poets entertained whole villages.

These traditional ways were replaced with political meetings and discussions organized by the Party. The huge social experiment of collectivization which Mao introduced in the 1950s was meant to destroy the time-honoured pattern of rural life.

Troupes of **agit-prop** performers toured the countryside putting on shows and plays which the villagers were required to attend. The shows took place in halls and public spaces. Sometimes the players arrived in brightly painted lorries carrying slogans and images extolling the wonders and benefits of the new Maoist world. The canvas sides of the lorry served as a screen on which propaganda films were projected.

The message in the propaganda

The insistent message of the films and the live performances was that the old days of cruel landlords and abused peasants had been replaced with a communal way of life perfectly suited to the new era of collective endeavour. The shows were played at knockabout pantomime level; the baddies were always bad, the goodies were always good. The landlords were obviously the worst of the baddies, but religious figures such as scheming Confucian officials and exploiting priests also appeared and were hissed at and jeered.

The patriotic churches

To give an illusion of toleration, the authorities allowed some churches to remain open provided that they 'did not endanger the security of the state'. What this meant in practice was they became state-controlled. Known as the 'patriotic churches', the clergy had to profess open support for the communist regime and accept that the authorities had the right to appoint priests and dictate the forms of worship. One consequence of this was conflict between the PRC and the **Vatican**, which refused to accept the validity of the patriotic churches.

Religious persecution during the Cultural Revolution

The PRC's decision to allow a semblance of religion to remain was a reluctant recognition that religious faith was too deep-rooted in Chinese tradition to be totally eradicated. Nevertheless, the persecution continued. During the Cultural Revolution, religion was denounced as belonging to the 'Four Olds' and the attack upon it intensified. Any clergy who had survived the earlier persecutions were rounded up and imprisoned.

Confucianism was denounced as representing all that was worst in China's past. The name of Confucius was linked to any person or movement that the authorities wished to denounce. 'Confucius and Co' became a standard term of abuse directed at any suspect group or organization. Significantly when Lin Biao was disgraced during the Cultural Revolution, the slogan coined to attack him was 'criticize Lin Biao and Confucius' (see page 136).

Religion and opposition in the provinces

A basic fear of Mao's government was that religion might encourage the breakaway tendencies in the PRC's provinces. From the beginning of its rule in 1949, the PRC let it be known that it would not grant independence to any of its regions. That was why in 1950 it sent the PLA into Tibet, Xinjiang and Guangdong to enforce its authority (see page 122). It claimed that the strength, indeed the survival, of the People's Republic of China as a nation demanded total unity and acceptance of central control.

> **🔑 KEY TERM**
>
> **Vatican** The administrative centre of the Roman Catholic Church in Rome.

Uighur, Kazakh, Hui, and Kirghiz peoples Ethnic groups, which in regard to race, culture, language and religion were markedly distinct from the Han people who made up over 80 per cent of China's population.

Patriarchal Male-dominated.

This had special reference to the PRC's outlying western provinces, Tibet and Xinjiang, areas larger in size than western Europe. It was Tibetan Buddhism that inspired Tibetan nationalism in its resistance to Chinese occupation. The PRC fretted that religion and nationalism would prove an equally dangerous mix in Tibet's northern neighbour, Xinjiang. Here the majority of the population was made up of the **Uighur, Kazakh, Hui, and Kirghiz peoples**, who were all devout Muslims.

What added to Chinese fears was the strategic position of Xinjiang, on whose western borders lay Pakistan, Turkistan and Kazakhstan, all of them strongly Muslim areas. The PRC's concern was that religious belief would combine with politics to create a dangerous separatist movement in Xinjiang, which would be backed by these border regions.

In a major effort to prevent this, the PRC condemned all independence organizations in China's border regions as 'handfuls of national separatists' with 'reactionary feudal ideas' who were in league with 'hostile foreign forces' and whose aim was to weaken the Chinese nation. The government adopted the same policy that it had in Tibet; it tried to dilute the Muslim element in the population by settling large numbers of Han Chinese in the region. This proved only partially successful. At the time of Mao's death in 1976, the Muslim proportion still formed a large minority of the Xinjiang population.

How did the status of women in China change under Mao?

The status of women

Imperial China, the nation in which Mao Zedong grew up, was a **patriarchal** society. Confucius had taught that to be harmonious a society must follow the rules of the *san gan*, which he defined as:

- loyalty of ministers and officials to the emperor
- respect of children for their parents
- obedience of wives to their husbands.

As a result women traditionally played a subordinate role in Chinese society. To counter this, the Chinese Communists officially proclaimed themselves to be advocates of female equality. One of the first acts of the PRC was to introduce a new marriage law in 1950. This laid down that:

- concubinage, the practice of men keeping women as mistresses, was forbidden
- arranged marriages were to be discontinued
- women who had been forced to marry were entitled to divorce their partners
- all marriages had to be officially recorded and registered.

Many women used their new freedom to divorce and remarry a number of times. There were cases of women taking as many as four different husbands in as many years. This threatened to prove so disruptive that a special clause was added to PLA regulations giving the soldiers the legal right to overrule their wives' pleas for a divorce.

The impact of collectivization on women

Further laws passed in the 1950s granted women the right to own and sell land and property. In the land redistribution which followed the seizure of the properties of the landlords (see page 123), women were actually granted land in their own name. However, much of this apparent gain was undermined by Mao's massive collectivization programme that accompanied the Great Leap Forward which abolished private property and required people to live in communes (see page 127). Interestingly, life in the communes did bring women one immediate advantage. The rule now was that everybody should eat in common in mess halls; this meant that women no longer had the daily burden of finding food and preparing it for the family.

Traditional prejudice against women

Yet for every gain that women appeared to make there seemed to be an accompanying disadvantage. Now that they were officially regarded in Mao's China as the equals of men, they could be called on to do the work of men. Between 1949 and 1976, the proportion of women in the workforce quadrupled from 8 to 32 per cent. This might bring them advantages if the work was suitable but if it was heavy physical labour then they were no better off than before.

Entrenched values and attitudes are hard to change in any country. China was by tradition a male-dominated society; no matter how genuine the new Communist regime might be in declaring that the sexes were equal, women still had to compete with deep-seated Chinese notions of female inferiority. This was clearly evident in the common prejudice against female babies. It was the wish of nearly all Chinese couples to have male children. The birth of a boy was thought to bring honour on the family, and the promise of another source of income; girls were seen as a drain on resources.

Unchanging peasant attitudes

Peasants complained that the new marriage laws were interfering with the established ways of life. Female subordination was the norm in all China's rural areas but especially so in the western provinces where there was a predominantly Muslim culture. In areas such as Xinjiang, families were tightly controlled by the men; female members were subject to the orders of husbands, fathers and brothers, and even brothers-in-law. Thirty years after Mao's death, the representative of the All China Women's Federation described the outlook of Xinjiang's 4 million women as being like a frog in a well: 'All they can see is a tiny bit of sky, so their outlook is very narrow. A woman is treated as a man's possession.'

Despite the CCP's public advocacy of women's rights, **feminists** observed that, in practice, Mao and his party operated a male-dominated system, an example being the infrequency with which women were granted government and party posts. During Mao's time, women made up only 13 per cent of the

KEY TERM

Feminists Supporters of the principle of full female equality with men.

membership of the Communist Party. The number of women who became members of the **National People's Congress** did rise under Mao from 14 per cent to 23 per cent between 1954 and 1975 but this was not at a rate to suggest that the CCP had made a priority of promoting females within its ranks.

Women and the family

In addition to females being denied a fuller political role, there was a deeper sense in which the policies followed under Mao prevented China's women from making a sustained advance. If anything, the radical character of Mao's reform programme increased their vulnerability. Collectivization entailed a direct and deliberate assault on the traditional Chinese family. Mao had already prepared the way for this as early as 1944 when he had stated that: 'It is necessary to destroy the peasant family; women going to the factories and joining the army are part of the big destruction of the family.' So determined was the Communist Party to undermine the family that in the communes men and women were made to live in separate quarters and allowed to see each other only for **conjugal visits**.

While in some respects this might be considered liberating since women were freed from the family ties that had restricted them, the enforced social change happened all too suddenly. The Chinese, a profoundly conservative people, became disorientated; women found themselves detached from their traditional moorings. Many felt unhappy that their role as mothers and raisers of families was now to be wholly devalued.

The impact of the Cultural Revolution

The devaluing of the individual and the family that came with collectivization was re-emphasized with particular force during the Cultural Revolution:

- The ownership of private property was now depicted as a crime against communist society.
- The enforced pooling of resources meant that the economic link that held individual families together was broken.
- Whereas in traditional China the **extended family**, which might in practice be a whole village, had been the main provider of help in difficult times, in Mao's China that role was taken over by the state.
- The provision of social welfare, such as education and medical care, was now to be organized and delivered by Communist Party officials and appointees.

The traditional **nuclear family** fell into one of the categories of the Four Olds that the young were sent to destroy (see page 133). Mothers were urged to teach their children that Mao Zedong and the Communist Party were their true parents, and, therefore, deserving of their first loyalty. Normal family affection was replaced by love for Mao. The young were asked to inform on those among their relatives who betrayed any sign of clinging, even in the slightest manner, to the decadent values of the past. In such an atmosphere, it was hard for mothers to continue their traditional role as homemakers.

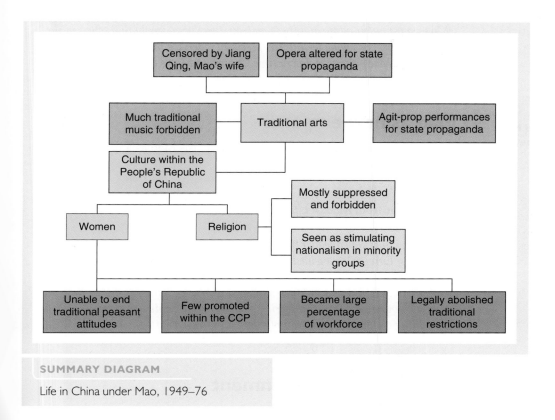

SUMMARY DIAGRAM

Life in China under Mao, 1949–76

 # Key debate

> ▶ *Key question: How far did Mao achieve a totalitarian state?*

Few analysts would dispute that Mao Zedong wielded enormous power. The debate and disagreements are over the use to which he put that power. Fascinatingly, Mao did not regard himself as being in total control, which is why even when he seemed at his most powerful he continued to believe he was surrounded by enemies. It was an aspect of his paranoid outlook.

Mao as unchallengeable leader

His leading colleagues had no doubts about the nature of his authority.

← **Why was there little challenge to Mao from within the government and party?**

According to Source O, why is Mao's sense of realism so important?

SOURCE O

Lin Biao writing in 1968, quoted in *A Critical Introduction to Mao*, edited by Timothy Cheek, CUP, UK, 2010, p. 103.

The thoughts of Chairman Mao are always correct. Chairman Mao's superiority has many aspects, not just one, and I know from experience that Chairman Mao's most outstanding quality is realism. I feel very deeply that when in the past our work was done well it was precisely when we thoroughly implemented Chairman Mao's thought. Every time Chairman Mao's ideas were not sufficiently respected there have been problems.

In what ways did Mao appear to be a new emperor?

Mao as new emperor

One of Mao's major Western biographers regards Mao as a new Chinese emperor ruling over a new empire.

SOURCE P

According to Source P, in what sense can Mao be regarded as a new emperor?

An excerpt from *Mao: A Life* by Philip Short, published by Hodder, UK, 1999, pp. 630–31.

He was unquestioned leader of almost a quarter of mankind, inhabiting an area the size of Europe. He wielded powers equalled only by the most awesome of Chinese emperors. Mao had an extraordinary mix of talents: he was visionary, statesman, political and military strategist of genius. To these gifts, he brought a subtle dogged mind, awe-inspiring charisma and fiendish cleverness. To Mao, the killing of opponents – or simply those who disagreed with his political aims – was an unavoidable ingredient of broader political campaigns.

In what ways did Mao exercise government?

Mao's style of government

It has sometimes been suggested that Mao was not in full control because on occasion he withdrew from politics and let others handle the affairs of state, as at the time of the famine and at stages in the Cultural Revolution. Jonathan Fenby, a modern expert on China, argues that this is to misunderstand the nature of Mao's authority.

SOURCE Q

According to Source Q, why did Mao's occasional withdrawal from the centre of politics never seriously diminish his power?

An excerpt from *The Penguin History of Modern China* by Jonathan Fenby, published by Allen Lane, UK, 2008, p. 378.

From time to time, Mao might choose to take a back seat and let others handle Party and state business. But when he wanted to assert himself, nobody could resist him. For the last three decades of his life, each directive he issued was regarded as gospel. The idea that Mao was ever seriously constrained once he had made up his mind holds little water. The ultimate proof of his dominance was how many things he got wrong, on a massive scale observable to all – and how he survived with the mantle of the great leader unchallenged by the tough figures around him, standing squarely in the line of all powerful first emperors.

Mao's use of his authority

A British authority on China suggests that by totally subordinating the CCP to his will, Mao deprived himself of an effective check on his policies. This resulted in the failure of his two great projects, the Great Leap Forward and the Cultural Revolution.

← **What was the consequence of Mao's style of government?**

SOURCE R

An excerpt from *Rebellions and Revolutions, China from the 1800s to 2000* by Jack Gray, OUP, UK, 2002, p. 378.

That Mao was an authoritarian ruler, prepared to be ruthless towards those he believed to be conspiring against the revolution is not in question. What is in question here is the idea that he was some sort of closed-minded orthodox fundamentalist. Why then did his two great campaigns fail? Beneath the many factors which contributed to the disaster lay one fundamental flaw; the authoritarian, totally unaccountable Party hierarchy which Mao himself had created was a useless instrument.

According to Source R, what is the basic explanation for the failure of Mao's two great campaigns?

In another revisionist treatment, Lee Feigon accepted that Mao was authoritarian but argued that the use to which he put this was creative not destructive (see Source S).

SOURCE S

An excerpt from *Mao: A Reinterpretation* by Lee Feigon, published by Ivan R. Dee, Chicago, USA, 2002, pp. 11–12.

The movements for which Mao is almost universally condemned today – the Great Leap Forward and especially the Cultural Revolution – were in many ways beneficial for the Chinese people: they forced China to break with its Stalinist past and paved the way for its great economic and political strides.

According to Source S, what were the positive aspects of the Great Leap Forward and the Cultural Revolution?

Mao as monster

The attempt at a balanced approach to Mao's policies and reputation was fiercely rejected in a study of Mao that appeared in 2005. It was written by Jung Chang, who had been a Red Guard but who had developed a fierce personal hatred of Mao because of the way her family had suffered during the Cultural Revolution. Her hatred suffused her book, which she co-wrote with her historian husband. She depicted Mao as a monster. A representative passage reads:

← **How helpful is it to regard Mao as a monster?**

SOURCE T

An excerpt from *Mao: the Unknown Story* by Jung Chang and Jon Halliday, published by Jonathan Cape, UK, 2005, p. 509.

What Mao had in mind was a completely arid society, devoid of civilization, deprived of representation of human feelings, inhabited by a herd with no sensibility which would automatically obey his orders. He wanted the nation to be brain dead in order to carry out his big purge – and to live in this state permanently.

According to Source T, why was Mao Zedong content for China under him to be an 'arid society'?

Jung Chang's argument was powerfully and emotionally advanced, but a number of Chinese and Western historians were quick to respond by pointing out that her book lacked balance and relied too heavily on suspect anti-Mao sources, which seriously lessened its value as an analysis. Jonathan Spence, widely acknowledged as the leading Western authority on Mao Zedong, made the following observation:

SOURCE U

Excerpt from 'Portrait of a Monster' by Jonathan Spence, in *Was Mao Really a Monster?*, edited by Gregor Benton and Lin Chun, published by Routledge, UK, 2010, p. 39.

By focusing so tightly on Mao's vileness – to the exclusion of other factors – the authors undermine much of the power their story might have had. By seeking to demonstrate that Mao started out as a vile person and stayed vile throughout his life, the authors deny any room for change, whether growth or degeneration, for subtlety or the possibilities of redemption. The Chinese who did struggle for change are denied any role in their own story, and become ciphers.

Spence's comment was not simply a criticism of Jung Chang but related to the problem all historians have in assessing the character of Mao's authority. Such was the scale of Mao Zedong's power, and so lethally disruptive were his uses of it, that it makes balanced appraisal especially difficult.

? According to Source U, why is it unhelpful to concentrate on Mao's vileness?

TOK Millions of people died in Mao's various programmes for improving the People's Republic of China. Can good occur through the destruction of people? (History, Ethics, Language, Reason)

Chapter summary

China under Mao Zedong, 1949–76

As a young revolutionary, Mao Zedong was attracted to Marxism and became a founding member of the CCP in 1921. By that time, two main revolutionary parties were in contention in China: the CCP and the Guomindang. Despite initially co-operating to destroy the warlords, the two parties were never united. The GMD's main aim under Chiang Kaishek was to destroy the Communists. In 1927 it launched an extermination campaign against them. Mao survived by retreating to Jiangxi where he established a Chinese soviet, dedicated to the furtherance of peasant revolution. Unwilling to accept dictation from the Comintern, he frequently rejected orders from Moscow.

Continually attacked by GMD forces, the Communists fled from Jiangxi in 1934 and undertook the Long March to Yanan. Mao used the influence he had gained while on the march to dominate the new soviet at Yanan, which he established between 1935 and 1949. He triumphed in a power struggle in which he overcame the pro-Moscow members of the CCP and asserted that China's communist revolution must be a peasant revolution. It was also during this time at the Yanan base, which he turned into a model Chinese soviet, that Mao led a spirited resistance to the Japanese occupation.

With the defeat of Japan at the end of the Second World War in 1945, the CCP turned on the GMD, engaging in a fierce four-year struggle which ended with the complete victory of the Communists. In 1949 Mao declared the People's Republic of China (PRC) to have come into being. As leader of the new nation, Mao tolerated no opposition to the CCP. All other parties were outlawed and total obedience was demanded of the people.

In 1958, in an attempt to modernize China, Mao implemented 'the Great Leap Forward', an economic project that failed and led to a disastrous famine. He withdrew briefly from politics, but returned to launch the Cultural Revolution (1966–76), an extraordinary movement that plunged China into a decade of deliberately engineered turmoil. His aim was to purge the CCP and leave his permanent revolutionary mark on China.

So pervasive was Mao's authority between 1949 and 1976 that it impacted upon every aspect of Chinese life, political, economic, social and cultural. Such was the extent of his authority that, by the time of his death, Chinese communism had become personally identified with him as Maoism.

Examination practice

Below are a number of different questions for you to practise. For guidance on how to answer exam-style questions, see Chapter 10.

1 Discuss the importance of Mao in the Chinese Communist Party's success in the Chinese Civil War by 1949.

2 Compare and contrast Mao's version of communism with that of any other members of the Chinese Communist Party who preferred a more Soviet style of communism.

3 What was the importance of the People's Liberation Army in Mao's People's Republic of China?

4 To what extent were religious and ethnic minorities affected by Mao's rule?

5 Discuss the importance of the '100 Flowers' campaign.

6 Analyse the successes and failures of the Great Leap Forward.

7 Explain the causes and effects of the Cultural Revolution in Mao's People's Republic of China.

8 How significant was propaganda in maintaining Mao's rule over the People's Republic of China?

9 Discuss the importance of the *laogai* in maintaining Mao's rule.

10 To what extent did Mao's government affect agriculture in the People's Republic of China?

 # Activities

1 Visit the website http://chineseposters.net/themes/mao-cult.php or another website featuring propaganda posters for Mao's People's Republic of China. Choose several posters as a class or in groups and then discuss common symbolism, the meaning of colours, and the role of Mao in each of these. Extend the activity by comparing and contrasting posters, looking at how these changed over time and their different themes.

2 Compare and contrast Mao's views on women, peasant farmers or education with those of Marx. A useful website is www.marxists.org which has quotations and writings by both of these individuals.

3 As a class, debate the following: Mao's peasant-based, nationalistically-oriented form of communism was a more realistic form than that envisioned by Karl Marx.

CHAPTER 5

Communism, Nazism and Maoism – a comparison

Following the Second World War, historians and political analysts began to use the term 'totalitarian' to denote the extreme authoritarianism that characterized particular regimes that had developed in Europe by the 1940s. Controversy arose when some analysts suggested that although communism and Nazism were sworn enemies, they were so similar in the methods they used that they were part of the same political phenomenon. Those on the Right and Left of the political divide (see pages 8 and 158) were outraged by the suggestion that their movements were the same in character as that of their bitter opponents. It is important, therefore, for historical balance when comparing the regimes to see how far they had common characteristics. Building on the analyses in the preceding chapters, this chapter offers a comparison of Stalin's Soviet Union, Hitler's Germany and Mao's China and a survey of interpretations of authoritarianism and totalitarianism.

You need to consider the following questions throughout this chapter:

✪ What similar or contrasting features of the regimes can be identified?

✪ What main interpretations have been advanced to explain authoritarianism?

 1 # Comparing Stalin's Soviet Union, Hitler's Germany and Mao's China

▶ *Key question: What similar or contrasting features of the regimes can be identified?*

Dominant leaders

In what ways did the three leaders dominate the movements they represented?

Each of the three regimes was led by a dominant individual who became identified with the cause he represented. Indeed, they were more than merely representative. All three individuals became the personification of the ideology they espoused:

- Stalin became Soviet communism (see page 49).
- Hitler became Nazism (see page 78).
- Mao Zedong became Chinese communism (see page 116).

No matter how far they removed themselves from the actual task of governing, as each of them occasionally did, their withdrawal did not diminish their authority. Hitler as *Führer*, Stalin as *Vozhd* and Mao as Chairman, were leaders in their own right as well as heads of the Nazi or Communist Party that ruled the nation. Theirs was always the ultimate authority.

Propaganda

What role did propaganda play in sustaining the position of the three leaders?

Having attained power, the three leaders were sustained by a continuous propaganda campaign by their party that raised them above normal politics. The term 'Red Tsar', for example, which was applied to Stalin, was particularly appropriate since the position he held was akin to the divine right claimed by the Russian tsars. The tsars had regarded their authority as being sanctioned by a power that went beyond ordinary politics and which, therefore, could not be challenged by ordinary politicians; Stalin claimed something very similar. As leader of the CPSU and heir to Lenin, he was the sole, rightful interpreter of the dialectical laws of revolution, thus putting him beyond challenge or criticism. It is one of the great modern political paradoxes that communism, a theory dependent for its meaning on the concept of the collective will of the people as the only true historical dynamic, has, in every society where it has come to power, resulted in the dictatorship of a single leader.

KEY TERM

Prophets Individuals endowed with divine insight, as honoured in the three main monotheistic (belief in one God) religions: Judaism, Christianity and Islam.

Revelation The disclosing of eternal truths.

Siegfried A legendary knight, regarded as representing the Germanic ideal.

Teutonic Relating to peoples of Germanic origin, interchangeable as a term with Aryan.

If Stalin set the pattern of communist dictatorship, it was Mao Zedong who most spectacularly continued it. His control of political ideas in China was such that he came to be regarded by the party theorists as the culmination of communist thought. Mao's ideologues described him in what amounted to religious terms. Communism was defined in China as Marxist–Leninist–Stalinist–Maoist thought, as if Mao were the last of the great **prophets** in a line of Marxist **revelation**.

Hitler also claimed a special affinity with history. He was portrayed in Nazi propaganda not simply as a peerless political leader, but as the incarnation of the spirit of **Siegfried**, the great hero of **Teutonic** tradition. Hitler, the representative of all that was best in the aspirations of the Aryan race, was fulfilling his historic role, leading Germany to its destiny as a great nation.

The leaders' special status

In what sense was the status of the three leaders raised above ordinary politics?

As dictators in their respective countries, Adolf Hitler, Joseph Stalin and Mao Zedong came to share a remarkable experience. Their political dominance and the adulation in which they were held by their peoples had the effect of removing them from reality. As they grew progressively more powerful, they became increasingly detached from the world around them. Their word was law and those permitted to have contact with them necessarily said only what they judged their leader wanted to hear. There is a strong case for saying that by their later years each of them had become irrational, as was evident from the extraordinary decisions they made:

- Facing defeat in the last stages of the war, Hitler preferred to see the Third Reich destroyed rather than surrender.
- Stalin launched further destructive purges (see page 44) even though his power was already absolute.
- Mao deliberately created national turmoil in a bid to defy the future and leave his permanent mark on China.

Organized hatred

All three regimes used organized hatred as a political weapon, directing it at selected groups of victims defamed as enemies of the state. The three regimes elevated the **scapegoat** principle into a central policy. They developed the notion that there was in the midst of society a corrupting force that had to be eradicated, a notion used as a justification for terror in all three regimes. In Hitler's Germany, it was the race enemy – the Jews. In Stalin's USSR, it was class enemies – the Kulaks. In Mao's China, it was class traitors – the rightists and revisionists (see page 124). From their earliest involvement in revolutionary politics, the three men had embraced terror as an essential mode of action.

> **In what sense were the three regimes based on organized hatred?**

> **🔑 KEY TERM**
>
> **Scapegoat** A sacrificial victim on whom blame for misfortune is placed.

SOURCE A

An excerpt from 'The National Revolution and the Peasant Movement' by Mao Zedong, 1 September 1926, quoted in *Mao's Road to Power 1912–1949, Revolutionary Writings*, edited by Stuart Schram, published by M.E. Sharpe, USA, 1997, vol. 2, p. 435.

All excessive actions have revolutionary significance. It is necessary to bring about a reign of terror in every rural area; otherwise we could never suppress the activities of the counterrevolutionaries in the countryside or overthrow the authority of the gentry. To right a wrong it is necessary to exceed the proper limits; the wrong cannot be righted without doing so.

> According to Source A, what is Mao's justification for the use of terror? **?**

SOURCE B

Excerpt from notes made by General Fritz Halder detailing Hitler's instructions to his generals on 22 August 1939, quoted in *Hitler* by Michael Lynch, published by Routledge, UK, 2013, p. 199.

Close your hearts to pity. Act brutally. The stronger has the greater right … Polish active force is to be destroyed again immediately … Continuous demolition to the point of complete annihilation.

> According to Source B, how did Hitler intend his forces to behave in Poland? **?**

According to Source C, what aspects of Stalin's character led him towards the use of terror?

An excerpt from *Stalin: A Biography* by Robert Service, published by Macmillan, UK, 2004, p. 344.

[Stalin's] capacity to turn on friends and subordinates and subject them to torture, forced labour and execution manifested a deeply disordered personality. He had a Georgian sense of honour and revenge. Notions of getting even with adversaries never left him. He had a Bolshevik viewpoint on Revolution. Violence, dictatorship and terror were methods he and fellow party veterans took to be normal. The physical extermination of enemies was entirely acceptable to them.

Why were all three leaders prepared to resort to terror?

Terror

There was an insistence among all three leaders that their goal of revolution could be achieved only through the use of violence. They contended that no class ever relinquishes power willingly; power has to be dragged from it by force. Even then, the dispossessed class will fight back; that is why there are always opponents who have to be terrorized.

There was also the perceived foreign threat. Notwithstanding their opposed ideologies, all the totalitarian regimes claimed that they were engaged in a struggle for survival in a hostile world, a struggle so pressing that it justified the resort to extreme measures. The need to consolidate and preserve the security of the state was paramount. Communism for Stalin became precisely this, the survival of the Soviet state; this is what he meant by his insistence on the priority of 'Socialism in One Country'.

The scale of terror was physically evident in one of the most fearful images of the twentieth century – the prison camp. Matching each other in their organized brutality were:

- the concentration camps in Hitler's Germany (see page 76)
- the *Gulag* in Stalin's Soviet Union (see page 43)
- the *laogai* in Mao's PRC (see page 136).

Motivation behind the Terror

Figures can never be precise, but conservative estimates suggest that Nazi Germany wiped out 6 million European Jews, that Stalin's purges resulted in the death of 20 million of his people and that a similar number died in China during Mao's various anti-movements. But it was not simply cruelty for its own sake. All three leaders believed that the destruction of opponents was a matter of duty. They judged that so pressing were the needs of the nation that they justified the use of the most remorseless methods.

Whether the leaders planned the destruction of life on the scale that it occurred is much debated. Arguments have been advanced to suggest that, while Hitler and Stalin were ultimately responsible for the carnage that took place under them, it reached the proportions it did because of the actions of enthusiastic underlings who seized the chance to indulge in the persecution of personal enemies. The particular charge against Mao is not that he actually willed the deaths that came with the Great Famine and the Cultural Revolution but that he permitted them to occur, first, by miscalculating the risks attached to his policies and, then, by refusing to acknowledge that the disaster was happening.

Cultural transformation

A prominent feature of the regimes was the way in which they moved from political revolution to cultural transformation. The Third Reich under Hitler sought to establish a set of norms which allowed only Aryan racial concepts to be expressed. 'Decadent influences' in the arts, by which the Nazis principally meant Jewish works, were to be expunged from German culture. In the USSR, Stalin and the Party asserted that Soviet communism would produce a new type of human being, *homo Sovieticus.* Decadent bourgeois values, therefore, no longer had any in place in the new state that was being forged; creative artists were required to produce works wholly relevant to the needs of the workers.

Mao took up that theme in China in his Cultural Revolution, which set out to destroy all remnants of China's artistic past. A major theme in his writings was that culture could not be separated from politics; it was an all-embracing phenomenon. It followed that if the arts were to continue as genuine expressions of Chinese communist culture they must carry no taint of the bourgeois past. State censorship became vital. This was the logic of his assault on the 'Four Olds' (see page 133), a form of nihilism intended to clear the way for an entirely new Chinese culture.

Noticeably in all the regimes, there was a complete dismissal of the liberal concepts of open artistic expression and intellectual freedom. In Nazi and communist society, such principles were regarded as an unacceptable indulging of the individual at the expense of the greater social good.

Religion

In regard to religion, Stalin and Mao shared the same attitude. Since they viewed it as a construct of the exploiting classes, employed in pre-revolutionary times as a means of enslaving the masses, religion would not be tolerated. As a mere set of superstitions that distracted the people from reality, it was to be persecuted out of existence. Hitler took a more nuanced approach. Although he had little respect for religion in itself, regarding its otherworldly values as a challenge to the secular principles of Nazism, he was conscious of the strength of both Catholic and Protestant traditions in Germany. This did not stop him from attempting in various ways to undermine the position of the Churches, but he stopped short of open persecution. That he felt constrained to do so is a corrective to the idea that Nazism always acted in a fully totalitarian manner.

> In what ways did the three regimes attempt to transform culture?

KEY TERM

Homo Sovieticus Perfect proletarian, Soviet man.

> Why did the three leaders regard religion as a problem in their respective countries?

🔑 KEY TERM

Sacrilege Degrading of something sacred.

Heresy Rejection of the basic political belief on which the movement depends, analogous to the rejection of a basic religious belief.

Secular faiths

There is an important sense in which the regimes may be described as secular faiths. Nazism, Stalinism and Maoism were regarded by their adherents as essential scientific truths, not merely political philosophies. In such circumstances, opposition was not simply a political act; it took on the character of a **sacrilege**. Dissidence became **heresy** and, since those guilty of it had affronted the values of the people, they had to be tried before the people. This was the rationale behind show trials, which were extensively used in all three regimes (see pages 40, 81 and 123). The accused were presented as heretics to be publicly shamed and humiliated before being condemned.

> **How freely were the populations in the three regimes allowed to move?**

→ Freedom of movement

The three systems clearly had much in common, but there were also distinct differences. An important one is that relating to the freedom of movement of the population. Under Stalin, passports were made compulsory for internal travel within the USSR. These were used as a means of hunting down Kulaks (rich peasants) and dissidents who tried to escape persecution by moving to different areas to hide. Passports permitting travel in and out of the country were rarely issued and then only to privileged groups, such as Party members and selected athletes and cultural representatives.

🔑 KEY TERM

Hukou Internal PRC passport or visa.

Similar restrictions were applied in Mao's China. Citizens had to carry a *hukou*, a document giving details of their place of residence. There was no absolute right to residence in a particular place and the *hukou* was applied by the authorities in a variety of ways either to prohibit or to enforce people's movement. Mao used it effectively, albeit unscrupulously, during the Great Leap Forward to shift huge numbers of rural Chinese from the land to the industrial centres.

In contrast, Hitler's Germany, up to the outbreak of war in 1939, was notably relaxed in its attitude to travel and movement. As was shown by its successful mounting of the Olympic Games in 1936, it was eager to welcome foreign visitors. It is true that its own people needed state-issued passports to leave and to re-enter the country, but that was the requirement in all European states at that time. Germans were encouraged to travel abroad and, although those who did so tended to be the well-to-do, the same was again true for the rest of Europe; cheap mass tourism did not develop anywhere in Europe until after 1945. Moreover, a distinctive feature of Nazi social policy was its *Kraft durch Freude* (see page 95) programme which provided its workers with holidays and opportunities for travel within Germany. Restrictions were, of course, placed on German Jews, but since this group made up barely 1 per cent of the population, it was possible both for visitors and Germans not to be fully aware of the situation.

> **How were economies in the three regimes revolutionized?**

→ Economic revolution

A further prominent aspect of the regimes was their commitment to centrally-directed economic transformation. Stalin's vast collectivization and industrialization schemes in the USSR (see page 35), copied by Mao in China in the Great Leap Forward, were meant to revolutionize the economy. Both men believed that without such transformation their regimes and their countries could not survive, since the hostile capitalist world would unite to crush them. Hitler's fears for Germany were not perhaps as intense as this. Nevertheless, he, too, saw economic advance as critical to his country's fortunes. Judging that war with the powers of Europe was a strong likelihood at some point in the future, he wanted Germany to develop an economy strong enough to meet the nation's military needs. That was the task he set his economic planners.

Nationalism

What now most impresses observers of the twentieth century is how powerful nationalism was as the great ideological driving force of its time. Right-wing movements such as Nazism and fascism were defined by their belief in the virtue and power of the nation-state. That also applied on the Left. To be sure, there were international communists such as Lenin who believed that the days of the nation-state were over and that class would become the determinant of all future societies. However, Lenin was in a minority. All the leaders of communist nations, including his own immediate successor in the USSR, Stalin, subordinated their communist ambitions to the needs of the states they led. Communism was the means to an end: the survival and development of the nation. In China, Mao Zedong adopted communism because it provided a political and social mechanism by which he could achieve his basic goal – the regeneration of the Chinese nation.

> **How powerful was nationalism as an influence in the three regimes?**

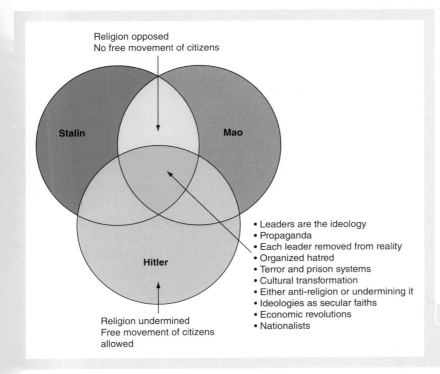

Religion opposed
No free movement of citizens

Stalin

Mao

Hitler

• Leaders are the ideology
• Propaganda
• Each leader removed from reality
• Organized hatred
• Terror and prison systems
• Cultural transformation
• Either anti-religion or undermining it
• Ideologies as secular faiths
• Economic revolutions
• Nationalists

Religion undermined
Free movement of citizens allowed

SUMMARY DIAGRAM

Comparing Stalin's Soviet Union, Hitler's Germany and Mao's China

Interpretations of authoritarianism and totalitarianism

> ▶ *Key question:* What main interpretations have been advanced to explain authoritarianism?

So central to modern history have the authoritarian regimes been that they have produced a range of interpretations that attempt to explain the outstanding political phenomena of the twentieth century. The following is a selection of some of the most influential analyses.

A rejection of individualism

Why did E.H. Carr regard the collective principle as a major influence?

The move towards totalitarianism was noted and approved of by the British scholar, E.H. Carr. As a Marxist, writing in the 1960s, he was strongly sympathetic towards Soviet communism, suggesting that it was 'the creed for which modern civilization is waiting'. He observed that the effect of the Second World War had been to stimulate the collective principle which could best be achieved in practical terms by governments taking increasing power at the centre. He believed that the Western liberal tradition with its emphasis upon the individual was no longer appropriate to the twentieth century: 'The trend away from individualism and towards totalitarianism is everywhere unmistakable.' With what was later shown to be a naive misjudgement, Carr regarded Soviet totalitarianism as successful because it had built a modern economy, and acceptable because its aim was to serve the interests of the people.

A factional struggle

Why did Friedrich von Hayek regard factionalism as a major influence?

Carr's views did not go unchallenged. Friedrich von Hayek, an influential Austrian analyst who had lived through the Nazi era, made a number of key observations in the 1970s. He stressed that the two major European totalitarian powers, the USSR and the Third Reich, were both socialist states. He saw their bitter rivalry as essentially a factional struggle between opposed wings of the same ideology. He argued that in politics, as in religion, it is disagreements between those who share the same basic faith that create the fiercest conflict. Neither National Socialism nor Soviet communism would admit the legitimacy of each other's interpretation of socialism. Each regarded the other as heretical.

An ideological conflict

On what grounds did Karl Popper defend liberal-democracy?

It was in protest against the notion that history was determined by iron laws of development that Karl Popper mounted a spirited defence of liberalism. Popper, whose long writing career lasted from the 1940s to the 1980s, was disturbed by the trend towards **collectivism** evident in all the countries involved in the Second World War, and which was at its most oppressive in the totalitarian states. He took a strongly moral line arguing that, for all its failings, liberal-democracy was the only system in which individual freedom could be maintained. He argued that human society was too complex and varied for it to be definitively analysed and suggested that the supposedly scientific methods used in the attempt to do so were essentially the prejudices and *a priori* assumptions of those with a political agenda. In a reversal of true scientific enquiry, the Soviet and Nazi totalitarian regimes had started with an ideology to which they then bent the facts to make them fit.

Totalitarianism as applied science

One of the most influential writers on the subject was Hannah Arendt, who advanced the persuasive thesis that totalitarianism was a specifically twentieth-century ideology which grew out of the scientific developments of the previous century. Producing her main works between the 1950s and 1980s, she explained the mass appeal of totalitarianism by pointing to the fact that science had made such great advances in so many areas that it was possible to believe that it held the answer to all life's problems. Ideologies had developed based on the conviction that human society could be scientifically analysed and the findings used to achieve directed social ends.

For Hannah Arendt, the outstanding example was Marxism (see page 19), which, claiming to have discovered the observable laws of social science, constructed a revolutionary programme around them. Nazism was also an appeal to science, but whereas Marxism was based on class struggle, Nazism was based on racial conflict. The striking point of similarity between them was that, since both claimed scientific validity, they were entitled to use violent, totalitarian methods to achieve their objectives. Possessed of the truth, they had no compunction about crushing their opponents, who, by definition, were always in the wrong.

Nazism and Soviet communism as branches of the same tree

Ernst Nolte, a Right-wing German philosopher of history, stirred controversy in the 1960s and 1970s by observing that, while Nazism and Stalinism were both undoubtedly totalitarian, Nazism had not developed independently. He suggested that Nazism came into being as a direct response to the growth of Soviet communism. Nolte's most provocative argument was that the Holocaust (see page 103) was directly modelled on the **annihilation policies** first adopted by the Soviet Union.

Without going as far as Nolte, there were other analysts who interpreted the right-wing dictatorships as essentially a reaction to the rise of communism, which in its international significance was a call for the revolutionary overthrow of capitalism and the capitalist nations. The terror that this excited explained the readiness of so many of the Western countries to be tolerant of

---

← **According to Hannah Arendt, how had scientific ideas encouraged the growth of totalitarianism?**

🔑 **KEY TERM**

Collectivism A system based on the idea that individuals must subordinate their private interests to those of society as a whole.

A priori Latin for 'from the first', a term in philosophy to describe the type of reasoning which assumes an assertion to be true before it has been proven so.

← **How similar were Nazism and Stalinism?**

🔑 **KEY TERM**

Annihilation policies The programme introduced by Lenin and continued by Stalin for destroying the Soviet Union's internal class enemies, beginning with the Kulaks, the rich peasants (see page 33).

Right-wing dictatorships. International socialism had the effect of closing the ranks of the Right against what it regarded as its greatest threat. The British historian, A.J.P. Taylor, a man of Left-wing sympathies, explained: 'Men were obsessed by fear of Communism and saw in Fascism the salvation of society.'

How great a difference was there between Nazism and Stalinism?

Nazism and Stalinism essentially different

Rejecting Nolte's contention, a number of German Marxist social historians, most notably Jurgen Habermas and Hans Mommsen, responded in the 1980s and 1990s by asserting that there was a distinct difference between Nazism and Stalinism. Without denying Soviet excesses, they argued that totalitarianism in the USSR had been an unavoidable reaction to the problems of sheer survival facing revolutionary Russia after 1917. In contrast, they argued, Nazism had been deliberately constructed as a front for the forces of the bourgeoisie. Rather than being a response to communism, Hitler and the Nazi movement had been created as a means of ensuring the survival and expansion of capitalism.

What contribution did the First World War make to the growth of totalitarianism?

Totalitarianism as a product of modern war and technology

A noted Polish-American scholar and statesman, Zbigniew Brzezinski, built on the work of Hannah Arendt by promoting the idea in the 1980s that totalitarianism was a particular product of the twentieth century. He viewed the First World War as having stimulated the growth of communism and fascism in two interconnected ways: the disillusion caused by the war had encouraged extremist ideas and the wartime advances in communication technology had enabled these ideas to be imposed on a mass audience. For Brzezinski, the defining elements in totalitarian systems of both Left and Right were dominant and charismatic leaders at the head of subservient parties, who were wedded to an ideology and employed terror to maintain control. The outstanding examples were the regimes of Stalin, Hitler and Mao.

Totalitarianism as a positive force

What positive aspects of totalitarianism have been emphasized by a number of revisionist historians?

Brzezinski established what may be called the mainstream interpretation of totalitarianism. But there were later notable shifts of emphasis. A revisionist school of historians who have been active since the 1980s and whose most representative figure is the Left-leaning Australian-American scholar, Sheila Fitzpatrick, have argued that the control exercised by Stalin in the USSR was markedly different from that of Hitler in Germany. For the revisionists, the Soviet Union was too poorly organized for it to have been a totalitarian state directly comparable to Nazi Germany. Fitzpatrick went further, asserting that the terror for which Stalin was notorious in the West had been exaggerated by **Cold War** propagandists. She suggested, moreover that despite its repressive image, Stalinism had been a positive experience for many Soviet citizens, the purges having helped to create a more socially mobile society.

KEY TERM

Cold War The period of political and diplomatic tension, 1945–91, between the capitalist USA and its allies and the communist USSR and its allies.

Modernization

For some scholars, totalitarianism as a phenomenon has to be understood as essentially a transition to modernization. The argument runs along these lines:

How important was modernization to the growth of totalitarianism?

- Communism, in both its Stalinist and Maoist forms, and Nazism were essentially responses to the demands of modernization.
- So pressing were those demands that to achieve them required the most rigorous and sweeping methods. Modernization could be achieved only through central control.
- Tsarist Russia, **Wilhelmine Germany**, Nationalist China: none of them had proved capable of successfully modernizing. They had lacked the necessary economic and political institutions and the resolve.
- It was the ruthlessness of Stalin, Hitler and Mao in their respective countries that allowed the remarkable economic transformation to be undertaken.
- So enormous was the task that to judge them by the traditional standards of the liberal-democracies is to assess them by the wrong measure. To achieve industrialization on the scale required left no room for the niceties of democratic politics. Coercion and repression were minor considerations when the nation was struggling to establish the base of its own survival.

> **KEY TERM**
>
> **Wilhelmine Germany** The German state during the reigns of Kaiser William I (1871–88) and William II (1888–1918).

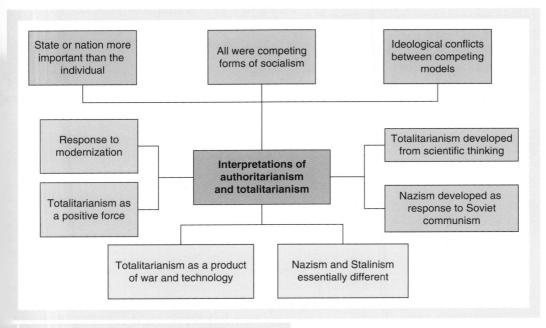

SUMMARY DIAGRAM

Interpretations of authoritarianism and totalitarianism

Chapter summary

Communism, Nazism and Maoism – a comparison

The outstanding feature of the three regimes that set the pattern for twentieth-century authoritarianism was the dominance of their leaders. All three regimes have been described as totalitarian since, despite their ideological differences, Hitler, Stalin and Mao asserted supreme authority in their respective countries and imposed dictatorial methods of control.

The three leaders were sustained in power by a continuous propaganda campaign that raised them to cult status. They also claimed a special relationship with history, each representing himself as the fulfilment of his nation's aspirations for progress and modernity. Such elevated claims tended to detach them from ordinary politics and made it impossible for legitimate opposition to form against them.

Intensely nationalistic in their aims, all three leaders identified dangerous elements within society – Kulaks in the USSR, Jews in the Third Reich and rightists in the PRC – who were then subjected to fierce persecution as a way of uniting the people in hatred of a common enemy. Sweeping reforms of the economy were another common feature as the regimes sought to become both industrially strong and militarily powerful. Unwilling to face challenge from alternative ideologies, the regimes suppressed religious worship and required that culture in all its forms must conform to the secular and artistic values of the state.

There were differences in the way the regimes operated, for example in the greater freedom of movement allowed in Hitler's Germany compared with the strict controls in the USSR and the PRC. But, overall, it is the similarities in methods of control that are the most evident.

It is how those similarities are to be interpreted that has divided scholarly opinion in a continuing debate over the character of totalitarianism. The Right has tended to stress how close the Nazi and communist regimes were in the violence of their methods, some writers going so far as to suggest that the movements were essentially the same, nihilistic Nazism being simply a reaction to nihilistic Soviet communism. The Left has countered by emphasizing the ideological differences and arguing that the extremism of Soviet and Chinese communism was forced upon those regimes by the demands of modernization and the sheer need to survive.

Examination practice

Below are a number of different questions for you to practise. For guidance on how to answer exam-style questions, see Chapter 10.

1   Compare and contrast the use of terror by Mao and Stalin.

2   For what reasons and with what results did Hitler and Mao utilize propaganda?

3   Analyse the importance of prison systems for two leaders of single-party states, each from a different region.

4   Compare and contrast the rise to power of either Hitler and Stalin or Stalin and Mao.

5   Explain the significance of the army for both Hitler and Mao.

6   To what extent did both Stalin and Mao alter their nations' economic systems?

7   Discuss the importance of political ideology for both Hitler and Stalin.

8   Why did no effective opposition form against Mao, Stalin or Hitler within their own states?

9   Analyse the impact of two leaders of single-party states, each from a different region, on their states' arts.

10 To what extent did both Mao and Hitler utilize nationalism in their ideologies?

 # Activities

1   How successful were Hitler, Stalin and Mao in creating a totalitarian state? Rank each of these rulers in terms of their personal success in creating a single-party state centred upon themselves using the following categories (and others you can think of):

● Economic policies

● Social policies

● Religious policies

● Structure of government

● Opposition

You will need to define what success in each of these categories actually means.

2   Compare and contrast the views and actions of Stalin and Mao on the role of agriculture for the state.

3   Review the use of propaganda for the governments of Hitler, Stalin and Mao.

● What themes and imagery did they have in common?

● What was different?

Create a display comparing and contrasting the various types of propaganda, with reference to the importance of symbolism, colours and the overall message.

CHAPTER 6

Egypt under Gamal Abdel Nasser, 1952–70

Between 1952 and 1970, Gamal Abdel Nasser revolutionized the politics of Egypt and the Middle East. Emerging from relative obscurity in the troubled Egypt of the 1930s and 1940s, he was one of a group of military personnel, known as the Free Officers, who in a revolutionary move overthrew the monarchy in 1952 and established military rule in Egypt. Within two years Nasser had become the dominant figure among the Free Officers and from then until 1970 he led an authoritarian single-party government which resorted to increasingly oppressive measures to impose its will. Starting with the aim of leading Egypt to full independence and modernity, Nasser expanded his ambitions to encompass his becoming the acknowledged leader of the Arab world, a move which resulted in Egypt's heavy involvement in the international complications of the Cold War.

You need to consider the following questions:

✪ What circumstances favoured the rise of Nasser?

✪ How did Nasser impose his authority on Egypt?

✪ What impact did Nasser's rule have on the lives of the Egyptian people?

✪ How far did Nasser achieve a totalitarian state?

① Nasser's rise to power, 1935–54

> ▶ **Key question:** *What circumstances favoured the rise of Nasser?*

Why were conditions so unstable in Egypt in Nasser's formative years?	**Egypt's struggle for independence**

 KEY TERM

Protectorate An area not formally taken over as a colony but still under protective jurisdiction.

Egypt's struggle for independence

Having been under Turkish control in previous centuries, Egypt fell under British domination in the late nineteenth century and became a British **protectorate** in 1914. At the end of the First World War, violent protests against the British occupation were organized by Egyptian nationalists; in 1922 the protectorate came to an end with the granting of independence for Egypt. However, it was limited independence. The British continued to claim the right to control the **Suez Canal** by stationing their troops in the Canal Zone and other areas of Egypt they considered strategically important. Over the next 30 years, the British armed presence became a constant source of bitterness to the Egyptians and there were recurrent demonstrations and serious disturbances in the main cities, Alexandria and Cairo.

What deepened the protesters' resentment was Britain's continued interference in Egyptian politics. A particular grievance was the manner in which the British saw fit to advise and direct King Faud (1922–36) and King Farouk (1936–52). It was in response to British diplomatic pressure that Farouk's government accepted the terms of the Anglo-Egyptian Treaty of August 1936 under which Britain, while withdrawing from other areas in Egypt, was granted the right to maintain a force of 10,000 troops in the Canal Zone. The Treaty intensified the anger of nationalist protesters not only towards the British occupiers, but also towards the monarchy and the government which had acquiesced in the humiliation. Demonstrations against British military occupation and political interference and against the weak Egyptian monarchy continued intermittently until 1952.

SOURCE A

Map of Egypt in 1945.

Study Source A and identify the areas in dispute between Britain and Egypt. **?**

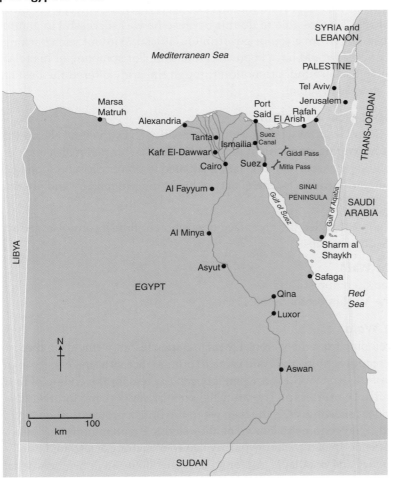

Nasser's early career

It was in this atmosphere of unrest and bitterness that Gamal Abdel Nasser grew to maturity. Born in Alexandria in 1918, the son of a post office official who was frequently moved from place to place, young Nasser had a very broken education, which meant he was largely self-taught. His frequent moves introduced him to different types of Egyptians and he became aware of the poverty and wealth that existed side by side. This led him, as a teenager, to become a member of the Egyptian Socialist party.

Nasser was also strongly influenced by the widespread anti-British sentiment; by the early 1930s, he was taking an active part in demonstrations against the British presence. He was arrested and detained on a number of occasions. In 1935 he suffered a head injury when a demonstration he was involved in was broken up by police. The experience strengthened his revolutionary resolve. Two years later, he took what was to prove a momentous step when he entered the army as an officer. He was able to do this because he was successful in gaining sponsorship from a senior government official. Without such backing, the officer class would have been closed to him. For someone of his relatively humble background, promotion through the army offered the best chance of a successful career.

Opposition to Britain

The Egyptian army, which was heavily politicized by the time Nasser joined it, provided the environment in which to develop his nationalist and revolutionary ideas. Once he had graduated to officer class, he soon became popular with cadets for the quality of his lectures in military and political history.

The army provided the organized opposition to British control, together with three other groups:

- the **Wafd**
- the Communist Party
- the Muslim Brotherhood.

The Wafd

Developing from the various Egyptian nationalist movements in the nineteenth century, the Wafd came to prominence as a single party at the end of the First World War when it began to press for the ending of British dominance over Egypt. This attracted popular support and for the two decades following 1922, the date when the British protectorate ended, the Wafd could genuinely claim to be the voice of Egyptian hopes for full independence. However, its willingness to compromise lessened its influence and popularity. Although it claimed to be an anti-monarchical party, its co-operation with the royal government in the signing of the

**KEY TERM**

Wafd Arabic for 'delegation', suggesting the Party's claim to represent the people.

Anglo-Egyptian Treaty in 1936 led many Egyptian nationalists to doubt that the Wafd truly represented the nation.

The Communist Party

Formed in Egypt in 1922, it modelled itself on the Bolshevik Party (see page 18). Its aims were both nationalist in that it wanted to remove the British presence, and revolutionary in that it wanted to overthrow the existing political and social system in Egypt. As a first step, it set out to take over the trade unions in order to cause industrial disruption.

The Muslim Brotherhood

Formed in Egypt in 1928, the Muslim Brotherhood had a distinctive attitude to politics. It regarded governmental and political systems as being of minor importance in the lives of the followers of the Prophet Muhammad, who had taught that obedience to Allah (God) was an obligation that came before all others. The Brotherhood took the fundamentalist view that the will of Allah, as revealed to the Prophet Muhammad and recorded in the **Qur'an** (or Koran), superseded all man-made laws and governments. It followed that there could be no such thing as a purely secular state since its absence of belief would render it illegitimate. Nor could there be a purely national state, based on ethnicity or geography, since the only bond that could give identity to a community was a shared belief in the truths of Islam. It also regarded Britain as an ungodly presence in Egypt.

> **KEY TERM**
>
> **Qur'an (also Koran)** The holy book of Islam, believed by Muslims to be the word of Allah as revealed to the Prophet Muhammad.
>
> **Axis forces** Drawn principally from Germany, Italy, and Vichy (unoccupied but pro-German) France.

Egypt and the Second World War, 1939–45

> In what ways did the Second World War increase tensions in Egypt?

British influence over the monarchy and government became stronger with the coming of the Second World War. Anxious to protect the Suez Canal and maintain Egypt as a base for their campaigns against the **Axis forces** in North Africa, the British regarded the Wafd as the main party that would keep Egypt loyal to Britain.

A critical event occurred in 1942 when Britain insisted that King Farouk appoint a pro-British Wafd prime minister. British troops surrounded the royal palace as Britain's Egyptian ambassador marched in on Farouk and demanded that the Prime Minister, Ali Maher, who was believed to have German sympathies, be dismissed and replaced with Mustapha Nahas. The King capitulated to the demand. An outraged Nasser declared: 'I am ashamed that our army has not reacted against this attack. I pray to Allah for a calamity to overtake the English.'

From that point on Nasser was convinced that Egypt could not progress unless it developed an army strong enough to defend its interests. It went beyond military considerations. The leadership of the army was necessary for Egypt to achieve its national aspirations. Here it should be stressed that the clear line of demarcation between politics and the military that existed in many Western countries did not operate in Egypt. The army in Egypt felt no

What impact did the Arab–Israeli War, 1948–49, have upon Nasser?

compunction to be politically neutral. For it to stand aside from politics and act only when instructed to by government was not part of the Egyptian tradition. The army was a political force, which was why ambitious young men like Nasser saw membership of it as a path to personal advancement.

Underground opposition movements

The ineffectiveness of the Wafd in the face of British pressure created internal party divisions and encouraged the spread of underground opposition movements, particularly on the Left (see page 7). Communists and socialists were vociferous in condemning what they termed the bourgeois elements in government who were more concerned with safeguarding their class privileges than in fighting for Egypt's independence. Violent recriminations were common and assassinations were frequent. The growth of an urban **guerrilla** force, the *Fedayeen*, added to the turmoil.

The aftermath of the Second World War

The 1940s were consequently a very disturbed time for Egypt, made worse by the aftermath of the Second World War. Egypt did not enter the war against Germany until February 1945, but this belated decision to join the Allies brought Egypt little benefit. To the angry disappointment of the Egyptians, Britain insisted on maintaining its military presence in Egypt and its hold of the Suez Canal. British anxieties over the German threat had been replaced with **Cold War** concerns. The Suez Canal was too strategically important for Britain to release its grip on it. The result was a sharp increase in Anglo-Egyptian tension.

The years 1945 and 1946 saw continual disturbances. In February 1946, nearly a hundred civilians were killed in anti-government and anti-British riots. The authorities tried to assert control by arresting the leaders of the various protest movements and outlawing their organizations. But Egypt was close to being ungovernable. No matter how often Farouk's cabinets were changed and new ministers appointed, they were unable to attract genuine support. Seven different governments were formed in the period 1945–50, but the changes did not bring stability. None of the administrations had an answer to the unrest and its root cause: the British military presence. The political system in Egypt was clearly inadequate to meet the demands placed upon it. The great dream of many nationalists in the 1920s that Egypt would develop into a workable **constitutional monarchy** was proving illusory. The chance of some form of anti-government revolution occurring became increasingly likely.

War in Palestine, 1948–49

The taut situation in Egypt was intensified by dramatic events in a neighbouring region that had immense repercussions for Egypt and the whole of the Arab world – the creation of the state of Israel in 1948. It has been remarked by a modern historian, Paul Johnson, that: 'There are few moments in the twentieth century so soaked in history as the establishment of Israel.' In personal terms, it was to affect Nasser for the rest of his life.

The Balfour Declaration

The founding of Israel in 1948 brought to a climax, though not a conclusion, a story which could be traced back to 1917 when, with the aim of enlisting Jewish support for the Allied war effort in the First World War, Arthur Balfour, the British Foreign Secretary, issued a formal declaration promising to back the establishment of a 'national home for the Jewish people' in Palestine. Balfour tried to achieve a compromise by adding that this Jewish home would not jeopardize the legitimate rights of the indigenous Palestinian Arabs. From the beginning the compromise proved unworkable. Between the two World Wars significant numbers of Jews moved into Palestine in the face of strong Arab resentment. Violence was met with violence.

SOURCE B

Excerpt from the Balfour Declaration, 2 November 1917, quoted in *The Making of the Modern Near East 1792–1923* by Y.E. Yapp, published by Longman, UK, 1991, p. 290.

His Majesty's government view with favour the establishment in Palestine of a national home for the Jewish people, and will use their best endeavours to facilitate the achievement of this object, it being clearly understood that nothing shall be done which may prejudice the civil and religious rights of existing non-Jewish communities in Palestine, or the rights and political status enjoyed by Jews in any other country.

> According to Source B, how are the rights of both Jews and 'non-Jewish communities' to be respected?

The British mandate

The British, mandated by the **League of Nations** as the supervising authority, refused to allow the development of political institutions since this would allow the Palestinian Arabs, the vast majority of the population, to cut or even end Jewish immigration into the area.

The British **mandate** was renewed under the United Nations in 1945. This was a critical year. The ending of the war in Europe revealed the horrendous scale of the **Holocaust**. Worldwide sympathy for the survivors of Nazi persecution added greater weight to the cause of **Zionism** and Britain found itself pressured, particularly by the USA, into allowing increased immigration of European Jews into Palestine. Even this was not enough; desperate Jewish refugees flooded into the area in defiance of the ineffectual British controls. Unable to prevent the influx, and still less able to pacify the Palestinian Arabs, who saw their land being taken from them by terrorist Zionist occupiers, the British handed their mandate back to the UN.

Arab reaction to the creation of Israel

On the very day that Britain withdrew from Palestine in May 1948, jubilant Zionists declared that the new state of Israel had come into being. Their

 **KEY TERM**

League of Nations The international body created in 1919 with the aim of peacefully resolving disputes between nations.

Mandate An authority granted by the League of Nations to certain countries to monitor and protect the interests of particular states and regions created at the end of the First World War.

Holocaust The systematic killing by Nazi Germany of 6 million European Jews between 1942 and 1945.

Zionism The movement for the creation of a Jewish state; the term is often used to denote Israeli expansionism.

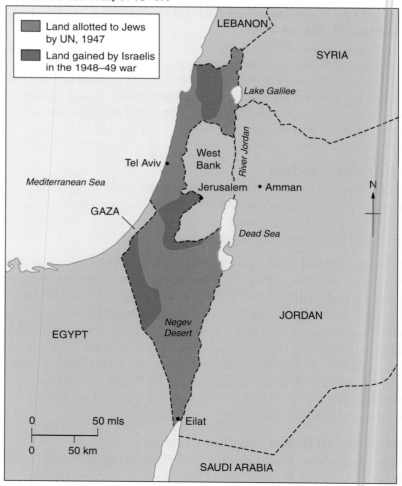

KEY TERM

Arab League Formed in 1945 with six member states – Egypt, Transjordan (Jordan after 1949), Iraq, Lebanon, Saudi Arabia and Yemen – it stood for collaboration between the members on 'the affairs and interests of the Arab countries'. From the beginning, Egypt was the strongest member.

euphoria was balanced by the searing anger of the Arab world which, believing itself to have been betrayed by the USA, Britain and the UN, pledged itself to the destruction of the new state. The lead was taken by Egypt through the **Arab League** in a joint plan to crush Israel. The war which followed saw Nasser's first active service as a soldier. He distinguished himself through the courage and leadership he showed as a brigade commander. Wounded in the stomach by shell shrapnel early in the war, he returned after treatment in Cairo to take part in one of the last Arab stands of the war. In the Falluja pocket near Gaza, Nasser led a resistance that lasted until the war came to an end in February 1949 and a truce was called which left the Israelis victorious.

Nasser returned from the war a heroic figure, but his personal success stood in marked contrast to the humiliation suffered by Egypt and the Arab League. Under-equipped, poorly led, outmanoeuvred by the Israelis strategically on land and in the air, and disunited among themselves, the

?

Study Source C. According to the map, what territorial gains did Israel make in the 1948–49 war?

SOURCE C

The Arab–Israeli War, 1948–49.

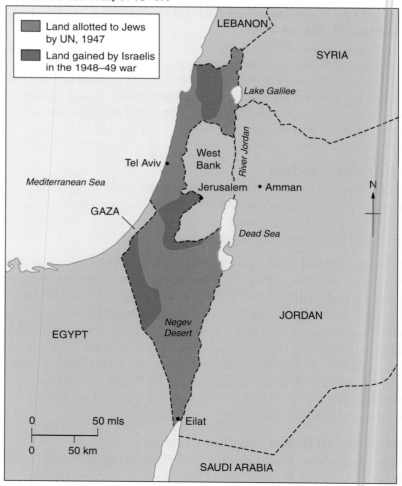

Land allotted to Jews by UN, 1947

Land gained by Israelis in the 1948–49 war

LEBANON

SYRIA

Lake Galilee

River Jordan

West Bank

Tel Aviv

Jerusalem   • Amman

Mediterranean Sea

N

GAZA

Dead Sea

JORDAN

Negev Desert

EGYPT

0   50 mls

0   50 km

Eilat

SAUDI ARABIA

member states had performed dismally. The Rhodes Agreement which formally ended the ten-month war left Israel not only in control of its original territories but master also of the lands it had overrun in the fighting.

While Nasser's detestation of Israel had meant he had gladly embraced the struggle, his initial doubts that Egypt was militarily ready for the war had been confirmed by defeat. He and other Egyptian army officers drew a number of lessons from the experience:

- Egypt's failure was a consequence of the corruption at the heart of the government led by King Farouk.
- Progress for Egypt depended on its developing an effective modern army.
- Israel could be overcome only if the Arab world united and marshalled superior military strength.
- Arab unity would not arise spontaneously – it required strong Egyptian leadership.

The Egyptian Revolution of 1952

Shortly after returning from Palestine, Nasser was elected chairman of a group known as the Association of Free Officers. He was now in a position to work towards the revolution which he was now more than ever convinced was necessary if Egypt was ever to rid itself of the weakness and corruption that denied it strength and progress. Circumstances were all in his favour. Egypt's humiliation at the hands of Israel, government corruption presided over by a self-indulgent king, permanent unrest on the streets, and the continued British presence at the Suez Canal created a situation in which revolution against the patently weak government was waiting to happen. In January 1952 a clash between British troops and Egyptian police in Ismailia, a town in the Canal Zone, resulted in the death of 50 policemen. A violent reaction followed in Cairo. Arson attacks saw much of the city in flames and the authorities seemed powerless to control the widespread disturbances. A French eye-witness described Egypt's desperate plight in the opening month of 1952 (see Source D).

> **What role did Nasser play in the 1952 Revolution?**

SOURCE D

Excerpt from *Nasser* by Jean Lacouture, published by Secker & Warburg, UK, 1973, p. 78.

*Egypt was a **triptych** of suffering, anger and humiliation. In the villages, the peasantry was being exploited unbearably. In the Canal Zone the guerrilla war against the British had assumed a ferocity very costly in human lives. In Cairo, the royal court pursued its depravity and intrigues to the point of nausea, and Egypt was about to vomit.*

> According to Source D, what made up Egypt's triptych of suffering in January 1952?

It may be said that the 'vomit' eventually came forth in the Revolution of July 1952, organized by the only force capable of mounting such an operation – the army. In that month, Nasser led a group of Free Officers in taking power. He did so in the name of General Mohammed Neguib, the

> 🔑 **KEY TERM**
>
> **Triptych** A painting made up of three separate panels, hinged together.

senior member of the group. Claiming they had been prompted to act by the news that Farouk intended arresting their leaders, the officers in a pre-emptive move forced the King to abdicate and leave Egypt. The Free Officers then set themselves up as an interim Revolutionary Command Council (RCC). Their declared aim in overthrowing the monarchy was to establish a democracy, not to install themselves as a military government. In June 1953, in a further step towards consolidating their hold, the RCC proclaimed that the monarchy was abolished and that Egypt was a republic. Neguib was declared to be president both of the Republic and the RCC, with Nasser named as vice-president.

There have been suggestions that the overthrow of Farouk was a plot hatched by the USA with the officers, but there is little evidence for this. It seems that the revolution of 1952 was essentially an Egyptian movement. The reality was that, by the time of his removal, Farouk had become such a diplomatic embarrassment that neither of the major Western powers involved, the USA and Britain, was prepared to keep him in power.

Neguib was the figurehead of the revolution but it was Nasser who directed it. Between 1952 and 1954, Nasser openly supported Neguib and, indeed, declined to stand against him when some of the other officers suggested he might push his own claims. Nasser calculated that Neguib, as an established elder officer with a proud Palestine War record, gave the new regime respectability, if not legitimacy.

Suppressing opposition to the revolution

During the two years of Neguib's leadership, Nasser, as vice-president, introduced a number of important measures, the critical one being agricultural reform (see page 192), but he was principally concerned to use the time to crush any political elements that might offer a serious challenge to the new Republic. In a preparatory move, he called for a 'national union', by which he meant the fusing of all the Egyptian parties under the leadership of the RCC. Nasser argued that the new Egyptian Republic would be best served by all the parties joining together in one major organization. What, in effect, he was pressing for was a one-party state which, by definition, would exclude all opposition groups.

It was such reasoning that provided the pretext for Nasser to embark on a policy of political repression. Groups such as the communists and extreme nationalists, who were unwilling to co-operate with the new government, were to be suppressed. Nasser made a particular target of the Muslim Brotherhood. Initially, the Brotherhood had welcomed the Free Officers' revolution since it expected that it would lead to the establishment of an Islamic republic. However, when Nasser made it clear that Egypt was to remain a secular state the Brotherhood quickly turned against him.

Although a Muslim himself, Nasser considered that the influence of the Brotherhood, which had a large following among ordinary Egyptians, had to be curtailed. He feared that it might present itself as an alternative power structure to the **National Union**, claiming the right to govern Egypt as a religious state that was entitled to the loyalty of all Muslims. When Nasser learned that a move against him was being prepared by the Brotherhood, he ordered it to be closed down in January 1954. In justification for such suppression Nasser pointed to the uncompromising opposition of the Muslim Brotherhood as powerfully expressed by Sayyid Qutb, one of its leading spokesmen (see Source E).

SOURCE E

Excerpt from *Milestones* by Sayyid Qutb, published by Kazi Publications, USA, 2003, p. 85.

Rather than support rule by a pious few, whether a dictator or democratically elected, Muslims should resist any system where men are in 'servitude to other men' – i.e. obey other men – as un-Islamic and a violation of God's sovereignty over all of creation. A truly Islamic polity would have no rulers since Muslims would need neither judges nor police to obey divine law.

According to Source E, what is the justification for Muslim resistance to authority?

Nasser's takeover, 1954

What steps led to Nasser's assumption of power in 1954

President Neguib was unhappy with Nasser's treatment of the Muslim Brotherhood but, despite being the country's nominal leader, he was becoming increasingly ineffectual. In contrast, Nasser's growing influence was evidenced by his becoming head of the RCC in March 1954. There was a feeling in government circles that Neguib was being tolerated only until Nasser saw fit to remove him.

The Anglo-Egyptian Treaty, 1954

Nasser's esteem rose still higher when he successfully negotiated a deal with Anthony Nutting, a British Foreign Office representative. A new Anglo-Egyptian Treaty was signed in October 1954. Under its terms, Britain undertook to:

- withdraw from the Canal Zone within two years
- abandon all connections with ex-King Farouk and the Egyptian monarchists
- accept the right of **Sudan** to independence from Britain and Egypt.

Assassination attempt against Nasser

Coinciding with his success in negotiating the Anglo-Egyptian Treaty, there occurred a remarkable event that sealed Nasser's popularity with ordinary Egyptians. Again, it involved the Muslim Brotherhood. In November, while Nasser was making a speech in Alexandria, an individual member of the Brotherhood attempted to assassinate him. The failure of the would-be

KEY TERM

National Union A title deliberately chosen by the RCC as representing Egypt itself. To oppose it, therefore, was to be anti-Egyptian. It had originally been called Liberation Rally.

Sudan Since 1899, Sudan had been jointly governed by Britain and Egypt as the Anglo-Egyptian Sudan. Nasser regarded Egypt's losing Sudan to be the necessary price for both countries' becoming independent from Britain.

assassin to hit Nasser, despite being only a few feet from him and firing a number of shots, led sceptics to conclude that the affair was stage-managed by Nasser's supporters. Whatever the truth, it was certainly the case that Nasser was quick to exploit the propaganda opportunity. He ended his interrupted speech with an impassioned declaration (see Source F).

According to Source F, what is the nature of Nasser's relationship with the Egyptian people?

SOURCE F

Excerpt from a speech by Nasser, November 1954, quoted in _The Arabs: A History_ by Eugene Rogan, published by Penguin, UK, 2009, p. 228.

My countrymen, my blood spills for you and for Egypt. I will live for your sake and die for your sake, for your freedom and honour. Let them kill me. It does not concern me as long as I have instilled pride, honour and freedom in you. If Gamal Abdel Nasser should die, each of you shall be Gamal Abdel Nasser. Gamal Abdel Nasser is of you and from you and is willing to sacrifice his life for the nation.

Rapturously received on his return to Cairo, Nasser felt justified in resorting to still fiercer repression. A mass round-up and imprisoning of Brotherhood members was carried out and six of the leaders were executed. With this strike, Nasser had removed the single greatest source of challenge to his regime. The communists had little popular backing and their threat was minimal. The Brotherhood, however, had contacts and support across a wide range of Egyptian society. Nasser's suppression of the movement in 1954 effectively ended the Brotherhood's open opposition. It is true that the organization still operated illegally as an underground movement but close secret-police surveillance resulted in its active members being arrested and sent to prison camps.

It is unlikely that Neguib was involved in the assassination attempt, but the suspicion among the Free Officers that he had been implicated further weakened his standing. Few of the Officers were prepared to struggle to save him. Neguib offered no resistance when a group of Officers placed him under house arrest. Such was Nasser's obvious popularity and influence at the highest levels that Neguib accepted that his own authority had now dissipated; he formally resigned the presidency in November 1954. Nasser was then invited by a deputation of Officers to take command. He accepted and became Prime Minister. It was the second revolution in Egypt within two years.

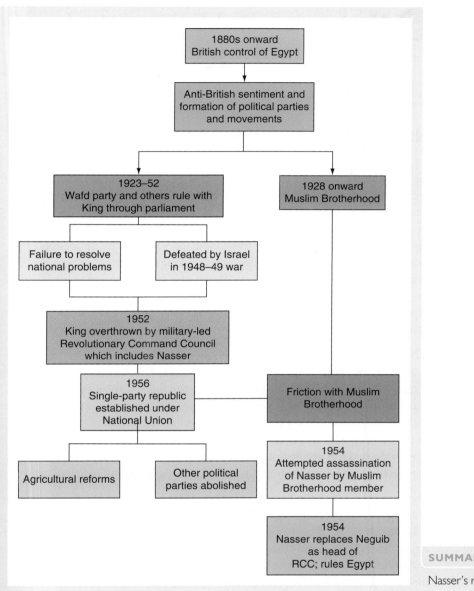

2 Nasser's establishment of an authoritarian state

▶ **Key question:** *How did Nasser impose his authority on Egypt?*

How did Nasser set about consolidating his authority?

Nasser's consolidation of power

Pending an election, Nasser was confirmed by the RCC as acting president of the Egyptian Republic in January 1955. Judging that there were still pockets of opposition to him, he continued with the repressive measures he had introduced as vice-president. However, he also sought to extend his popular base by going on a series of tours of the country. His aim was to present himself as the genuine leader of the people whose needs he understood. His journeys were punctuated by rallies at which huge, exuberant crowds demonstrated their support for him. The media also championed him. Nasser cleverly pushed the idea that he represented not merely Egyptian, but Arab aspirations towards freedom and economic advancement. This caused jealousy among Arab leaders elsewhere, but was highly attractive to Egyptians.

The Gaza problem

In February of 1955, a disturbing reminder of Middle-Eastern realities cut across Nasser's triumphant progress when the Israelis seized part of the Gaza Strip, a region in which a large number of Palestinian refugees had gathered after the 1948–49 war. The Israelis justified the action by referring to Egypt's constant use of the region as a base for raids against their people. Nasser denied the accusation, but there was little doubt he had encouraged the Egyptian *Fedayeen* in their guerrilla actions against the Israelis.

The ease with which the Israelis had taken Gaza confirmed Nasser's belief that, until Egypt was properly organized militarily, any thought of regaining Palestine was unrealistic. Such reorganization, however, required heavy expenditure and Egypt at this stage simply did not have the capital. This made Nasser willing to accept finance from both the West and the **Soviet bloc**. Egypt would take its money where it could find it, regardless of Cold War divisions.

The Bandung Conference, 1955

Nasser recovered from the temporary dip in his reputation following the Gaza incursion by figuring prominently at the Bandung Conference in Indonesia in April 1955 as representative, not simply of Egypt, but of the wider Arab world. It was at Bandung that he helped develop the **non-aligned movement (NAM)**, whose basic attitude was expressed in the term, 'positive neutralism' – the idea that independent countries could stand aside from both the United States and the Soviet bloc. As a result of Bandung, Nasser became associated with major world figures such as **Nehru** of India and **Tito** of Yugoslavia, leaders who declined to take sides in the Cold War.

The imposition of authoritarian control

Early in 1956, Nasser moved towards his strongest position yet when the new republican constitution was ratified, creating a single-party system.

What means were employed to impose Nasser's authority?

The adoption of single-party rule

Nasser's National Union was declared to be the only legitimate political party. For opponents, the prohibition on all other parties was proof that Egypt was adopting an autocratic form of government, despite its claim to be a republic. Of course, such adjectives were rejected by the National Union and Nasser himself. His justification for single-party rule ran along these lines:

- At its current stage of development Egypt's great need was unity.
- Therefore, to engage in opposition was to be irresponsible to the point of treason.
- The one-party system was not an attack upon democracy; it was its fulfilment.
- Democracy could take many forms. It did not have to take a multi-party form.
- Democracy, after all, was the will of the people and, in Egypt's case, the will of the people was represented in the enlightened rule of the National Union.

There was the added consideration that democracy was suspect in Egyptian minds since it was associated with the colonial West whose grip Egypt had only just broken. It has also to be remembered that, even in Europe, democracy in historical terms was a relatively recent development. It was unrealistic to expect Egypt to embrace a system that had not been fully implemented in the UK and the USA until the late 1920s.

Nasser's justification for repression

In Nasser's only major written work, published in 1955, *Egypt's Liberation: The Philosophy of Revolution*, he argued that centuries of foreign domination had drained the Egyptian people of their real sense of identity and unity. He saw it as his duty to redirect the revolution to its true task, that of instilling into the Egyptian people a new sense of purpose and of ending division between them. He confessed to having been disturbed by the way the first stage of the revolution had been distorted. The overthrow of the monarchy had been followed not by harmony, but by vindictiveness.

SOURCE G

Excerpt from *Egypt's Liberation: The Philosophy of Revolution* by G.A. Nasser, quoted in *Nasser* by Anthony Nutting, published by Constable, London, UK, 1972, p. 51.

The vanguard performed its task … threw out Farouk and then paused waiting for the serried ranks to come up in their sacred advance towards the great objective, but the masses that came were disunited. Every man we questioned had nothing to recommend except to kill someone else. Every idea we listened to was nothing but an attack on some other idea. We were deluged with demands

According to Nasser in Source G, what had disappointed him about the Egyptian revolution?

for revenge as though the revolution had taken place in order to become a weapon in the hands of hatred and vindictiveness. If anyone had asked me in those days what I wanted most, I would have answered promptly – to hear an Egyptian speak fairly about another Egyptian.

Nasser's dissatisfaction with what the first revolution had produced strengthened his notion that Egypt's progress depended on the enlightened rule of a one-party government, capable of providing the discipline and leadership the nation needed.

Nasser's aims as leader

A referendum held in June 1956, asking for acceptance of the new constitution with Nasser as president, won an overwhelming vote in favour. This confirmed for Nasser that the second revolution and the creation of the single-party system had truly ushered in government by the people. He announced his aims, which were to:

- rid Egypt of the legacy of monarchy
- destroy the vestiges of **colonialism**
- end **feudalism**
- end **monopoly capitalism** in Egypt
- create **social justice**
- establish democracy
- build up Egypt's armed forces.

Suppression of opposition

Nasser was very much a realist. He believed that his regime needed sufficient force at its disposal to meet its internal and external enemies. Without such force, he argued, political aspirations were unachievable. In politics Nasser was a pragmatist. He judged that ideology, no matter how well founded, amounted to very little unless it was backed by the means to impose it. That was why, once in power, he did not rely simply on popular appeal but continued to suppress opposition and develop mechanisms for enforcing political and social control. His chief instruments for suppressing opposition were:

- the armed forces
- the Mukhabarat – the secret police and intelligence agencies, the main instruments for maintaining state security. Growing into a large bureaucracy, with a staff of 10,000 officials, the Mukhabarat stood outside the law and had the power to interfere with any of the other state organizations
- the bureaucracy – Nasser deliberately governed through an extensive bureaucracy in order to suggest that his authority had a much wider base than simply his own individual power
- the government-controlled trade unions
- the *Fedayeen* – now regarded as representing Nasser's popular following and capable of controlling Egypt's internal dissidents
- the government-controlled media which acted as Nasser's propaganda machine.

KEY TERM

Colonialism The take over by European powers of territories whose people were too weak militarily to prevent their political and economic subjection.

Feudalism A system in which privileged landowners oblige the landless to work for them.

Monopoly capitalism A system in which the state interferes with the working of the economy in order to protect large commercial and industrial interests from competition from smaller concerns.

Social justice A system in which the law operates to create equal rights for all and prevent exploitation of the weak by the powerful.

All these bodies were either directly concerned with carrying out his wishes or were compliant with them. They were a formidable set of controls which effectively stifled public criticism of Nasser and made open opposition to him or the regime virtually impossible. Protest was necessarily furtive and clandestine. By 1960, 8,000 Islamists and 10,000 communists had been imprisoned along with hundreds of army officers.

Nasser set the tone for repression when he declared to a committee of the **Arab Socialist Union (ASU)**: 'We do not allow any deviationists to remain among us. Should a person deviate in any committee of the ASU, this committee must speak up and seek to expel him.'

Nasser sometimes personally intervened to condemn the excesses of the Mukhabarat, when they came to light. He declared on one occasion, following the death of a political prisoner under torture by the security forces, that such methods had no place in the new Egypt. But his protest seems to have been issued for form's sake rather than being a genuine expression of outrage. As observed by Said K. Aburish, one of Nasser's major Arab biographers: 'As long as Nasser was alive and well and capable of overwhelming the people around him, the chances of creating a democratic or semi-democratic system had little chance of success.'

The character of Nasser's rule

Revolutionary though he considered himself to be, Nasser's personal leadership was a continuation of Egypt's historical tradition that government was a matter of power exercised from the centre. Even after the overthrow of King Farouk there was a residual respect, if not for kingship, at least for central, one-person rule. It was part of Egypt's history and Nasser in applying a despotic grip was not really reversing the tradition, he was restoring it. Nasser did use state terror to enforce authority, but it was never mass terror of the type associated with Stalin's USSR, Hitler's Germany and Mao's China.

Prison camps

There were six known prison camps where thousands of opponents were incarcerated. The most notorious was Kharga in the remote Western Desert, specially reserved for Egyptian communists, who were routinely starved and beaten. The camp system was not on the scale of the *laogai* in China or the *Gulag* in the USSR (see pages 136 and 42), but the principle of maintaining places of terror both to punish the supposedly guilty and strike fear into the innocent was the same. Collectively, the camps were filled in the main with a mixture of communists, Muslim fundamentalists and assorted dissidents, arrested in the periodic rounding-up of opposition groups.

The media

During Nasser's rule, the state took over the main aspects of the media. Radio, television and newspapers became the chief means by which government propaganda was spread and Nasser's image projected. By 1970 most homes in

KEY TERM

Arab Socialist Union (ASU) The new name given in 1962 to the National Union, the sole party allowed to function legally in Egypt.

Laogai The term, which means 're-education through labour', came to be used to describe the extensive prison-camp system which operated under Mao in the PRC.

Gulag An extensive system of penal colonies spread across the USSR.

the urban areas and most villages in rural regions had access to television and radio broadcasts which presented the news from a pro-government aspect. Not all non-government newspapers were closed down but the secret police put pressure on dissident journalists to make them conform.

Treatment of the Jews in Egypt

Officially there was no overt persecution of Egypt's 200,000 Jews. Nasser's nationalization programme (see page 192) was not specifically directed at Jewish commercial interests in Egypt, although the takeover of companies did lead to a number of Jewish businesses leaving Egypt. It was never Jewishness itself but Zionism that Nasser condemned. His objection was to the European Jews who had come to Israel to deprive the Arabs of their lands. The Jews of Egypt he regarded as Egyptians (see Source H).

According to Nasser in Source H, why is it wrong to regard Egyptians as anti-Semitic?

SOURCE H

Excerpt from an interview with Nasser, February 1969, quoted in *Nasser* by Jean Lacouture, published by Secker & Warburg, UK, 1973, p. 365.

The Jews are our cousins. Moses was born in Egypt. The Israelis say that we are anti-Semitic, which is absurd. We are Semites ourselves and we consider the Jews of our country to be Egyptians.

However, this apparent generosity of spirit did break down in times of crisis. For example, it did not prevent Nasser from ordering the imprisonment of 500 innocent Egyptian Jews in an act of retaliation after the Six-Day War in 1967 (see page 186).

Nasserism as an ideology

> **Did Nasser's ideas amount to a political ideology?**

KEY TERM

Pan-Arabism A transnational movement for the unification of the Arab peoples in order to pursue their common interests and improve their conditions.

Historians of modern Egypt tend to agree that Nasser did not develop a political philosophy or ideology. He had ideas, of course, and justifications for the measures he took, but, apart from his one book, *The Philosophy of Revolution*, Nasser did not produce a substantial set of theories. For Nasser, Egyptian nationalism and **Pan-Arabism** were self-evident values. The task was not to theorize but to act.

Reaction to Zionism

There is no doubting the sincerity of Nasser's distaste for Zionism. Yet Zionism was also important to him politically. He used anti-Zionism as a powerful rallying call in Egypt. As long as Israel was the main political and very visible sign of Arab subjection, then he could always refer to the need for Egyptians and Arabs to unite in the struggle against the great affront to Egyptian and Arab pride – the existence of the state of Israel.

Reaction to colonialism

Similarly, Nasser could refer to the old colonial past, the colonialism of Britain in particular and of the West generally, in creating the Egypt that he had inherited. He could claim that the problems that Egypt faced were not primarily of Egyptian making, that they were the legacy of colonialism. While this elicited a powerful emotional response in the Egyptian people, it did not amount to an easily defined philosophy or ideology. It was in essence a set of reactions against the problems that confronted Egypt. It was Nasser himself, his character and his personality, that gave definition to what is sometimes called Nasserism.

The Suez Crisis, 1956

It was Nasser's repeated claim that, in spite of the seemingly harsh means that sometimes accompanied its imposition, his rule took its legitimacy from the support of the people. At no stage was that support more genuine and intense than at the time of the Suez Crisis. This central episode in his leadership brought Nasser to the brink of disaster, but ended by giving him his greatest triumph and elevating him to hero status in Egypt and winning him the admiration of the Arab world.

Despite his earlier struggle against Britain, Nasser had developed relatively harmonious relations with the UK since the 1952 revolution, as the Anglo-Egyptian agreement of 1954 indicated. Of especial significance was that he had been promised US and British loans for the construction of **the Aswan High Dam** on the upper Nile, a project on which he had staked his own and Egypt's future. However, when the Western powers learned that Nasser had also approached the Soviet bloc countries for aid, they suspended their original offer. Facing political and economic ruin if the Dam were not completed, Nasser used the only means left to him for raising the necessary finance: he nationalized the Suez Canal.

The nationalization of the Suez Canal

In July 1956, to massive popular acclaim in Egypt, he announced that Egypt was taking over the Canal Company and all its assets. In addition, foreign ships would have to pay to pass through what was now an Egyptian waterway. The fees raised by this would go not to the Company shareholders but directly to the Egyptian government to pay for the Aswan Dam's construction.

Nasser had four main motives in seizing the Canal, which were to:

- acquire desperately needed finance
- inspire the Egyptian people
- impress the Arab world
- strike at European **neo-colonialism**.

The British Prime Minister Anthony Eden regarded Nasser as a 'Middle-Eastern Hitler'. Such a man, he said, must not be allowed 'to leave his thumb on Britain's windpipe', a reference to the threat to the essential oil supplies that came to Britain from the **Middle East** through the Canal. He began to plan ways to bring Nasser down. The French, long resentful of Egypt's support of Arab nationalists in **French Algeria**, were very willing to join the British in opposing Nasser. Eden had been led to believe that the USA would give at least moral backing to Anglo-French attempts to free the Canal and the USA did, indeed, join Britain and France in seeking to put pressure on Egypt by the creation of a Canal Users' Association.

What impact did the Suez affair have on Nasser's leadership?

KEY TERM

The Aswan High Dam A vast construction intended to modernize Egypt by preventing the recurrent, destructive Nile floods and by providing a limitless supply of hydro-electric power.

Neo-colonialism An attempt by the former colonial powers to re-impose their control on their previous possessions.

Middle East Never an exact term, it includes such countries as Libya, Egypt, Turkey, Israel, Palestine, Syria, Jordan, Saudi Arabia, Iraq and Iran. Objections are sometimes raised to the use of the term on the grounds that it perpetuates the language of colonialism.

French Algeria Algeria, part of the French empire, had a large Muslim population, most of whom supported the Algerian independence movement. French forces became involved in a bitter struggle against Algerian nationalists (1954–62).

SOURCE I

Nasser waves to the crowds in Alexandria after announcing the nationalization of the Suez Canal.

Nasser, however, despite the international line-up against him, refused to budge. In truth, he could do little else, short of climbing down and destroying his leadership. Britain and France then referred the issue to the **UN Security Council**. This proved fruitless, since the Soviet Union used its **veto** to block proposals in the Council to have Egypt condemned internationally.

The invasion of Egypt, 1956

Eden's failure to gain UN support confirmed him in his belief that only force could shift Nasser. He began secret discussions with the French and the Israelis, who were eager to launch a major strike against Egypt. Plans were prepared for a combined military invasion of Egypt. The strategy, finalized in mid-October 1956, was that the Israelis would attack Egypt across Sinai. Britain and France, after allowing sufficient time for the Israelis to reach the Canal, would then mount a joint assault on the Canal region from the north, under the pretence of forcing Egypt and Israel to observe a cease-fire. On

29 October, the Israelis duly attacked across the Gaza Strip; on 30 October the Anglo-French ultimatum was delivered and on the following day the two European allies began their invasion of Egypt.

On the eve of the attack, Nasser said 'I do not intend to fight them. I intend to stand back and wait for world opinion to save me.' This policy of inaction was the only option open to him. Militarily, Egypt had no chance of surviving the tripartite attack had it been sustained as originally planned. As Nasser knew, his country did not have the means to resist and there were no significant moves in the Arab states to come to Egypt's aid. As it happened, it was indeed world opinion, or at least the opinion of the superpowers, that saved Egypt and Nasser.

SOURCE J

Map of the Suez invasion, 1956.

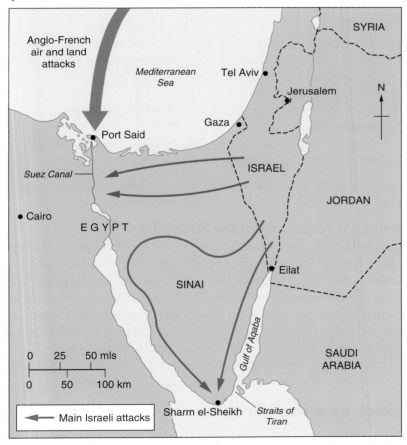

What information is conveyed by Source J about the tripartite attack upon Egypt in the Suez Crisis of 1956?

The UN's response

The United Nations hurriedly called an emergency debate in which the US government, infuriated by Eden's failure to inform them of the intended invasion, led the condemnation of Israel and her two allies. Deprived of US backing, Britain used its veto for the first time to defeat a UN resolution demanding an immediate cease-fire. Besides resentment at not being previously informed of Britain's intentions, what angered the USA was the fear that Eden's actions would allow the Soviet Union to seize the initiative. And, indeed, after some days' delay while it dealt with **the Hungarian Uprising**, the Soviet Union made a dramatic move. On 5 November, it issued a diplomatic note to Britain, condemning the Anglo-French invasion of Egypt and warning that the USSR was prepared to use nuclear missiles against the cities of the Western invaders.

It is unlikely that the USSR would have risked carrying out its threat, but it was one of a number of considerations that combined to break Eden's resolve, namely:

- the opposition of the USA, which feared the tripartite attack would allow the USSR to exploit the situation to gain influence in the Middle East
- UN condemnation of the action
- deep divisions within Britain over it
- opposition to it from the majority of members of the **British Commonwealth**
- a devastating withdrawal of their British funds by foreign investors, which threatened to leave Britain bankrupt.

Faced with such factors, Britain accepted the UN demand for disengagement and Israel, France and Britain began withdrawing their invading forces.

Benefits for Nasser from the Suez affair

If Nasser's decision not to fight had been a gamble, it was one that brought him huge returns. Eden's decision to personalize the Suez Crisis had a remarkable unintended result for Nasser. Eden had stated 'Our quarrel is not with Egypt – still less with the Arab world; it is with Colonel Nasser.' In saying that and then losing the war, Eden made Egypt's survival a great personal victory for Nasser. Disregarding how close they had been to defeat, Egyptians hailed their leader as the man who had successfully defied Western imperialism and repulsed Zionism. What was seen as his victory over neo-colonialism meant that his reputation also soared in the Arab world.

Nasser as a Pan-Arabist

Nasser's outstanding personal success in the Suez Crisis encouraged him in his long-held ambition to become leader of Pan-Arabism. His aim was two-fold: to strengthen his position at home and to achieve Arab unity under Egypt's guidance. In pursuit of this policy Nasser travelled widely in the Middle East and became diplomatically involved in the affairs of many of

In what ways was Nasser's adoption of Pan-Arabism an extension of his ambitions as Egyptian leader?

the Arab nations. In all this activity, there were three key episodes which helped both to define his policy and explain why it ultimately failed:

- the formation of the United Arab Republic (UAR), 1958–62
- the war in Yemen, 1962–67
- the Six-Day War, 1967.

The formation of the UAR, 1958–62

What seemed to be an important step towards the furthering of Nasser's Pan-Arabism was the formation in 1958 of the United Arab Republic (UAR), based on these terms:

- Egypt and Syria would merge as one nation
- Egypt would form the 'Southern province', Syria the 'Northern province'
- Nasser was recognized as Head of State
- Egypt would control the joint military forces.

The appearance of genuine union proved deceptive. From the beginning, Syria chafed at not being treated as a true equal; its officials were denied positions of importance in government and Egypt took precedence in decision-making. Syrians began to regret forfeiting their independence by, in effect, subordinating themselves to Nasser and Egypt. The result was that in 1962, Syria unilaterally declared that it was withdrawing from the UAR. There were fears that Nasser would use the Egyptian army to prevent Syrian secession. He seems to have considered such a move, but decided eventually that the sight of Egypt's forcibly imposing itself on another Arab state would seriously undermine his advocacy of Pan-Arabism. He publicly accepted Syria's withdrawal and acknowledged that mistakes had been made.

The war in Yemen, 1962–67

It was in part to redeem the prestige lost over the UAR debacle, that Nasser became entangled in the affairs of Yemen. In 1962, rebels in Yemen sought to overthrow the monarchy there and set up a republic. The pro-monarchists resisted fiercely and a bitter civil war ensued. On the principle of supporting Arab nationalist movements against reactionary forces and seeking to restore his waning reputation in the Arab world with a quick, decisive victory, Nasser committed Egypt to the rebels' cause.

It proved a bitter experience: the struggle lasted from 1962 to 1967, involving at any one time between a third and a half of Egypt's armed forces and costing the lives of large numbers of Egyptian soldiers. The expensive intervention ended in failure in 1967 when Nasser, accepting that the monarchists were too strong to be defeated, dejectedly withdrew his forces. Jordan and Saudi Arabia, both of them monarchies, had opposed what they regarded as a Yemeni rebellion not a nationalist movement. They considered that Egypt's intervention had provoked a civil war in the Arab world.

Egypt's involvement in Yemen has been described as 'Nasser's **Vietnam War**'. His backing of the Yemeni rebels had certainly damaged Egypt's and his own standing. It had:

- undermined the Arab unity he was committed to achieving
- pre-occupied the Egyptian army for five years
- diverted money and resources from vital domestic projects
- weakened the army by using up military resources, thus making it less capable of fighting the Israelis in the imminent Six-Day War.

The Six-Day War, 1967

Nasser did not plan the specific war which broke out in June 1967, but, from 1956 on, he expected another war with Israel at some point. His Pan-Arab diplomacy and his build up of the Egyptian army were based on the assumption that another major conflict with Israel was inevitable. He also believed that there were three key factors on his side:

- The USSR would back Egypt in any war with Israel.
- The USA would prevent Israel from attacking Egypt.
- The Egyptian army would be ready for war with Israel.

He was to be proved wrong on all three counts. With a disregard for Cold War alignments and diplomatic conventions, Israel seized the initiative in June 1967. Asserting that an Egyptian blockade of the **Straits of Tiran** (see Source K), Egyptian army manoeuvres in Sinai, and a recent military pact between Nasser and King Hussein of Jordan were evidence of an intended joint Arab attack, the Israelis claimed they had to strike pre-emptively. This was their justification for launching well prepared assaults on various Arab positions. Within three hours, Israeli aircraft had attacked Egyptian airfields and practically destroyed the whole of Nasser's air force while it was still on the ground. Syria and Jordan also suffered crippling Israeli ground and air attacks. Within six days the Israelis had achieved overwhelming success; the combined Egyptian, Jordanian, Iraqi and Syrian forces had been defeated. As in 1948–49, lack of effective liaison between the Arab commands, inferior equipment, and strategic naivety had made the task easier. Israel now had control of these vital areas:

- the Sinai peninsula and the Gaza strip, taken from Egypt
- East Jerusalem and the West Bank, taken from Jordan
- the Golan Heights, taken from Syria.

The humiliation for Nasser could not have been greater. It was a disaster from which he never fully recovered. Always contingent upon his being able to guide the Arabs to victory over Israel, his reputation as the great Pan-Arabist was now shredded. The respect and gratitude of the masses for what

SOURCE K

Map showing the aftermath of the Six-Day War.

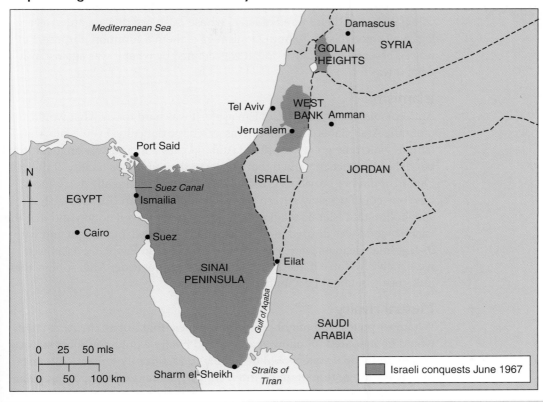

Israeli conquests June 1967

he had previously done to raise Arab consciousness and self-esteem did not entirely evaporate, but his leadership was now compromised.

Nasser's difficulties as a Pan-Arabist

An unremitting problem for Nasser in his attempt to lead a Pan-Arab movement, which his 1956 Suez victory had done so much to promote, was the basic fact of disunity between the Arab states. The Syrian episode had illustrated this. It should be mentioned here that the word 'Arab' is a very loose term. It is the equivalent of saying 'European'; it encompasses a wide range of ethnicities, nations, cultures and languages. When considering the Arab world, disparity is as important a factor as similarity. Indeed, the term 'Arab world' has its own problem. In journalistic shorthand, it is often used as a synonym for the Middle East. Both terms are imprecise, and they certainly do not equate. The striking example is Iran whose people are not Arabic but Persian. It is a particular irony that as a Semitic people the Jews of Israel were ethnically closer to some of their Arab enemies than those enemies were to each other. It is also notable that many Egyptians did not think of themselves as Arabs, but as a wholly separate group identified by their unique culture and history.

What does Source K indicate about the scale of Israeli success in the Six-Day War?

What factors
undermined Nasser's
chances of achieving
Arab unity?

→ Arab disunity

The only sure bond between the Arab states was their rejection of Western colonialism and their hatred of Israel whose existence they regarded as a legacy of colonialist rule. Anti-Zionism gave them a common purpose, but it was an essentially negative one; it was defined by what it was against, not what it was for.

Islamism

Anti-colonialism and anti-Zionism aside, it was hard to say what would unite the Arab states. Therein lay Nasser's basic difficulty. Even Islam, the faith to which the great majority of Arab peoples adhered, was an insufficient bond. Nasser once remarked that whatever the numinous quality of the Qur'an, it did not provide a practical guide to politics; 'I really don't know how one could possibly govern according to the Qur'an.' Experience had shown him that Islamic religious identity was not a fixed notion and that the Islamic world was divided in terms of what it believed and taught and who its legitimate leaders were. He judged that, just as in Egypt, the Islamists were a divisive force if left unchecked, so too, in the wider Arab sphere, their influence would not be a unifying one.

Mutual rivalry

Whatever policies he might promote, he knew that not all the Arab states would be prepared to follow. Jealousy and rivalry would doubtless surface and no individual state would be willing to sacrifice its separate interests merely for the notion of unity. Interestingly, Nasser was far more popular with the ordinary people of the Arab states than he was with their leaders. This was why his relations with the key Arab states of Jordan, Saudi Arabia, Iraq and Lebanon were never smooth. There was a feeling among the leaders of those countries, particularly in Iraq and Jordan, that Nasser's brand of Pan-Arabism was really a cover for a form of Egyptian imperialism.

The Israeli question

The issue that ultimately determined the success or failure of Nasser's foreign policies was Israel. For as long as he was seen as the great Pan-Arabist standing up to the Western powers, which were still trying to assert their old colonialism, the Arab nations lauded him as their champion. But the greatest test would be whether he could successfully resolve the issue of Israel. That was the question on which his ambition to lead the Arab world rested. To Arab nationalists the state of Israel, the creation of Western intrigue, was an open wound which would be healed only when Israel ceased to exist. Conscious of this, Nasser between 1956 and 1967 promoted or supported a range of Arab anti-Israeli movements, the most significant of which was the **PLO**.

KEY TERM

PLO Palestinian Liberation Organization, formed in 1964 under Egyptian auspices and pledged to 'prohibit the existence of Zionism' through the use of terror tactics against Israeli targets.

Anthony Nutting regarded Nasser's misunderstanding of the true nature of the esteem he gained in the larger Arab world as the explanation for his failure to fulfil his dream of leading a Pan-Arab movement. Misreading the tumultuous welcome he received from the people on his visits to other Arab states, he did not grasp that the leaders of those states had no wish to subordinate themselves to his leadership. They lionized him as a potent symbol of Arab nationalism, anti-colonialism and anti-Zionism, but they had no intention of letting Egypt control them.

SOURCE L

Excerpt from *Nasser* by Anthony Nutting, published by Constable, UK, 1972, p. 479.

*Used to handling his own relatively docile subjects, he failed to see that, with their different backgrounds, even those Arabs who shared his ideological leanings – such as the Syrian **Baathists** – were bound to resent being dictated to by Cairo. He did not realize until it was too late that his initial success in spreading the message of Arab nationalism had been achieved by example rather than pressure. And when he sought to exploit these early achievements he found he had grossly overestimated his capacity to impose Egypt's leadership upon the rest of the Arab world.*

> According to Nutting in Source L, why had Nasser's Pan-Arab policy not been a success?

> **KEY TERM**
>
> **Baathists** Members of a Pan-Arab socialist party which was particularly strong in Syria and Iraq.

Nasser's miscalculations led to the failure of his policies towards Syria, Iraq and Jordan, where his intelligence forces were unable to exploit the situation to Egypt's advantage. Nutting saw this as the explanation for his lack of success in the 1960s and his declining influence on the course of Arab affairs. Nasser once described his policy as leader of Egypt as three intersecting circles: Arab, Islamic and African. But in the event his enforced pre-occupation with Arab problems and the opposition he encountered from Islamic forces within Egypt left him little opportunity to engage in African affairs. His dream of Egypt's leading some form of pan-African movement remained but a dream.

Nasser's decline

> What issues dominated Nasser's last years?

Acknowledging the disaster that defeat in the Six-Day War in June 1967 had been, Nasser immediately resigned the presidency. In a resignation speech broadcast on radio, he told the Egyptian people that he accepted 'the whole responsibility' for the failure. The response was a mass outpouring of affection and support for him. Cairo was brought to a standstill as millions filled the streets and squares, shouting Nasser's name. The scene was captured by a French correspondent for the French newspaper, *Le Monde* (see Source M, page 190).

According to Source M, what is the nature of Nasser's relationship with the Egyptian people?

SOURCE M

Excerpt from a statement by Eric Rouleau, 9 June 1967, quoted in Raymond Flower, *Napoleon to Nasser: The Story of Modern Egypt*, published by AuthorHouse, UK, 2002, p. 220.

I've never seen a whole people plunged into mourning like this and crying in anguish as they did. The answer was given to me by one of them who in the morning wanted Nasser out, and in the evening was shouting for him to stay: 'For us Nasser is a sort of father. One can be angry with one's father and criticise him, but one doesn't want him to go. I felt lost without him.'

Faced with such adulation, Nasser agreed after only one day to withdraw his resignation and continue as president. However, his last three years were very much a post-script. Depressed by the outcome of the Six-Day War and physically ailing, he was no longer the dominant figure he had been. He continued to tour Arab countries where he was invariably well received, but although he still preached the need for unity his message concerning Israel was much less openly belligerent. He advised against trying to resolve the Palestine question by direct conflict with the Israelis and hinted that attrition was the more realistic approach. This led to his accepting the **Rogers Plan**. But basically Nasser still believed that military conflict with Israel was ultimately unavoidable: 'We are all aware that Israel does not want peace. War is inherent in the construction of Israel itself. It is part of its plans and policy.'

In Egypt in 1968, disturbed by demonstrations demanding greater democracy, Nasser continued to back the use of force to repress dissident elements, but he also made concessions to assuage public anger. In a form of apology for the recent military defeat, high-ranking officers were put on trial. A 'March 30 Manifesto' was introduced in 1968, promising further political reforms. These, however, remained promises rather than actions; at his death in 1970, the authoritarian nature of the regime of Gamal Abdel Nasser remained intact.

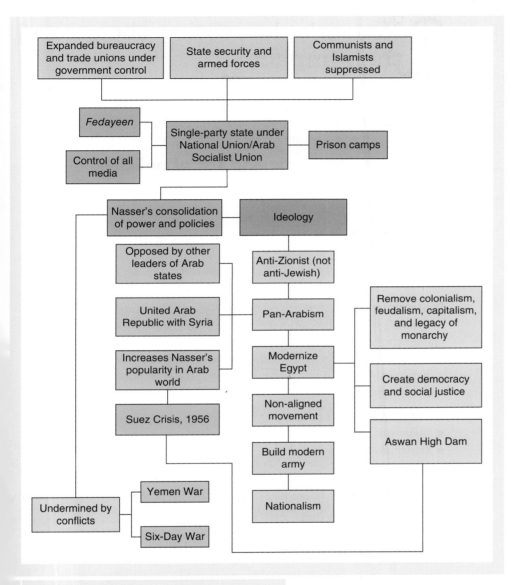

Nasser's domestic policies and their impact

> **Key question:** *What impact did Nasser's rule have on the lives of the Egyptian people?*

How successful were the economic and social policies followed by Nasser?

Nasser's economic and social policies

Considered as an economic programme, Nasserism had four essential aspects:

- nationalization
- agrarian reform
- industrialization
- finance.

Nationalization

In keeping with his proclaimed objective of following a socialist approach, Nasser considerably increased the role of the state in economic planning. Prior to his taking power in 1954, state ownership had been limited to railways, irrigation and oil refining. By 1967, the enterprises under state control included:

- banks and finance houses
- insurance companies
- transport
- hotels
- large shopping stores
- the press
- the export–import trade.

In addition, following the seizure of the Suez Canal Company in 1956, Nasser took over British and French commercial properties and extended the expropriations to include the holdings of a number of foreign companies and concerns.

Agrarian reform

During Nasser's lifetime, Egypt's population rose from 23 to 33 million. Since Egypt was overwhelmingly a rural society, agriculture was the basic form of economic activity. Barely 20 per cent of the people lived or worked in urban areas. Agriculture policy was, therefore, a vital part of economic planning. A number of key agricultural measures were introduced:

- To redress the imbalance on the land where 75 per cent of the land was owned by only 6 per cent of the landowners, a limit of 200 *feddans* was placed on the amount of land an individual could legally hold. This was later reduced to 100 *feddans*.

- Land was redistributed to encourage smaller landowners. As a result 320,000 *feddans* had been reallocated to the peasants by 1961.
- Rents were reduced and frozen.
- The wages of agricultural labourers were raised.
- Taxes were lowered to reward efficient farmers.

The land reforms Nasser introduced, although criticized by some for not going far enough, were important measures. Poverty was significantly reduced under him. Farming also became more efficient in some areas, a critical development since Nasser wanted food to be produced not simply to feed the people but to create a surplus that could be sold to acquire foreign capital.

Industrialization

Appreciating that no nation can modernize without having a strong productive base, Nasser's major objective was to achieve industrial growth. If industry could be made more productive, this would address a besetting weakness – Egypt's trade imbalance. The country imported too much and exported too little. If that gap could be reduced or even reversed through Egypt's becoming more self-sufficient, then the capital that was saved could be invested in industrial expansion. Major changes on the industrial front were made in an effort to achieve this:

- Industrial corporations were nationalized with the aim of making them more responsive to national needs. Their profits would be used both to redistribute wealth and provide capital for government projects.
- Two thousand new factories were built in Egypt in Nasser's time.
- A government Economic Agency was formed in 1957 to implement and monitor industrial growth plans.

The Aswan High Dam

All the schemes that were devised were dependent on one economic essential: the availability of energy supplies. The generation of electricity was central to Nasser's **modernization** plans. This was why the Aswan High Dam loomed so large in government thinking and propaganda. It was intended to provide electricity for large areas of Egypt and so be a major industrial stimulus. However, although the physical construction of the Dam was in itself a major achievement that symbolized Egypt's bid for modernity, the Aswan High Dam as an economic venture delivered less than it promised. By the time of Nasser's death in 1970, it had not met the economic and social expectations that accompanied its construction.

> The original hope had been that the disruption caused by the need to relocate hundreds of thousands of people, mainly **Nubians**, would be offset by the Dam's effect in bringing over a million *feddans* into cultivation. In the event, barely half that amount of land became available for farming and the displaced Nubians were left impoverished. Instead of producing the expected 10 million **kWh** of electricity each year, only 7 million were generated.

 **KEY TERM**

Modernization The movement of a nation from a rural, agricultural society to an urban, industrial one.

Nubians A group of people living in southern Egypt and northern Sudan with a distinct culture, language and history.

kWh Kilowatt hours, the main measurement of electrical output.

- The estimate that some 4,000 Egyptian villages would be electrified by the end of the 1960s proved seriously inaccurate. Barely half that figure was reached.
- The ability to complete the Dam's construction by 1969 depended in the end on borrowing heavily from the USSR, Western bankers and governments being unwilling to loan to Egypt following its earlier seizure of foreign assets.

'The Aswan Dam is no more than a monument to Nasser's autocracy and megalomania … it pawned Egypt's resources to the Soviet Union.' This verdict by political scientist P.J. Vatikiotis may be harsh, but it was certainly true that Nasser, in his determination to break free from Western capitalist domination, had put Egypt at the financial mercy of the Soviet Union. Aware that after its defeat by Israel in 1967, Egypt would need to make up the heavy losses in arms and equipment it had suffered, the Soviet Union struck a hard bargain: it demanded that in return for Soviet supplies Egypt had to sell its cotton crop at a low, fixed, non-negotiable price to the USSR for the next five years.

Finance

In regard to finance, Nasser operated what was essentially a closed system. Since there was no outside scrutiny, his government was not accountable. Nevertheless, it is now known from Egyptian and Western sources that during the period 1952–66, Egypt received the following amounts:

- $1.335 billion from the Soviet bloc for the construction of the Aswan Dam and for industrial development
- $400 million from the Western countries for industrial projects
- over $4 billion was raised from the seizure of foreign assets.

In the same period the Egyptian government claimed to have spent $6 billion in the public sector developing Egypt's infrastructure. But while there were spectacular signs of investment, as in the construction of transport systems, these did not explain the gap between the large amounts the government received and the relatively small amounts it spent. This led some observers to suggest that the money not accounted for had been used corruptly by Nasser's government as bribes to buy political support.

Economic changes

Nasser's Egypt saw undoubted economic improvement. As a result of land reform and other economic measures, agricultural and industrial production rose. An important shift occurred in the pattern of Egypt's exports. Traditionally, Egypt's foreign exports had been dominated by cotton. During Nasser's time such exports dropped by 50 per cent, but this was partly compensated for by an increase in the sale abroad of industrial manufactures. Of equal significance was the number of Egyptians who went as oil workers to neighbouring Arab countries. Since these countries, as well as paying the guest workers directly, also paid Nasser's government for the privilege, this provided a substantial income for Egypt. By 1970 there were over 3 million such workers, based mainly in the Arabian Peninsula.

Positive aspects

Despite the disappointments attaching to such developments as the Aswan High Dam, millions of Egyptians did experience a significant increase in the quality of their living and working conditions. By 1970, Egypt could boast a **GNP** growth rate of over 4 per cent, which, according to World Bank figures, was well above the international average. Among the major benefits for the Egyptian people were:

- A growing number of schools and universities were built or improved.
- The number of children attending school in Egypt quadrupled during Nasser's regime.
- Modern science, which included the teaching of evolution, was developed as a subject in schools and universities.
- Housing developments were planned in the major cities.
- Clean water was provided in many areas.
- New or improved hospitals and clinics were developed.

Negative aspects

The achievement of economic growth was impressive, but there were negative consequences and it is debatable whether the economic gains offset the failure to advance the political and social freedoms that the regime had initially promised. Nasser's government fell short of developing Egypt as an ordered, civil society:

- Debt increased, making Egypt heavily dependent on the Soviet Union.
- The expanding state bureaucracy resulted in a costly public sector wage bill.
- Corruption became endemic in the state institutions.
- **Patronage** and **nepotism** continued to operate as they had before the revolution.
- Poor financial management resulted in the state incurring large losses.
- Military costs remained high as a result of the Yemen and the Six-Day Wars.
- Government controls restricted private enterprise and investment.
- Population increase intensified overcrowding in the urban areas.
- To meet the food demands of a growing population, Egypt became heavily dependent on the importing of foreign grain.
- Authoritarianism was enforced through the mechanisms of the police state.

The National Charter, 1962

In 1962, Nasser introduced a National Charter (constitution), which he claimed as a major reorganization of Egypt's political and economic structures in response to the popular will. Among its provisions were the following:

- To emphasize that Egypt was based on socialist principles, the National Union Party was replaced with the Arab Socialist Union (ASU). The ASU was opened to all members of society and thus became a mass party. An elected National Assembly was established to provide representative government. Youth groups were extended to provide sporting and cultural activities to a wider range of young people.

> **KEY TERM**
>
> **GNP** Gross National Product, the annual total value of goods and services produced by a country at home, added to the profits from its export trade.
>
> **Patronage** Providing government approval and support and extending privileges to selected individuals and groups.
>
> **Nepotism** The granting of positions and privileges to family members or close associates.

> ← **How far did the Charter address the needs of the Egyptian people?**

Agricultural co-operatives The pooling of local resources and farming for shared profits.

Jihad An Islamic term meaning a committed struggle of believers against unbelievers.

Jahiliyya A state that has rejected Allah.

- **Agricultural co-operatives** were started in the localities.
- Universal health care was introduced.
- Houses and schools for the poor were constructed.
- The Suez Canal was widened to take the largest oil tankers and thus increase revenue.
- Measures to limit the growth of bureaucracy were adopted.

Political implications

Although celebrated by Nasser and his supporters, the Charter was simply a merging of various piecemeal measures introduced earlier. The notion that it was a major extension of democracy was belied by the fact that Nasser's party, the National Union, albeit under the new name ASU, remained the only party legally allowed to operate. The single-party system was to continue as Egypt's political structure. No known opponent was ever allowed to become a member of the National Assembly. The clearest evidence that the Charter was little more than propaganda was the severe political oppression that accompanied its introduction. Muslim fundamentalists were again the major victims of a clampdown in 1962, with thousands being arrested.

Nasser's most courageous and persistent opponent was the Muslim Brotherhood's chief spokesman, Sayyid Qutb. Despite being frequently imprisoned, Qutb continued for a decade after 1956 to attack Nasser and his policies. Nasser's patience finally ran out in 1966 when Qutb published a book calling for a *jihad* against the Egyptian state, which he condemned as a *jahiliyya*. On Nasser's instruction, Qutb was tried for conspiracy and treason and then executed. It has been suggested that the judicial killing of Sayyid Qutb marked Nasser's final victory over the extreme religious right.

> In what areas did conditions improve for Egyptian women?

The status of women

Nasser made it one of his declared aims to advance female emancipation, remarking, 'Woman must be regarded as equal to man and she must shed the remaining shackles that impede her freedom of movement, so that she can play a constructive and vital part in shaping Egyptian society.' His approach angered the Muslim Brotherhood which condemned such moves as un-Islamic. This was one of the issues in his continual struggle with the movement. As a devout Muslim himself, he rejected their claim to speak for Islam. As part of his clampdown on the Brotherhood, he insisted that the religious courts be brought under the jurisdiction and authority of the secular courts. This gave him the leverage to introduce such measures as:

- the compulsory schooling of all Egyptian children, girls and boys
- the modernizing of divorce laws so that wives had equal rights with husbands to separation
- the introduction of family planning services to limit the number of children to those a family could financially support
- granting women the right not to have to wear the veil in public
- denying religious authorities the power to censor films and television programmes.

Conclusion

With all its failings, Egypt under Nasser was the most advanced of all the Arab states in terms of technology and social improvement. Yet despite this apparent advance, a contemporary Egyptian account, written in 1963, argued that Nasser's regime had not succeeded in addressing the issue which had been one of its central revolutionary aims – the improvement of the lot of the ordinary Egyptian: 'Egypt's human resources have been hardly tapped relative to those not only of advanced, but even of comparatively backward countries.'

← **How far had Nasser's regime improved the conditions of ordinary Egyptians?**

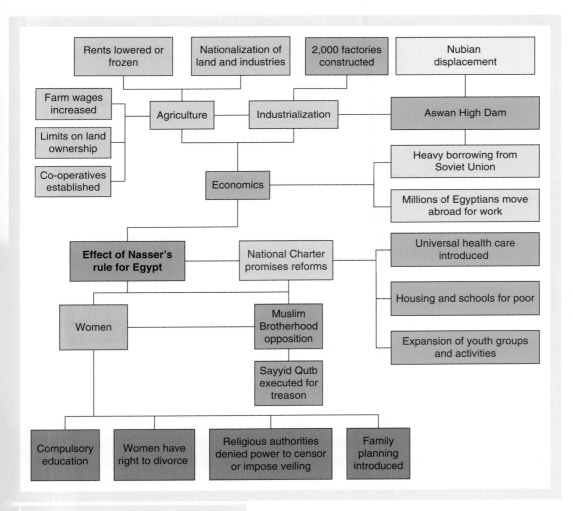

SUMMARY DIAGRAM

Nasser's domestic policies and their impact

▶ **Key question:** *How far did Nasser achieve a totalitarian state?*

An English historian makes a strong case for describing Nasser's regime as totalitarian. Raymond Flower writes of Nasser:

SOURCE N

? According to the author of Source N, what evidence is there to suggest that Nasser's regime was totalitarian?

Excerpt from *Napoleon to Nasser: The Story of Modern Egypt*, by Raymond Flower, published by AuthorHouse, UK, 2002, p. 202.

He had all the reins of government in his power and his snake-like gaze seemed to take in everything that was going on down to the most trivial detail. If some one applied for an exit permit to leave the country his approval had to be sought. If an import permit was given, Gamal Abdel Nasser had vetted it first. All promotions and appointments were decided by him. He alone knew the ramifications of the three separate secret intelligence systems dealing with espionage and counter-espionage inside the country and abroad, each of which had an order to keep a close check on each other's activities.

How did Nasser broaden the basis of his support?

The base of Nasser's power

Flower's obvious exaggeration of Nasser's powers of surveillance is intended to emphasize the range of state control exercised by his regime. The Egyptian scholar Tawfiq al-Hakim does not directly challenge this, but points to the way in which the governing and political class broadened its composition as a consequence of Nasser's domestic policies. This did not lessen Nasser's authority but it showed that he was prepared to give it a wider base. People who had been excluded before 1952 now took a role, sometimes of particular significance, in the new regime. This expansion has sometimes been defined as an aspect of 'Nasserism' insofar as government under Nasser can be thought of as introducing a specific system identified with him.

How did Nasser exercise secret government?

Secret government

Louis Awad, another Egyptian scholar, accepts that there was a broadening of the administrative system but argues that this was essentially an increase in numbers of personnel rather than a widening of its class intake. He suggests that the changes were in fact a means of consolidating Nasser's power since they involved collusion between the new government and the pre-revolution social elites who saw the opportunity to maintain their privileges by committing themselves completely to the new regime. Awad sees this as a reason why opposition to Nasser was so muted, describing Nasser's technique as the exercise of 'secret government'. He is also critical of Nasser's claim, used to justify continued repression, that his was the only viable or legitimate government available to Egypt in the circumstances.

Awad contends that this was Nasser's excuse for imposing an autocratic, one-party system. There were alternatives, but Nasser declined to pursue them: 'All of Nasser's career was in the context of destroying this or that, not in creating something.'

Control from the centre

Awad develops his case by stressing that even when the two major enemies Nasser had identified, the monarchy and the old land-owning elite, had been removed he still maintained the autocratic regime. Moreover, because Nasser ran a closed system, his government was not accountable and this is particularly evident in regard to finance. The conclusion that Awad draws from all this is that, despite its original claims, the Nasser government did not introduce socialism into Egypt, but rather a form of state-directed economic planning, which was control from the centre, rather than control from below with a redistribution of resources to Egyptian people.

Awad goes on to suggest that Nasser's embracing of Pan-Arabism was a form of compensation. Unable to satisfy the expectations he had helped to arouse in the Egyptian people, he covered this by extending his mission to include the Arab world itself.

> **How far did Nasser adopt socialism?**

A hierarchic society

Fuad Zakaryya, another Arab scholar, takes the view that, notwithstanding Nasser's wish to introduce equality into Egypt, in practice very little was done to improve the lot of the lower orders in Egyptian society. Instead there was an increase in the privileged classes' hold on society: 'The net practical result was an increase in the number of masters.' Zakaryya suggests that society under Nasser, rather than being more egalitarian, became more hierarchic and structured. The intended spread of power downwards did not occur and the privileged elites became more entrenched in their positions. The state was not accountable to the people and there was no popular control over the government. The three main organs of Nasser's state – the bureaucracy, the army and the secret police – dictated the character of that society and so the claim to egalitarianism is unfounded.

> **How far was authority distributed under Nasser?**

Corruption

Zakaryya goes on to highlight the corruption that came to characterize Nasser's system of rule. It was this that prevented the revolution from being a truly liberating experience for ordinary Egyptians. Once people in the administration were allowed to make money out of the new system, the idealism with which they had entered the revolution quickly dissipated and the interests of the people were neglected. It is true that there were occasional campaigns against corruption, an example being the trials of military leaders after the Six-Day War, but by then corruption had become endemic.

One of the best informed studies of Nasser's Egypt was made by Anthony Nutting, a British minister who came to know Nasser personally. Nutting, after initially hoping that Nasser would use his power to lead Egypt along a more democratic path, grew disillusioned with what the regime had done. Nutting's regret was that the gains made by Nasser on the industrial and social front were not repeated in the political field. Egypt under Nasser became a military dictatorship organized around a bloated and corrupt bureaucracy.

Nutting adds, however, that the responsibility for the way conditions had developed in Egypt went beyond Nasser. Stressing the importance of considering basic Egyptian attitudes, Nutting suggests that veneration of the strong leader was an ingrained practice among the people. The Egyptian populace had, as was their tradition with leaders from time immemorial, deified Nasser. If, therefore, he responded more as a **Pharaoh** of old than as a constitutional ruler of the twentieth century, they were as much to blame as he was.

This is a view supported by Said Aburish, who regards Nasser as an 'odd type of dictator', explaining that Nasser 'manifested a need to be loved, or followed because he was loved, which most dictators do not have. His dictatorial ways were a mixture of **populism** and a need to be accepted as a man of principle'. Like Nutting, Aburish refers to the way in which the political tradition among Egyptian people made them complicit in the imposition of dictatorship over them. 'The problem was not in the spread of oppression and privileged exceptions, but in the fact that the Egyptians became used to them to the point that they considered them as normal.'

The role of failure in Nasser's bid for power

Aburish makes the further striking suggestion that Nasser was not an authoritarian by nature and was not turned into one by the exercise of power. The key to understanding Nasser's rule, Aburish argues, is failure. Nasser would have loved to have governed by popular consent, but having failed in his over-ambitious aims he was reduced to exerting dictatorial control. 'He failed in Egypt. He failed in the Arab world. He failed in his confrontation with Israel. He failed in building institutions that would outlast him. Eventually he became a petty dictator.'

Nasser's popularity

A British commentator on modern Egypt, Anne Alexander, speaks of Nasser's '**metaphysical union**' with the Egyptian people, and it is certainly true that, for all Nasser's authoritarianism, the great majority of Egyptians felt great warmth towards him. Sceptics might say this was the result of his very efficient propaganda machine, his image appearing everywhere in newspapers and on billboards and TV screens, but the affection was genuine

Tawfiq al-Hakim commented: 'Nasser became the First man in the country, loved by everyone. When the masses love, they do not question or discuss. There was nothing else but to believe and applaud him.'

Pointing to the darker side of this, al-Hakim observed: 'The beloved ruler became accustomed to unquestioned rule until an Iron Curtain fell between the people and the Absolute Ruler. We knew no more about the affairs of our country or those of the outside world than what he communicated to us.' Ordinary Egyptians were given so little real information about what was really going on that they accepted without question the stories they heard from the leader they idolized. This helps to explain the utter disbelief that overcame them when Egypt was defeated in 1967.

Arbitrary rule

There was initially much sympathy for Nasser among Western observers, particularly those on the political Left. Here, it seemed, was a leader with his own brand of home-grown socialism, breaking his country free from its colonial past and showing a freshness of vision in foreign policy by taking a non-aligned stance. But such admiration tended to become muted when it was realized that behind this apparently progressive front Nasser was engaged in establishing his own personal power.

Nasser himself endeavoured to play down the personal nature of his rule, claiming that it represented a genuine expression of the Egyptian popular will: 'Government is now by the people. There is no need for rules. Governments in the past were against the people. Today government is one – fused with the people.' However, P. J. Vatikiotis suggests that, contrary to Nasser's claims, Egypt experienced a decline in political freedoms under his regime: 'Egyptians after 1952 moved from some freedom under law to greater autocracy and servitude; from a degree of legality to almost plain arbitrariness. Arbitrary rule is by definition, tyrannical.'

← **Why did autocracy expand rather than diminish under Nasser?**

T O K

Many Egyptians believed Nasser was a successful ruler in comparison to King Farouk. Why is it important for people to judge the success of a nation's ruler? (History, Language, Ethics, Reason)

Chapter summary

Egypt under Gamal Abdel Nasser, 1952–70

Growing up in a turbulent Egypt struggling for full independence, Nasser was attracted to nationalist ideas and became involved in anti-British protests. He trained as a soldier and saw front-line service in the Arab–Israeli War of 1948–49. Having risen up the ranks he was a key member of the group of officers who overthrew the Egyptian monarchy in 1952 and established a republic. As leader of Egypt from 1954, he greatly enhanced his authority at home and won the admiration of the Arab world by triumphantly resisting the Israeli–British–French invasion at the time of the Suez Crisis in 1956.

Nasser began the process of modernizing Egypt along socialist lines by using the construction of the Aswan High Dam as the centrepiece in a series of agricultural and industrial reforms. However, opposition from such groups as the communists and the Muslim Brotherhood led him to introduce repressive social and political measures, including the outlawing of all other parties except his own National Union.

A prominent figure in the non-aligned movement, which avoided association with either of the Cold War blocs, Nasser was a pan-Arabist, believing that under Egyptian leadership the Arab states could be united in a common effort to improve the conditions of their people. However, his hopes in this regard were undermined by his being drawn into a number of conflicts within the Arab world which led to the suspicion that Egypt under him was aiming at dominance. Nasser's decision to intervene in Yemen proved particularly damaging. It entailed an unsuccessful five-year struggle which depleted Egypt's military resources and left it incapable of responding effectively to the attack by Israel in 1967.

Egypt's defeat in the Arab–Israeli War of 1967 was a blow from which Nasser never recovered. Although he remained leader until his death in 1970, retaining the basic loyalty of his people, he acknowledged that he had not realized his hopes for Egypt and the Arab world. Egyptian and Western scholars are in broad agreement that, whatever Nasser's ambitions may have been, conditions and problems at home and abroad led him to construct an increasingly authoritarian regime. However, they also concur in viewing him as an iconic figure who advanced the interests of Egypt and the wider Arab world in unprecedented ways.

Examination practice

Below are a number of different questions for you to practise. For guidance on how to answer exam-style questions, see Chapter 10.

1　Discuss the importance of nationalism for Nasser's economic and political policies.

2　To what extent did opposition form within Egypt against Nasser?

3　How successful were Nasser's economic policies?

4　Explain the importance of the Suez Crisis of 1956 for Egypt's Nasser.

5　Analyse the impact of Nasser's rule on Egyptian society.

6　Assess the importance of Nasser's rule on the status of women in Egypt.

7　Discuss Nasser's rise to power between 1952 and 1954.

8　What was the importance of Israel for Nasser's rule between 1956 and 1970?

9　For what reasons and with what results did Nasser and his government construct the Aswan High Dam?

10　To what extent was Nasser of Egypt a totalitarian ruler between 1954 and 1970?

Activities

1　Research Nasser's use of Egyptian cinema and radio for propaganda purposes. Examples of films that might be studied include, in English translation, *The Noble Thief*, *Saladin*, and *The Anglo-French Aggression Against Egypt*, as well as others. Counter-propaganda films by the British government might also be studied to extend this research: *The Facts about Port Said*, *Report from Port Said*, and *Suez in Perspective*. Consider the imagery, message, and historical accuracy.

2　By all accounts, Nasser was an extremely popular ruler in Egypt. Discuss as a class why it might be important for a ruler to be popular, what the basis of a ruler's popularity is, and at what point can popularity be a hindrance to one's decision-making.

3　Pan-Arabism was a philosophy advocated by many in the Middle East in the early twentieth century. Nasser was one of these people. Investigate the origins and meanings of Pan-Arabism. What was it and what was it not? Why would many Egyptians find Pan-Arabism appealing and why would many find it unacceptable?

CHAPTER 7

Cuba under Fidel Castro, 1959–2006

In 1959, Cuban revolutionary Fidel Castro led a small band of rebels to victory over the dictator Fulgencio Batista. From that date on, Castro was the ruler of the sugar island of Cuba until his retirement in 2006, establishing one of the twentieth-century's longest periods of unbroken political control. During that near half-century, he created a regime which his supporters hailed as a great liberating movement and his opponents condemned as a ruthless tyranny. Against the backdrop of the Cold War, Castro followed policies that both alienated the USA and won the support of the Soviet Union. The ending of the Cold War in the early 1990s raised the question as to whether, now that Cuba was internationally isolated, the system that Castro had created could survive.

You need to consider the following questions throughout this chapter:

✪ What circumstances favoured the rise of Castro?
✪ How did Castro impose his authority on Cuba?
✪ What impact did Castro's rule have on the lives of the Cuban people?
✪ Did Castro have an ideology?

1 Castro's rise to power

▶ *Key question: What circumstances favoured the rise of Castro?*

> Why were conditions so unstable in Cuba in Castro's formative years?

 **KEY TERM**

Latin America South American countries which historically had been settled or controlled by Spain or Portugal.

→ ## Cuba under Batista

In the middle of the twentieth century, Cuba, a large Caribbean island 90 miles (145 km) from the US mainland, was one of the richest countries in **Latin America**. Its weakness was that its wealth was largely dependent on one home-grown crop – sugar – which accounted for three-fifths of the workforce and one-quarter of all the island's exports. Without sugar there was no Cuban economy. The USA, Cuba's largest and most powerful neighbour, was the main purchaser of the crop, which meant that the USA had a hold on the Cuban economy. When relations between Cuba and the USA were amicable, the islanders had a guaranteed buyer and a source of income to pay for needed imports. However, if relations became strained, it was not easy for Cuba to find a comparable market elsewhere should the USA cease or significantly cut its purchases.

Cuba's relations with the USA

The USA's influence was not limited to economic matters. Developments around the beginning of the century had also given the USA a strong political influence. In the Spanish–American War of 1898, the United States had wrested control of Cuba from Spain and subsequently granted Cuba its independence. However, independence came at a price. Under **the Platt Amendments** of 1901 and 1903, the Cuban government had to accept the following terms:

 **KEY TERM**

The Platt Amendments
Named after Senator Orville Platt, who introduced them into the US Congress in 1901, the amendments became the basis of what was, in effect, a binding treaty between Cuba and the USA.

- Cuba could not enter into an agreement with a third power.
- The United States had the right to intervene militarily in Cuba.
- Guantanamo Bay on the eastern tip of Cuba was leased to the United States.

Given Cuban subordination to the USA, it followed that all national movements seeking Cuba's complete independence regarded the breaking of US dominance as a necessary first step. However, this political aim had to take second place to Cuba's economic needs. Cuban governments could not afford to antagonize the island's main trading partner. This was the lesson learned by Fulgencio Batista, Cuba's president from 1952 to 1959.

Mafia An underworld crime syndicate, particularly strong in Florida.

Batista's regime, 1952–59

Batista had begun his political career as a dedicated defender of Cuban rights against the USA. Head of the Cuban army, he had held power legitimately as president in the early 1940s, during which time he had adopted enlightened social and economic policies to limit the privileges of the landowners and reduce poverty. But, after losing office, he had gone to live for some time in the USA. He returned to Cuba in 1952 and, rather than wait to be legally re-elected, seized power in a military coup. He then proceeded to reverse his earlier policies by embarking on repressive measures aimed at gaining the support of the island's privileged elites, such as the owners of the large sugar plantations, most of whom had strong links with business interests in the USA. Corruption, which had long been a feature of Cuba's government and in which Batista was personally involved, worsened.

It was in this context that the contacts Batista had made both officially with US government representatives and covertly with the American **mafia** during his years in the USA proved important. In return for dollars for the regime, Batista allowed corruption to flourish. One aspect of this was that during Batista's seven-year presidency Cuba, especially the capital Havana, became a playground for rich Americans who crossed from Florida. The Americans brought plentiful dollars to Cuba but they also brought vice. Drugs, prostitution and racketeering flourished. It was two-way traffic. The common practice was for wealthy Cubans to visit the USA for long periods and to send their children to be educated there. They copied American ways and fashions and in doing so tended to detach themselves even further from their poorer Cuban compatriots.

Hugh Thomas, a celebrated British authority on Cuba, described the corrupting effect of Batista's regime: 'Havana was a paradise if one was rich, liked easy women, rum drinks and flashy nightclubs and casinos. The ruling class was predominantly white and of Spanish extraction, the poor underclass was mostly black with African roots. The disparity in wealth was shocking.' During his campaign for the US presidency in 1960, John F. Kennedy declared that Batista had 'turned Democratic Cuba into a complete police state – destroying every individual liberty'.

Opposition to Batista

Batista's policies after 1952 offended his former Cuban political allies who saw him as a turncoat who had sold out to the USA for financial benefit. He then gained a reputation as a fierce dictator as his rule became increasingly coercive. The reaction to all this was that a number of opposition groups formed which, whatever their differences, were united in opposition to Batista. These included:

- student organizations
- rural agricultural workers
- the Communist Party.

Yet, despite the severity of his rule and the growth of opposition to it, Batista had initially been able to draw on three main sources of support:

- the army
- the **labour unions**
- the USA.

However, over time the support from these groups lessened. Rivalry and corruption within the armed services weakened morale and Batista could no longer rely on their loyalty. Although he claimed an affinity with ordinary Cubans, his popularity waned as the harshness of his regime went unchecked. The labour unions continued to back him, but since large numbers of workers did not belong to unions, this was of diminishing help to him as industrial troubles spread. Particularly damaging to Batista was his loss of favour with important sections of opinion in the USA. After 1952, anti-government dissidents had fled to the United States where their denunciations of government corruption in Cuba influenced some members of **Congress** to turn against Batista's regime.

How did Castro seek to undermine Batista's regime?

Fidel Castro's challenge

The deep unrest caused by the increasing repression and corruption of Batista's regime created growing opposition. Prominent among those prepared to challenge Batista was Fidel Castro.

Castro's early politics

Castro had been born in 1927, the illegitimate son of a farmer of Spanish stock, who had become a relatively wealthy sugar plantation owner. Fidel had the conventional education for boys of his class, attending a Catholic school. From the first, he seemed naturally rebellious, going as far on one occasion as to champion the plantation workers when they went on strike against his father. At Havana University, where he studied law, his organizing of demonstrations and protests on behalf of underpaid workers cemented his reputation as an anti-establishment troublemaker.

In 1947, Castro left Cuba for the first time to join in what proved to be a badly mismanaged attempt to bring down Rafael Trujillo, the ruler of the **Dominican Republic**. A year later, Castro involved himself in equally unsuccessful risings in **Columbia**. Back in Cuba, Castro practised as a lawyer for a time, pointedly choosing to represent the poorest clients from whom he took no fee. He said that it was his experience working with such people that opened his eyes fully to the social and economic inequalities blighting Cuba. He was also angered by the evident grip that US business interests exerted on the Cuban economy. Acknowledging that he was a socialist, though not yet a communist, Castro joined the *Partido Ortodoxo* in the late 1940s.

By the early 1950s, Castro had begun to consider standing for election to the Cuban Congress. However, that avenue was rapidly closed to him by a dramatic turn of events. In 1952, Batista destroyed the constitution by seizing power in a military-backed coup and appointing himself a presidential dictator. The only way Castro could now operate was as an anti-Batista rebel. His initial hope was that the rebellion he contemplated would 'unite all the different forces against Batista'.

> **🔑 KEY TERM**
>
> **Columbia** One of the most northerly of the South American countries, the Colombian Republic underwent a period of bloody political conflict in the 1940s and 1950s, known as 'the Violence'.
>
> *Partido Ortodoxo* Literally 'Orthodox Party', better translated as 'People's Party'.

> Study Source A and, after reading pages 208–12, identify the key areas associated with Castro's rise to power. **?**

SOURCE A

Map of Cuba in 1962.

Why was the
Moncada attack a
pivotal event in
Castro's rise?

The Moncada Barracks attack, 1953

Castro's first major move against Batista was an attempted seizure of the Moncada military barracks outside Santiago, which housed units of Batista's army. His intention was to strike a blow against the new regime before it had consolidated itself and thus rally all the hesitant opponents of Batista to act together against him. It was a bold but unrealistic aim. The number of attackers led by Castro has been variously estimated between 160 and 180. It was a pitifully small contingent, composed largely of poor agricultural and factory workers and containing only two known communists. Lacking weapons and military experience, it was no match for the thousand professional soldiers who defended the barracks. A number of the attackers were shot in the fighting, 48 escaped, and the rest were captured, including Castro and his younger brother Raúl.

Castro's trial and imprisonment

Fidel Castro used his subsequent trial as a platform for defending himself as a committed Cuban patriot fighting for the liberty of the Cuban people. In a memorable phrase, he claimed 'History will absolve me', words he later used as the title of a pamphlet in which he developed the ideas he had expressed in his trial speech. Cuba, he claimed, needed to:

- restore the constitution destroyed by Batista
- redistribute land to the people
- extend education to all the people
- end corruption in politics and in business
- grant 30 per cent of the profits of industrial enterprises to the workers
- cut wasteful government arms expenditure.

Given that he had been the leader of the attack, Castro was treated surprisingly leniently. He had expected to be executed. His survival was due less to his captors' clemency than to Batista's wish not to turn the rebels into martyrs. There had been an angry reaction from Cubans and foreign observers at the ferocity with which those captured in the rising had been treated. Perhaps ten had been killed in the actual engagement but over 60 were summarily shot after the fighting had ceased. To lessen the tension this had caused, Castro, rather than receiving the expected death penalty, was sentenced to a fifteen-year prison term. This was later commuted under an amnesty and he was released in 1955 after serving less than two years.

The 26 July Movement

Although the Moncada attack had proved a hopeless enterprise, Castro regarded it as so expressive of his anti-Batista, pro-Cuba crusade that he adopted the title '26 July' to describe his rebel movement. His early release did not lessen his revolutionary ardour; he simply resolved to be better prepared when he next openly challenged Batista's rule. To that end, he went to Mexico soon after his release and began training a small band of fellow exiles. It was in Mexico that he met for the first time an individual who was

KEY TERM

Marxist Relating to the ideas of Karl Marx, a German revolutionary, who had advanced the notion that human society developed historically as a continuous series of class struggles between those who possessed economic and political power and those who did not. He taught that the culmination of this dialectical process would be the crushing victory of the proletariat over the bourgeoisie.

o have a big impact upon his subsequent career, an Argentine doctor and Marxist revolutionary, Ernesto (Che) Guevara.

Guevara's influence

purning his middle-class upbringing in Argentina, Guevara embraced evolutionary politics. He travelled across a number of Latin American ountries, supporting a variety of anti-government organizations and using is medical knowledge to assist rebel militia groups. He became intensely nti-capitalist, asserting that interference by the imperialist USA was the root ause of the poverty and political repression of the peoples of Latin America. his notion was intensified by his experience in **Guatemala** in 1954, where e witnessed what he regarded as the bringing down of the legitimate evolutionary government by a conspiratorial group of reactionary army fficers backed and funded by the **CIA**. When Guevara and Castro met in Mexico in late 1955, they quickly became comrades. Guevara's ideas and xperience helped to give focus to Castro's broad objective of overthrowing atista. The points that Guevara impressed upon Castro were that:

to remove a powerful military government, the basic strategy must be to avoid direct conflict where possible and fight only on advantageous terms **guerrilla** warfare would undermine the government's superior strength effective guerrilla warfare depended on the rebels making common cause with the ordinary people who would then provide them with supplies, shelter and information
the USA was basically a malign force that would always back reactionary and repressive governments in any country with which it had dealings.

The *Granma* attack, 1956

ager to be part of the Cuban revolution against Batista, Guevara joined the 6 July Movement and returned to Cuba with Castro. The return itself became piece of folklore. Hoping for simultaneous risings by his followers in other arts of the island, Castro sailed from Mexico intent on taking Santiago, Cuba's econd largest city and a key southern port, which would provide a base for hallenging Batista in the rest of the island. But things went wrong from the tart. The boat the party sailed in, the *Granma*, was overloaded with 82 men and heir weapons. The party barely survived their hazardous crossing and when hey did finally stagger ashore, they found that government troops were waiting or them. News of the intended landing place had been leaked by informers. tanding no chance against the prepared defenders, Castro's party scattered. All ut twelve of them were captured. The group of twelve, which included the two astro brothers and Guevara, eventually found sanctuary in the hills of the ierra Maestra. This region was to provide their shelter for the next three years s Fidel Castro set about rebuilding the 26 July Movement.

nitially the Cuban Communist Party did not support Castro. As their bsence from the Moncada attack had shown, the Communists did not

---

How did Guevara's ideas influence Castro as a revolutionary?

KEY TERM

Guatemala A central American state bordered by Mexico and Belize.

CIA Central Intelligence Agency – the USA's espionage and counter-espionage organization.

Guerrilla A style of warfare in which mobile troops, who live off the land, harass the enemy with surprise attacks while avoiding pitched battles.

What was the importance of the *Granma* attack to Fidel Castro's revolutionary movement?

KEY TERM

26 July Movement Castro's name for his revolutionary movement, chosen in commemoration of the Moncada Barracks attack, which had taken place on that date in 1953.

Sierra Maestra A mountain range running across the province of Oriente in eastern Cuba.

? What image of Castro and Guevara does Source B project?

Che Guevara (left) and Fidel Castro (right) in 1961 during a popular meeting in Havana.

🔑 KEY TERM

Putschista Someone willing to engage in violent struggle but lacking a true understanding of the revolutionary process.

regard him as a natural ally. Indeed, they referred to him as a *putschista*. What eventually made them willing to join him was his brother's influen Raúl Castro, like Che Guevara, was a fully-committed Marxist and the far association was enough to make the Communists suspend their doubts about Fidel and follow him. The fact was that for Fidel Castro revolutiona theory was unimportant at this stage. His approach was very simple; he v driven by an intense love of Cuba, a deep distaste for Batista's regime, an genuine desire to elevate the conditions of the people.

How did Castro use propaganda to promote his revolutionary aims?

Castro's early propaganda

An important aspect of Castro's rebuilding of the 26 July Movement was effective use of propaganda, which he targeted at both Cubans and a wid audience. In a series of interviews with sympathetic US reporters who fou their way to his rebel base, Castro projected an image of himself as the patriotic freedom fighter desperately struggling to defend a poor and oppressed people against Batista's corrupt regime. Liberal opinion in the USA and western Europe was impressed not just with the message they heard from him, but also with the passion with which he presented it. Physical appearance also mattered. The photographs that the journalists brought back and which found their way into popular magazines showec

Castro and his 26 July followers as rugged young men, dressed in battle fatigues and living off the land in their forest encampments as they trained themselves to overthrow tyranny and corruption. There was a heroic quality about them that appealed, particularly to the young in the West. Indeed, it was the rebels' youth that was so striking. Until John F. Kennedy became US President in 1960, the world seemed to be run by tired old men who had little to offer the modern world. As young revolutionaries, the photogenic Castro and Guevara made an attractive, romantic contrast with them.

Batista's overthrow

In his interviews, Castro exaggerated the scale of his popular support, but there was no doubt that it was increasing. Between 1957 and 1959, what amounted to a civil war raged in Cuba. Anti-Batista riots and protests, invariably suppressed with great brutality by government forces, were common. While these disturbances were not all in support of the 26 July Movement, Castro obviously benefited from them. As his rebel units grew larger and better armed, Castro launched a series of disruptive guerrilla attacks on Batista's forces, which were becoming weakened by outbreaks of mutiny in the ranks and by disputes among rival officers. Batista attempted to tighten his hold by resorting to fiercer repression, but as the situation deteriorated it became apparent that he lacked the ability to enforce his leadership. In historian Hugh Thomas's description, 'Batista was less himself a torturer than a weak man surrounded by cruel ones he could not control.'

Withdrawal of US support

Aware that Castro was gaining support and Batista losing it, the CIA suggested to the **State Department** that the USA switch its support from Batista to the Cuban opposition groups. Though such views were controversial in the USA, they were influential enough to persuade President Eisenhower's administration to withdraw military supplies at a critical time in 1957 when Batista was trying to deal with a mutiny at a naval station in Cienfuegos. This had the double effect of dispiriting Batista, who desperately needed US backing, and giving hope to the Cuban opposition. Castro was able to intensify his challenge to the regime. In the summer of 1958, he easily resisted a concerted attempt by government forces to entrap him and his followers in Oriente, one of the provinces in the Sierra Maestra. Having been the region where he had been forced to hide to survive, the Sierra Maestra had now become Castro's stronghold from which he was to advance to overthrow Batista.

Castro's autumn offensive

The government's summer campaign proved to be Batista's last effort to keep control. Its failure opened the way for Castro to take the offensive in the autumn. A number of factors combined to doom Batista:

- An election called by Batista in a desperate attempt to give popular backing to his government failed when 75 per cent of the electorate boycotted it.

What factors led to Batista's overthrow?

KEY TERM

State Department
The USA's foreign ministry.

Sierra Cristal A mountain range in northern Cuba.

Escambray A mountain range in central Cuba.

- Raúl Castro was in effective control of the **Sierra Cristal** region in the south east of the island.
- Che Guevara was dominant in the **Escambray** region of central Cuba.
- Fidel Castro was master of Oriente in the east.
- Now that the 26 July Movement seemed unstoppable, the other opposition groups, which had declined to support it earlier, came over to its side.
- The Catholic Church, to which the great majority of the Cuban people belonged, had begun openly to condemn the savagery of Batista's rule.

The rebels were now free to advance on Havana. By the end of 1958, Batista's position was beyond recovery. Abandoned by the USA, deserted by his senior officers, and faced with a seemingly united opposition, Batista fled to the Dominican Republic on New Year's Day 1959. Guevara's units moved into Havana on that same day. A group of generals made a bid to cling onto power by forming another military government, but their plan was thwarted when the workers supported Castro's call for a general strike in protest. The generals accepted defeat and withdrew. On 8 January, Fidel Castro entered Havana to a rapturous reception from its people. He had achieved a revolution.

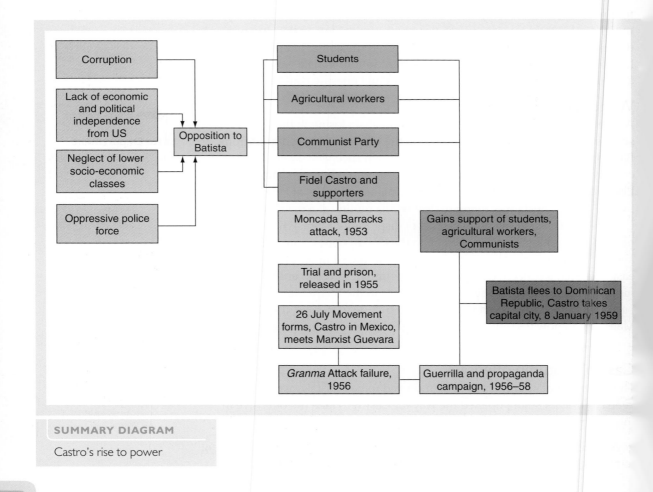

SUMMARY DIAGRAM

Castro's rise to power

2 Castro's establishment of an authoritarian state

▶ *Key question: How did Castro impose his authority on Cuba?*

All the Cuban revolutions prior to Castro's had begun with great optimism, only for them subsequently to founder. Determined to avoid similar failure, Castro judged that no matter how high his ambitions for Cuba he could achieve them only if he had complete, controlling power.

Castro's consolidation of power

Castro made a number of key moves to consolidate his position at home:

- A Fundamental Law of the Republic decreed that authority now rested in a **Council of Ministers**, led by Castro as Prime Minister.
- Press freedom was severely restricted.
- The University of Havana lost its autonomy and came under government control.
- Public **show trials** were held of ministers, officials and previous supporters of Batista. Many were subsequently executed.
- The Communist Party was invited to join the 26 July Movement in government by providing officials from its ranks.
- Huber Matos, a key military figure in the 26 July Movement but a strong anti-communist, was removed and imprisoned for treason.
- The moderate leaders of the labour unions were removed and replaced by pro-Castro communists.

Relations with the USA

In seeking to consolidate his power after the revolution, Castro knew that relations with the USA were the biggest problem. Anticipating that there might be a breakdown, he had already begun moving to the Left (see page 7) at the time he took power. That was why he drew closer to the Cuban Communist Party, offering them minor posts in government. There was also a practical reason. The 26 July Movement which he had led to victory lacked the trained officials necessary for running the government in the new Cuba. The flight of the majority of the managers and officials who had worked for the Batista regime left large administrative gaps. To help fill these, Castro turned to the communist **cadres** from whose ranks officials could be drawn.

Cuban–US problems

Had it been only a matter of politics, some form of accommodation might have been possible between Castro and the USA. Initially, his revolutionary government had American backing. At the time of his toppling of the Batista regime in 1959, Castro described himself as a 'humanist' rather than a

> How did Castro first seek to consolidate his power?

KEY TERM

Council of Ministers A governing Cabinet.

Show trials Special public court hearings, meant as propaganda exercises, in which the accused were paraded as enemies of the people.

> Why was the issue of Cuba's relations with the USA so important to Castro's consolidation of power?

KEY TERM

Cadres Dedicated Communist Party workers trained to take over as officials in the event of a revolution in Cuba.

KEY TERM

Washington A term commonly used to refer to the US government, which is located in that city.

Cold War The period of political and diplomatic tension, 1945–91, between the capitalist USA and its allies and the communist USSR and its allies.

Commercial agreement Signed between the USSR and Cuba in February 1960, according to which the Soviet Union was to buy the bulk of the island's sugar crop in return for selling oil and industrial machinery to Cuba.

Cuban *émigrés* Anti-Castro elements who had fled the island after the 1959 revolution.

communist, a category **Washington** found acceptable. For a time, indeed, he was something of a hero figure to the US public. The admiration did not last long, however. As a means of uniting the Cuban people, Castro, influenced by Che Guevara, chose to adopt a strong anti-Americanism, asserting that the poverty of Cuba was a direct result of the USA's imperialism. This became the justification for the expulsion or takeover of a large number of US business concerns. By the end of 1960, the refineries and assets of the following oil companies in Cuba had been seized:

- Royal Dutch Shell
- Standard Oil
- Texaco.

Along with this went the takeover of these major foreign companies:

- Coca-Cola
- Moa Bay Nickel Company
- Roebuck
- Sears.

The first response of the USA was to apply diplomatic and financial pressure. When this did not budge Castro, Washington withdrew its diplomatic recognition of the new Cuba. Fearing that they were now dealing with a communist island only 90 miles (145 km) off the Florida state coast, many high-ranking Washington officials turned their thoughts towards armed intervention in Cuba. They were disturbed by the realization that Castro's revolution had become a considerable **Cold War** coup for the USSR. Following the expulsion of US companies from Cuba, the Soviet Union had been quick to sign a **commercial agreement** and to offer diplomatic and economic assistance. The USSR hoped, and the United States feared, that the establishment of a Soviet-backed Marxist state in Cuba would be the prelude to the rapid spread of Soviet-style communism throughout central and Latin America. A US Congressman declared that 'for the first time since 1917 free America has the toad of Communism squatting on her very doorstep'.

The Bay of Pigs, 1961

Early in 1960, Eisenhower authorized a covert CIA programme for using Guatemala as a training base for **Cuban *émigrés*** in preparation for a future attack on Castro's Cuba. The hope was that this would provoke a popular rising that would topple the regime. A secret mission statement defined the CIA's aims (see Source C).

? According to Source C, what is the essential aim of the programme as outlined?

SOURCE C

Excerpt from a paper prepared for the Senate Foreign Relations Committee, Washington, 16 March, 1960, quoted in *The United States and the Origins of the Cuban Revolution* by Jules R. Benjamin, published by Princeton University Press, USA, 1992, p. 207.

The purpose of the program outlined herein is to bring about the replacement of the Castro regime with one more devoted to the true interests of the Cuban people and more acceptable to the US in such a manner as to avoid any appearance of US intervention. Essentially the method of accomplishing this end will be to induce, support, and so far as possible direct action, both inside and outside of Cuba, by selected groups of Cubans.

The attack was launched in April 1961 soon after Kennedy, the incoming president, who had earlier been a Castro admirer, had given it his approval. It proved a fiasco. The invaders failed to receive the support they had expected from either the local Cubans or, more critically, the USA, and were killed or captured as soon as they landed. Forewarned of the attack, Castro's forces were waiting for them. It was obviously a military disaster for the USA, but an even greater diplomatic and political one. The Soviet Union could barely contain its joy and the young President Kennedy his embarrassment.

A victory parade was held in Havana. *Life,* a popular US magazine, described how 'Havana gleefully noted the wealth of the captured invaders: 100 plantation owners, 67 landlords of apartment houses, 35 factory owners, 112 businessmen, 179 lived off unearned income, and 194 ex-soldiers of Batista.' In a grand gesture of defiance to the USA, Castro announced to the cheering crowds at the parade that Cuba would now become a fully communist state. What he meant by this soon became apparent when elections were declared to be no longer necessary now that Cuba was effectively a one-party state.

Relations with the USSR

Castro's stand against one of the world's superpowers was hugely popular in Cuba but it was fraught with risk. The hard reality was that his adoption of communism had further compromised Cuba's independence and ability to compete commercially. It had already mortgaged its sugar crop to the USSR. Clearly, the USA would no longer be the main purchaser of Cuba's other goods. The only alternative was to sell to the Soviet Union, the only buyer comparable to the USA. The result was that, far from being free to do as it wished, Cuba now became wholly reliant on the other superpower, the USSR.

The Soviet Union was swift to build on the moves it had already made. Within a month of Castro's declaration of Cuba as a communist state, Nikita Khrushchev, the Soviet leader, formally promised to defend Cuba against any future aggression by the USA, accompanying his promise with the pronouncement that 'the **Monroe Doctrine** is dead'. Supplies of Soviet arms to Cuba were on their way, in addition to the Soviet Union's advancing of millions of dollars worth of credit and equipment to the island.

The Cuban Missile Crisis, 1962

Emboldened by Kennedy's embarrassment over Cuba, Khrushchev's USSR took its most provocative step so far in the Cold War. During the 19 months following the Bay of Pigs fiasco, the Soviet Union's increasing arms provision to Cuba culminated in the installation on the island of Soviet nuclear

> **⚷ KEY TERM**
>
> **Monroe Doctrine** A warning given by President Monroe in 1823 that the USA would not allow other powers to colonize or interfere in any part of the Americas, and would regard itself as the protector of the region.

> What was at stake for Castro and Cuba in the missile crisis?

missiles with a capability of striking every major state in the USA. Che Guevara led the Cuban negotiations over their positioning. In October 1962, US reconnaissance aircraft brought back photographic evidence of the missiles and their silos in an advanced stage of construction.

The Soviet explanation was that the devices were there to defend Cuba against further foreign intervention but, since this claim followed a previous denial that the USSR had installed any missiles at all in Cuba, it served only to increase US fears. Kennedy announced that a naval blockade of Cuba would operate until the missiles were dismantled and removed. He added that, if any attempt was made to use them against the United States, he would order retaliation in kind. Kennedy backed his ultimatum by putting the United States Air Force (USAF) and the **Polaris** submarine fleet on war alert.

When Khrushchev likened the proximity of Soviet missiles in Cuba to that of US ones in Turkey, Kennedy replied that the US commitment to European defence, which the Turkish bases represented, was in no sense comparable to the Cuban missiles whose only conceivable purpose was to threaten the United States.

The critical decision was Khrushchev's. Would he be prepared to continue at the risk of full-scale nuclear confrontation? The answer came on 28 October, the day when the course of the Soviet vessels would bring them within the exclusion zone imposed by the US navy. From the **Kremlin** came the order to the Soviet ships not to enter the zone. In the following days, a number of contacts were made by letter and telephone between Kennedy and Khrushchev. Subsequently, the Soviet leader let it be known that the Soviet missiles would be removed from Cuba. For its part, the USA undertook to reduce its bases and missiles in Turkey.

The outcome of the crisis

Soon after the crisis had passed, Guevara asserted that had the Cuban leaders been in control of the missiles, they would have used them against the USA. This may have been bravado after the event but it was clear that Castro and Guevara felt betrayed by the Soviet withdrawal. There was no hiding the reality that Castro had been merely an onlooker in the crisis. The drama had been played out between Kennedy and Khrushchev. In an attempt to preserve his status, Castro sought to claim a moral victory. He expressed great pride in the enthusiastic mass response of the Cuban people to his call for them to prepare to defend their island against the expected US invasion. He made adroit use of the missile metaphor to claim a form of parity for Cuba with the superpowers (see Source D, page 217).

SOURCE D

Excerpt from a speech by Castro, November 1962, quoted in *The Rise and Decline of Fidel Castro* by Maurice Halperin, published by University of California Press, USA, 1973, p. 199.

The Cuban people is invincible and has a right to maintain its dignity and prestige unsullied! Because we possess long-range moral projectiles that cannot be dismantled and will never be dismantled! And these are our strategic weapons, our defensive strategic weapons, and our most powerful offensive strategic weapons!

> According to Source D, what weapons do the Cuban people possess? **?**

Economic policy

> What did Castro aim to achieve through his economic policies?

The economic policies that Castro adopted were an integral part of his attempt to consolidate his authority. He had inherited a series of economic problems that were not of his making.

Economic problems

- Cuba's vital sugar industry had suffered significant shrinkage on the world market.
- The sugar refiners had failed to modernize their industry by mechanization and adequate investment. The result was that in 1959 the island was producing only 10 per cent of the world's sugar, compared with 25 per cent twenty years earlier.
- In that same period, US investment in Cuba's sugar production fell from 60 per cent to 35 per cent.
- The decision of most of the industrial managers to leave the island when Batista was overthrown deprived Cuba of crucial expertise and so undermined Castro's plan for reinvigorating the economy.

Castro's economic reforms

To tackle these problems, Castro adopted the following measures:

- Large landowners were deprived of their land and an Institute of Agrarian Reform was created with the main purpose of breaking up the *latifundias* and 'returning the land to the people'.
- The sugar industry, Cuba's major source of revenue, was nationalized.
- Government subsidies were introduced in order to lower the rents and rates paid by the poor.
- State investment was directed into Cuba's infrastructure to improve communications and public services, including communal housing in urban areas.
- Plans to redistribute income and raise workers' wages were introduced.
- To save on expenditure, cuts were made in the imports of food and consumer goods.
- Rationing was introduced to lessen food shortages.

 **KEY TERM**

Latifundias The Cuban landowners' great estates.

Diversification

Castro's original plan had been to diversify the Cuban economy so that it would no longer be wholly dependent on sugar. But by the mid-1960s, he realized that this was unworkable. The attempt to develop different crops that could be marketed as profitably as sugar had proved a failure. Furthermore, the plan to develop industrial programmes as alternatives to sugar production had not been successful. This was partly a result of the flight of so many managers from Cuba immediately after the revolution; the skilled personnel required for successful diversification were simply not available.

A further reason was the decision Castro had made soon after coming to power to break economic ties with the USA. The move had left Cuba heavily reliant on the Soviet Union for economic survival, as exemplified in the Soviet purchase of the island's annual sugar crop. Cuba did not possess the economic freedom to diversify. The consequence was that, for much of Castro's era, Cuba became a sugar-based, industrially inefficient economy with the only financial backing coming from the Soviet Union.

Having accepted that the attempt to diversify had been ineffective, Castro tried to go back to sugar as the traditional **staple**. But his earlier actions had created their own problems. Much of the sugar cane had been destroyed or ploughed up in preparing the soil for the new crops, such as cotton or soya bean. In some cases it took up to four years to replant effectively and even then the yields did not match the good years of the late 1950s and early 1960s. Adding to the difficulties was the dilapidated state of the mills and refineries which had been allowed to run down. Nature also played a part, with unusually bad weather contributing to disappointing sugar harvests. The 1960s saw an 8 per cent drop in sugar production across the decade.

The '10 million ton harvest', 1970

The poor agricultural performance did not prevent Castro from launching a scheme intended to sustain the revolutionary momentum that had propelled the 26 July Movement to power. The drive towards his brand of Cuban communism was intensified. Further agrarian reforms resulted in two-thirds of the land coming under government control in the form of state farms. This move towards greater centralization was similar to the **collectivization** programme in Stalin's Russia and Mao's China (see pages 32 and 127). Castro proposed making the 1970 sugar harvest, expected to be abundant, the centre of a great popular rallying. He asked the Cuban people to look beyond selfish material considerations and see the new socialism as a moral movement, where individual advance was meaningful only if it occurred as part of the communal whole. Labelled the '10 million ton harvest' before it had actually been gathered, the 1970 harvest was presented as a symbol of what was achievable through collective endeavour.

KEY TERM

Staple Basic crop or commodity on which an economy relies.

Collectivization Depriving the peasants of their land and requiring them to live and work in communes.

In the event, '10 million ton harvest' was a major disappointment, not simply because it fell short of the projected figure by some 2 million tons, but also because the desperate means used to try to make the yield meet its target damaged the soil and the cane, severely reducing the prospects for future harvests:

- The underlying problem was that the migration of land workers to the factories that had occurred under the government's prompting in the 1960s had removed skilled cane cutters from the sugar plantations.
- Those brought in to gather the harvest lacked the knowledge and technique to perform the task adequately.
- In some areas, corrupt officials distorted the figures in order to suggest that they had achieved better results.

The 1970 harvest came to symbolize the new Cuba, but not in the way Castro had intended. It revealed the economic dislocation and continuing corruption in administration that the revolution was supposed to have eradicated.

The harvest failure was part of a larger problem. If planning was to work, there had to be expert planners, but these were in short supply. There was abundant enthusiasm among the revolutionaries who now ran things, but enthusiasm was not enough. It was not a substitute for managerial skill. The consequence was poor decision-making which stifled rather than encouraged expansion.

Opposition to Castro

The combination of failed economic policies, increasing authoritarianism and a growing sense of disappointment with the way the revolution was working in practice led to the growth of opposition. Those who had regarded Castro's 26 July Movement as a movement for liberation now began to have doubts.

The worldwide adulation among liberals for the Cuban leaders (see box below) served to make it additionally troubling to the idealists in Cuba when they realized that the admiration felt by outsiders for Castro's revolution was based on a misunderstanding of the actual situation. Unfulfilled hopes were, therefore, an important element in the formation of opposition. The same idealism that had motivated support for Castro now aroused opposition to him.

> **KEY TERM**
>
> **Maoism** The identification of Chinese Communism with Mao personally.
>
> **Eastern bloc** The countries of central and eastern Europe which were dominated by the Soviet Union between the late 1940s and late 1980s.

← **Why did opposition to Castro's regime develop?**

International icons

Internationally the 1960s had been a period when many people, particularly the young, had begun to challenge the old established governments and the ideas on which they were based. The challenge was not always clearly articulated; it tended to be a protest movement rather than a defined set of objectives, but it had taken its inspiration from such developments as **Maoism** in China (see page 156) and Castroism in Cuba, which were interpreted as representing a new form of politics liberated from the corrupt capitalism of the West and the rigid communism of the **Eastern bloc.** It was in this atmosphere of youthful rebellion that Castro and Guevara became iconic figures. Posters bearing their words and images became commonplace on Western university campuses.

Disaffected groups

The disaffection was strongest among:

- landowners who had been forced off their land
- industrialists who had had their factories taken over by the state
- peasants who felt aggrieved at having been forced into collectivization
- pro-Americans who had been forced to break their commercial and financial links with the USA
- those badly affected by the failure of Castro's economic diversity programme
- those who were offended by the ineffectiveness with which Castro's government operated
- those who considered that the political constraints and repression imposed by the regime were unjustified by any of the internal or external threats supposedly facing Cuba
- writers and artists whose works were subjected to government censorship
- editors and journalists who objected to the curtailment of their press freedoms
- academics who resented the government's encroachment on university freedoms
- the trade unions, which had lost their independence
- professional bodies and associations, such as those representing businessmen, solicitors and teachers, who were angered at their being brought under state control
- lawyers who chafed at the government's asserting the right to appoint judges, a move that amounted to state control of the judiciary; their objections were voiced by Manuel Urrutia, a judge who had previously opposed the Batista regime and who, despite his re-appointment to the bench by Castro, chose to resign in protest at the new regime's suspension of elections
- those who were dismayed by the way Cuba's revolutionary government became centred in the person of Fidel Castro himself; such personalizing of authority undermined the notion of the 1959 revolution as a movement of the people
- those among Castro's former supporters who were disturbed by his insistence on fighting wars abroad on behalf of liberation movements in such far-off countries as Angola, Zaire (later renamed the Congo) and Ethiopia, as well as closer to home in Latin America; they found his pre-occupation with anti-imperialist campaigns merely drew attention to his failure at home to extend to his own people the rights that Cuban soldiers were fighting and dying for elsewhere
- those who had fled the island because they knew their days of privileged living were over or because they simply felt they could not live in the repressive society Castro was creating
- those in the cultural scene who resented the regime's restrictions on artistic freedom. Often expressed in protest songs, a main target of their complaint was the bureaucracy that had grown up under Castro,

interposing itself between him and the people. A popular representative of this view was the folk singer Silvio Rodriguez who bitterly berated the bureaucrats, describing them as 'bosses who said one thing and did another … establishment cowards who were ruining the revolution'.

Émigrés

By 1968, 350,000 Cubans, nearly 5 per cent of the population, had left the island. Most went to the United States where many of them formed cells planning to return to reclaim Cuba by force should the opportunity arise. It was the existence of such *émigrés* abroad and their contacts with disaffected groups remaining in Cuba that gave Castro his justification for imposing surveillance and controls on the people.

Although the opposition groups looked to be a large and formidable array, they were never as serious a threat as appearance suggested. It was only the US-backed émigrés who represented real resistance, and when they did openly challenge Castro, as at the Bay of Pigs, they were decisively beaten.

Opposition weaknesses

- Opposition was never a united, organized body and the disaffected groups were unable to concert their efforts, even had they ever seriously planned to challenge Castro.
- Castro's status as the embodiment of Cuban aspirations meant that opposition to him seemed unpatriotic and so rarely gathered popular support.
- The firmness with which Castro dealt with challenges rendered it a hazardous venture to try to oppose him.
- Cuba's close-knit society made it easy to monitor opposition movements through eavesdropping and surveillance. The **DGI**, an organization which operated under Fidel Castro's direct control, was a highly effective means of detecting his enemies in Cuba and outside.

Assassination attempts

Castro was a leader who excited either intense affection for the way he attempted to elevate the poor and the dispossessed, or profound dislike for the way he was prepared to destroy rights and liberties. One of Castro's long-term bodyguards, Fabian Escalante, claimed to have counted 638 assassination attempts on the man he was guarding. Allowing for the likely exaggeration, since so many failures would reflect well on Escalante, the number suggests the danger Castro was constantly in and the degree of hatred towards him. He once joked that, if surviving assassination attempts were an Olympic event, he would be a multi-gold-medal winner. Unsurprisingly, the CIA was thought to have been behind most of the attempts.

Castro's treatment of opposition

Initially Castro had made little effort to stop people leaving; if they did not want Cuba, he said, Cuba did not want them. He had deliberately encouraged criminals, the insane and anti-social types to go. (US refugee

KEY TERM

DGI Dirección General de Inteligencia (General Directorate of Intelligence) – an internal security agency, concerned with enforcing conformity within Cuba. It was especially active as an anti-US spy network.

agencies in Florida complained of Castro's dumping his unwanted population on the USA.) Subsequently, however, Castro grew concerned that Cuba was losing too many of the skilled personnel it needed. Regulations were introduced forbidding Cubans to leave without acceptable reason. The restriction added to the feeling that Cuba was a closed, authoritarian society.

Occasionally, however, in order to reduce political tension, Castro would allow large numbers of Cubans to leave. One such moment occurred in 1980 when 10,000 people, reacting against food rationing, besieged Cuba's Peruvian embassy appealing for asylum. But Castro always accompanied such occasions with vast propaganda displays of support for himself and the regime. His intention was to show that the overwhelming mass of the population backed the revolution, contrasting with the relatively tiny number of selfish individuals who refused to stay and continue the struggle to achieve Cuba's destiny. 'Let them depart in shame' was his dismissive reference.

How did Castro modify his style of governing?

Changes in Castro's style of government, 1970–90

No longer able to turn for advice to Che Guevara, who had left Cuba in 1965 and was killed in Bolivia two years later, Castro had hard decisions to make. Conscious of the limited economic gains the revolution had made in its first decade and of the opposition that had developed in reaction to the economic measures, Castro responded by increasing political repression. But he also took major steps to adjust the organization of the government. Admitting that the failed 1970 harvest programme had revealed the limitations of the previous approach, he decided on a policy of depersonalizing the revolution. This did not mean he gave up power; he still retained ultimate authority, but he chose to delegate more while at the same time spreading the base of government. His response to criticism of the growth of bureaucracy was not to cut bureaucracy but to make it function more efficiently.

The Cuban Constitution, 1975

To give greater formal authority to the system which had been created since the 1959 revolution, a new constitution was adopted. Its most prominent clauses stated that:

- Fidel Castro, as First Secretary of the Cuban Communist Party and President of the Council of Ministers, was head of government
- Cuba was a socialist state, with the Communist Party as the only recognized political group
- local assemblies, drawn from members of the Communist Party, were to provide delegates for the National Assembly, an elected body of 600 members
- the Council of Ministers was to be drawn from the National Assembly.

Political and administrative changes

Under the terms of the new constitution, a number of important administrative and political changes were introduced:

- Ministers had greater freedom to act on their own initiative.
- Clearer lines of responsibility were drawn between departments and services.
- The police force was made part of the armed services.
- The 26 July Movement and the Communist Party were merged as one party.
- The legal system was streamlined to make court procedures simpler.
- While not given full independence, the trade unions were entitled to sit on tribunals concerned with workers' rights and to make recommendations regarding economic planning.

Rectification

Castro was sincere in his wish to broaden the base of his authority and to make his personal role in government less obviously dominant. However, it was clear that, whatever the adjustments he allowed, the reins of power remained firmly in his hands. He also knew that the political and administrative alterations would be mere tinkering unless they were accompanied by genuinely productive economic changes. It was to that end that the government under him initiated what became known as *rectification*, an approach intended to combine revolutionary idealism with hard practical realism. It was meant to apply especially to the economy.

- To enable Cuba to keep pace with modern technology, computers were introduced into factories and offices.
- Incentives were reintroduced into the workplace. Productive workers and managers were to be rewarded with pay increases and bonuses.
- Studies were conducted to make work practices more productive.
- A quota system was introduced, laying down targets to be achieved in designated areas of production.
- Priority in the supplies of materials and labour was to be given to areas and plants where the evidence suggested they would be most productively used.

Effects of rectification

Rectification as an economic programme had mixed results:

Between 1971 and 1976, Cuba's **GNP** grew each year by 10 per cent, which compared favourably with less than 4 per cent annually in the preceding five years.

However, in the following half decade, 1976–81, the growth figure fell back to 4 per cent annually.

Under the drive for efficiency, workers with higher skill levels received bonuses, but the less skilled remained on basic or decreased wages and were obliged to move to other jobs or locations.

> **KEY TERM**
>
> **Rectification** A revitalizing of the Cuban revolution by the correction of past errors.
>
> **GNP** Gross National Product, the annual total value of goods and services produced by a country at home, added to the profits from its export trade.

Austerity

The economic decline in the late 1970s led Castro's government to reappraise its policies for the 1980s. A major difficulty was that there was little room for manoeuvre commercially, a result both of Cuba's dependence on the Soviet Union and of the US embargo applied to Cuban trade since 1962. By the early 1980s, Cuba was in a predicament:

- The US trade embargo restricted the outlets for Cuban products to a limited number of countries, which resulted in Cuba's trade balance always being in deficit.
- Since sugar was its main export, Cuba was particularly susceptible to adverse changes in world sugar prices. This increased Cuba's need for the Soviet Union to continue to buy the bulk of its sugar crop at a fixed price.

SOURCE E

Castro speaks to thousands of Cubans on the Plaza de la Revolución in Havana, 1968.

? What information about Castro does Source E provide?

- Practically all Cuba's oil purchases were from the USSR.
- Cuba was in debt to the USSR by some 7 billion dollars.
- It owed a further 3.5 billion dollars to international banks.

Castro's response was to call for more austerity. Cubans had to make sacrifices for the national good. He repeated his familiar 'moral' appeal to the people, urging them to consume less, which would reduce the need for expensive imports, and to work for lower pay or for no financial return at all. He claimed that the need for this arose from the plain fact that Cuba had a surplus of labour. Some of this could be soaked up by increasing the size of the army and by encouraging young revolutionaries to go abroad, but the basic answer lay in the Cuban people settling for less in material terms.

Although a declared communist, Castro was not an orthodox Marxist. In 1974, he modified Marx's maxim 'from each according to his ability, to each according to his needs' to read, 'each Cuban should receive according to the work effort he applies'. His desire to improve the conditions of Cuba's poor was genuine but he believed the improvement had to be achieved not by government handouts but by individual and communal effort. Hence the severity with which slackers and saboteurs were treated by the regime.

The Special Period – Cuba after 1991

In the late 1980s and early 1990s, a series of resistance movements brought down the communist regimes in all the Eastern bloc countries. The climax came in 1991 with the collapse of the communist government in the USSR itself. Having been heavily dependent on Soviet assistance since 1959, Castro now had a major problem. The fall of the Eastern bloc and the disintegration of the USSR left communism a broken system. Castro's adherence to the Soviet Union was now his handicap, not his safeguard. The new Russia that emerged from the old USSR maintained contacts, but felt no obligation to honour the Cuban–Soviet agreements. Castro could no longer rely on the purchase of his sugar or the financial subventions he had hitherto enjoyed.

← **Why did the collapse of communism in the USSR prove so significant for Castro's Cuba?**

The impact on Cuba of the USSR's collapse

The consequence was increasing strain in the Cuban economy as it sought to adjust itself to the new situation. This era of hardship was dubbed 'the Special Period', its particular features being:

- Cuban income dropped by nearly 50 per cent between 1989 and 1992.
- In that same period, Cuba's annual supply of oil from Russia dropped from 13 million tons to under 2 million.
- In a desperate bid to save energy, power supplies to homes and factories were cut and there was a return to horse-drawn vehicles and bicycles as the main means of transport.

- The fuel shortage seriously handicapped the production of nickel, one of Cuba's main exports after sugar and tobacco; output fell from 47,000 tons to 29,000 between 1990 and 1994.
- Cuban commerce was further damaged by the USA's extension of its trade embargo to include US **subsidiary companies** operating in other countries.
- Strict rationing was introduced to cope with food shortages and people were discouraged from eating meat; locally grown rice, beans and fruit became the standard fare.

Castro's response

Faced with the collapse of communism in Europe, Castro was quick to assert that Cuba's revolutionary aims remained unaltered. This was where his consistent refusal to embrace orthodox **Marxism** stood him in good stead. His earlier insistence that his communism was a Cuban creation born of Cuban conditions was a reassertion of his right not to have to conform to any external interpretation of what a communist revolution should be. It was another area where his outlook mirrored that of Mao Zedong in China (see page 114).

Despite Castro's restatement of his commitment to Cuba's revolution, there were hopes among some in the government and many outside that the Special Period would lead to a liberalizing of his regime. There were signs that these hopes might be realized. In 1992, the National Assembly made a number of changes in the constitution, a significant one being an adjustment of the electoral rules so as to allow voting by secret ballot in the election of Assembly deputies. But to avoid any suggestion that the Assembly was challenging Castro, Carlos Lage, the Vice-President, emphasized that whatever reforms might be adopted they would not change Cuba's 'socialist essence'.

Castro himself made a number of adjustments to indicate that in the post-Soviet era he was prepared to make concessions in Cuba's interests:

- He allowed the US dollar to operate again as legal currency in Cuba.
- He encouraged tourists to come to Cuba, particularly from the wealthy USA.
- In 1994, he made an agreement with US President Clinton permitting an annual quota of 20,000 Cubans to leave for the United States.
- In 1998, a similar agreement allowed Cubans to receive unlimited amounts of American dollars from their *émigré* relatives in the USA.
- In 1998, Pope John Paul II visited Cuba at Castro's personal invitation. One consequence was Castro's agreeing to lift the restrictions on the **Varela Project**.
- Better relations were established with the European Union which had earlier criticized Castro for his repressive policies.

- Judging that Mao's China was now the only remaining force in international communism, Castro was keen to increase economic and political ties with it.
- In the wake of the widespread destruction caused by a hurricane that struck Cuba in 2001, Castro authorized the buying of massive food supplies from the United States. It was the first time in 40 years that the American embargo had been officially suspended. Castro maintained his principles, however, by refusing to accept the supplies as part of a US government humanitarian aid package. He insisted upon a commercial agreement.

Increased authoritarianism

Despite the concessions, Castro let it be known that he was far from ready to allow Cuba to become a fully open society, certainly not politically. In 2002, he began reversing his earlier tolerance at the time of the Pope's visit, by clamping down again on the Varela Project when it openly pressed for greater civil rights in Cuba. In March 2003, in what Castro's opponents called the 'Black Spring', 40 Varela members were imprisoned for receiving money from hostile foreign countries and using it to campaign against the Cuban government.

In suppressing the Varela Project, Castro was reacting as much to US censures as to developments in Cuba. In 2002, President George W. Bush had added Cuba to a list of countries he regarded as forming '**the axis of evil**'. Based on dubious intelligence reports, Bush's belief was that Castro was allowing biological weapons to be developed in Cuba.

There were stronger grounds for Bush's animosity in 2003 when, in what was regarded internationally as an unnecessarily vindictive act, Castro ordered the execution of a group of Cuban dissidents who had seized a ferry in an attempt to escape to the USA. This time the EU was sufficiently angered to order economic sanctions to be placed on Cuba.

Castro's retirement

How fragile Cuba's economy was became evident in 2004 when a spike in world oil prices caused a severe fuel shortage in Cuba, forcing the closure of over one hundred factories; these included sugar refineries and steel mills. A partial recovery came a year later, however, when Castro did an exchange deal with Venezuela's President, Hugo Chavez, under which, in return for oil, Cuba sent teams of doctors to practise in Venezuela. It was one of Fidel's last clear initiatives. His growing frailty led to his increasing withdrawal from the centre of things. In 2006 he effectively stood down from government in favour of his brother, Raúl.

 **KEY TERM**

The axis of evil Originally used by US President George W. Bush to refer to those countries which he regarded as supporting terrorism or developing weapons of mass destruction – Iran, Iraq and North Korea.

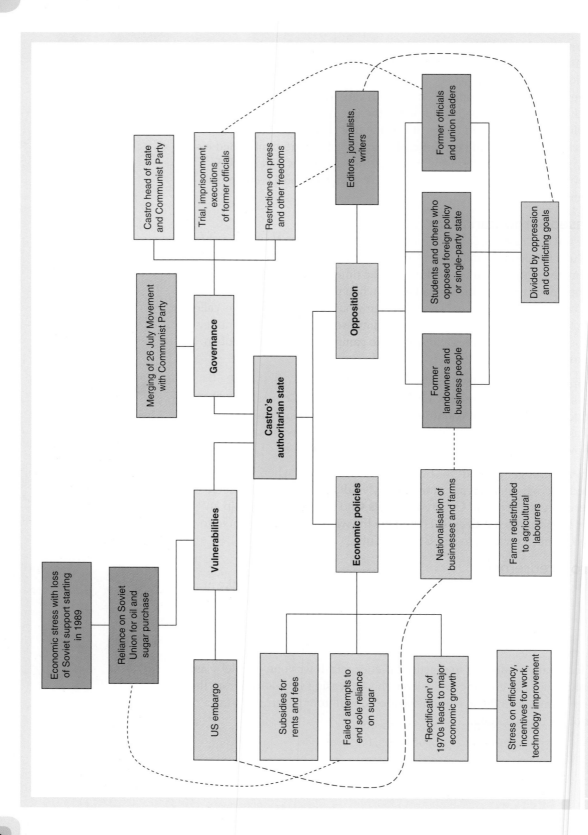

Castro's authoritarian state

Governance
- Merging of 26 July Movement with Communist Party
- Castro head of state and Communist Party
- Trial, imprisonment, executions of former officials
- Restrictions on press and other freedoms

Vulnerabilities
- Economic stress with loss of Soviet support starting in 1989
- Reliance on Soviet Union for oil and sugar purchase
- US embargo

Economic policies
- Nationalisation of businesses and farms
- Farms redistributed to agricultural labourers
- Subsidies for rents and fees
- Failed attempts to end sole reliance on sugar
- 'Rectification' of 1970s leads to major economic growth
- Stress on efficiency, incentives for work, technology improvement

Opposition
- Editors, journalists, writers
- Former officials and union leaders
- Students and others who opposed foreign policy or single-party state
- Former landowners and business people
- Divided by oppression and conflicting goals

3 Life in Cuba under Castro, 1959–2006

▶ **Key question:** *What impact did Castro's rule have on the lives of the Cuban people?*

Castro's long career as leader significantly altered the conditions in which the Cuban people lived. This section describes the main changes.

The condition of the people in Castro's Cuba

◄ **How had the Cuban people fared under Castro?**

An examination of some of the key statistics suggests that the main gains for the Cuban people were economic and social, with the main losses being political.

Improvement of people's conditions

As measured in 2002:

- Castro's Cuba was 55th out of the 187 countries listed in the **UN's Human Development Index**, a rise of ten places in five years.
- By the same measurement, Cuba was fifth in the list of South American countries.
- Cuba's **GDP** annual growth rate by the year 2000 was 5.6 per cent.
- Cuba had a universal, free welfare service (including health care and social security) and gained international renown for the quality of its medical treatment and welfare provision.
- Cuba had a remarkable number of doctors serving the population, 530 for every 10,000 people, the second-best ratio in Latin America.
- Cuba's **infant mortality rate** (7 deaths for every 1,000 births) was the lowest in South America.
- Average **life expectancy** was 77.6 years.
- Of the 88 nations classified as the '**developing world**', Cuba was ranked fourth in its success in tackling poverty.
- Cuba's **adult literacy rate** in 2008 stood at 98 per cent, the highest in South America and on a par with levels in the advanced world.
- Cuba spent 13.6 per cent of its GDP on education. This compared with 5.5 per cent in the USA.

The scale of Cuba's advance can be judged by comparing conditions in 1959 with those in 2000. The comparison shows:

- improvements had occurred in living conditions
- despite, or perhaps because of, rationing, far fewer people went hungry by 2000
- housing had improved in quality and availability
- unemployment had dropped to zero

KEY TERM

UN's Human Development Index A system operated by the United Nations from 1990 for measuring the relative economic and social development of individual states.

GDP Gross Domestic Product, the annual total value of goods produced and services provided, the standard way of measuring a country's economic strength.

Infant mortality rate The number of children who die within eighteen months of birth.

Life expectancy The age to which an individual was likely to live from birth.

Developing world (sometimes 'Third World') Nations with limited financial resources, low industrial growth rates, and poor living standards.

Adult literacy rate The percentage of the adult population with basic reading and writing skills.

KEY TERM

Mixed-race persons
Those with one black and one white parent.

Human Rights Watch (HRW) An international non-governmental organization which monitors and reports on countries which breach human rights.

Labour camps Prisons and detention centres in which the inmates are required to perform heavy work.

- free education up to higher level became available even for the poorest
- racial discrimination had been outlawed and equality between blacks and **mixed-race persons** (35 per cent of the population) and whites (65 per cent of the population) became a legal and social norm
- women were given equal rights as citizens and workers.

Totalitarianism

The obvious achievements that the figures above indicate have to be set against the restrictions on human rights that became a notorious feature of Castro's rule. In a series of reports produced between 2000 and 2008, **Human Rights Watch (HRW)** listed Cuba as being guilty of a series of violations of basic rights, which included:

- arbitrary arrest
- imprisonment without trial
- summary executions
- suppression of all forms of political dissent
- denial of the right of 'free expression, association, assembly, privacy, movement, and due process of law'.

HRW joined with other monitoring bodies in 2008 to point out the following:

- Cuba was second only to the People's Republic of China in the number of journalists it imprisoned.
- Ordinary Cubans had very limited access to the internet, the right to use it being restricted to selected government-monitored locations. Unauthorized web-users risked a five-year prison term.
- By the end of the 1990s, Cuba's prison system, proportional to the size of the island's population, was the most extensive in Latin America, containing 40 maximum-security prisons, 30 other prisons, and 200 **labour camps**. In the majority of cases, prisoners were held in conditions which fell below international standards for such penal institutions.
- Cubans did not have the right to free movement, being unable to leave or return to Cuba without official government permission.

Some observers have argued that the violations of these rights justify describing Cuba as a totalitarian state under Castro. The figures strongly support that contention. While it has to be added that totalitarianism was not Castro's declared aim, that his purpose was not personal power but the regeneration of Cuba in the interests of its people, his leadership of Cuba between 1959 and 2006 bears all the hallmarks that are associated with regimes such as Stalin's, Hitler's and Mao's. His motives might have been more elevated than theirs but the methods of achieving his ends were similar:

- the one party-state
- strict censorship
- control of the legal system
- intolerance of dissent

- persecution of minorities (see below)
- an extensive prison-camp system
- centralized control of the main institutions of society and the state.

Treatment of minorities

Although Castro often stated that one of his objectives was to extend equality to the Cuban people, his treatment of minorities did not always fulfil that ideal.

How tolerant was Castro's regime of ethnic and social minorities?

Black Cubans

When black political movements adopted Marxism in the twentieth century they replaced class with race as their defining motivation. They were seeking equality and the end of white dominance over them. This was certainly the aim of black Cuban communists. In 1959, black Cubans, who were the descendants of the slaves brought from West Africa in the eighteenth and nineteenth centuries to work on the island's sugar plantations, made up 10 per cent of Cuba's population of 12 million. Although slavery had been abolished in Cuba in 1886, the status of blacks had not risen to the level of the whites, their former masters, who were of European, largely Spanish, origin. Blacks invariably had the lowest incomes and lived in the poorest conditions.

Castro's taking power in 1959 had been immediately followed by an exodus of hundreds of thousands of Cubans from the island. It was overwhelmingly a flight of white Cubans. The great majority of blacks supported Castro, believing that their status and conditions would improve under him. They were to be disappointed. A black Cuban from Oriente province commented in 1963: 'We are still black and a minority. They free us on paper but there is a lot of separateness in our lives still.'

The leader of Cuba's black communists, Carlos Moore, noted in 1969 that the improvement of conditions for blacks had not figured in Castro's declared pre-revolutionary aims and that black Cubans had made more progress in the last ten years of Batista's rule than they had under Castro. Furthermore, a number of the members of Moore's black communists had been imprisoned for declining to co-operate with Cuba's official Communist Party. Moore argued that Castro's claim that he supported black advancement had been made more as an attempt to embarrass the USA, where the **civil rights movement** was a sensitive issue, than a genuine commitment. In Moore's judgement:

- the revolution had changed little since the white middle class was still in control
- anti-black prejudice continued
- blacks still played little part in Cuban politics
- the regime deliberately played down the contribution blacks had made to Cuba.

 **KEY TERM**

Civil rights movement
A powerful movement in the USA in the 1960s and 1970s, which campaigned for full political and economic equality for the country's ethnic minorities.

Social minorities

There was a strong puritanical aspect to Castro's regime which made it intolerant of homosexuality. Known homosexuals were classified, along with **Jehovah's Witnesses** and corrupt officials, as 'social deviants'. Such groups were placed in special army units for what was termed 'rehabilitation', the notion being that hard military labour would cure them of what the authorities regarded as their perverse behaviour and turn them into productive contributors to the revolution.

The role of the military in imposing conformity

The army played an important social and economic role in Castro's Cuba. Young Cuban males were conscripted into a three-year programme of **national service**. An organization, Military Units to Aid Production (UMAP), had the responsibility not only for the training of the conscripts as soldiers, but also for directing them into vital civilian work, the harvesting of the sugar cane crop being a key example. The UMAP quickly gained a fearsome reputation for the way it operated. Stories of soldiers being regularly brutalized, some fatally, became so widespread that Castro eventually felt obliged to disband UMAP and order that a number of senior officers be put on trial for having allowed the excesses to occur.

Legal freedoms

By 1973, the independence of the judiciary was effectively ended when the courts were brought under direct government control. Believing that lawyers were basically conservative in outlook and, therefore, unlikely to be reliable supporters of Cuba's revolution, Castro discouraged legal studies in the universities. By 1974, Cuba had the lowest number of law students of all South American countries. Private law practices were also frowned upon and solicitors who wished to continue representing clients in court had to belong to state law firms. As a way of suppressing political opposition, Castro's regime encouraged the courts to adopt a **presumption of guilt** in dealing with cases against those charged with state crimes. Defence lawyers were instructed 'to avoid making use of defence motions that prevent justice from fulfilling its social function'.

Tribunals

Minor courts were replaced with revolutionary tribunals, presided over not by trained magistrates but by government-appointed 'people's representatives' who in most instances were members of the local branch of the Communist Party. This was presented by the government as a study in popular revolutionary justice. The tribunals had the authority to deal with 'misdemeanours', the type of case which affected people at a local everyday level – drunkenness, neighbourhood disputes, youth misbehaviour, etc. The punishments they could impose included:

- fines
- house arrest

Were the Cuban people protected or oppressed by the law as it operated under Castro?

- curfews
- confiscation of property.

Regardless of how effective the tribunals were as a means of law enforcement, their chief value to the regime was in providing ways of monitoring local populations and so increasing the government's powers of surveillance.

Committees for the Defence of the Revolution (CDRs)

An important set of local bodies that provided the government with an extra-judicial means of controlling the population were the CDRs. They provided a form of communal activity intended to consolidate the revolution by giving the people a sense of identity with the regime. Functioning ostensibly as social clubs, the committees were organized by the Communist Party and were supposedly meant to illustrate how well the people pulled together under Castro. The government's effectiveness in promoting the CDRs as a social instrument for uniting the people behind the regime, whether willingly or under duress, could be seen in their numerical growth (see Source F).

SOURCE F

Membership totals in Committees for the Defence of the Revolution.

Year	Number of members
1961	798,703
1965	2,001,476
1970	3,222,147
1975	4,800,000

What do the figures in Source F suggest about the popularity and influence of the CDRs?

Since the population of Cuba was around 12 million in 1976, the figures show that well over a third of the people belonged to CDRs. Clearly, this provided the regime with a formidable mechanism for maintaining control.

The 'exemplary parenthood' programme

An interesting example of the social role the CDRs were called upon to play was the 'exemplary parenthood' programme started under their direction in the late 1960s. Under this parents had to show that they were actively involved in their children's education. They were required to:

- make regular parental visits to the school.
- supervise their children's learning and explain such failings as bad behaviour and low marks
- ensure their children missed school no more than 5 days in a 100.

Other prominent aspects of the 'exemplary parenthood' programme were schemes aimed at:

- increasing the number of blood donors
- encouraging people to recycle glass and plastic as a means of meeting Cuba's commodity shortages.

→ # The role and status of women

Women's contribution to the revolution

Woman had played a critical part in Castro's rise. In the 1950s, teams of them had worked in urban and rural areas to promote his revolutionary ideas. It had been a female lawyer, Haydée Santamaria, who had defended Castro at his trial following the 1953 Moncada attack (see page 208). During Castro's subsequent imprisonment, women were prominent in maintaining the 26 July Movement. A special women's guerrilla brigade had been formed under Celia Sanchez and had fought in the hills. One example of their propaganda role was their printing and distributing of over 10,000 copies of Castro's 'History Will Absolve Me' speech.

The Cuban Women's Federation

Given the contribution of women to the revolution, it followed logically that Castro would turn to them to assist in building the new Cuba. Formed in 1960, the Cuban Women's Federation (FMC) complemented the work of the CDRs, involving itself in the organization of a range of activities at local level, including:

- implementing Cuba's literacy drive
- training women and girls in domestic skills
- retraining former domestic servants for industrial work
- raising health standards by promoting hygiene programmes
- organizing day-care centres for women and infants
- enlisting and supervising unemployed women for voluntary work on the land.

? What main trend is evident in Source G?

SOURCE G

Numbers in the Cuban Women's Federation.

Year	No. of members	Number of branches
1961	17,000	340
1965	584,797	10,694
1970	1,324,751	27,370
1975	4,800,000	46,146

By 1975, three-quarters of Cuba's female population had joined the FMC. In that same year a Family Code was introduced which granted wives and husbands the same rights to be educated and pursue a career. The result of such measures was that by the year 2000 women made up:

- 43 per cent of Cuba's workforce, compared with 13 per cent in 1959
- 58 per cent of workers in technology
- 85 per cent of secretarial workers
- 63 per cent of workers in service industries.

However, these figures should not read as implying that women had made significant political or social progress under Castro. Indeed, the most characteristic feature of the FMC was its conservatism. Its leader, Vilma

Espin, stated in 1969: 'What one needs is to place five women where there were four men, to let those men go to fill a place where they are needed more. Let women be employed even though a higher number may be required.' Five years later, she declared directly that the FMC was 'feminine, not **feminist**'.

This outlook may explain why only 25 per cent of managerial posts were held by women, and why, despite their contribution to Castro's success in 1959, only one in three of Cuba's **National Assembly** delegates were women. It was not until 1986 that a woman became a member of the Communist Party's **Politburo**. Lower down the organizational hierarchy, females played a still smaller role; in local party branches only one position in six was filled by a woman. It should be added that in comparative international terms these are not startling figures. In Europe around this time women were markedly unrepresented in formal politics.

KEY TERM

Feminist The principle of full female equality with men.

National Assembly The Cuban National Assembly of People's Power, a parliament of 614 members elected every five years.

Politburo An inner core of some twenty leading members of the Communist Party.

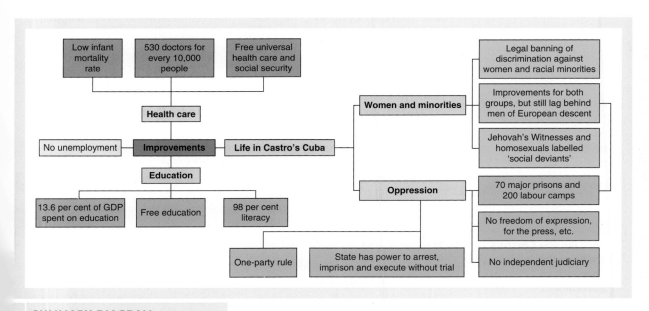

SUMMARY DIAGRAM

Life in Cuba under Castro, 1959–2006

4 Key debate

▶ **Key question:** *Did Castro have an ideology?*

> **How important was nationalism to Castro?**

→ Castro as nationalist

There is a well-founded argument put forward by some leading commentators, such as British historian Hugh Thomas and Eric Williams, a Caribbean scholar, that Fidel Castro did not have a definable political philosophy. Thomas in *Cuba* (1971) said that Castro lacked a 'fixed or coherent ideological point of view'. It is true that Castro claimed to be a communist after 1959, but this was done largely to spite the USA and attract the USSR. He was never a committed Marxist in the sense that Stalin and Mao Zedong were. Castro began with the notion that the people of Cuba could achieve their freedom by overthrowing a corrupt regime and replacing it with popular government. For the rest of his long career he kept to that belief and did not develop his ideas in any significant way. What inspired him was simple nationalism not complex political theory. Writing in 1970, Williams commented:

> **?** According to Source H, why is the Cuban Revolution best understood as Castro's Revolution?

SOURCE H

Excerpt from *From Columbus to Castro: The History of the Caribbean 1942–1969* by Eric Williams, published by André Deutsch, UK, 1970, p. 486.

Castro is for revolutionary action. Marxist or not, the Cuban Revolution remains Castro's revolution, and the Communist party has no power in Cuba. For the rest Castro's programme is pure nationalist, comprehensible to and acceptable to any other Caribbean nationalist.

> **How far was Castro a traditionalist in his approach to government?**

→ Castro as traditionalist

Other writers have developed this theme by stressing that Castro's approach was **populist** rather than ideological. Historian Leycester Coltman suggests that Castro believed he had a special affinity with the Cuban people and that by appealing to their basic patriotism he could lift them to heights of endeavour and accomplishment. It was a matter of feeling rather than argument. His long public speeches were not philosophical treatises; they were rallying calls to the public. A fascinating aspect of this was the way Castro used Cuban religious tradition to appeal to the people (see Source I).

> **🔑 KEY TERM**
>
> **Populism** A political approach that seeks to create a direct relationship between the leader and the people, based on the idea that the leader has a special understanding of the people's needs.

Excerpt from *The Real Fidel Castro* by Leycester Coltman, published by Yale University Press, USA, 2003, p. 140.

Castro was seen by many as a Christ-like figure, the pure one descending from the mountains to clean away the dirt and corruption of the cities. Even the sinful and unworthy could now redeem themselves by demonstrating their support for the Revolution. Castro was a Marxist and an atheist but he knew how to exploit the religious feelings of others. He encouraged the legend that the movement had started with twelve men, the temptation to create a parallel with Christ's apostles was too great to be resisted.

> According to Source I, how was Castro raised above politics in the eyes of many Cubans? **?**

Guevara's influence

> ← How important was the influence of Guevara on Castro?

Spanish historian Juan Lopez, in his *Democracy Delayed the Case of Castro's Cuba* (2002), and American historian Thomas Wright, in his *Latin America in the Era of the Cuban Revolution* (2000), have argued that it was Che Guevara who gave Castro such ideology as he had. They suggest that Guevara brought to Cuban politics not simply a sense of idealism but the notion that Cuba could rebuild itself by making its population 'the new men'. Guevara also used religious tradition when he claimed that historically the Spanish occupation had given Cuba the notion of a redeemed people. The Spanish priests, rather than patronize the people, had seen them as instruments for God's purpose in developing a new brand of human goodness. Translated into secular terms, this sense of re-creation had a powerful political impulse and it was this that pushed Castro towards the idea that he was not simply dealing with the grievances of the Cuban people; he was giving them a higher aspiration.

Castro's pre-occupation with the USA

> ← Why did Castro's relations with the USA prove so important?

A number of scholars, most notably Eric Williams and Hugh Thomas, insist that Castro's ideas and policies cannot be understood unless they are put in the context of the Cold War, which was at its most intense when he came to power in 1959. It was impossible for the USA to see Cuba in isolation. Its concern was always how developments in Cuba would impact upon the international scene. Initially Castro's ideas did not stretch much beyond Cuba itself. However, given the times in which he lived and the hopes he had for Cuba, he was unavoidably drawn into global affairs. By the 1950s, the world had become **bi-polar**; neutrality was not a real option. A country or a bloc was either for or against the USA, for or against the USSR. There was no middle ground. It is in that context that Cuban politics and Castro's thinking have to be understood. He had a stark choice: either to continue with the US connection, which meant subordination to the USA, or turn to the Soviet Union which would be a new relationship but would still be as restrictive as the old. In short, he was in the position of all the Latin American leaders since the Monroe Doctrine – unable to be genuinely independent.

> **🔑 KEY TERM**
>
> **Bi-polar** Divided between the two power blocs, the USA and its allies and the USSR and its allies.

Castro made Cuba more independent of US control – a move which was welcomed by many Cubans. Do individual leaders drive history or do they reflect the will of their people? (History, Language, Emotion, Reason, Human sciences)

An interesting slant has been offered on Castro's attitudes by a US analyst, Ann Louise Bardach. Building on the ideas of Williams and Thomas, she suggests in her *Cuba Confidential* (2003) that his distaste for US imperialism, which he regarded as the source of all Latin America's problems, obsessed him and conditioned his whole political outlook. For him, the development of the Cuban revolution was really a running battle with the United States. His severity towards his own people, not simply the Cuban *émigrés*, was reactive defiance against the USA. Castro was drawn towards the Soviet Union and Mao's China not because he necessarily admired their systems but because they shared his enmity towards his great foe.

Why did Castro adopt repressive policies in Cuba?

Castro's authoritarianism

On the issue of the severity of Castro's rule, other analysts argue that its repressive character was there from the beginning. While not discounting the idea of it as a product of his relations with the USA, they emphasize that stern control was regarded by Castro as essential to the effective government of Cuba (see Source J).

According to Source J, what means were used by Castro's regime to impose central control?

SOURCE J

Excerpt from *Cuba: Order and Revolution* by Jorge Dominguez, published by Belknap Press, USA, 1978, pp. 260–61.

In revolutionary Cuba, all levels of the mass organizations, the subordinate units of the party, and all elections lack important aspects of political autonomy and are subject to externally imposed restraints on the selection of leaders, election procedures and policy making. The fact of dependence remains constant.

*The revolution and its leaders legitimate the Constitution, the courts, the administration, the party, the mass organizations, and the elections – and not vice versa. Elections are deliberately set up to be unrepresentative politically in order to facilitate the **routinization of Fidel Castro's charisma** by bringing forth as candidates people who are said to resemble him in some way.*

KEY TERM

Routinization of Fidel Castro's charisma A process which, by constant emphasis, created a common outlook among the Cuban people that Castro's gifts as leader were the standard by which to judge all other politicians.

Social historian Dayan Jayatilleka, in *Fidel's Ethics of Violence* (2007), also regards Castro's repressive approach to politics as defining his rule. Since Castro believed that his authority was basically for the good of the Cuban people, he felt entitled to use force and repression to maintain his authority. The end justified the means.

Why did Castro adopt communism?

Castro's communism

Castro's authoritarianism is a major feature of the debate over the source of Castro's communism. Some historians, for example Julia Sweig, in her *Inside the Cuban Revolution* (2002), suggest that it was an essential accompaniment of his early revolutionary thinking, but that, to avoid being seen taking sides in the Cold War, he chose not to stress his basic ideology. Others, including Brian Latell in his *After Fidel: the Inside Story of Castro's Regime* (2005), judge that he adopted communism for expedient reasons after coming to power, largely in order to win the support of the Soviet Union. A third notion, advanced, for example, by Jorge Dominguez, is that the rigours of the communist system appealed to Castro once he realized the scale of the problems confronting Cuba after he had come to power. US enmity and the need for strong government in Cuba made it a logical progression for him. It justified his totalitarian methods.

An interesting gloss is put on the debate by the British Marxist historian, Eric Hobsbawn, who suggested that it was practical necessity not free choice that led Castro to adopt communism in Cuba. His populist style left him no alternative (see Source K).

SOURCE K

Excerpt from *The Age of Extremes* by Eric Hobsbawm, published by Michael Joseph, UK, 1994, p. 440.

Fidel's form of government by informed monologues before the millions, was not a way to run even a small country or a revolution for any length of time. Even populism needs organization. The Communist party was the only body on the revolutionary side which could provide him with it. The two needed each other and converged.

According to Hobsbawm in Source K, what led Castro to adopt communism?

In another insightful observation, Hugh Thomas observed that there was perhaps too great a desire among Western historians to define Castro's communism. He thought it a mistake to label Castro by political terms that properly belong only in a European context. To make his point, Thomas suggested that it was equally possible to describe Castro's regime as fascist as it was to call it communist.

SOURCE L

Excerpt from *Cuba or the Pursuit of Freedom* by Hugh Thomas, published by Eyre & Spottiswoode, UK, 1971, pp. 1490–91.

It is tempting to compare Cuban communism with fascism. There is the willingness of large sections of the population to surrender their individuality as men did to Fascist leaders. There is the persistent elevation of the principle of violence and there is the cult of leadership … and the continual denigration of bourgeois democracies …

Fascism was a heresy of the international socialist movement and several fascist leaders had once been men of the Left … it is possible to imagine Castro moving from extreme Left to extreme Right.

According to Source L, what is the evidence for regarding Castro as a fascist?

Thomas was quick to add that that these were superficial resemblances and he did not in fact believe Castro was a fascist. Thomas stressed that context is everything. Castro's communism was a specific phenomenon, particular to him and to Cuba.

Chapter summary

Cuba under Fidel Castro, 1959–2006

After a number of early failures, the young Cuban revolutionary, Fidel Castro, finally overthrew the corrupt regime of Fulgencio Batista in 1959. With the aid of another influential revolutionary, Che Guevara, Castro proceeded to create a new, authoritarian political system in Cuba. He had initially been well disposed towards the USA, but Cold War fears led the US government to regard him with suspicion. Castro reacted by declaring Cuba to be a communist state. This broke Cuba's vital economic link with the USA, which had been the major purchaser of the island's agricultural and manufactured products. Castro turned perforce to the USSR, which became Cuba's essential economic partner.

Overcoming military attempts by US-backed Cuban *émigrés* to remove him, Castro resorted to increasingly dictatorial methods to impose his control. Opposition was not tolerated and Cuba became a one-party state. Heavily dependent on Soviet aid, Castro allowed Soviet missiles to be sited in Cuba, a decision which put the island at grave risk of invasion by the USA at the time of the Missile Crisis in 1962. With the crisis resolved peacefully, Castro returned to his attempts to develop the Cuban economy: he introduced policies aimed at diversifying industry, a process that involved the nationalization of domestic and foreign companies and businesses. The failure of a major effort to modernize Cuban agriculture persuaded Castro to adopt a new set of policies, which, between 1970 and 1990, went some way towards improving Cuba's economy. However, under an approach known as *rectification* Castro made it clear there was to be no lightening of political control.

Cuba's economic vulnerability was exposed by the collapse in the early 1990s of the Eastern bloc communist governments. Deprived of Soviet support, Castro was obliged to adjust his policies. During the 'Special Period' which began in 1991 Castro did not abandon Marxism but did allow more progressive moves to be made in order to cope with Cuba's food and other supply shortages. However, he never fully relaxed his central hold on Cuba and opposition groups continued to protest against his authoritarian methods.

At his retirement in 2006, Castro could look back on a record of chequered but basically successful leadership. Cuba had survived as an independent nation, albeit at the price of political repression, and the Cuban people had begun to enjoy substantial improvements in many aspects of their living and working conditions.

Examination practice

elow are a number of different questions for you to practise. For guidance on how to answer exam-style
uestions, see Chapter 10.

1 What was the importance of Che Guevara for Castro's rule?

2 To what extent were Castro's economic policies successful?

3 Explain the importance of communists in Castro's early government.

4 Assess the impact of Castro's rule on women.

5 Analyse the importance of emigration for Castro's Cuba.

6 Discuss the reasons for Castro's successful rise to power by 1959.

7 To what extent was Castro a totalitarian ruler between 1959 and 2000?

8 Why did little effective opposition form against Castro within Cuba during his rule?

9 What was the importance of the Cuban Missile Crisis for Castro's rule?

10 Discuss the successes and failures of Castro's agricultural policies.

Activities

I Create a timeline of Castro's rise and rule. You could expand this to include visual images, biographies
and historiography.

2 Cuba was almost totally reliant on sugar for its economy. Research the history of sugar with special
focus on its economic impact on Caribbean islands and connection to slavery.

3 Castro adapted communism to address the specific needs of Cuba. Compare and contrast Cuba's form
of communism with that found in the Soviet Union and the People's Republic of China. Which form of
communism was Cuba's most closely aligned with? Explain.

CHAPTER 8

Argentina under Juan Perón, 1946–74

In 1943, Juan Perón was one of a group of nationalist officers in the Argentinian army who seized power in a coup and set themselves up as a government. Within three years, Perón had been elected President and proceeded to govern Argentina from 1946 to 1955. He adopted a populist approach, enlisting the support of workers and ordinary people, while subjecting opponents to fierce repression. Successful though he was in three separate elections, he was always reliant on the support of the army for his retention of authority and it was an army coup that forced him from office in 1955 after two terms as President. In 1973, he returned from exile for a third term, but was dead within a year, having added little to his earlier accomplishments.

You need to consider the following questions throughout this chapter:

✪ What circumstances favoured the rise of Perón?

✪ How did Perón impose his authority on Argentina?

✪ What impact did Perón's rule have on the lives of the Argentinian people?

✪ Was Perón a Right-wing or a Left-wing leader?

Perón's rise to power

▶ **Key question:** *What circumstances favoured the rise of Perón?*

Argentina before Perón

> **Why were conditions so disturbed in Argentina in Perón's formative years?**

KEY TERM

Chauvinist Militant ultra-nationalist.

Patriotic League An Argentinian nationalist group created to fight the immigrant organizations responsible, so the League claimed, for the strikes and industrial unrest and for bringing communism into the country.

Having been a Spanish colony since the sixteenth century, Argentina had gained its independence in 1818. As a free nation, it made slow economic progress until the 1880s when it began to develop its railways, receive foreign investment, and open itself to large-scale immigration from Euro[pe]. Argentinian nationalists grew concerned that their country was changing [in] ways they could not control. They were especially concerned by the inflo[w of] immigrants. Organized by such **chauvinist** groups as the **Patriotic Leag[ue]**, intermittent outbursts of violence against the newcomers occurred, the m[ost] serious taking place in 1919 during the *la Semana Trágica*. The objectior[ns of] the nationalists and moderates, as well as those on the far Right derived from certain main concerns about:

- the scale of immigration
- foreign monopolies controlling key aspects of Argentina's economy, fo[r] example, meat packing and sugar refining

- the evasion of tax by foreign companies
- foreign manipulation of exchange rates to the detriment of Argentina
- US protectionism made it impossible for Argentina to operate a free trade system.

Despite the disturbances, government in Argentina remained in the hands of a conservative landowning **oligarchy**. However, constitutional changes early in the twentieth century, including the introduction of universal male **suffrage**, resulted in the growth of political parties, the largest being the radicals. By the late 1920s, the previously unshakable governmental grip of the conservatives began to be challenged.

The decade of infamy, 1930–43

In the 1930s, Argentina continued to be ruled by a landowning elite, the *estancieros*, which enforced its control by violent means. In theory, Argentina was now a democracy, but elections were decided by bribery and intimidation and the results were invariably falsified. Unsurprisingly, the mixture of chicanery and repression provoked serious public disorder as the only means of protest. Such was the corruption and oppression that the period earned the epithet 'the decade of infamy'.

Economic problems

Argentina also faced severe economic difficulties. The impact of the Great Depression, which affected all countries in the 1930s (see page 14), created particular problems for Argentina, a country which derived its income largely from the sale of manufactures and food products, particularly processed meat. The Depression of the 1930s saw a sharp drop in international demand for Argentina's goods. The result was a fall of over 40 per cent in the country's exports. Foreign investments fell sharply, which rapidly reduced the government's income and led to a mounting deficit and rising inflation.

One consequence was a call from Argentinian nationalists for the country to move towards **autarky**. They argued that a self-sufficient economy would end Argentina's dependence on the uncertainties of world trade cycles and allow it to modernize at its own pace. The state would become the main agency directing the economy. This resurgence of nationalism was a general response to the uncertainties of the international economy. It was also a specific reaction against Britain's dominance in its trade relations with Argentina. Despite the advantages it brought, the **Roca-Runciman Agreement** of 1933 was considered by many Argentinians to be an illustration of their country's relative weakness. The agreement was very much in Britain's favour, since it required Argentina to open itself to British companies, which were to be excused taxation and given priority in bidding for contracts.

Growing discontent

The disturbed times led dispossessed land workers to migrate to the major cities, including the capital, Buenos Aires, where they joined the thousands

> **KEY TERM**
>
> ***La Semana Trágica*** The 'week of tragedy' in January 1919 when nationalist gangs roamed the streets of Buenos Aires, beating up foreigners, the main targets being Jews and communists.
>
> **Oligarchy** Rule by a privileged elite.
>
> **Suffrage** The right to vote.
>
> ***Estancieros*** Owners of the *estancias*, the great landed estates in Argentina.
>
> **Autarky** An economically self-sufficient nation.
>
> **Roca-Runciman Agreement** Agreement between Britain and Argentina in 1933 under which Britain gave preferential treatment to Argentina's meat exports in return for Argentina's increasing its imports of British products.

of factory workers who had lost their jobs in the Depression. The government's response to this volatile situation was to use state funds to buy up the unsellable produce so that the landowners' wealth was maintained and to use increased force to contain disorder. At the same time, the government appealed to the *estancieros*, both to provide funds from their own resources and accept higher levels of taxation. However, since their primary concern was to safeguard their own economic status, the *estancieros* declined to co-operate. Such obduracy led to renewed protests from the workers and their unions against the privileged classes for putting their interests before those of the nation.

There was some economic improvement in the late 1930s, which saw an increased demand for manufactures, but this served to give greater opportunity for the unions to press their demands, since they were now a key element in the nation's attempt at recovery. The main organization representing the workers, the **General Confederation of Labour (CGT)**, became an influential movement. It was at this point that dramatic developments elsewhere cut across domestic affairs. The Second World War, which began in Europe in 1939, impacted significantly on Argentina. The disruption caused to international commerce by the various blockades which the warring sides imposed on each other deprived Argentina of markets and supplies. By the early 1940s, it was becoming evident that a conflict was approaching between the established ruling classes who wanted to retain power and the middle classes and workers who wanted an end to privilege.

KEY TERM

General Confederation of Labour (CGT) An alliance of Argentinian trade unions, collectively numbering over a third of a million members.

Junta Government by military generals.

Corporate state A society whose various economic and social elements are integrated and controlled by the central government.

How did the coup by the GOU contribute to Perón's rise?

The military coup, 1943

A basic fact in Argentina was that government ultimately rested on military support. The army was always in a position to intervene directly. In June 1943 it made that choice. Declaring that the dangerously disturbed circumstances could not be allowed to continue, an army faction, the Group of United Officers (GOU), seized power in a coup and set up a ruling **junta**. One of the officers involved was Colonel Juan Perón.

Perón's background

Born in Buenos Aires in 1895, Perón was of Italian emigrant stock. He always took pride in his origins and, despite his later troubles with the Catholic Church (see page 259), always described himself as a devout Catholic. He became a cadet in military school in 1911 aged sixteen and showed a single-minded determination to rise up the ranks as an infantry officer. He was adept at cultivating relations with those of his superiors who could help his promotion. In the late 1930s and early 1940s, Perón travelled extensively in Europe as a military observer and was impressed by Nazi Germany and Fascist Italy. As a professional soldier with a strong belief in the virtues of social order, he admired the apparent economic efficiency and political stability achieved by the Italian leader, Mussolini, in converting Italy into a centralized **corporate state**.

Perón as Labour Minister and Vice-President

Perón's reward for his contribution to the junta's takeover was to be given the post of Minister of Labour in December 1943. His appointment proved to be a momentous stage in his political advance. Believing that government–worker relations were of fundamental importance in the shaping of the new Argentina, he turned the Ministry into the government's most effective and significant department.

The speed of Perón's rise was clear in his elevation to Vice-President early in 1944. This followed his backing of General Edelmiro Farrell in the removal of the incumbent President Pablo Ramirez. Perón now combined his vice-presidential position with that of Labour Minister. His eyes were now set on the presidency itself.

SOURCE A

Perón shakes hands with Edelmiro Farrell after becoming Vice-President, 1944.

What information is conveyed by Source A about Perón?

Perón's populism

Perón's position as Minister of Labour led to his forming close contact with workers and organized trade unions. Disturbed by what he learned of the difficulties faced by the workers, he pressed for new laws to protect their rights. In return for the trade unions' promise of electoral and political support, Perón brought in measures raising wage levels and extending

How did Perón project himself politically?

welfare benefits. Significantly, he saw this as a way not merely of helping the workers, but also of avoiding revolution from below.

According to Source B, what steps are necessary to avoid 'Violent Revolution'?

SOURCE B

Excerpt from a speech by Perón, April 1945, quoted by David Rock in *The Cambridge History of Latin America*, vol. viii, edited by Leslie Bethell, published by CUP, UK, 1996, p. 67.

If we fail to carry out the Peaceful Revolution, the People themselves will take the road of Violent Revolution. The solution to the whole problem is social justice towards the masses. Naturally this is not a popular idea among rich men. But they are their own worst enemies. Better offer 30 per cent now, than within two years, or perhaps even months, to risk losing all they have, including their ears.

Perón drew increasing attention to himself by the impassioned nature of his attack on the reactionary classes who had ruled Argentina for too long. He asserted that the new government to which he belonged was attempting to return Argentina to its people: 'We've passed social reforms to make the Argentine people proud once again to live where they live.' Perón's affinity with ordinary people was spectacularly shown in his efforts to relieve the victims of a devastating earthquake which struck San Juan in 1944. As an energetic fundraiser, he showed a talent for making himself popular with high society and with show-business celebrities. Perón was developing an impressive **populist** style.

Creating mass support

Perón's chief concern was to develop his contacts with the workers and peasants. Unlike Argentina's pre-1943 rulers, Perón regarded the masses as a critical force in politics. Rather than despise them, he chose to attract them by showing sympathy towards their difficulties. He regarded the workers as inexperienced in politics, but judged that this made them a potentially highly useful force. If he could enlist them in his cause, their sheer numbers and economic importance would be a huge asset.

Perón's policy amounted to more than simply backing workers' rights in theory. His officials actively encouraged strikes as a way of forcing employers to accept union demands. While this obviously sustained Perón's popularity with the workers, it also created lasting resentment among employers who were unconvinced by Perón's assurances that it was a way of keeping the workers in order and preventing social unrest.

Defeat of army opposition, October 1945

It was jealousy of Perón's growing popularity and worries about his close relations with the *descamisados* that led a group of his opponents within the army to order his arrest and imprisonment on the grounds that he was creating public disorder. The extent of Perón's popular following was immediately revealed in a large-scale protest outside the prison which forced the authorities to release him after only four days. Of particular significance in the episode was the part played by Eva Duarte, a prominent female

🔑 KEY TERM

Populist A political approach that seeks to create a direct relationship between the leader and the people, based on the idea that the leader has a special understanding of the people's needs.

Descamisados 'The shirtless ones', a term first used pejoratively by the upper class to describe Argentina's manual workers. Eva Perón's application of the word to the workers and the poor of Argentina turned it into a term of respect rather than abuse.

supporter. Eva, or Evita ('little Eva'), as she became better known, was to prove to be one of his greatest political assets. In this instance, she had not organized the protest, but, once it had begun, she was foremost in supporting him. The couple were married soon after his release.

SOURCE C

An extract from a letter written in 1951 from a young girl asking Eva Perón for her help, quoted in *The Argentina Reader*, edited by Gabriela Nouzelles and Graciela Montaldo, published by Duke University Press, Durham and London, UK, 2002

My dear Evita, I'm not going to ask you for anything the way everybody else around here does, cause the only thing I want is for you to read this letter and remember my name. I know that if you keep my name in your mind even if it's just for one little minute nothing can happen to me and I'll be happy and not have any ailments or miseries. I'm 17 and I sleep on the mattress you left at my house for a present last Christmas. I love you lots, pretty Evelina.

> What information does Source C convey, regarding the relationship that Eva Perón had established with ordinary Argentinians by the 1950s?

Perón's bid for the presidency

← **Why did Perón's presidential campaign prove successful?**

The popular backing he had received encouraged Perón to believe that the presidency itself was within his grasp. It was as a member of Partido Laborista (the Argentine Labour Party) that Perón stood for election in February 1946. His close relations with the workers led some of the conservative officers to continue to oppose him. Significantly, they were joined in this by the US ambassador in Buenos Aires, Spruille Braden, who, in effect, campaigned against Perón by openly supporting the Democratic Union, the Labour Party's main challenger.

US hostility towards Perón was a consequence of the strained post-war relations between Argentina and the USA. Braden represented the prevalent fear in the USA that South America was in danger of falling under Soviet influence. Ironically, the USA had previously been concerned about Perón's supposed fascist leanings, a sign of how difficult it was to be precise about Perón's political attitudes.

In the event, Braden's intervention actually helped Perón, who was able to play upon nationalist feelings to suggest that he stood for Argentine independence in a battle against US domination. In the run up to the presidential election, Perón further appealed to nationalist sentiment by successfully pressing the government to nationalize Argentina's Central Bank. To this shrewd move, he added what was practically an electoral bribe by using his authority as Minister of Labour to grant special Christmas bonuses to the workers. Against such astute populist touches, the opposition groups were unable to block the wave of support for Perón. In the election, he gained a popular vote that was 11 per cent ahead of his nearest rival. He now began a presidency that was to last nine years during which he created a new form of government – Perónism.

What ideas formed
Perón's political
outlook?

Perón's ideology

Juan Perón was the first Argentinian leader to make the will of the people a principle of government. He made a direct personal identification with the people, an approach which stood in marked contrast to the disregard shown towards the masses by leaders previously. This did not make Perón a democrat; he did not regard popular support as indispensable to his authority. But in his judgement, it did elevate his leadership to a higher plane than the merely political. He was not simply a leader of Perónism, the movement which took his name; he *was* the movement. Early in his first presidency he attempted to give the movement a philosophical base by making it synonymous with *justicialismo*, a system for providing justice for the people. It was said to rest on three fundamental principles:

- **social justice**
- autarky
- national political sovereignty.

Insofar as there is a definitive statement of Perónism as a political theory, it was contained in what Perón described as the 'the Twenty Truths', a list drawn up before he came into office in 1946 (see Source D).

What is notable about the Twenty Truths is that they are a set of assertions, not a developed philosophy. Neither do they form an economic programme. This is why Perónism in action often had a pragmatic quality to it. In practice, it became a mechanism for staying in power. This did not prevent the supporters of Perónism, the term being used interchangeably with *justicialismo* in the Twenty Truths, from ascribing high ideals to it. Ironically, Perónism was at its most appealing as an ideology during the two decades between 1955 and 1973 when Perón was in exile, the reason being that his followers could invest in it their own aspirations and intentions. This over the years led to splits in the movement, the main division being between the far Left and the nationalist Right, both wings believing that ultimately the party could be shaped to its own particular design.

There is a fascinating sense in which Perónism, the movement that bore Perón's name, was a greater force than he was. This was because those who called themselves **Perónists** imparted to the term their own expectations and beliefs rather than slavishly embracing Perón's ideas.

KEY TERM

Justicialismo A Perónist system said to rest on three fundamental principles: social justice, autarky and national sovereignty.

Social justice A system in which the law operates to create equal rights for all and prevent exploitation of the weak by the powerful.

Perónists Supporters of Perón and Perónism.

SOURCE D

'The Twenty Truths' quoted in *Perón Meidante*, by Guido Indij (translated by Mitchell Abidor), published by La Marca Editora, Argentina, 2006, p. 40.

According to Source D, what social values do Perónism and justicialism represent?

The Twenty Truths, 1946

1. *True democracy is when the government defends only one interest: that of the people.*

2. *Perónism represents the will of the people.*

3. *The individual Perónist works for the Perónist Movement.*

4. *For Perónism there is only one class: those who work.*

5. *In the New Argentina work is both a right and a duty. Justice requires that no one should consume more than he produces.*

6. *For the Perónist there is nothing better than another Perónist.*

7. *No Perónist should feel that he is more than he is, nor less than he should be. When a Perónist begins to feel that he is more than he is, he begins to change into an oligarch.*

8. *In political action, the Perónist accepts the following order of values: first the Fatherland, then the movement and then the men.*

9. *Politics for us is a means not an end. The end is the good of the Fatherland, which means the happiness of its children and national greatness.*

10. *The two arms of Perónism are Social Justice and Social Welfare. These embrace the people with justice and love.*

11. *Perónism seeks national unity not strife. It needs heroes but not martyrs.*

12. *In the New Argentina the only privileged ones are the children.*

13. *A government without doctrine is a body without soul. For this reason Perónism has a political, economic, and social doctrine: Justicialism.*

14. *Justicialism is a new philosophy, simple, practical, popular, profoundly Christian, and profoundly humanist.*

15. *As a political doctrine, Justicialism seeks a balance between the rights of the individual and the rights of the community.*

16. *As an economic doctrine, Justicialism puts capital to the service of the economy, which in turn serves the well being of society.*

17. *As a social doctrine, Justicialism seeks social justice, which is the guarantee of the people's rights.*

18. *Perónism seeks an Argentina socially just, economically free, and politically sovereign.*

19. *Perónism constitutes a central government, an organized state and a free people.*

20. *Argentina's greatest asset is its people.*

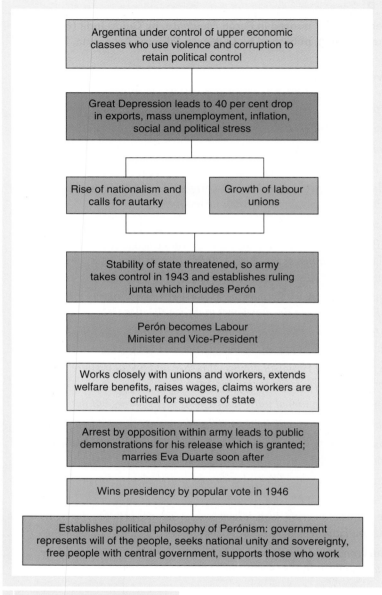

Argentina under control of upper economic classes who use violence and corruption to retain political control

Great Depression leads to 40 per cent drop in exports, mass unemployment, inflation, social and political stress

Rise of nationalism and calls for autarky

Growth of labour unions

Stability of state threatened, so army takes control in 1943 and establishes ruling junta which includes Perón

Perón becomes Labour Minister and Vice-President

Works closely with unions and workers, extends welfare benefits, raises wages, claims workers are critical for success of state

Arrest by opposition within army leads to public demonstrations for his release which is granted; marries Eva Duarte soon after

Wins presidency by popular vote in 1946

Establishes political philosophy of Perónism: government represents will of the people, seeks national unity and sovereignty, free people with central government, supports those who work

SUMMARY DIAGRAM

Perón's rise to power

Perón's establishment of an authoritarian state

> ▶ *Key question: How did Perón impose his authority on Argentina?*

Following his formal installation in June 1946, Perón had two consecutive terms as President. The first ran from 1946 to 1951; the second, following his re-election in 1951, lasted until his overthrow in 1955.

Perón's consolidation of authority, 1946–55

At the start of his presidency, Perón judged that his obvious first need was to retain the support of four key institutions: the army, the police, the civil service, and the Catholic Church. Perón's technique was to cultivate all these groups by confirming their rights and privileges and extending his **patronage** towards them. He was also determined to retain the support of a key political organization: the Argentine Labour Party.

The army

Having been opposed earlier by a military faction, Perón set about purging the army of suspect officers. Those who were too well entrenched to be removed he endeavoured to win over by promising that if they stayed loyal to him they would be rewarded with promotions and increased army salaries. As events would later show, his patronage did not guarantee permanent support, but it enabled him to establish his authority during his first presidential term, 1946–51.

The police

In similar style, Perón won the police over by offering loyal officers rapid promotion and financial benefits. His relationship with the police proved critical when he began to suppress opposition. The willingness of the law enforcement agencies to implement Perón's tough line gave them a dominant and feared place in society.

The civil service

Patronage again proved successful in the civil service; Perón granted privileges to officials willing to implement his plans. He calculated that well-rewarded bureaucrats were more likely to remain loyal. This was undeniably a form of corruption, but without it government was scarcely possible.

The Catholic Church

In return for their official approval of his regime, the higher ranks of the Catholic clergy were granted recognition of their status and of the Church's special place in Argentine society in such fields as education and moral guidance. The right of the Church to lay down the principles which should

> **How did Perón establish his authority?**

KEY TERM

Patronage Providing government approval and support and extending privileges to selected individuals and groups.

govern society in such sensitive areas as relations between the sexes, family life and the upbringing of children was recognized. Church teachings condemning contraception, abortion and divorce were not to be challenged.

The Perónista Party

Perón had used the Argentine Labour Party effectively to further his presidential ambitions. But, once he had achieved office, he was opposed to its continuance as an independent political organization. He, therefore, dissolved it in 1946 and replaced it with the *Partido Perónista* (the Party of Perón). As its name indicated, the new party took its identity from him. It was he who gave it its character and purpose. To ensure that this remained the case, Perón insisted that the party's constitution formally recognize him as the ultimate authority by accepting that he had:

- the right to approve the party's candidates for election and to appoint its officials.
- the power to overrule any decision made by the party.

The party's constitution served as the model for Argentina's National Constitution which was formally adopted in 1949, endowing Perón with complete authority over the Argentinian state.

The governmental system

In theory, the system was an electoral hierarchy, with Perón owing his authority to the vote of the people. In practice, Perón's monopoly of the media, his ability to manipulate the voting system, and his right to appoint ministers and key officials made him all powerful. Under the terms of his constitutional powers, Perón established a state security bureau which acted as a secret police service whose main task was the identifying and suppression of opposition.

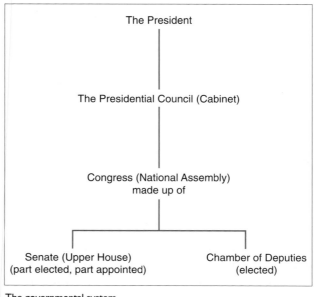

The governmental system

The unions

Perón linked his destruction of a separate labour party with a similar attack on the trade unions. They had helped him greatly in his rise to the presidency but he had no wish to see them develop as an independent socialist force. He wanted them to regard him as their essential leader with total control of their organization, the General Confederation of Labour (GLF). To that end, he closed down the existing unions and replaced them with **syndicates**. He stressed that he did this not to weaken trade unionism but to strengthen it. He claimed that since he understood the workers, he would now be the instrument through which their hopes would be realized. It was a logical aspect of his **populism** and was a critical move in his assumption of power.

To hide the repressive nature of his policy, Perón emphasized the benefits that would follow from the syndicates which operated under the banner of the CGT:

- greater freedom for workers to negotiate
- state protection of workers against employers
- higher wages
- improved working conditions.

Cipriano Reyes and Luis Gay, heads respectively of the Meat-packers Union and of the Telephone Workers Union, had been enthusiastic Perón supporters but they protested against his dictatorial authority over the unions. Perón reacted angrily. He had both men arrested in 1947 and tortured on false charges of spying for the USA and issuing death threats against the President and his wife. Some union leaders in the CGT resigned in protest, but the majority chose to conform. The result was as Perón had intended: deprived of leaders willing to speak out, the CGT became a subservient department of state carrying out Perón's demands.

Perón's policies during his first term, 1946–51

In 1946, Perón inherited a healthy economy. The nation's trade was in balance, allowing Argentina to begin settling its debts. Encouraged by this, Perón announced that his objective was to turn Argentina into a socially just and an economically self-sufficient nation. The major step towards this was the introduction of a **Five-Year Plan**.

The Five-Year Plan, 1946–50

A large portion of national income was to be redistributed among the workers, which led to **real wages** rising by over a third between 1946 and 1951.

A social welfare programme was drafted, which included the provision of medical services and unemployment and sickness benefits.

Levies were imposed on Argentina's main exports, meat and wheat, in order to provide greater quantities for domestic consumption.

KEY TERM

Syndicates State-controlled worker organizations.

Populism A form of politics that seeks to create a direct relationship between the leader and the people, based on the idea that the leader has a special understanding of the people's needs.

Five-Year Plan A programme for industrial development based on a set of production quotas.

Real wages Earnings measured not by their nominal value but by their purchasing power.

What were Perón's aims for Argentina during his first term?

Institute for the Promotion of Argentine Commerce (IAPI) – A state-controlled organization empowered to use government funds to promote Argentina's trade.

ISI Import Substituting Industrialization – replacing imported goods with home-produced commodities.

GATT General Agreement on Tariffs and Trade, an international body established in 1947 with the aim of making world commerce fairer and more profitable for all concerned by reducing tariffs and removing trade barriers.

IMF International Monetary Fund – a scheme which began operating in 1947 with the aim of preventing nations from becoming insolvent. Member states made deposits into a central fund from which they could draw in time of need.

Third Way An approach that avoids the extremes of communism and capitalism.

? According to Source E, what impact did the Marshall Plan have on Argentina?

- The **Institute for the Promotion of Argentine Commerce (IAPI)** became the guaranteed buyer of the bulk of Argentina's grain.
- Foreign-owned enterprises, such as the railways, the telephone system, the docks, public transport and utilities, were nationalized with the aim of raising government revenue.
- A state-organized **ISI** scheme was adopted to restrict imports and promote domestic production and consumption.
- Schemes were adopted for the improvement of Argentina's infrastructure with special attention given to communications, transport and energy provision with the aim of developing both the public and private sectors.
- To retain Argentina's economic and financial independence, Perón declined to join **GATT** and the **IMF**.

The Third Way

In 1949, Perón summed up his policies as the pursuit of a '**Third Way**', a policy that ran between the extremes of communism and capitalism and was aimed at making Argentina a self-sufficient industrial power. This was a striking attempt at creating balance, but in practice the Third Way satisfied neither Left nor Right. Socialists and conservatives came to look on Perón with disfavour and suspicion.

As to the idea of self-sufficiency, economic historians now stress that in the twentieth century it was impossible for any nation to be a genuine autarky. Perón soon had to abandon his attempted isolationism (see page 243), one feature of which had been his rejection of the **Marshall Plan**. By declining the USA's offer of large-scale financial assistance, Perón had sacrificed a major opportunity of acquiring investment for growth. Joseph Page, a leading Perón biographer, stressed the significance of this (see Source E).

SOURCE E

Excerpt from *Perón: A Biography* by Joseph Page, published by Random House, UK, 1983, p. 139.

The Marshall Plan drove a final nail into the coffin that bore Perón's ambitions to transform Argentina into an industrial power. As a non-beneficiary, Argentina was denied vital resources and markets and did not have the means to compensate for these from its own resources.

Perón's re-election

Opposition to Perón rose towards the end of his first term, but it was not strong enough to prevent his re-election in 1951. Greatly aided by the affection felt by the masses for his wife, Eva, as a social reformer (see page 270), Perón was able to claim that by continuing as President he would be able to fulfil his promise to the nation. It had been his original intention that Eva should be his running-mate as Vice-President, but a combination of resistance from a faction within the army and her rapidly declining health made this impossible. Nevertheless, in the election, the first in which women in Argentina had the vote (see page 270), Perón won easily gaining 64 per cent of the 7 million votes cast. This compared with 1946 when he had won 2.4 million votes (54 per cent). However, a detail that puts Perón's 1951 victory into perspective was that in the election campaign, his control of the media prevented the opposing candidates from receiving coverage in the press or on radio.

Perón's second term, 1951–55

During Perón's first term, the government's support of the unions' pay claims had increased the purchasing power of the workers. But, by the time of Perón's second term, the demand for goods that this created could not be met. There were not enough commodities available. Argentina's industry had not developed to the point where it could meet domestic needs. Demand outstripped supply. The result was rising inflation as too much money chased too few goods.

As a consequence, the IAPI could no longer afford to subsidise wages. It now reversed its policy and called for them to be reduced or frozen. As a result, real wages fell by 40 per cent between 1950 and 1954. Inflation reduced the profits previously enjoyed by employers and manufacturers and wiped out the value of fixed incomes and pensions. The worst affected were the industrial workers and the lower middle class, which included such groups as shopkeepers, local traders and teachers.

The Second Five-Year Plan, 1953

In an attempt to prevent further decline Perón introduced a second Five-Year Plan in 1953, setting a number of key objectives:

- State subsidies to farmers were introduced, the aim being to increase surplus produce, which could be sold as exports, thus lessening Argentina's trade deficit.
- To prevent the extra food produce being domestically consumed, a freeze on workers' wages was imposed so as to restrict their purchasing power.
- To encourage investment from outside, Perón allowed foreign companies to establish themselves in Argentina. One example was Standard Oil, the US company which was granted extraction and refining rights in return for cheaper oil prices for Argentina. However, the expected benefits proved double-edged. The advanced machinery the company used reduced the number of manual workers required with the result that unemployment rose.
- To make up for falling revenues, Perón ordered the printing of more paper currency. The result was rapid inflation. Between 1950 and 1955, the Argentinian peso lost over half its value against the US dollar. In 1950 the exchange rate was $1 to 16.5 pesos; in 1955 it was $1 to 36 pesos.

Perón's U-turn

The remarkable aspect of the Second Five-Year Plan was that it amounted to a U-turn.

← **Why did problems mount for Perón in his second term?**

 **KEY TERM**

Marshall Plan A plan adopted by the USA in 1947 under which it offered to provide substantial amounts of dollars to any country willing to grant trade concessions to the United States in return.

- Without openly abandoning his claim to a special relationship with the *descamisados*, Perón had, in effect, asked the traditional conservative elite of the *estancieros* and big business to form a common front against the demands of the workers.
- Perón had also sharply modified his attitude towards foreign capital. Contrary to his earlier aim of achieving economic independence, he began to appeal for international investment in both private and nationalized enterprises in Argentina. He invited the USA to look upon his country as an area where major US concerns, such as the automobile and oil industries, had a lucrative future because of the favours Argentina was now prepared to offer them.

Weakness of the policies

Critics of the U-turn pointed to the contradictions between the two Five-Year Plans:

- By encouraging a shift during Perón's first term from **heavy** to **light engineering** and manufacturing, the first plan had limited the chances of Argentinian industrial growth.
- An attempted reversal of this policy after 1951 was insufficient to recover the lost opportunity. Farming, industry, power generating and transport all lacked up-to-date machines.
- However, these could be bought only if there was adequate investment, the funds for which simply did not exist, largely because of the problems Perón had created by his pursuit of autarky.
- Having tried to follow 'a middle way', which included a refusal to join such bodies as the IMF and GATT, Argentina could not borrow easily in the international market and its accumulation of domestic capital fell far short of its needs.

Perón's call for unity

The rapid inflation hit the workers hard by greatly reducing the real value of their wages. The fall in purchasing power made worse by the imposed wage freeze caused great bitterness. Aware from the increasing number of strikes that the workers resorted to that his policies were alienating those elements in society, the middle and working classes, on whose support his popularity had been based during his first term as president, Perón sought to repair the damage. He issued an appeal for national unity and a willingness to make sacrifices so that justice for all could be achieved. But in the straitened circumstances, the response fell short of what he expected.

Opposition to Perón

During his first presidential term, Perón had won over or pacified the major institutions (see page 251). He had played off potential opposition factions against each other and drew strength from three particular factors:

- his relations with the workers whose hero he had become
- the backing of the army
- the support of the Church.

KEY TERM

Heavy engineering
Large-scale manufactures based on the use of iron and steel.

Light engineering Skilled, specialized activities such as precision tool-making.

Why did opposition to Perón develop during his second presidency?

SOURCE F

Perónist propaganda poster, presented in the form of a cinema bill. It is headed, 'Now showing – Evil Ones' and reads: 'A man who lives but does not work is a despicable parasite, preying on those who do work.' Top left, it shows loyal workers entering a factory called 'New Argentina'.

What information does Source F provide concerning Perónist attitudes towards the workers?

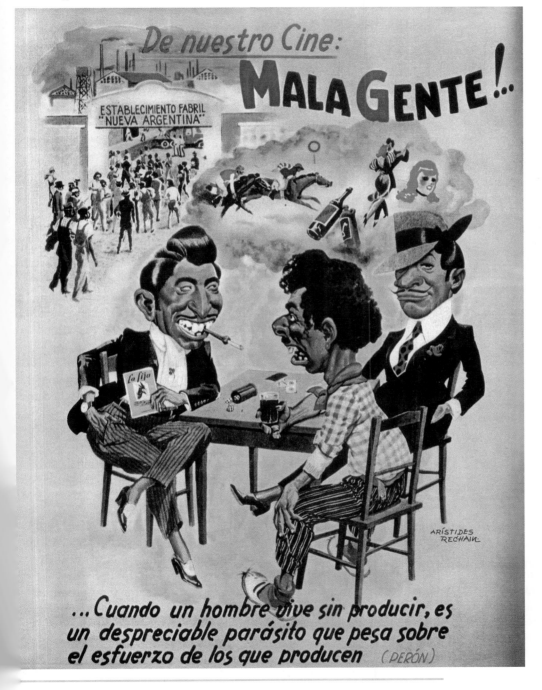

Those factors ceased to be a source of support during his second term. A particular tragedy was the death of Eva in July 1952. With her passing, Perón lost not only a wife and companion but someone who had become an icon to the mass of the Argentinian people. Perón's popularity had become dependent on hers. In some ways she had been his greatest asset and her absence after 1952 was a political loss as well as a personal bereavement.

Reasons for opposition

Perón's second-term policies aroused anger among all the underprivileged classes in Argentina. The measures had in a sense broken what had earlier seemed a special bond between the regime and the people. The result was the formation of an angry opposition to Perón. This was sometimes expressed as opposition to Perónism as separate from Perón as a person. The distinction enabled the adulation of Perón to continue even after his policies had been found wanting.

Opposition to bureaucracy

The government bureaucracy grew markedly during Perón's time in power. He used his authority over the appointment of officials as a technique for buying and maintaining political support. This worked as a broad strategy but it produced a bloated and costly administration and inadvertently provided a target for opponents to attack.

Opposition from the workers

Having earlier removed those trade union leaders who had opposed him (see page 253), Perón had turned the workers' representative body, the CGT, into a means of suppressing them. Most of its top officials were Perónist appointees with the result that worker–state or worker–employer negotiations and settlements were in effect dictated by government bureaucrats who declared that strikes were forbidden. In protest against this, rank and file members of the unions ignored their leaders and took to the streets. The two largest demonstrations, a sugar workers strike of 1949 and a transport workers strike of 1951, were broken up by the army and police with great brutality. An ominous development was the assistance given to the police by squads of Perónists, who, calling themselves the National Liberation Alliance (NLA), roamed the streets assaulting the strikers and their families.

Opposition from the upper classes

Perón's policy of appealing to the *descamisados* by introducing policies that favoured their interests caused lasting resentment among employers. By tradition, Argentina's upper classes had only contempt for those they regarded as the lower orders. Class division was engrained in Argentinian society. Perón's challenge to this earned him the bitterness of the privileged who did not believe his claim that he was seeking a balanced, harmonious society. They saw his pro-worker reforms as a threat to their traditional status. Ernesto Sammartino, leader of the **Radical Civic Union**, dismissed

KEY TERM

Radical Civic Union A conservative group, to which many businessmen belonged, formed in opposition to Perón.

Perón's supporters as animals in a zoo. Knowing that his objection to Perón's policies would lead to his arrest, Sammartino fled the country.

Opposition from the Catholic Church

Perón had been on good terms with the Catholic Church when he had first become President in 1946 (see page 251). He had been willing to recognize its rights and privileges, but relations soon soured. Churchmen were unhappy with the way Perónist propaganda urged the people to idolize their leader. Perón's reputation as a womanizer was also strongly criticized by the clergy, who were further angered in 1954 by government measures legalizing divorce and prostitution. For his part, Perón was embittered by the Church's refusal to consider Eva Perón for immediate **canonization** after her death in 1952.

A more directly political issue arose when Perón tried to ban the Christian-Democrat Party which the Church had helped found. Perón's government and the **Church hierarchy** traded insults. The Catholic clergy used **pastoral letters** to denounce Perón to their congregations. Religious processions were turned into anti-Perón demonstrations. Perónists responded with mass gatherings at which the Catholic clergy were denounced for their interference in politics. Crisis point was reached when Perón expelled a bishop and two priests from the country for what he regarded as treasonable opposition. The Church's response went beyond Argentina. In June 1955, Pope Pius XII, as head of the Catholic Church, formally **excommunicated** Perón.

Excommunication

For Perón, the most worrying feature was not excommunication, but the way in which the Church in Argentina used its influence with the people generally, and the army in particular, to undermine his position. He was right to be anxious about the build up of opposition. While speaking at a Perónist rally in Plaza de Mayo in Buenos Aires, following his excommunication, a mutinous air force squadron flew over and bombed the crowd, killing over 350 people. The attempted coup failed but it set in motion a series of military challenges to Perón's authority. Blaming the Church as much as the military for this, his supporters reacted by wrecking churches and assaulting clerics. Arson became a common method used by both sides to attack opponents.

Perón tried to rally popular support through propaganda and mass meetings. He made a direct appeal to his followers to regard themselves as saviours of the Argentine state and to be prepared to work to a **5:1 destruction ratio**. But these were acts of desperation that could not hide the fact that Perón had lost the support of key sections of the military.

Perón's overthrow, 1955

Of all the opposition groups that formed against Perón, the critical one was the army. Never a united body, it was composed of factions that could easily splinter or turn against someone they had originally supported. To retain the loyalty of his officers during his presidency, Perón had lavished favours on

KEY TERM

Canonization The conferring of sainthood by the Catholic Church.

Church hierarchy Argentina's Catholic bishops who had authority over the clergy and laity.

Pastoral letters Formal addresses from the bishops read out to the people attending Sunday mass.

Excommunicated Formally dismissed from membership of the Catholic Church.

5:1 destruction ratio Perónist policy of killing five opponents in retaliation for every one of their own number killed.

them. But this was never enough to gain the support of all the military. It was an army faction which joined with the Church to form the strongest opposition grouping. The bishops gave their backing to a combination of anti-Perón army and navy units, which, led by General Eduardo Lonardi, moved against Perón openly in September 1955.

Unable to rally sufficient military support, Perón thought of arming his loyal trade unionist followers and forming a civilian counter-force but it was all too late. Fearing for his life as the revolt grew, he fled by river boat to safety in Paraguay. After nearly a decade, he had been forced from power. It was to be another eighteen years before he returned to Argentina.

How did Perónism continue to affect Argentina during his exile?

Perón's continuing influence, 1955–73

Perón's exile did not end military rule in Argentina. It was only the personnel who changed. The governments after 1955 were still essentially military in character. Perón's influence was still felt; the governments that wrestled with Argentina's problems after him were operating within the system that he had fashioned. Besides creating a large bureaucracy, whose members still expected to receive the privileges that came with their posts, he had also lifted the aspirations of many groups in society including the middle and working classes. He may not always have met their expectations but he had aroused them; the consequence was that all the governments that succeeded Perón's were judged by comparison with his. So powerful did his influence remain that one of the later presidents, Arturo Frondizi, chose to describe his own policy as 'Perónism without Perón'.

The Perónists

A major destabilizing factor was that the Perónists remained a political force. Although they were periodically proscribed as a party, they continued to be active, dreaming of their leader's return, and ready to challenge all the interim governments, which they necessarily regarded as only temporary. Nor was Perón quiet during the time he was away from Argentina. He was in continual contact with his supporters in Argentina, including trade unionists giving them instructions and directions and offering advice.

A troubled interlude, 1955–73

For the eighteen years after Perón's departure in 1955, the story was of short-lived administrations wrestling unsuccessfully with the social unrest that confronted Argentina. Short periods of relative calm were interspersed with disturbed times when strikes proliferated and city riots were common. A vivid example of the unrest that did occur was the *cordobazo* in 1969 when a loose combination of communists and Perónists joined striking car workers in a two-day riot. Although the rioters were eventually dispersed by troops, the troubles helped to bring down the government of the day. As had been the case since the 1930s, the army held the key to power. It was because influential officers supported Perón that he was able to return to Argentina in June 1973.

KEY TERM

Cordobazo A violent rising in the Argentinian city of Cordoba in May 1969.

Perón's third term, 1973–74

Half a million ecstatic supporters greeted Perón at the airport on his arrival. But such were the fierce political divisions in the Argentina to which he returned, the fiercest being between opposing Perónist factions, that his return became the scene of a savage clash between trade unionists and *montoneros*, which resulted in hundreds of deaths. Nevertheless, within four months of his return, he had been elected president for the third time.

Perón's aims

As president for the third time, his intention was to return to the policies that he regarded as having been successful in his earlier terms. He still believed that he could unite Argentina under his leadership and guide it towards progress and greater self-sufficiency. His first steps included the following:

- Banks and selected industries were nationalized.
- Foreign investment was discouraged.
- Local businesses received state subsidies.
- Welfare schemes were reintroduced.
- State loans were advanced to urban workers for house purchase.
- Taxes were imposed on land values.
- The IAPI was re-established.

Attempts to reassert authority

Appreciating that none of his economic reforms would be successful unless political stability was restored, Perón set about imposing his authority. His greatest problem was the deep division between his own followers. During his eighteen-year absence, the Left-wing of the Perónist groupings, the *montoneros*, had become a predominant element. They had supported Perón's return in the belief that he would crush both the conservatives and the trade unionists and turn Argentina into a fully socialist society. But Perón resolved instead to crush the *montoneros*. Backed by the moderates and conservatives in the army and the party, he authorized extra-legal measures to be used against them. At the same time he appealed for an end to the violence that was disfiguring Argentina (see Source G).

SOURCE G

Excerpt from a speech by Perón in June 1973, quoted by Juan Torre in *The Cambridge History of Latin America*, vol. viii, edited by Leslie Bethell, published by CUP, UK, 1996, p. 145.

We have a revolution to make, but for it to be valid it must be a peaceful reconstruction. We are in no condition to keep destroying in the face of a destiny pregnant with ambushes and dangers. It is necessary to return to what in its time was our maxim: from work to home and from home to work. Justicialismo was never sectarian or exclusive and today it calls upon all Argentines without distinction so that all of us, with solidarity, will join together in the task of national reconstruction.

Why did Perón's last presidency prove unsuccessful?

KEY TERM

Montoneros Formed in 1970 in the wake of the *cordobazo*, they were an extreme Left-wing Perónist group who believed in waging urban guerrilla warfare; arson and assassination were among their preferred methods.

According to Source G, how is national reconstruction to be achieved?

Perón's problems

Perón's appeal for national unity did little to satisfy his followers:

- The *Perónistas* who had worked for his return found that he had lost his revolutionary drive.
- The middle class and the trade union members in the party were disturbed by Perón's declared aim of seeking 'an integrated society'; which they took to mean that he intended to remove the privileges he had previously granted them in return for their support.
- He upset another of his traditional props, the military, by intimating that while he intended to build up the army as a modern professional force he also planned to lessen its political influence.

KEY TERM

Triple A The Argentine Anti-communist Alliance.

Feudal A hierarchical system in which power is in the hands of an absolute ruler who distributes land and positions in return for required civil or military duties being performed.

Absolutism A governmental system in which the levers of power are exclusively in the hands of a group or an individual.

For all his apparent wish to see Argentina become an integrated democracy, Perón was still prepared to use his customary methods of repression. In order to destroy the Left-wing organizations of which he disapproved, he gave his backing to an undercover unit, known as the **Triple A**, whose methods for crushing communists and socialists included kidnapping, torture and assassination.

Whatever Perón's intentions may have been when, in October 1973, he became president for the third time, the reality was he was no longer in a position to direct events. He was 78 years old and had less than a year to live. During his last months he rapidly lost his sharpness of mind and political acumen, a consequence of the Alzheimer's disease which had begun to afflict him. He relied heavily on his third wife, Isabel Cartas, whom he had married in 1962 and who had been elected as his Vice-President. By the time Perón died from a heart attack in July 1974, she was, in effect, running the presidency, something which she then did formally in her own right as President after his death.

How far did Perón achieve a totalitarian state?

A totalitarian state?

It has been suggested that rather than being totalitarian, Perón's rule is better described as **feudal**, the notion being that he behaved in the manner of a medieval European monarch, who, backed by a powerful army, distributed patronage and privilege but always retained absolute authority for himself at the centre of things. This is a striking image, but the analogy breaks down in relation to the **absolutism** that lay at the heart of historical feudalism. Perón was never absolute. It is true that Perónism grew into a powerful movement that engaged the emotions of the Argentinian people and created a cult around Perón and his wife, Evita. At its highest point, Perón's popularity was greater than any Argentine, possibly any South American, leader in history. Yet, as his being forced from office in 1955 proved, when opposition became too strong he did not have the means to retain control. Patronage was effective in buying support at given times but was never a guarantee of permanent authority.

The character of Argentinian government

Argentina was by tradition a corrupt political system. Preferment and favour were bought and sold. This did not change under Perón; indeed, he exploited it. But just as he was its manipulator, so, also, he was its victim. When he upset the nation's strongest residual institutions, the Church and the army, and they combined against him, he did not have the resources to resist them. He could call on no tradition or constitutional precedent strong enough to overcome them. It was not a matter of his failing a democratic test. Argentina was not a working democracy. Elections were not genuinely free. That had worked to his advantage. But, since the system was subject to the play of politics, it could also, as events showed, work to his detriment. This weakness applied also to the economy. Unless they have absolute power to call on, all regimes are dependent for their strength on the state of the economy. Despite his remarkable innovations and experiments in this field, Perón was ultimately overtaken by economic problems he could not solve.

Authoritarian government, invariably of a military character, was the norm in South American countries, including Argentina. The chronic failure to establish civilian government conditioned the population to accept military rule as the only workable system. Civilian administrations were seen as lacking the strength to impose their policies. Therefore, even when military rule was not in itself genuinely popular it was regarded, *faute de mieux*, as the only system with a realistic chance of meeting national needs. Perón's regime was a continuation of that tradition. But, while authoritarian, Perón was never powerful enough to be totalitarian.

A number of factors prevented Argentina from being a totalitarian state under Perón:

- The frequency with which opposition formed against him and his awareness of how fragile his hold was over the nation undermined any idea of his achieving absolute authority.
- The success of his early policies together with the severity with which he crushed dissent tends to make his power appear greater than it was. But the ferocity of the challenge to him during his second term, his eventual overthrow in 1955, and his long wait in exile before his return in 1973 indicated how limited his power was.
- Perón's authority was always contingent upon events over which he was not the master. Had he not been a soldier he could not have come to power. Military force sustained him in office but, since it was the final arbiter, it was also the reason why he was rejected.

 **KEY TERM**

Faute de mieux In the absence of a better alternative.

Consolidation of authority:

– Promotions, salary increases and granting of privileges to army, police and civil service.
– Grants Catholic Church control of education, agrees to accept Church teachings on contraception, abortion and divorce.
– Partido Perónista established with Perón in control of all of the party.
– 1949 constitution gives Perón control over all aspects of state.
– Unions abolished and replaced with state-operated syndicates.

Perón's rule

First term: 1946–51

Third Way:

- Redistribution of national income to workers; 33 per cent rise in real wages.
- Medical, unemployment, sickness benefits established.
- Taxes on exports to allow more local consumption.
- Nationalized foreign businesses, plus transportation, utilities, communications, etc.
- Invested in infrastructure.
- Declined to join international economic organizations such as GATT and Marshall Plan.

Second term: 1951–55

Reverses many first-term policies:

- Reduced worker wages by 40 per cent to reduce consumption from 1951–54.
    - Increased consumption meant high inflation for the few goods available for purchase.
    - Need to increase exports to pay debts.
- Foreign companies allowed to re-enter economy, granted privileges.
- Money printed in large quantities; major inflation as currency lost value.
- Sought political and economic assistance from upper economic classes.

Opposition builds from:

- betrayed workers; protests attacked by army and police
- upper economic classes who resented earlier support for workers and higher taxes
- Catholic Church after Perón legalized prostitution, divorce; opposed Church-supported party; exiled Church officials
- pro-Church military officials forced him to flee to Paraguay, September 1955.

Third term: 1973–74

Returns from exile, elected President shortly afterwards.

Reinstitutes many former policies:

- Nationalizes banks and selected industries.
- Discourages foreign investment.
- Subsidises local businesses.
- Reintroduces welfare programmes.
- Issues state loans to workers to purchase housing.
- Taxes land values.
- Backs anti-communist Triple A that attacks opponents.

Dies in July 1974.

Life in Argentina under Perón, 1943–74

▶ **Key question:** *What impact did Perón's rule have on the lives of the Argentinian people?*

From early on in his first term, Perón began the process of intensifying his grip on Argentina.

Perón's repression of opposition

← **What methods did Perón's regime use to enforce control over the people?**

Contrary to his often-declared belief in freedom of speech, Perón became increasingly dictatorial as opposition to him grew. This amounted to an attack on press, academic and cultural liberties.

Control of the media

A new law, **desacato**, was introduced, requiring newspapers, journals and radio stations to abandon all criticism of the regime. Censorship was imposed and editors and journalists who declined to conform were arrested and imprisoned. Argentina's radio network was compulsorily purchased by the government so that only pro-Perón news was broadcast. The country's major newspaper, **La Prensa**, which had represented contrary opinions, was taken over by the CGT and transformed into a mouthpiece for the regime. With the media largely silenced, it became difficult for organized protest to make itself heard as the authorities stifled legitimate political complaint by a series of restrictive measures:

- Editors were required to submit their copy to the authorities before publication.
- Unco-operative national and regional newspapers were closed down.
- The arbitrary arrest, interrogation and torture of editors and journalists became common.
- A prohibition was imposed on the reporting of public meetings disapproved of by the government.

The Perón cult

A controlled and subservient media allowed Perón to develop a **cult of personality**. His and Evita's name and image appeared everywhere as what amounted to a propaganda machine extolled the regime's virtues. There was no doubt that Perón became hugely popular. The reality was that Perón, as with Hitler in Germany (see page 71) and Mao Zedong in China (see page 146), established an affinity with ordinary people that went beyond politics and elevated him to a position where he was regarded as personal representative of the aspirations of large sections of the population.

It was the bond between leader and people which was the most characteristic feature of Perónism. It was a relationship that survived the

KEY TERM

Desacato Contempt – a legal restriction which was placed on opinions of which Perón's government disapproved.

La Prensa 'The Press' – a widely circulating newspaper that claimed to represent ordinary Argentinians.

Cult of personality A consistent use of mass propaganda to promote the idea of the leader as an ideal, heroic figure elevated above ordinary people and politics.

mistakes and failures of Perón as a political figure. Perónism outlived Perón, as was clear from the victory of Perónist parties in eight of the ten general elections held in Argentina in the thirty years after Perón's death.

Control of the courts

To prevent possible legal objections to his regime, Perón brought the nation's courts under government control. The most significant move was against the Supreme Court, Argentina's highest legal authority, responsible for overseeing the whole legal system. Angered by its resistance to his early reforms, such as land redistribution and imposed wage rises for workers, he persuaded the National Congress to charge the Court with treason and corruption. The majority of the Court's 50 members were dismissed and replaced with Perónist supporters. At a lower level, magistrates in local courts were dismissed if they were suspected of being anti-government. This was done under the pretence of reorganizing the courts to make them more responsive to the needs of the people.

Suppression of academic freedom

KEY TERM

Intelligentsia Persons of influence in the intellectual world; for example, academics and writers.

Angered by criticism of his regime among Argentina's **intelligentsia**, Perón mounted a direct attack on the universities:

- University departments were closed, including the School of Philosophy and Literature in Buenos Aires. Other suspect departments, such as History, had their state funding slashed.
- Over 1,500 university academics and administrators were dismissed, many of whom fled to the USA.
- Student unions were disbanded and individual students obliged to sign a pledge of loyalty to Perón.
- Academic publications were censored to remove criticisms of the regime.

Suppression of artistic freedom

As was to be expected, the increasing censorship that Perón imposed aroused the anger of writers and artists. His response was to threaten those who openly spoke out against the regime. A number of those who may be regarded as Argentina's cultural leaders, such as the actress and singer, Libertad Lamarque, chose to leave Argentina rather than stay and risk imprisonment. Prominent among those who were persecuted were:

- comedy actor, Nini Marshall, who sometimes mocked the government
- publisher, Victoria Ocampo, who allowed subversive literature to appear
- pianist, Osvaldo Pugliese, who declined to perform at Perónist rallies
- film director, Luis Saslavsky, whose works contained strongly implied criticisms of Perónism.

Jose Luis Borges

The regime's attitude towards culture was vividly displayed in Perón's treatment of Jose Luis Borges, Argentina's most celebrated writer at that time. Borges' reluctance to give his whole-hearted support to Perón led to his inclusion in a list of artists and writers who began to be persecuted. He was treated in a particularly humiliating way, with ridicule being used as a form of oppression. The holder of a prestigious public position in Argentina's main cultural centre, the Miguel Cane Library, Borges in 1946 was informed by the authorities that he was being 'elevated' to the position of chief inspector of poultry at a Buenos Aires meat market. Faced with this insult, he immediately resigned from government service. To show its solidarity with Borges, Argentina's main intellectual forum, the Society of Argentinian Writers (SADE), organized a dinner in celebration of his literary accomplishments. Borges could not attend the function, but he sent an address which he asked to be read out (see Source H).

SOURCE H

Excerpt from a 1946 address by Jorge Borges quoted in *Borges: A Life* by Edwin Williamson, published by Viking Books, UK, 2004, p. 295.

*Dictatorships breed oppression, dictatorships breed servility, dictatorships breed cruelty; more loathsome still is the fact that they breed idiocy. Bellboys babbling orders, portraits of **caudillos**, prearranged cheers or insults, walls covered with names, unanimous ceremonies, mere discipline usurping the place of clear thinking. Fighting these sad monotonies is one of the duties of a writer.*

According to Source H, what is the main duty of a writer under a dictatorship?

⚷ KEY TERM

Caudillos Political military leaders, such as Perón.

Borges became regarded as the main representative of artistic dissent during the Perón years. Against his own inclination, but judging that it might be a gesture of defiance to the regime, he allowed himself to be nominated and then elected President of SADE in 1951. What depressed Borges was the thought that the only reason the organization had not yet been closed down was that Perón regarded it as of barely peripheral influence in an Argentina in which the government controlled the press, radio and television.

However, government indifference turned to direct interference following Eva Perón's death in 1952. Borges and other writers had been as scathing of her as they had been of Perón, and the President did not tolerate criticism of his wife. Borges was told that the SADE offices had to put large photos of the President and the First Lady on permanent display. When Borges refused, as the authorities expected him to, he was placed under house arrest. Soon after, SADE was prohibited as an organization and its offices closed down. Borges joined in the celebrations that followed Perón's overthrow in 1955 and used his time as a free man to renew his condemnation of the fallen regime.

With the coming of Perón's third presidency in 1973, artists, writers and academics feared renewed repression. However, the brevity of the ailing Perón's last period in power meant that the all-out attack that had occurred in the earlier periods was not repeated. That Borges was totally blind by this time may also have been a factor explaining the apparent clemency.

Control of education

Education played a major part in Perón's attempt to impose himself on Argentinian culture. Schools were required to adapt the curriculum so that it incorporated *justicialismo* as a guiding influence on the young. Perón's and

Eva's speeches and writings were regularly circulated. The substance of these texts was less important than the image they were trying to project – namely that the leader and his wife represented the Argentinian ideal which the young should strive to emulate. Perón awarded himself the title of 'Liberator of the Republic' and Eva was referred to as 'The Spiritual Chief of the Nation'. Schools which did not willingly join in this cult of the Peróns were put under pressure; teachers who did not conform were dismissed and institutions that did not co-operate were closed.

Perón's increasing interference in educational matters intensified the conflict between the regime and the Catholic authorities who protested that the Perón cult was an affront to true spiritual values. The Catholic Church had been the traditional providers of schooling in Argentina, a situation that Perón at the start of his regime had willingly supported (see page 251). In 1945, he had made the teaching of Catholic religion and morals compulsory, followed a year later by the establishment of the Department of Religious Teaching, a move which confirmed the Church's educational monopoly. However, between 1954 and 1955, Perón completely reversed these policies in a series of restrictions on Catholic education:

- Religious teaching in state and private schools was prohibited.
- State funding of the Catholic schools was cut, causing a number to close.
- The right to appoint teachers to posts in universities and schools was taken over by the state.
- The Department of Religious Teaching, established by Perón in 1946, was abolished.
- The teaching of Catholic religion and morals was to be no longer compulsory.
- Catholic magistrates known to be opposed to Perón were dismissed.
- The National Congress declared that the link between Church and state in Argentina was dissolved and that the President and Vice-President were no longer required to be Catholics.

How did Argentina's minorities fare under Perón?

→ Treatment of minorities

Homosexuals

Same-sex relations, conducted in private between consenting adults, had been legal in Argentina since 1887. Perón did not attempt to change this and there was no direct persecution of homosexuality during his leadership of Argentina. However, it is known that he personally disapproved of the practice. His distaste for writers and artists may well have derived from his fear that homosexuals were beginning to play too prominent a role in Argentinian culture. His wish to see prostitution decriminalized was part of his campaign to reassert heterosexuality as the social norm. The growing appeal of football worried him, not because he disliked it as a sport, but because it was an all-male activity. For similar reasons, he was anxious to see the **tango** restored to its central place in popular public entertainment as a

 KEY TERM

Tango A traditional, stylized, erotic Argentinian dance, said to be the vertical expression of a horizontal desire.

dance that dramatically expressed the traditional image of the virility of Argentina's men and the femininity of its women. Special state subsidies were granted to film companies willing to produce cinema that celebrated the tango as a defining aspect of national life.

Jews

There were occasions when opponents accused Perón of being anti-Semitic. The charge was largely based on the fact that he allowed Argentina to be a sanctuary for Nazi war criminals who had fled Germany at the end of the Second World War in Europe. It was certainly true that among the most prominent escapees given residence in Perón's Argentina were Klaus Barbie, the notorious head of the **Gestapo** in France, Adolf Eichmann, one of the main organizers of the **Holocaust**, and Joseph Mengele, the notorious 'doctor of death', who experimented on prisoners at **Auschwitz**.

Yet there are no sure grounds for describing Perón as being actively anti-Semitic. Indeed, his actions indicated a marked lack of prejudice against the Jews:

- No restrictions were placed on Jews in Perón's Argentina and many of them held public office.
- Jews were to be found within Perón's own party and it was common for Jewish organizations in Argentina to give open electoral backing to Perón.
- A number of Perón's chief government advisers were Argentine Jews.
- Perón appointed the first Jewish professor at Argentina's National University, a gesture that met with the disapproval of the Catholic hierarchy.
- Argentina was also the first South American country to give formal diplomatic recognition to the state of Israel in 1948.
- Perón appointed a Jew as Argentina's ambassador to the new state of Israel.
- Perón's government negotiated a trade agreement which offered generous exchange terms to the Israelis.

Ethnic minorities

In 1960, Argentina's population was made up of the following ethnic categories:

- 54 per cent European descent
- 31 per cent mestizo (mixed European and Native American) descent
- 9 per cent Amerindien (Native American) descent
- 4 per cent Arab or Asian descent
- 2 per cent black African descent.

Historically, the non-white population had the poorest jobs and lived in the poorest conditions. Perón made no specific moves to improve the status of the non-whites. However, neither did he follow overt racial policies. It was always his claim that he saw all Argentinians as equals and that his policies for the improvement of living and working conditions were intended to embrace all the poor, regardless of ethnic differences. His attempt, therefore,

> **KEY TERM**
>
> **Gestapo** *Geheime Staatspolizei*, special state police in Germany and German-occupied Europe.
>
> **Holocaust** The systematic killing by Nazi Germany of 6 million European Jews between 1942 and 1945.
>
> **Auschwitz** The Nazis' main death camp in occupied Poland.

to awake a sense of self-worth in the poor and traditionally despised lower classes necessarily included the non-white minorities.

The role and status of women

What influence did Perónism have on the status of women in Argentina?

It would be no exaggeration to say that the status of women under the Perón regime can be measured by reference to one particular woman, Eva Perón. Such was her fame and stardom during her seven-year marriage to Perón that she brought attention to Argentina's women in a way that feminism as a general movement could not have done.

Evita made it one of her main concerns to advance the rights of women. She wrote articles in magazines and gave talks on radio in which she presented her case. She helped to give prominence to the parliamentary bill passed in 1947 granting female suffrage. The press made much of a specially arranged ceremony which saw Perón formally sign the bill and then pass it to Evita to hold it aloft. It was one of those gestures that helped identify her with the presidency. The public were being encouraged to regard Juan and Evita Perón not simply as man and wife, but as a progressive presidential team. It was propaganda, but showed a feel for public relations.

Evita as a women's role model

Coming from humble origins but possessed of a driving sense of ambition, Evita exploited her good looks and winning personality to charm officials and politicians into accepting her direct involvement in public affairs. Her personal touch, as much as her active promotion of women's rights at a formal level, helped to advance female emancipation. Here was a woman successfully breaking the conventions of a traditionally male-dominated society and actively entering national politics.

Although Evita had innate charm, there was also a toughness about her, which she explained as a product of her hard upbringing. Born illegitimately to a poor immigrant family which was then abandoned by her father, she had gone as a teenager to Buenos Aires where she earned a living as a nightclub hostess and dancer and played small parts in radio plays and films. Unashamed of the aggressive style of some of her speeches, she justified it by reference to her personal experience of poverty.

She embarked on a series of foreign tours, including one to Europe in 1947 during which her elegance and stylish dress sense elevated her to international celebrity status. Building on her growing popularity and influence, Evita used her contacts to establish the Women's Perónist Party in 1947, her declared purpose being to guarantee that in future 'no Argentine woman would any longer be denied the privilege of being a Perónist'. She stressed that 'just as only workers can wage their own struggle for liberation, so, too, only women can be the salvation of women'. She was concerned to stress, however, that her particular form of feminism was an adjunct, not a challenge, to Perónism.

SOURCE I

Excerpt from *My Mission in Life* by Eva Perón, published by Vantage Press, USA, 1953, p. iii.

I was not, nor am I anything more than a humble woman, a sparrow in an immense flock of sparrows, but Perón was, and is, a gigantic condor that flies high and sure among the summits and near to God. If it had not been for him who came down to my level and taught me to fly in another fashion, I would never ... have been able to contemplate the marvellous and magnificent immenseness of my people ... All that I am, all that I have, all that I think and all that I feel, belongs to Perón.

According to Source I, why was Eva Perón so concerned to give the credit to her husband for what she had achieved?

The Women's Perónist Party

Within four years of its foundation, the Women's Perónist Party had gained over half a million members represented by over 3,000 branches across Argentina. Numbers alone do not indicate the party's importance. It proved to be a consciousness-raising exercise, whose message was that women could now participate in public life. It was a remarkable achievement on Evita's part, but it has to be emphasized that she could not have done it without Perón. It was a two-way affair. She undoubtedly brought glamour and an appealing common humanity to his regime. But had she not been the wife of a man of military and political authority, her influence would have remained marginal. Her marriage to him in 1945 had proved a shrewd career move.

The Eva Perón Foundation

An initiative that proved especially popular and established the Peróns' credentials as committed social reformers was the founding in 1948 of the Eva Perón Foundation, a programme for relieving the lives of the poor. The statistics tell the story of its impact. Presented as an example of Perón's Third Way in action, the Foundation:

- established and managed 8,000 schools
- created 1,000 kindergartens
- set up 4,200 clinics, hospitals and care homes for the elderly
- built 25,000 homes for the poor in an area of Buenos Aires that became known as 'Evita city'
- provided holiday resorts for the workers and their families
- built special theme parks and play areas for children
- provided education scholarships and bursaries
- handed out basic food stuffs to the needy
- employed 14,000 staff, including doctors and nurses
- was allocated an annual government grant of over 50 million US dollars.

Perón had hoped to have Eva as his vice-presidential running mate in the 1951 election but her failing health as she fought against cervical cancer made this impossible. His original nomination of her offended some in the military and a number of officers used his supposedly unconstitutional step as a pretext for moving against him. Their attempted coup in September 1951 failed, however. Yet how much Perón's popularity was tied up with Eva's

? What information does Source J offer regarding the relationship between Juan and Eva Perón?

became evident after her death when he struggled as an individual to retain the popular acclaim that he and she had jointly enjoyed.

It is notable that the advance of women in the Perónist movement tended to stall after Eva's death, but the impact she had on a wider front was clear from the spread of women's rights groups particularly among the poor. By the 1980s, organizations devoted to the welfare of women were to be found in nearly every urban area. An interesting post-script is that it was women who were foremost in the protests on behalf of the **'Disappeared'** in the 1980s.

SOURCE J

Eva acknowledges the crowd's applause at a gathering of Perón's supporters in October 1951. Too frail to stand on her own, she has to be held upright by Perón.

The advancement of women's rights under the Peróns

1943–45	As Minister of Labour, Perón created the Department of Women's Labour, a recognition that nearly a million women were in the industrial workforce and needed special consideration.
1944	A minimum wage was introduced for piece-work done at home, which was overwhelmingly an occupation in which women engaged.
1947	The franchise was extended to women.
1947	Measures were adopted to improve the rights of girls and women in secondary and higher education.
1947	Steps were taken to ensure better wages and improved conditions for female industrial workers.
1949	Females made up 46 per cent of the workforce.
1949	Equal pay was granted for female textile workers.
1950	By this date the number of women at university had doubled in six years.
1951	Women vote for the first time. There was a turnout of 90 per cent among those registered to vote and 65 per cent of them supported Perón.
1951	Twenty-four women took their seats as elected members of Congress and seven women entered the Senate.

Perón's record

Perón was always a controversial figure and opinion remains divided over his accomplishments and legacy. It is helpful to list the points that Perón's contemporary supporters and later sympathizers applauded and set them against the points which Perón's contemporary opponents and later critics condemned.

← As leader of Argentina, what had Perón achieved for the people?

Achievements and positives

- Perón raised Argentina's national self-esteem by suggesting that its people were capable of advancement by their own efforts.
- He broadened the social base of public participation in national life by appealing to the working classes to think of themselves as contributors to the national endeavour.
- He and Eva Perón awoke a sense of self-worth in the poor and traditionally despised lower classes.
- Women received the vote and recognition of their rights to education and employment.
- Wage rates rose and working conditions were improved.
- Health care and welfare were introduced for the workers.
- The education system was improved with a marked rise in literacy.
- New homes were built for over 2 million people.
- Argentina's infrastructure was modernized.
- Significant land redistribution helped lessen poverty.

Failures and negatives

- Perón's attempts at tackling poverty were only superficially successful.
- Living standards rose for some but the gap between rich and poor widened.
- Perón remained reliant on military power in order to stay in power.
- He encouraged the development of a corrupt bureaucracy that expected to retain its privileges regardless of the state of the nation.
- He governed through dictatorial methods, using coercion to subdue opposition.
- His supposed popularity was created by the Perónist-controlled media.
- He employed threats and censorship to suppress free cultural expression.
- Argentina's underlying economic problems were not solved under him.
- He used patronage as a technique of government, which undermined the idealism he espoused in the Twenty Truths.
- Argentina remained a divided society under him.
- Argentina under him became violently polarized between conservative and progressive elements.

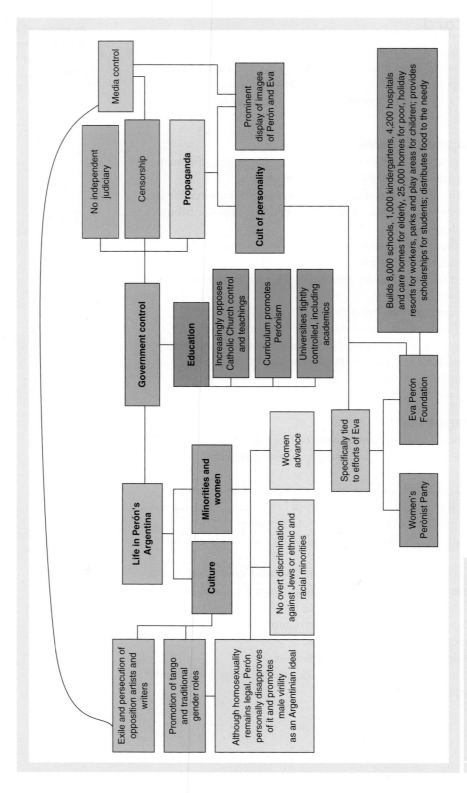

SUMMARY DIAGRAM

Life in Argentina under Perón, 1943–74

Life in Perón's Argentina

Government control

Media control

No independent judiciary

Censorship

Propaganda

Prominent display of images of Perón and Eva

Cult of personality

Education

Increasingly opposes Catholic Church control and teachings

Curriculum promotes Perónism

Universities tightly controlled, including academics

Minorities and women

Women advance

Specifically tied to efforts of Eva

Eva Perón Foundation

Women's Perónist Party

Builds 8,000 schools, 1,000 kindergartens, 4,200 hospitals and care homes for elderly, 25,000 homes for poor, holiday resorts for workers, parks and play areas for children; provides scholarships for students; distributes food to the needy

No overt discrimination against Jews or ethnic and racial minorities

Culture

Exile and persecution of opposition artists and writers

Promotion of tango and traditional gender roles

Although homosexuality remains legal, Perón personally disapproves of it and promotes male virility as an Argentinian ideal

Key debate

> ▶ **Key question**: *Was Perón a Right-wing or a Left-wing leader?*

Left-wing?

A pamphlet, distributed by the Catholic clergy to their congregations in the autumn of 1954 began, 'Perónism, the Instrument of Soviet Communism in Argentina!' The clergy's desire to characterize Perón's regime as part of a communist conspiracy was understandable given the ferocity of the regime's clash with the Catholic Church, but as a definition of Perón's politics it was wholly inaccurate. Perón was never a communist. But he did appear, at least at first, to have Left-leaning views. His early support of the workers and his attacks upon the *estancieros* seemed to indicate that he was following socialist policies. An Argentinian **Marxist** writer, Ernesto Laclau, saw Perón as a man of the Left because 'in contrast to European fascism, Perónism empowered workers against the ruling class'. Laclau added, however, that most European political terms were unhelpful when applied to Argentina, which made any attempt to make a comparison between Perón and a European Left-wing leader, such as Stalin, problematical.

What superficially might make Perón appear Left-wing were his close relations with the trade unions and his restrictive policies towards employers and landowners. However, these polices belonged to his first period as President and he reversed them after 1952. Historian David Rock notes that as his power grew stronger:

SOURCE K

Excerpt from *Authoritarian Argentina* by David Rock, published by University of California Press, USA, 1993, p. 204.

Perón seemed to distance himself from the workers, steadily abstracting himself from their day-to-day affairs and behaving as if the state and himself were separate from and suspended above society at large. His opponents interpreted this as further confirmation that Perónism was simply a form of fascism, but Perón's mix of several authoritarian-populist styles defied easy labels or characterizations.

Perón's attempt to be classless and populist in his approach makes it difficult to regard him as a socialist in any fixed sense, a point stressed by two US analysts (see Source L, page 276).

The seemingly socialist tendencies in Perón's rule were restricted to his first presidency when things went relatively well for him. Juan Carlos Torre, an Argentinian historian, considers that Perón's supposed socialism was only ever superficial and that his real feelings became apparent in his second term when, confronted by economic decline and growing opposition, Perón resorted to the repression of opponents in keeping with the basic authoritarianism he had first expressed in 1945.

> How appropriate is it to describe Perón as Left-wing?

> 🔑 **KEY TERM**
>
> **Marxist** Relating to the ideas of the German revolutionary, Karl Marx, who had advanced the notion that human society developed historically as a continuous series of class struggles between those who possessed economic and political power and those who did not. He taught that the culmination of this dialectical process would be the crushing victory of the proletariat over the bourgeoisie.

> According to Source K, what was the consequence of Perón's distancing himself from the workers?

According to Source L, how had Perón undermined his attempt to create a multiclass coalition?

SOURCE L

Excerpt from *A History of Latin America* by Benjamin Keen and Keith Haynes, published by Houghton Mifflin, USA, 2004, pp. 332–34.

Perón managed to win over a considerable sector of the dependent middle class through his use of government patronage. He kept the military happy by providing it with generous salaries. One of Perón's greatest allies was his beautiful and stylish wife Eva, who relished her role as his liaison to the working class …

[However] in struggling to extricate the nation from an economic quagmire, Perón undermined the multiclass coalition that had brought him to power. When the final successful revolt took place in 1955, enough of the working class were alienated to assure the military's success.

SOURCE M

In Source M how does Perón justify the use of violence?

Excerpt from a speech by Perón in August 1945, quoted by Juan Carlos Torre in *The Cambridge History of Latin America*, vol. viii, edited by Leslie Bethell, published by CUP, UK, 1996, p. 92.

With our exaggerated tolerance, we have won the right to repress them violently. And from now on we establish as a permanent rule for our movement: Whoever in any place tries to disturb order against the constituted authorities, or against the law and the Constitution, may be killed by any Argentine. The watchword for every Perónista, whether alone or within an organization, is to answer a violent act with another violent act.

How appropriate is it to describe Perón as Right-wing?

Right-wing?

Authoritarianism was certainly an aspect of Perónism, but this does not necessarily make him Right-wing, since authoritarianism is associated with regimes of both Left and Right. What makes Perón sometimes appear Right-wing is that his regime possessed a number of the characteristics of the Right-wing systems elsewhere, Nazi Germany and Fascist Italy being obvious examples:

- a corporate, centralized system of government
- an authoritarianism maintained by armed force
- a political conformity imposed by extra-legal security forces
- a strongly nationalistic outlook
- cult of the leader as an icon.

These were undeniable features of Perón's regime, but since the same features can also be identified in Stalin's Soviet Union, Castro's Cuba and Mao's China, countries which were not Right-wing, it would be inappropriate to apply the term to Perón's Argentina as if it were an accurate description. Argentinian scholars, such as Mariano Plotkin in *Politics of Consensus in Perónist Argentina, 1943–1955* (1992), rejects as too superficial the idea of Perón's regime being Right-wing. Plotkin suggests that Perón's practice of taking up whatever ideas seemed to be applicable in a particular situation makes it impossible to apply a single definition to his politics.

It was understandable that, in the 1940s and 1950s, when memories of Hitler and Mussolini were still very fresh, Perón's populist style should have been likened to theirs. Perón's rousing speeches and the marches and demonstrations of his supporters had echoes of the Nazi and Fascist rallies. Perón also claimed, as Hitler had, that he represented a movement for national unity that went beyond mere politics. There was a powerful emotional element in the mass appeal of Perónism, which Evita helped to sustain. The US historian, Robert Potash, offers this explanation (in Source N):

SOURCE N

Excerpt from *The Army & Politics in Argentina: 1928–1945* by Robert A. Potash, published by Athlone Press, London, UK, 1980. p. 91.

The identification of many Argentines of modest circumstances with the Perón administration rested on emotional as well as pragmatic considerations. Evita Perón's charitable activities and her many public appearances helped create a sense of personal contact with the President. The trade unions, through Evita's influence and the frequent presence of the secretary-general of the CGT at high level meetings, could give their members a sense of participation in the making of policy. The linkage between the masses of the workers and the Perón government was further strengthened by its frequent denunciations of exploitative property owners and of foreign imperialists.

According to Source N, how did Perón establish a special relationship with ordinary Argentinians? **?**

Yet that link between Perón and masses was quickly broken when Perón reversed so many of his earlier policies. British historian Robert Alexander suggests that the range of opponents who came in time to oppose Perón undermines any attempt to label Perón precisely as a Right-wing leader. Alexander argues that the repressive methods Perón used obscured his political objectives and reduced his rule to personal authoritarianism. It was rule for its own sake rather than an applied ideology.

SOURCE O

Excerpt from *An Introduction to Argentina* by Robert J. Alexander, published by Pall Mall Press, UK, 1969, p. 98.

As a result of the dictatorial nature of the Perón regime all opposition parties – Communists, Radicals, Socialists, and Progressive Democrats – conspired jointly and separately to overthrow the regime. They joined forces with military men who were against the Perón government. Few of the opposition political leaders, not even the Socialists, were willing to concede that Perón had done anything on behalf of the organized workers.

According to Source O, why did a coalition of interests form against Perón? **?**

Two Argentine historians make the illuminating observation that what seemed to support the notion of Perón's being Right-wing was not so much the policies he followed but what was made of them subsequently by Perónists.

According to Source P, what was the 'historical twist' that led the radicalized young to join the Perónist movement?

SOURCE P

Excerpt from 'Argentina since 1946' by Juan Carlos Torre and Liliana De Riz in *The Cambridge History of Latin America*, vol. viii, edited by Leslie Bethell, published by CUP, UK, 1996, p. 141.

The youth radicalized at the end of the 1960s in the struggle against the military regime had adopted peronismo *as a way of identifying themselves with the people. In a historical twist, the sons of those who had firmly opposed Peron turned their backs on their parents to embrace the very cause they had fought against. Under the spell of the ideas of Che Guevara, the protagonists transformed* peronismo *into the militant embodiment of a national socialism.*

> How far did Perón have a structured ideology?

Neither Left nor Right?

The striking feature of Perón in government was his lack of a structured ideology. There was in his case nothing comparable to Hitler's National Socialism, Stalin's Marxist–Leninism or Mao Zedong's Chinese Communism (see pages 64, 57 and 114). Attempts to interpret *justicialismo* as set out in the Twenty Truths as either a Left- or Right-wing political philosophy founder on the difficulty of making clear sense of it. Some scholars view the Twenty Truths as being too vague to merit being described as a programme. Indeed, historian David Rock in *Argentina, 1516–1982* (1986) dismisses *justicialismo* as simply 'vapid'.

 **KEY TERM**

Reactive pragmatism Responding to events as they occur rather than working to a prescribed plan.

New Deal A set of programmes introduced by US President Franklin D. Roosevelt's administration to tackle the effects of the Great Depression in the 1930s.

Liberal-based programmes In the UK, between 1945 and 1951, the Labour government implemented a welfare-state programme based on ideas originally advanced by the Liberals.

Perón's approach can more appropriately be described as **reactive pragmatism**. The USA's **New Deal** policies were as much a model for Perón's actions in government as were those of the Right-wing dictatorships in Europe. The social welfare schemes he implemented had much in common with the **liberal-based programmes** adopted in Britain in the late 1940s. This eclectic approach can be summarized by saying that Perón genuinely wished to improve the conditions of the people but was open-minded in his methods.

British historian Jill Hedges, in *Argentina: a Modern History* (2011), sees Perónism not as a recognizable movement that easily fits into a Left or Right category but as essentially a nationalist reaction against what were commonly perceived to be Argentina's failings. The reason why Perón was able to return to office in 1973 was not primarily because of his positive appeal but because in the eighteen-year interval no other leader or party had proved capable of providing effective government: 'Perónism represented the failure of any other figure or movement to capture the [Argentinian] imagination.'

T O K
Perón was partly successful as the result of his wife's popularity. Do all leaders need to be popular to be successful? (History, Language, Reason, Emotion)

Perón had certainly admired what he regarded as the efficient administration of Italian Fascism and German Nazism, but this did not make him either a Fascist or a Nazi. It was possible for him to be impressed by certain features of the systems without his accepting the ideologies that underlay them. The truth is Perón's politics defy simple description. He had principles but he wa pragmatic in his application of them. His nationalist fervour led him to adopt an approach that was intended to appeal to all Argentinians, Left and Right, across the political spectrum. It is this that makes it difficult to give a precise definition to his attitude. Perón claimed to follow the 'Third Way'. The result was that at times he appealed to all the classes but at other times he met resistance from a wide cross-section. His politics was a hybrid, a mixture of Left and Right policies.

Chapter summary

Argentina under Juan Perón, 1946–74

Juan Perón emerged onto the troubled political scene in the 1940s when Argentina was bitterly divided between oligarchic government, workers and middle classes. Trained as a soldier, he had been impressed in the 1930s by the efficiency with which Right-wing government appeared to operate in Europe. Resolved to restore stability to Argentina, he played a leading part in a successful military coup which took power in 1943. As Minister of Labour he established close relations with the workers and developed a populist form of politics which helped carry him to the presidency in 1946.

Consolidating his authority over the next ten years by repressive means, he nevertheless sought to create social harmony by following a 'Third Way', a set of polices which included the attempt to achieve a fairer distribution of national wealth among the people.

Using propaganda to project himself as the benign leader, Perón was greatly aided by his wife, Evita, who became hugely popular as an iconic figure personifying the nation's highest aspirations. Her death removed one of Perón's greatest political assets. That loss, combined with growing opposition among groups from the upper, middle and lower classes, the army and the Catholic Church, all of whom felt variously let down by his economic and social policies, led to his overthrow in 1955. Even in exile, his influence remained strong as his supporters, the *Perónistas,* continued to be active in Argentina. Perón returned briefly for a third term as President, 1973–74, but by then he was a sick man and died in office with little new accomplished.

Perón remains a controversial figure. Historians differ over whether he had a distinctive ideology, whether he should be described as Left- or Right-wing, and whether his undoubted successes in helping to modernize Argentina by improving its social and economic conditions were outweighed by the dictatorial methods employed to achieve this.

Examination practice

Below are a number of different questions for you to practise. For guidance on how to answer exam-style questions, see Chapter 10.

1 To what extent did Perón's rule affect women in Argentina?

2 Explain the importance of the working class on Perón's rise and maintenance of power in Argentina.

3 For what reasons and with what results did opposition form against Perón in Argentina?

4 Discuss Perón's political ideology and explain its significance.

5 What was the role of Perón's wife Eva in his rise and rule?

6 Assess Perón's economic policies and programmes in terms of their success.

7 Explain the significance of the army for Perón's rise and rule in Argentina.

8 Analyse the role of the *estancieros* in Perón's political system.

9 What was the impact of Perón's rule upon the arts?

10 To what extent was propaganda used to maintain Perón's control of Argentina?

 # Activities

1 Make a table or chart comparing and contrasting Perón's views on trade unions, the army, women, and other factors between his first and second terms in office.

2 As a class, research and discuss the extent to which Perónism was just another form of fascism. Extend this by investigating to what extent Perónism is still a factor in Argentina's politics today.

CHAPTER 9

Tanzania under Julius Nyerere, 1961–85

Julius Nyerere, having led Tanganyika to independence in 1961, ruled the new nation, which became Tanzania in 1964, for the next quarter century. His initial aim was to modernize Tanzania by abandoning its colonial past while retaining its essential African character. However, the political, economic and social problems he faced obliged him to adopt increasingly authoritarian methods of government. He found that he could not continue with his idealistic plans for his country. Matters were made more difficult for him by the conflicts that developed in neighbouring states into which Tanzania was drawn diplomatically and militarily. By the time he retired from office in 1985, his economic and social policies had largely failed.

You need to consider the following questions throughout this chapter:

✪ What circumstances favoured the rise of Nyerere?
✪ How did Nyerere impose his authority on Tanzania?
✪ What impact did Nyerere's rule have on the lives of the Tanzanian people?
✪ How positive in its effects was Nyerere's leadership of Tanzania?

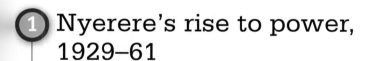

1 Nyerere's rise to power, 1929–61

▶ Key question: What circumstances favoured the rise of Nyerere?

Before 'the scramble for Africa' occurred in the late nineteenth century, there were some 800 tribal or regional units on the African continent. One critical consequence of European colonization was the formation by 1914 of over 40 distinct areas that were to become the future nations of Africa. These were often arbitrary and careless of native territorial traditions, but they had the effect of establishing a concept of African nationhood.

Tanganyika's colonial past

German East Africa

During the scramble, Germany took possession of the regions that later became known as Tanganyika, Rwanda and Burundi. These were then grouped together as German East Africa. However, at the end of the First World War, these colonies were taken from defeated Germany and formed into a set of new states. To provide guidance and protection for the new

> **KEY TERM**
>
> **The scramble for Africa**
> During the period 1870–1914, the major European powers vied with each other in colonizing various parts of Africa.

> **What developments led to an increasing demand for the independence of Tanganyika?**

? Examine Source A and identify German East Africa.

SOURCE A

Map showing the partition of Africa between the European powers by 1914.

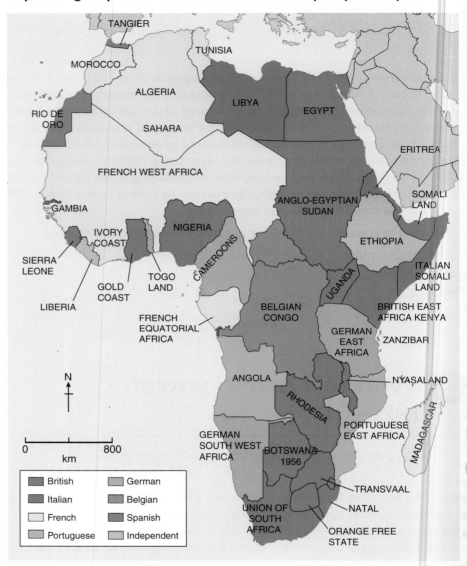

🔑 **KEY TERM**

Tanganyika The large mainland area of what became Tanzania, when the neighbouring island of Zanzibar was incorporated in 1964.

states until they had achieved full self-determination, the League of Nations placed them under the authority of certain mandated powers, principally Britain and France. It was under the terms of a League mandate that **Tanganyika** was transferred to British control. An important side effect was that some 6,000 European and Asian businessmen came to Tanganyika after 1919. Believing that British indirect rule would create stable conditions for their businesses to flourish, they were also attracted by the availability of cheap resources and low-cost native labour.

The impact of the First World War

The First World War played a formative role in the development of African nationalism. According to US President Woodrow Wilson, the main spokesman for the victorious Allies, the war, in which many African troops had played a conspicuous part, had been fought 'to make the world safe for democracy'. Self-determination and the right of all peoples to be free were principles enunciated in the **League of Nations** charter. Logic and justice meant the principles could not be denied to the African peoples. The terms of the **mandates** required that the new territories be administered with the interests of the native population as paramount. However, as many African nationalists saw it, the mandates were merely a cover for continued **colonialism**. The colonial powers were reluctant to admit this and continued to develop their territories without regard to awakening African aspirations. The colonizers still thought in terms of tribal units and regions linked together solely by their dependence upon colonial **patronage**.

Problems for east African nationalists

Initially, African leaders were diffident about challenging the continuation of colonial authority. Indeed, the African response, excluding the regions of Arab settlement, such as Zanzibar, was to imitate the lifestyle of the Europeans. Ambitious Africans copied the dress, religion and education of the Europeans. As a native Tanganyikan said in 1925, 'to the African mind to imitate Europeans is civilization'.

A basic difficulty for nationalists in east Africa was the lack of a broad popular following. For the most part, the native peoples of the region were poorly educated members of a peasant community whose basic social unit was the family and the tribe; it would take time before they would become responsive to nationalism. Nevertheless things were changing. Money as a form of exchange began to be used increasingly frequently and this, in turn, produced a **cash crop economy**. An industrial labour force was also developing as land workers were attracted to the towns where jobs and wages were becoming available. Such trends were of obvious political significance; people began to think of themselves not simply as members of a tribe but as Tanganyikans. This developing sense of nationalism was highly welcome to those leaders and movements who wanted east Africa to become truly independent.

The impact of the Second World War

Despite the difficulties in its way, African nationalism began to gather strength after 1919. Native politicians were gaining experience, organizations were forming, and change was being discussed. What turned this potential for change into actuality was the advent of the Second World War. Fought by the Allies as a struggle for freedom against subjugation, it reinforced the principle of self-determination that had emerged from the First World War and destroyed any lingering justification for refusing the demand of a people for the right to govern themselves. Eighty-seven thousand Tanganyikans

🔑 KEY TERM

League of Nations The international body created in 1919 with the aim of peacefully resolving disputes between nations.

Mandate An authority granted by the League of Nations to certain countries to monitor and protect the interests of particular states and regions created at the end of the First World War.

Colonialism The takeover by European powers of territories whose people were too weak militarily to prevent their political and economic subjugation.

Patronage Providing government approval and support and extending privileges to selected individuals and groups.

Cash crop economy Arable farming for financial profit rather than for mere subsistence.

were conscripted into the British forces between 1940 and 1945; they fought in Somaliland, Ethiopia, Madagascar and Burma. The effort and sacrifice this entailed strengthened the idea that Tanganyika could no longer be kept in subjection. The British inadvertently promoted this by employing the Swahili word *Uhuru* to describe their struggle against Germany. Used by the British to mean 'war for freedom', *Uhuru* was eagerly taken up by nationalists as an expression of their own desire for liberation from colonialism.

SOURCE B

Excerpt from an anonymous letter in a Tanganyikan newspaper in 1947, quoted in *A Modern History of Tanganyika* by John Iliffe, published by CUP, UK, 1979, pp. 376–77.

Now is the time for the British to fulfil their promise that when the war ended the world would be made new and all men would gain freedom ... The line of progress must be planned not by the tutors [British administrators] alone, but by the co-operation of the tutors and the taught [Tanganyikans] ... Civilization started in Africa long before the other countries of the world awoke, but Africa's progress was retarded by the awakening of the other countries ... Now she is awakening from her long siesta.

? According to Source B, what obligation has the Second World War placed upon the British in their relations with Tanganyika?

The strength of this demand was vividly illustrated in the case of British India. Economically drained by the costs of war, Britain no longer had the financial resources to continue to control India. Moreover, it accepted that it had lost the moral authority to do so since it was evident that the great majority of the Indian people wanted Britain's withdrawal. In 1947, Britain duly granted full independence to the Indian sub-continent. The wider significance was that the giving up by the British of India, their most prized imperial possession, undermined the justification and the will for Britain to retain its other territories. A process of decolonization began. This would take decades to complete, depending on the strength of nationalism in the various colonies. What also slowed the process was that in some areas, such as Kenya, Britain delayed granting independence until the interests of the European settlers had been guaranteed.

The European settler problem

A particular problem for all the African colonies as they approached independence was the attitude of the European settlers, many of whom came from families that had lived in Africa for generations. Would they be willing to adapt to the changed world in which they were a minority? Would they be willing to cede power or would they try desperately to preserve their privileged status? However, notwithstanding these obstacles, the question now for Britain's remaining territories was not whether they would obtain independence but when. In the case of Tanganyika the 'when' question began to be forcefully and eloquently put by Julius Nyerere. It was he who gave the movement for Tanganyikan sovereignty its vital leadership.

SOURCE C

Map of Britain in Africa, 1947–68.

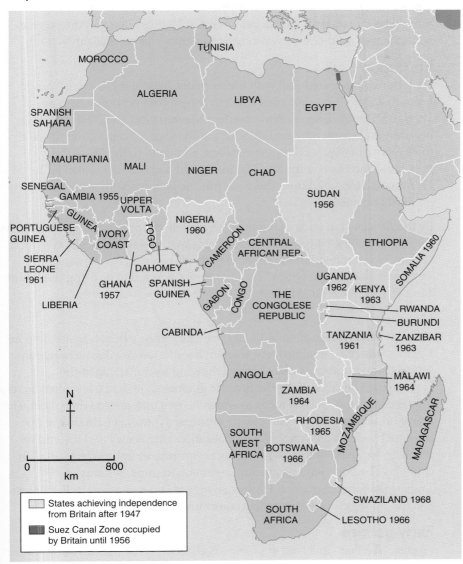

Study Source C.
Identify Tanzania,
Zanzibar, Kenya,
Uganda and the
Congolese
Republic.

States achieving independence from Britain after 1947

Suez Canal Zone occupied by Britain until 1956

KEY TERM

Paramount chief The formal title given by British administrators to an African tribal leader who was recognized and respected by the tribe's members as having legitimate authority over them.

ulius Nyerere

Cultural background

ulius Kambarage Nyerere, the son of a **paramount chief** of the Zanaki tribe, nherited from his forebears, particularly from his mother, an understanding hat tribal lore and tradition rested on the concept of a relationship between uman beings and the natural world. Every facet of nature and every human ttribute were interconnected. There was nothing alien between humankind nd nature. The animals and the fruits of the earth gave human beings their

What characteristics of Nyerere's personality and upbringing fitted him for leadership?

physical sustenance. The winds, the forests, the rivers: these were natural gifts whose contemplation gave humans their spiritual understanding and sense of wonder. Life was a totality; there was a chain of continuity linking those who had died and those yet unborn with those living in the present. Veneration of its ancestors was central to a tribe's sense of identity.

Education

Such thinking blended well with the form of Christianity Nyerere learned from the Catholic missionaries who ran the primary schools which he attended. The Christian notion of an omnipotent God, the creator and benefactor of mankind, fitted smoothly with tribal concepts of nature as a force whose benign workings gave shape and unity to the life of the individual and the community. The moral and social values which Julius Nyerere had inherited from these sources, he later made the basis of his political principles.

By the African standards of the time, Nyerere had a privileged upbringing. As the son of a chief, he had from his earliest days an elevated position in local society. He attended Tabora, a school that was reserved for the sons of Tanganyika's elite and which Nyerere himself referred to as being 'as close to **Eton** as you can get in Africa'.

University

After Tabora, Nyerere attended Makerere University, a British foundation in Uganda, where he qualified as a teacher. Back in Tanganyika, he taught in schools for a number of years before taking up a scholarship at the University of Edinburgh. By the time he graduated, he had been considerably influenced by the socialist ideas to which he was introduced while there. The brand of socialism which particularly impressed him was **Fabianism**, a movement whose advocacy of nationalization, democracy and the end of privilege appealed to him as providing the principles upon which a nation could best be built. He was already beginning to think in terms of Tanganyikan independence. He saw an accord between Western Fabianism and the traditions of African tribal **communalism**.

Early politics

Nyerere had been involved in politics as a student at Makerere, but it was on his return from Edinburgh that he took up the cause of national independence as his main political objective. His first significant step was to join the Tanganyika African Association (TAA) which had been founded by the British in 1929 as an organization where elite Taganyikans could discuss social and political issues without ever becoming a threat to the colonial administration. Nyerere rapidly transformed TAA from a mere social club into an organization to agitate for the ending of colonial rule over Tanganyika. In 1954, Nyerere formally turned TAA into the Tanganyika African National Union (TANU), an overtly political organization with the central aim of achieving independence for Tanganyika.

Nyerere's nationalism

Nyerere soon gave up his teaching post and entered full-time politics on behalf of TANU. His skill as a public speaker and his dedication to national independence soon earned him an enthusiastic following. His approach was modelled on that of Mohandas Gandhi, the outstanding nationalist leader who led the movement against Britain's control of India (see page 284). Nyerere conducted a series of tours of Tanganyika discussing local issues and gaining the support of the tribal leaders. He also travelled abroad; on one notable occasion he spoke on behalf of TANU to the **Trusteeship Council of the UN**, presenting the case for Tanganyikan independence. His speech delighted his supporters but angered the British authorities who responded by placing a temporary ban on Nyerere's speaking in public.

Nyerere's rise to leadership

Nyerere was not of course the only nationalist in Tanganyika. Among others who became prominent because of their committed opposition to colonial rule were two medical doctors, Vedast Kyaruzi and Luciano Tsere, members respectively of the Haya and Iraqw peoples, and Steven Mhando, a teacher from the Bondei tribe. But the reason why such men never attained Nyerere's status or matched his following was that they remained essentially tribal and regional leaders. Nyerere was the only truly national figure who emerged in late colonial Tanganyika. Describing Nyerere's dominance in this respect, British historian John Iliffe writes:

SOURCE D

Excerpt from *A Modern History of Tanganyika* by John Iliffe, published by CUP, UK, 1979, p. 509.

[A]lmost alone among Tanganyikans he had the knowledge of world events and the understanding of political theory to organize a movement which did not grow from local necessities. Nyerere was racially sensitive, hated foreign rule, feared Conservative complicity with settler ambitions and knew that Africa was moving towards conflict and liberation.

After 1954, Nyerere led TANU as the main organization for achieving independence on native Tanganyikan terms. It is important to emphasize that there was little resistance from any quarter to independence itself. By the late 1950s it had become accepted that this would be achieved at some point in the future. Nyerere calculated that if the Tanganyikans could set up a workable representative system, no matter how rudimentary, the British parliament would be obliged to accept it as meeting the basic democratic norms required for the granting of independence. The question was how soon it would be granted and on what terms. Nyerere had long been aware that the relations between European settlers and the native people in Tanganyika were a potential problem. He had written on this while a student in Edinburgh (see Source E, page 288).

KEY TERM

Trusteeship Council of the UN The new United Nations organization which took over from the old League of Nations body which had administered the mandates (renamed trusts).

How did Nyerere come to represent Tanganyikan nationalism?

According to Source D, what particular attributes fitted Nyerere for leadership of the nationalist movement?

According to Source E, what significance does the term 'the people' have for Nyerere?

SOURCE E

Excerpt from a 1952 essay 'Freedom and Unity', by Julius Nyerere, quoted in *Two African Statesmen* by John Hatch, published by Secker & Warburg, UK, 1976, p. 31.

Our problem in east and South Africa is a problem of a White minority which sincerely believe that democracy's cardinal foundation is the will of the people, but which refuses to let the term 'the people' include non-Europeans.

For a small white minority to come to our country and tell us that they are the people of the country and we are not is one of those many insults which I think we have swallowed for far too long. The sooner we tell them that we will no longer tolerate such monstrous impudence the better for all of us. It is even more to their interest than ours that we should refuse to tolerate such insult now when we can still so refuse peacefully, rather than let them grow so chronically insulting that any peaceful means or reparation will seem inadequate.

Nyerere and Lennox-Boyd

While committed to the eventual granting of independence, the British authorities were reluctant to move quickly. In 1957, while on a visit to Tanganyika, Alan Lennox-Boyd, Britain's **Colonial Secretary**, remarked that progress towards independence was 'in danger of becoming too rapid rather than too slow'. He added that the British government was determined not to grant power to 'irresponsible people or to any government under which responsible people of all races in Tanganyika would not feel secure'. Lennox-Boyd did not mean to sound racist; his intention was to include all those Tanganyikans, whether indigenous, European or Asian, whom he regarded as responsible. However, his choice of words was interpreted by native Tanganyikans as implying that they were judged as being not yet capable of responsible self-government.

Lennox-Boyd's lack of political judgement added to the difficulties confronting Nyerere, who had set himself the task of putting pressure on the British authorities so as to oblige them to grant independence as early as possible. But he was also intent on restraining the militants among the nationalists who were becoming increasingly frustrated in the face of what they regarded as Britain's obstructive methods. Nyerere's fear was that peaceful transition to self-government for Tanganyika would be jeopardized if extremism took over the movement. In 1956 it had been announced by the **Governor-General** that, in 1958, for the first time in Tanganyika's history there would be free elections to the **Legislative Council** in which Africans could take part. Seeing this as a mere gesture, there were TANU members who wanted to boycott all elections held under British auspices. But Nyerere dissuaded them from such a course by setting a personal example. In 1957, he accepted an appointment to the Legislative Council, and although he subsequently resigned, he announced that TANU would participate in the elections. This was in spite of the regulation that only one-third of the elected Council members could be African.

SOURCE F

Distribution of seats in the Legislative Council.

	Population of Tanganyika in 1958	Total number of seats on the pre-1958 legislative
African	8,665,336	0
European	20,598	14
Asian	76,536	6

Examine the figures in Source F. What do they indicate regarding the inequalities of the voting system in Tanganyika before 1958?

Nyerere opposed a TANU boycott of the elections not because he accepted the injustice of the regulation but because he was concerned that, if TANU did not stand, its rival African parties, the United Tanganyika Party (UTP) and the African National Congress (**ANC**), would gain undue influence. His fundamental aim was to make TANU the only acknowledged representative of the Tanganyikan people.

The libel case, 1958

How difficult a path Nyerere had to tread became clear in a remarkable incident in 1958. By that date, Nyerere had emerged as the outstanding figure in the nationalist movement. While he was on friendly terms with some of the British administrators, both in Tanganyika and at the Colonial Office in London to which he had made a number of visits, his growing popularity, as evident in TANU's election victories, disturbed the British Governor-General Edward Twining, who shared Lennox-Boyd's reluctance to see independence advance too swiftly. Twining's attitude was a factor in the late 1950s in a proliferation of strikes and protests, some of which became violent. The British authorities reacted by arresting and prosecuting demonstrators and by banning TANU from operating in certain regions.

Nyerere published an angry article in which he condemned government officials not only for their attempt to restrict political freedom but also for using illegal court-room tactics in the trials of the protesters. He went so far as to accuse two district commissioners of having encouraged witnesses to commit perjury so that guilty verdicts would be returned and TANU vilified. In a desperate move to silence Nyerere, the government charged him with **criminal libel**. The situation was now very tense. It seemed that the authorities were becoming more obdurate and that Nyerere had abandoned his moderate approach. If he were to receive a severe sentence, the chances of a peaceful transition to Tanganyikan independence would be destroyed.

Nyerere and Richard Turnbull

What helped to prevent a crisis was the appointment of a new Governor-General. The trial of Nyerere happened to coincide with the scheduled retirement of Twining and his replacement by Sir Richard Turnbull. Despite a reputation for toughness, Turnbull showed an immediate willingness to compromise. Even before the trial of Nyerere had been concluded, the new Governor-General had invited him for talks. The two men established an immediate rapport and agreed that they would co-operate in the process towards independence. Reflecting the new optimism that such amity created, the court convicted Nyerere, but offered him a choice between a fine and imprisonment. It had been his original resolve to go to prison as a gesture of defiance to the British authorities. However, accepting that to do this might unnecessarily incite his nationalist supporters to acts of violence, Nyerere now opted for the fine instead. It was an act of goodwill towards Turnbull that was greatly appreciated by him and undoubtedly helped smooth the way to independence.

By what steps did Tanganyika gain independence?

The achievement of independence, 1959–61

Nyerere's objectives

Julius Nyerere was re-elected in 1959 to the Legislative Council. He advanced what he called a non-racial candidacy rather than a multi-racial one. He meant by this that he wanted people to regard themselves primarily as Tanganyikans rather than as members of an ethnic group. He explained that he wanted the independent Tanganyika that was imminent to avoid dividing politically along racial lines. He achieved considerable success in this; his TANU party gained mass support from African Tanganyikans. Equally significantly, 40 per cent of those from a European or Asian background voted for TANU. Nevertheless, Nyerere asserted that in purely democratic terms, African Tanganyikans as the largest sector of the population had an indisputable claim to political predominance.

British acceptance of TANU's demands

Governor-General Turnbull recognized that TANU overwhelmingly represented Tanganyikan opinion. In all free elections the party never gained less than two-thirds of the popular vote. Turnbull accepted that 'in terms of population the Africans always will be an overwhelming majority in Tanganyika'. It followed, therefore, that 'African participation both in the legislature and in the executive should steadily increase'. The principle of **majority rule** made this an absolute requirement.

Turnbull's acknowledgement of Nyerere's stated principle was a critical moment in Anglo-Tanganyikan relations. It meant, in effect, that the British government accepted the right of Nyerere and his TANU party to lead Tanganyika to independence. Nyerere listed the elements that independence had to contain:

- universal adult **suffrage**
- majority rule
- an elected legislature with blocks of reserved seats for the minority European and Asian Tanganyikans
- an elected **Council of Ministers**.

The role of Iain Macleod

The objections of the European settlers to majority rule were largely overcome when Iain Macleod became Colonial Secretary in 1959. Macleod, who declared that genuine democracy had to operate, accepted Nyerere's proposals and agreed that independence for Tanganyika must be granted at the earliest feasible time. Conscious of the opposition to majority rule among whites in other African states approaching independence, such as Kenya and Uganda, Macleod announced unequivocally that 'Tanganyika would not be held back because of possible repercussions in other territories'.

KEY TERM

Majority rule The right of the largest group to have the largest representation in government.

Suffrage The right to vote.

Council of Ministers A governing Cabinet.

Elections to the Legislative Council in 1960 saw TANU win another overwhelming victory, gaining over 90 per cent of the popular vote. Neither of the other two main parties, UTP and ANC, won a single seat. TANU's victory was clear proof of the dominant political position achieved by its leader Nyerere. The Council, which was increased to 81 members, was renamed the Legislative Assembly. Reflecting Tanganyika's ethnic make-up, it contained 52 Africans, 16 Europeans, 12 Asians and 1 Arab.

Nyerere became Chief Minister of the Council and appointed his own ministers, nine Africans, two Europeans, and one Asian. In the United Nation's Trusteeship Council, Nyerere was described as 'an outstanding political leader – indeed a great African statesman'.

Independence gained, 1961

In 1961, at a constitutional conference attended by Nyerere and British officials in Dar es Salaam, the final details for independence were agreed. On 9 December that year the Republic of Tanganyika came into being. Britain formally withdrew, handing over full powers of self-government to the new sovereign state. Nyerere took office as its Prime Minister. In the euphoria that accompanied these events, he declared, 'This is a triumph for Tanganyika. I rejoice to say it is not a day of triumph *over* anybody. It is a happy victory in which we are all winners.'

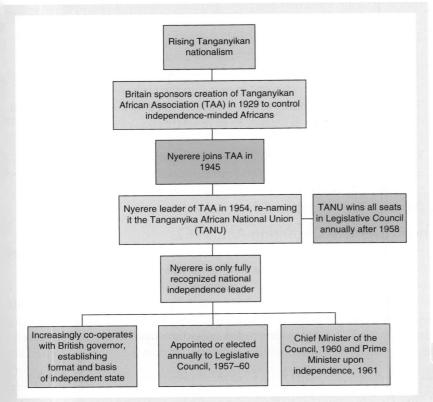

SUMMARY DIAGRAM

Nyerere's rise to power, 1929–61

Nyerere's control of Tanzania

> ▶ **Key question:** *How did Nyerere impose his authority on Tanzania?*

The sense of excitement and optimism that accompanied the transition to independence could not hide the reality of the problems Nyerere now faced. Could he lead an economically poor and politically inexperienced African country to prosperity and stability?

What steps did Nyerere take to suppress opposition?

Nyerere's consolidation of authority

Having become leader of the new nation, Nyerere, in 1961, made an appeal for national unity, but he was conscious that he was likely to face opposition from the following groups or sectors:

- **The tribes:** there were 130 separate tribes in Tanganyika. Their chiefs were disturbed that Nyerere, as a Zanaki tribe member himself, had warned that tribal interests would have to take second place to the needs of the new nation.
- **Europeans:** who were worried that as a minority their former privileged position would be undermined.
- **The trade unions**: composed predominantly of indigenous Tanganyikans, they were concerned that Nyerere's promise of a non-racial approach implied a threat to their bargaining powers as a majority group.
- **The army:** which was essentially British in its structure and the majority of its officers were British. There were fears among the non-British personnel that, if Nyerere abandoned the system of allocating promotions to ethnic groups, their chances of rising up the ranks would be limited.
- **The other political parties:** who were disturbed by the stranglehold that the monolithic TANU appeared to have established over the governmental system.
- **Writers and journalists:** who feared that artistic and press freedoms were at risk. They were perturbed by rumours that Nyerere would demand that in the interest of national unity the media must be non-critical and deferential towards him and the government.

The Preventive Detention Act, 1962

Nyerere moved quickly to prevent any possibility of the groups becoming an organized opposition. One of his first moves was the introduction of the Preventive Detention Act of 1962, a measure which had first been used by the British administrators. Under its terms, the authorities were empowered to arrest anyone on suspicion of anti-state activity without having to issue a formal charge. The Act was targeted at opposition leaders and the press as a way of removing or silencing them.

Another set of intended victims were the trade unions. Nyerere had initially been keen to gain the support of the unions but, fearing that worker protest and strikes gave his government a bad image at home and abroad, Nyerere had over one hundred union officials arrested and held indefinitely. According to a number of world bodies concerned with monitoring international violations of civil rights, thousands of Tanganyikans were **'disappeared'** under Nyerere. As a gesture of solidarity with the victims, **Amnesty International** took up the cause of some selected 150 Tanganyikan 'prisoners of conscience', its term for those held illegally.

SOURCE G

Excerpt from a 1978 Amnesty International report, quoted in 'Human Rights in Tanzania' by James S. Read, in *Mwalimu: The Influence of Nyerere*, edited by Colin Legum and Geoffrey Mmari, published by British-Tanzania Society, 1995, UK, p. 140.

Indefinite detention without trial continues to be the means favoured by the Government to deal with any alleged offence (including corruption) when it fears that it has insufficient evidence for a trial.

According to Source G, how was the law relating to detention misused in Tanzania under Nyerere?

 **KEY TERM**

'Disappeared' A term that came into common use to describe how authoritarian regimes simply removed people they disapproved of without leaving any trace or offering any explanation. The logical deduction was that the 'disappeared' were killed by the regime.

Amnesty International A charity created in 1961 to call attention to the plight or fate of prisoners of conscience and to apply moral pressure to regimes which transgressed legal and ethical codes.

Labour camps Prisons and detention centres in which the inmates are required to perform heavy work in the toughest conditions.

Villagization The collectivization of the peasantry, based on the programme adopted by Mao Zedong in the PRC (see page 127), which Nyerere had observed at first hand on his visits to China.

Labour camps

A development that damaged Nyerere's reputation, particularly among those who had invested great hope in his leadership, was the spread of **labour camps** in Tanganyika during his regime. Accounts, substantiated by bodies such as Amnesty International, which interviewed inmates after their release, described the regular use of torture in the camps. It was reported that conditions were deliberately made as unpleasant as possible. Solitary confinement and electric shock treatment were routinely used to break the spirit of any dissidents who defied camp rules. So poor was the food provided and so insanitary and overcrowded was the camp environment that outbreaks of diseases such as dysentery were common. The main victims were unco-operative trade unionists and those who resisted **villagization** (see page 300). As many as 10,000 prisoners were held in the camps at any one time.

When Nyerere was challenged over the severity of the labour camp regime, he claimed that the stories were exaggerated and that where there were examples of ill-treatment these were lapses on the part of individuals who failed to follow proper procedures.

Suppression of army mutinies, 1964

In January 1964, the Tanganyikan Rifles, the only regiment in Tanganyika, mutinied. The chief complaint of the troops was that independence had not improved their chances of promotion; there were still only a handful of native Tanganyikans in the officer class, which was predominantly European. Some of the mutineers also spoke for disgruntled industrial workers who complained of a similar discrimination operating against black Africans in the job market. Nyerere was fearful on two counts. The obvious first concern was that, if unrest spread through the army, Tanganyikan security and his capacity to control the country would be gravely at risk. His second worry was that, since it was indigenous Tanganyikans who were at the heart of the troubles, this might be a sign of ethnic rivalry, one of the developments he was so eager to prevent in his dream of a non-racially conscious state.

The mutiny was serious enough for Nyerere to enlist outside British forces to contain it. He did so reluctantly since it seemed to suggest that Tanganyika was not yet fully independent of its old master. However, the immediate need was to suppress the mutiny. Once this was successfully accomplished, Nyerere moved quickly to order the arrest and court-martial of the mutineers. He claimed that a tough response was merited since the mutiny, if not quelled, could turn into a coup against him and the government.

Reform of the army

The mutinies convinced Nyerere of the need to establish the armed services along British lines as a force wholly subordinate to the state. He instructed that the development of the armed services would in future fall under the authority of TANU or, more precisely, the authority of TANU Youth League (TYL). Where his approach differed from the British model was in the politicizing of the army rather than the neutralizing of it. He was making the army an integral part of the nation's political system. However, since that system was a one-party affair, the net effect was to leave the army under the control of Nyerere and TANU.

A key part of the army reform undertaken by the TYL was conscription; the country's young men were required to perform two years' **national service** in uniform. Nyerere's purpose was not simply the forging of a larger and better trained army. He wanted the conscripts to have inculcated into them the concept of national as opposed to tribal identity and an understanding that their first loyalty was to the state.

Student opposition

Unsurprisingly, Nyerere's introduction of national service upset the country's university students of whom there were some 6,000 in Tanzania in 1965, based mainly on the campus of University College Dar es Salaam. Over half of these became actively involved in a series of disruptive demonstrations. Nyerere, however, was unmoved by their protests. When they denounced compulsory national service as an affront to their dignity, he stressed that students were among the most privileged in society. They should, therefore, see it as a matter, not merely of duty, but of honour, to contribute to the common good without thought of material reward. He announced that, while he saw the young as Tanzania's future and wanted them to be as well trained as possible, he would not allow them to interfere with his planning. Students would serve in the armed forces before they began their civilian careers. If they dared defy the authorities by continuing with their protests, they would be imprisoned. Nyerere's ideas here were similar to Mao Zedong's, who had required students and **intellectuals** in China to go into the fields and work with the peasants in order to learn the dignity of labour (see page 135).

KEY TERM

National service A period of compulsory military training.

Intellectuals A term stretched to encompass all those whose way of life or work was judged to have given them privileges denied to the people.

Tanganyika becomes Tanzania, 1964

The neighbouring island of Zanzibar, which had gained independence from Britain in December 1963, was ruled by a sultan. Barely a month after Zanzibar's independence had been declared, a coup, organized by the socialist Shirazi Party, overthrew the sultan and installed Abeid Karume, the Shirazi leader, as President. Within little more than a year Zanzibar had entered into a formal union with Tanganyika to form the state of Tanzania in April 1964. Nyerere was declared President, with Abeid Karume his Vice-President. Not all Tanganyikans approved of the move, but Nyerere assured them that it was a progressive move from which both parts of the new nation would benefit. It certainly increased Nyerere's stature in Africa and the wider world.

SOURCE H

Nyerere signing the document declaring the joining of Zanzibar and Tanganyika to form the state of Tanzania in 1964.

What information regarding Nyerere's leadership of Tanzania is conveyed by Source H?

One-party state

In 1965, Tanzania was formally declared to be a one-party state. TANU was to be the only recognized political party. There was little organized objection to this. When foreign correspondents queried why Tanzania under him had not developed as a multi-party democracy, Nyerere responded by pointing out that multi-party democracy was not the only form of legitimate democracy. He referred them to a speech he had made in 1963 (see Source I, page 296).

He argued that to create a multi-party system simply to satisfy an abstract concept of democracy would make no sense; it would ignore the political realities of Tanganyika. There was no need for any another parties; TANU as representative of all the people could accommodate all their hopes and wishes, and even their complaints, in its programme.

?

According to Nyerere in Source I, why was a one-party system more democratic for Tanganyika than a two-party system?

SOURCE I

Excerpt from speech by Nyerere in 1963 to the TANU conference, quoted in _Africa: A Modern History_, by Guy Arnold, published by Atlantic Books, UK, 2005, pp. 132–33.

Our own parties were not formed to challenge any ruling group of our own people; they were formed to challenge the foreigners who ruled over us. They were not, therefore, 'political parties' – i.e., factions – but nationalist movements.

I would say that we not only have an opportunity to dispense with the disciplines of the two-party system but that we would be wrong to retain them. I would say that they are not only unnecessary where you have only one party but they are bound, in time, to prove fatal to democracy.

In 1977, TANU and Zanzibar's Shirazi Party (see box on page 295) were merged to become 'the Party of the Revolution', the only party permitted in Tanzania.

Nyerere's justification for repressing opposition

Nyerere consistently claimed that the maintenance of order was the first requirement of the new state of Tanzania. Before taking power, he had emphasized that the creation of stability would have primacy in the structuring of Tanganyika: 'There will be no change in TANU's attitude to law and order, except to enforce even more respect for law and order.' Nyerere was also sensitive to the fears of the European settlers whose skills as officials and administrators Tanzania still needed. He wanted to assure them that disorder would not be tolerated in the new state.

Nyerere's hard line has to be viewed in context. It was certainly the case in all the emergent African states that the breakdown of civil order was the greatest threat to their development. Vivid in the minds of leaders like Nyerere was the tragedy of what had been the Belgian Congo. Becoming independent in 1960 on the withdrawal of the Belgian colonial administration, the Congo had swiftly collapsed into violent disorder. Regional and tribal rivalries became so destructive that **UN forces** had to move in to attempt to restore some semblance of peace. Given the immediacy of those events in the Congo, it was understandable why Nyerere should have demanded effective government control in Tanganyika and Tanzania as a central requirement, even if that meant repression of opposition.

Nyerere strengthened his argument by asking that his country should not always be judged in reference to western European values. He rejected the notion that Africa had to meet standards set by outsiders. Africa's peoples were entering a unique phase in their development. They had to have the time and freedom to develop in their own way.

African and foreign affairs

An important factor in Nyerere's consolidation of authority in Tanzania was his standing as an African statesman. As a champion of African freedom, Nyerere came to represent the cause of the newly independent states. He wanted to remove what he regarded as the harmful legacy of colonialism in

KEY TERM

UN forces Military units brought into being by a formal UN Resolution and composed of troops from a number of member states.

In what ways did developments in foreign affairs assist Nyerere in maintaining his authority in Tanzania?

Africa, which included political and economic dependency on the West. This was the most enduring aspect of his leadership of Tanzania. His unmatched reputation as an African statesman, influencing the policies of the **PAC** and the **OAU** in their anti-colonial struggles, won him admiration abroad and strengthened his position at home.

Mozambique

Tanzanian forces actively supported **FRELIMO** in its struggle against Portuguese colonial control of Mozambique. Founded under Nyerere's auspices in the Tanzanian capital of Dar es Salaam in 1962, where its headquarters remained, FRELIMO eventually won its struggle in 1975 when Portugal withdrew. Nyerere was recognized as having played a pivotal role in ending Portuguese colonialism.

Zimbabwe

In 1965, in an act of defiance against Britain's insistence that **Southern Rhodesia** could be granted independence only on the principle of black majority rule, Ian Smith's white minority government declared a Unilateral Declaration of Independence (UDI) and claimed the right to nationhood on its own terms. From that point on, Tanzania under Nyerere gave its diplomatic and military backing to the Zimbabwe Africa National Liberation Army (ZANLA) which took up arms against Smith's regime until it finally accepted majority rule in 1979.

Seychelles

In 1977, the Tanzanian army under Nyerere was involved in the deposing of James Mancham who the previous year had been elected as President of the ex-British colony of Seychelles in the Indian Ocean. He was replaced by another European, France Albert René, who went on to impose an oppressive one-party Marxist regime on the Seychelles. Although Nyerere was not responsible for this development, the part he had played in removing a democratically-elected president compromised, but ultimately did not damage, his position as a supporter of **libertarian** movements in Africa.

South Africa

Nyerere defined his approach to South African affairs when, in 1969, with fellow African President Kenneth Kaunda of **Zambia**, he issued the **Lusaka Manifesto** in which the two leaders stated their desire to see post-colonial Africa develop towards democracy by a peaceful route. They stressed, however, that if the peaceful route was closed then the African people were entitled to use such force as was necessary in the pursuit of independence. The country they had in mind was South Africa, whose **apartheid** policy deeply offended the other African nations.

It was under the terms of the Manifesto that Nyerere gave support to the variety of organizations in and outside South Africa such as the PAC, OAU and the ANC, that challenged the white government there. However, his record was regarded by some anti-apartheid activists as inconsistent since, while at times he took a tough line against the white South African government, on other occasions he advised moderation rather than

KEY TERM

PAC Pan-African Congress, founded in 1900 to campaign for African freedom from colonial rule.

OAU The Organization of African Unity, founded in 1963, with essentially the same objectives as PAC.

FRELIMO 'Liberation Front of Mozambique', a guerrilla movement made up of a number of anti-Portuguese resistance groupings.

Southern Rhodesia A British colony 1923–64, became Rhodesia in 1964, and Zimbabwe in 1980.

Libertarian Belief in the need to guard individuals and institutions from excessive government control.

Zambia Formerly Northern Rhodesia.

Lusaka Manifesto A communiqué condemning racism, presented by Kaunda and Nyerere at the Conference of East and Central African States in April 1969, and signed by all the heads of state attending.

Apartheid A system formally adopted by the white South African government for the 'separate but equal' political and economic development of the different races. In practice it was a method for maintaining white minority rule.

confrontation. He was accused of effectively suppressing the PAC in 1980 after it had rejected his suggestion that the time had not yet come for an armed rising in South Africa.

Relations with China

Early in his presidency Nyerere had warned his fellow African leaders that they might have to face another 'scramble for Africa', a new brand of colonialism. He was referring to the danger of the attempt by the great communist rivals, the Soviet Union and the People's Republic of China (PRC), to infiltrate Africa in their own interests. As the African countries became independent, the Soviet Union and the PRC provided them with personnel and resources in an attempt to establish a predominant influence in African affairs.

However, despite his warning about another scramble, Nyerere veered very much to the PRC's side. During visits there in the 1960s, he developed close relations with its leader, Mao Zedong, and encouraged Chinese investment in Tanzania. It was PRC capital and workers which helped create the prestigious **TANZAM** railway. Financed by a PRC grant of $400 million and running 1,160 miles (1,870 kilometres) from Dar es Salaam in Tanzania to Kapiri Mposhi in Zambia, the line was constructed between 1971 and 1976 by 75,000 labourers, a third of whom were Chinese.

KEY TERM

TANZAM Tanzania–Zambia railway.

Importance of Nyerere's foreign policy

The significance of Nyerere's foreign policy was that it elevated his standing as an African, indeed world, statesman. Such stature increased the difficulty for domestic politicians in Tanzania to oppose him since, for them to do so looked as if they were challenging the nation's greatest asset. Nyerere began to be referred to by Tanzanians as the 'Father of the Nation' and *Mwalimu* (great teacher).

What forms did government take under Nyerere?

The structure of government under Nyerere

The government structure under Nyerere was a hierarchy with the following main features:

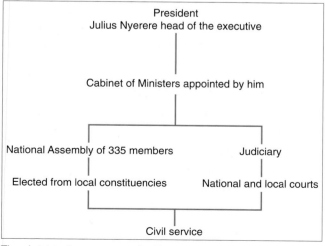

The administrative structure under Nyerere

The determining factor was that from 1965 on Tanzania was a one-party state. Only TANU members could stand for election to the National Assembly. Moreover, one-third of the Assembly's members were appointed, not elected. Effectively, all appointments were made by Nyerere or the ministers and officials to whom he delegated power to act in his name. He possessed ultimate authority. All political and administrative appointments were under his control.

Bureaucracy

All modern states need a functioning civil service. Unfortunately for Tanzania, Nyerere's period in power saw the civil service become a state bureaucracy which proved both meddlesome and inefficient. It interfered with privately-owned businesses but seldom with productive effect. A representative example was the **sisal** industry, which accounted for 40 per cent of Tanzanian exports. Its sales and output could have been 15 per cent to 20 per cent higher had government departments not intervened in an attempt to extract higher tax from a profitable concern.

As well as being a drain on government finance, since its members were among the highest paid of state workers, the civil service also became tainted with corruption. Misappropriation of public funds and tax revenue became standard practice. **Nepotism** and favouritism prevented those of real talent rising to the top and the awarding of government contracts depended more on whom the contractors knew than on the quality of the service they offered. The right of officials to grant permits to those bidding for contracts meant they issued them in return for what were, in effect, bribes. Those officials who became the fattest cats in this system acquired the name '**Wabenzi**'.

Some attempt was made in the early 1970s to limit the number of bureaucrats but this proved little more than a gesture. Between 1975 and 1985, the number of officials in government departments swelled by 35 per cent from 21,000 to 28,300. Since nearly all the officials were TANU party members who owed their position to Nyerere's patronage, they were highly unlikely to oppose him on any major issue, a situation which was obviously much to his liking. A quiescent civil service is a necessary part of any modern authoritarian system.

Nyerere's ideology – *Ujamaa*

Julius Nyerere had entered politics in the 1950s committed to socialism, but socialism interpreted in a particular African way. His word for it was *Ujamaa*, which he defined as a form of socialism based on Tanzania's traditional rural way of life. He wanted the co-operative communalism of tribal tradition to be used to help turn Tanzania into a modern African nation (see Source J, page 300).

← What ideas inspired Nyerere's politics?

KEY TERM

Sisal A fibre that can be cultivated and processed into rope and twine.

Nepotism The granting of positions and privileges to family members or close associates.

Wabenzi The 'Benz people', a pejorative term used to describe Tanzanian officials in mocking reference to their buying luxurious Mercedes-Benz cars.

Ujamaa The word in Swahili, Tanzania's national language, for 'familyhood' or community.

? According to Source J, what does Nyerere understand by the term *Ujamaa*?

SOURCE J

Excerpt from 'Ujamaa – the Basis of African Socialism', a pamphlet by Julius Nyerere, 1962, quoted in *Two African Statesmen* by John Hatch, published by Secker & Warburg, UK, 1976, p. 182.

Modern African socialism can draw from its traditional heritage the recognition of 'society' as an extension of the basic family unit. Ujamaa *describes our socialism. It is opposed to capitalism, which seeks to build a happy society on the basis of the exploitation of man by man; and it is equally opposed to doctrinaire socialism which seeks to build its happy society on a philosophy of inevitable conflict between man and man.*

The Arusha Declaration, 1967

In 1967, at Arusha, a village in northern Tanzania, Nyerere issued his 'Arusha Declaration' in which he set out what the philosophy of *Ujamaa* meant in practical terms. It was a programme for the development of Tanzania, based on egalitarian, socialist principles. The key elements in the programme were the:

- abandonment of capitalism in favour of communal values
- development of Tanzania as a single-party democracy
- elimination of class discrimination
- nationalization and central direction of the economy
- villagization of the land in order to develop communal methods of production
- replacement of tribal loyalties with a sense of a Tanzanian national identity
- achievement of national self-reliance through collective effort
- assertion of national independence by throwing off the colonial legacy
- provision of free, compulsory education to train the young as workers and instil in them the values of *Ujamaa*.

Villagization

A central feature in *Ujamaa* was the programme of villagization. A typical village contained some 250 families; these were now to be grouped to work together as one unit. This programme proved the most controversial and the most disruptive of Nyerere's policies. His initial belief had been that collectivization would improve agricultural efficiency and production. He calculated that the sharing of tools and supplies would make communal farming a success. But this proved a misjudgement. The Tanganyikan peasants found themselves unable to adapt to enforced collectivism. While it was true that communal ways were a feature of tribal culture, these did not extend to work on the land; by tradition, farmers were independent. Officials were directed by Nyerere to go into the countryside and teach the benefits of villagization, but they largely failed. Despite the offer of privileges to village elders if they embraced the new system, it proved difficult to persuade reluctant peasants to co-operate. Nevertheless, 10 million villagers (90 per cent of the rural population) had been collectivized by 1979.

SOURCE K

The villagization process.

Year	Number of villages collectivized
By 1968	180
By 1969	800
By 1972	2,500
By 1973	5,500
By 1975	6,500
By 1979	7,650

Examine Source K. What trend is evident in the villagization process?

Enforcement of villagization

At Arusha, Nyerere had said '*Ujamaa* is a state of mind; you can arrange for people to live together, but you cannot force them to behave co-operatively.' However, contrary to this statement, when the Tanzanians were slow to respond to the call to collectivize, Nyerere sanctioned the use of force:

- The police and the army were sent out to prevent protests and physically dispossess peasants who resisted.
- 203 leading organizers of resistance were arrested and imprisoned.
- 319 villages were forced, under guard, to move to **collective farms** elsewhere.
- Crops were seized or destroyed and livestock was killed or scattered.

Despite the repression with which it was occasionally enforced, the notable feature of villagization, given the scale of the operation, was how seldom force needed to be used. The fact was there was little organized resistance. Over the course of villagization, only 300 villages mounted sustained protest. Some government officials interpreted this lack of resistance as willing acceptance of collectivization, but it was more likely to have been stoic resignation. It was the threat of force and the knowledge among the villagers that they had little chance of resisting it that made them conform. Chiefs were removed from the headship of tribes to prevent their becoming a focus of opposition. Of the 130 tribes there were only twenty instances where chiefs resisted persuasion and threats and had to be physically removed. The relative smoothness of the overall operation was the result of the subtle methods the TANU officials adopted. They found that the method least likely to cause trouble in the villages was simply to prevent the election of a new chief on the death of the existing one. This needed time, of course, which is why the enforced removals tended to happen in the late 1970s after the programme had been running for over a decade.

The results of villagization

The failure of collectivization economically was plain from the figures. Between the late 1960s, when collectivization had been introduced on a

KEY TERM

Collective farms Farms run as co-operatives in which the peasants shared the labour and the wages.

voluntary basis, and the late 1970s, by which time it had become compulsory, agricultural production in Tanzania had dropped by half. In some areas the local economy collapsed altogether. The most telling statistic that revealed the failure of *Ujamaa* as a land policy was that the areas collectivized by 1980 held 90 per cent of Tanzania's rural population yet produced barely 5 per cent of the country's arable and dairy output.

It is important to emphasize that for Nyerere the whole purpose of villagization was to improve the life of Tanzanians. He was distressed when presented with accounts of villagers' misery; his hope was that these were isolated cases, the result of excess zeal among the officials imposing the programme. Yet he came to recognize that the villagization programme had not fulfilled his idealistic hopes for it. Though he never formally abandoned it, he acknowledged at the time of his retirement that villagization had largely been a failure (see Source L).

SOURCE L

Excerpt from the 'The Goal of an Egalitarian Society' by Colin Legum, in *Mwalimu: The Influence of Nyerere*, edited by Colin Legum and Geoffrey Mmari, published by British-Tanzania Society, 1995, UK, pp. 189–90.

While many villages engage in communal co-operative activities, very few farm co-operatively … I once asked [Nyerere] how many of the 7,650 villages could be described as true Ujamaa *communities. He answered by holding up both hands and said: 'If I said as many as the fingers on both hands I would not be exaggerating.'*

> According to Source L, what was the scale of the failure of villagization?

Economic planning under Nyerere

Nyerere's economic policy was based on a series of **Five-Year Plans** (FYPs).

First Five-Year Plan, 1964–69

The aim of the First FYP was to attract private and foreign investment in Tanzanian agriculture and industry. Emphasis was laid on developing the country's transport system and modernizing its harbours. Schemes for diversifying and improving such traditionally productive factories as sisal plants and food-processing canneries figured prominently. Nyerere calculated that the projects under the plan would require a capital expenditure of half a billion dollars. He openly stated that, given the country's limited financial reserves, more than half of the capital would have to come from outside Tanzania.

> How far did Nyerere achieve his economic objectives for Tanzania?

KEY TERM

Five-Year Plan A programme for industrial development based on a set of production quotas.

GDP Gross Domestic Product, the annual total value of goods produced and services provided, the standard way of measuring a country's economic strength.

The planners who worked under Nyerere had calculated that the first FYP would achieve a 6.8 per cent annual **GDP** growth rate. They were to be disappointed. The figure reached was only 5.3 per cent. The principal reason for the shortfall were:

- the rapid rise in population, which increased during the course of the plan by nearly a third from 10.7 million to 13.2 million, creating a demand for food and commodities that could not be met

- villagization, which disrupted the production and distribution of supplies of food and commodities.
- a drop in world prices, which lessened the value of such key Tanzanian exports as coffee, tobacco and sisal
- a shortfall in the amount of foreign aid received.

SOURCE M

Population growth in Tanzania 1960–85, from Population Division of the Department of Economic and Social Affairs of the United Nations Secretariat, World Population Prospects: 2010, http://esa.un.org/wpp

Year	Total population
1960	10,740,000
1965	11,683,000
1970	13,605,000
1975	15,978,000
1980	18,686,000
1985	21,848,000

Examine Source M. What population trends are discernible in Tanzania between 1960 and 1985?

The Second Five-Year Plan, 1969–74

The Second FYP is best understood as an attempt to introduce into the economy the principles of *Ujamaa* as announced by Nyerere in the Arusha Declaration in 1967. With respect to agriculture, the hope was that the programme of villagization would lead to a major increase in food production which would, in turn, lead the nation to self-sufficiency. There was certainly an increase in crop yield. The Second FYP began a process that, by the late 1970s, saw tea, cotton and tobacco production reach impressive levels. However, these could not have been achieved without the financial help of the **International Development Association (IDA)** which, by 1981, had advanced $670 million to Tanzania. Moreover, the successes in cash crop production were overshadowed by the failure to grow adequate supplies of food. This was evident in the statistic which showed that, during the years of the Second FYP, Tanzanian food imports rose in cost from $243 million to $771 million.

Throughout Nyerere's time as leader, Tanzania remained chronically short of **staple** cereals, such as sorghum, millet and maize; the annual shortfall approached a million tons. The shortages led to disturbances and protests in a number of regions but the unrest did not become a serious threat to the government largely because it was able to call on foreign aid from such bodies as IDA and the **CDC**, which paid for the import of food.

Nationalization

The outstanding feature of the Second FYP's industrial programme was nationalization. As stated in the Arusha Declaration (see page 300), the economy was to be centralized and nationalized. In keeping with the *Ujamaa*

KEY TERM

International Development Association (IDA) Created in 1960 and funded by the USA, it aimed to reduce poverty in the poorest countries by providing them with grants to stimulate economic growth.

Staple Basic crop or commodity on which an economy relies.

CDC (Commonwealth Development Corporation) Created by Britain in 1948 with the aim of financing self-sufficient agriculture and industry in the poorer countries of the Commonwealth.

principle that the needs of the people collectively had priority over the making of profits by self-seeking individuals, a range of enterprises were taken over by the state. Large concerns, such as banks, finance houses, insurance societies, transport companies, major manufacturing firms and import–export companies were among the private concerns that were nationalized. The government announced that it would be responsible for 85 per cent of all industrial development in Tanzania.

Nyerere's belief was that the state's takeover of large parts of the private sector would provide a basis of national unity and economic growth. The practice fell short of the ideal envisaged. The government had set itself a target of a 7 per cent increase in industrial productivity; the figure reached was only 4 per cent. Poor planning of the nationalization process, which was disrupted by lengthy disputes over the compensation to be paid to the dispossessed companies, and poor administration afterwards undermined incentive and encouraged corruption. Money that should have been invested back into the national economy ended up in private hands. By 1975, the nationalized part of the economy was producing less than one-third of the revenue it had contributed when privately owned.

Wage disparity

In the areas of industry that did experience growth, the workers did relatively well. To the satisfaction of the trade unions, whose support Nyerere was eager to keep, wages rose. Yet this created a problem by emphasizing the disparity in income between industrial and agricultural workers, who, on average earned five times more than their rural counterparts. The discrepancy undermined the *Ujamaa* principle of national unity. There were strikes and protests among land workers but these were contained largely because of two factors:

- The police and army responded quickly to suppress signs of trouble.
- There were no independent trade unions. The organizations representing agricultural and industrial workers were controlled by TANU, which, as the party of government, used its influence to prevent unrest spreading.

The Third Five-Year Plan, 1976–81

Nyerere approached the Third FYP much more soberly. The plan concentrated on developing Tanzania's infrastructure, improving basic facilities, such as water and electricity supplies, and developing scientific and technological research. Nationalization was not abandoned but Nyerere made it clear that the private sector was now fully acceptable in the nation's economy. His more conservative approach was explained by events in Africa and the wider world which cut across developments in Tanzania.

The impact of the international oil crisis, 1973

The worldwide recession created by the rapid increase in oil prices in the 1970s impacted particularly severely on the Tanzanian economy. Despite cutting back on its purchase of oil from abroad by 20 per cent, Tanzania still saw the cost of its fuel imports quadruple between 1972 and 1977. This coincided with the income from Tanzania's exports (mainly coffee, cotton and tobacco) dropping by over 30 per cent in the same period. Falling profits led to companies cutting back on production and laying off workers.

The collapse of the East African Community (EAC), 1977

EAC was a common market and trading partnership formed in 1967 between Burundi, Kenya, Rwanda, Uganda and Tanzania. It lasted a decade until its collapse in 1977, caused largely by the disruptive behaviour of Uganda's Idi Amin (see below). The EAC had provided Tanzania with cheap resources, particularly for its aviation and telecommunications industries. With the EAC's disintegration, Tanzania now had to purchase these resources at a higher price from Europe and North America. This involved spending its limited foreign exchange reserves to import materials and equipment. Tanzania suffered losses of $200 million.

The Ugandan War, 1979–81

Idi Amin had seized power in Uganda in a military coup in 1971. Over the next eight years, he ran a fierce dictatorship which resulted in the death of more than 300,000 people. Responding to appeals from Ugandan exiles who fled to Tanzania, Nyerere sent his troops into Uganda in 1979 to aid the rebels. This was also in retaliation for the occupation of a part of Tanzania by Amin's troops a year earlier. Although Amin was overthrown in 1979, the war dragged on for another two years before Tanzanian forces finally withdrew following the return to power of Milton Obote, the leader whom Amin had originally toppled. The conflict, which caused the death of 700 Tanzanian troops and the serious wounding of a further 500, drained Tanzania of $600 million in military costs.

Natural disasters in the 1960s and 1970s

Tanzania's financial problems were deepened in this period by a series of droughts and floods. These caused a fall in harvest yields made worse by the damage to the road and rail networks, which disrupted the distribution of dwindling food supplies. To cope with the crises, Tanzania had to appeal for international food aid. The total losses had to be met by borrowing $250 billion.

Faced with such a list of deficits, Nyerere's reaction was to cut expenditure which slowed down economic expansion. *Ujamaa* remained an ideal, which he continued to advocate in his public pronouncements, but in his remaining years as President he became much more realistic and accepted that his original objectives were unrealizable.

Tourism

An interesting development that went some way to off-setting the financial costs of the floods and droughts was the growth in tourism. The natural beauty of Tanzania and the splendour of its wildlife made tourism an obvious economic resource to exploit. By 1979, foreign visitors to the national parks, such as the Serengeti, numbered over 400,000, bringing the equivalent of $12 million into the country.

Nyerere's last years as President, 1981–85

There were signs that long before his retirement in 1985 Nyerere had become disillusioned by the inability of his socialist policies to achieve the national objectives he had set himself. Convinced that the failure of *Ujamaa*, particularly in regard to villagization, had been caused by the corrupt way it had been handled by officials, he belatedly introduced an anti-corruption campaign. Over a thousand officials were arrested on such charges as diverting public funds into their own accounts and appropriating supplies for their own use. The campaign was broadly popular but it created opposition among those who feared their vested interests were threatened. An attempt to overthrow Nyerere occurred in January 1983 when a group of some 30 disaffected army officers and officials tried to remove him. They failed; the coup was poorly organized and aroused little support. But it was enough to confirm Nyerere in his resolution not to stand again for the presidency, an intention he had announced at the time of his re-election victory in 1980. He did not formally abandon his economic and social policies, but he left the way open for his successors to modify his socialism and allow market forces to operate.

Nyerere's acknowledgement of failure

Nyerere's willingness to promote Ali Hassan Mwinyi as his successor, even though he knew that Mwinyi intended to reverse many features of *Ujamaa*, was his tacit admission that the programme had failed. The policies then adopted by Mwinyi after becoming President are an instructive commentary on where Nyerere had gone wrong. Among the key changes were the:

- introduction of a multi-party electoral system
- scrapping of the collectivization of agriculture
- releasing of a number of political prisoners and detainees
- lessening of central government control of the economy
- dismantling of the nationalization programme.

Relative growth

Despite Nyerere's sense of disappointment with his country's economic performance during his time as leader, a comparison with other African countries in the same period shows that, though there had undoubtedly been decline in Tanzania, this was a general economic phenomenon (see Source N)

SOURCE N

? Study the figures in Source N. Taking GDP as a measure of growth, examine how well Tanzania compared with other African countries in its economic development between 1961 and 1984.

World Development Indicators for Tanzania, *Bank/Tanzania Relations, 1990*, PFPs, IMF RED (1999).

GDP growth (%), 1961–84	Tanzania	Ghana	Kenya	Malawi
1961–66	6.0	1.9	5.4	7.0
1967–72	4.0	3.7	9.0	5.7
1973–78	2.3	0.8	4.9	5.9
1979–84	−1.0	−1.4	3.0	1.9

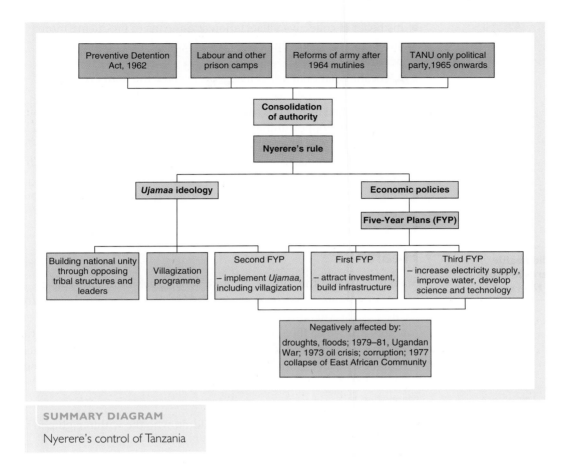

Nyerere's control of Tanzania

3 Life in Tanzania under Nyerere, 1961–85

▶ **Key question:** *What impact did Nyerere's rule have on the lives of the Tanzanian people?*

After Nyerere's retirement in 1985, it became common to regard his years in office as a failure since his plans for the improvement of his people had not been realized. It was suggested by critics that he had too often allowed his idealism and political conviction to obscure reality. Among the failures and limitations cited by critics were that:

• Nyerere's imposition of one-party government restricted the growth of democracy

- his belief in collective villagization as a means of producing more and better food proved mistaken and created an embittered peasantry
- advocating national self-reliance overlooked the hard economic reality that Tanzania had limited natural resources to exploit and, therefore, had to rely heavily on imports for essential supplies, which restricted the opportunities for the people to advance themselves materially
- Nyerere did not tackle poverty effectively, forcing Tanzania to rely too heavily on foreign aid and loans
- nationalization and government control of the economy had not produced growth
- bureaucratic corruption had been allowed to develop.

How did health standards improve under Nyerere?

Health

Statistics suggest that one of Nyerere's major achievements was an increase in the people's general standard of living, despite the privations created by the villagization programme. Analysts and historians often use a category known as the Quality of Life Index (QLI) to measure a nation's economic performance. The emphasis in QLI is not on purely financial or economic considerations but on social ones. Have conditions improved for the people? The answer to that question is assessed by three main measures:

- *infant mortality* – the number of children who die within eighteen months of birth per thousand of live births
- *life expectancy* – the age to which an individual was likely to live from birth
- *adult literacy* – the percentage of the adult population with basic reading and writing skills.

Tanzania's QLI record in comparison with its neighbours, Uganda and Kenya, with western Europe and with the USA and Canada combined is shown in Sources O, P and Q.

SOURCE O

? Study Sources O, P and Q. How favourably does Tanzania's QLI compare with its neighbours and with western Europe and North America?

Infant mortality rates in different countries and regions.

Date	Tanzania	Uganda	Kenya	Western Europe	USA and Canada
1962	225	215	189	31	23
1967	161	201	163	28	20
1975	154	182	129	23	18
1978	152	183	115	20	16
1985	110	183	96	17	8

SOURCE P

Life expectancy in different countries and regions.

Date	Tanzania	Uganda	Kenya	Western Europe	USA and Canada
1962	37	47	50	68	70
1967	40	49	53	70	71
1975	63	52	56	72	72
1978	48	52	59	74	73
1985	54	51	62	76	74

SOURCE Q

Literacy rates in different countries and regions.

Date	Tanzania	Uganda	Kenya	Western Europe	USA and Canada
1962	20	24	26	86	83
1967	44	45	47	89	88
1975	63	60	64	91	89
1978	78	69	79	92	90
1985	84	75	85	93	91

While these figures were not impressive initially by the standards of the USA or western Europe, they show a notable advance for Tanzania over the period. Nyerere's record as measured by QLI is striking. Despite the food shortages and continuing poverty, many more children were surviving, people were living longer and were being better educated. This was not an accident; it was a result at least in part of the health provision programmes introduced under Nyerere. Not all public money was frittered away in failed schemes and bureaucratic corruption. There was investment in positive planning:

- In 1961, in a population of 10.7 million, there were only 12 fully trained professional doctors, a ratio of one doctor to 870,000 people. By 1985, in a population that had more than doubled to over 27 million, there were 1,065 trained doctors, a ratio of one doctor to 26,000 people.
- In addition, over a ten-year period between 1976 and 1985, over 6,000 nurses and medical assistants entered the public health services.
- By 1985, half of all Tanzanian families had access to a health centre, a considerable achievement by African standards.
- By 1985, under a state immunization programme, half a million children had been vaccinated and inoculated against a variety of diseases.
- Notwithstanding the criticism of collectivization as social policy, there were aspects of villagization that were distinctly progressive. One example is that by the time of Nyerere's retirement every village had been provided with a primary school.

Study Source R. What information do the figures provide regarding the provision of health facilities between 1961 and 1985?

SOURCE R

Health care provision.

Year	No. of hospitals	No. of health centres/clinics	No. of pharmacies
1961	98	22	975
1985	149	239	2,644

How did educational standards improve under Nyerere?

Education

A remarkable increase in educational provision took place during Nyerere's years. A major feature was the growth in literacy (see Source Q, page 309), a result of the increased school provision for children.

SOURCE S

Study Source S. What trend is observable regarding school provision between 1961 and 1984?

Number of children attending primary school.

Year	Number of children attending primary school (7–14 year olds)
1961	500,000 (25%)
1977	2,287,000 (72%)
1984	3,756,000 (98%)

Teacher training

By 1984, 35 training colleges had been created or developed, producing 2,000 teachers each year. Despite this, the problem of over-large classes persisted; in 1984 the teacher–pupil ratio was 1:53.

The curriculum

In keeping with the philosophy of *Ujamaa*, Nyerere required that education be based on the principle of Education for Self-Reliance (ESR), which he defined in these terms:

SOURCE T

According to Source T, what does Nyerere understand by the term 'self-reliance'?

Excerpt from a pamphlet, 'Education for Self-Reliance' by J.K. Nyerere, 1967, quoted by A.G. Ishumi in *Mwalimu: The Influence of Nyerere*, edited by Colin Legum and Geoffrey Mmari, published by British-Tanzania Society, 1995, UK, p. 51.

The education provided by the colonial government was not designed to prepare young people for the service of their own country; instead it was motivated by the desire to inculcate the values of the colonial society. Our education must therefore inculcate a sense of commitment to the whole community. Schools must, in fact, become communities and communities that practise the precept of self-sacrifice. The teachers, workers and pupils must be members of a social unit.

To further his educational aims, Nyerere established the Institute of Curriculum Development (ICD) whose tasks included:

- overseeing the preparation, printing and distribution of textbooks promoting self-reliance and written at varying levels of difficulty so as to cover primary, secondary and tertiary education
- ensuring that science, history and politics were taught as core subjects
- monitoring the teaching and lifestyle of the teachers in order to check they were carrying out their principal task of inculcating self-reliance
- liaising with the existing Church schools (mainly Catholic mission foundations) to find effective ways of incorporating self-reliance into the teaching of traditional Christian values, such as self-control, unselfishness and respect for others.

The status of women

Tanzania, as was the case with most African states, was a **patriarchal** society. Eighty-five per cent of the population lived in rural areas in extended families in which women did most of the work in the house as well as assisting men working in the fields. They provided 80 per cent of the labour force in rural areas. The subsistence level of farming, in which the hoe remained the basic implement, gave women little opportunity for breaking free of traditional ways. Nyerere was very aware of this. In 1968, he observed:

SOURCE U

Excerpt from a speech by Nyerere in 1968, quoted in *Africa's Liberation: The Legacy of Nyerere*, edited by Chambi Chachage, published by Pambazuka Press, South Africa, 2010, p. 154.

In the villages, women work very hard. At times they work for twelve or fourteen hours. They even work on Sundays and public holidays. Women who live in the villages work harder than anybody else in Tanzania. But men who live in villages are on leave for half their lives.

Nyerere's understanding of the situation led him to a series of initiatives which included:

- a declaration that women were the equal of men before the law
- the legal requirement that women as workers were to receive equal treatment and pay
- outlawing of unfair discrimination against women when applying for employment and promotion
- removing restrictions on the right of women to vote
- granting women equal rights to stand for parliament
- opening positions in the civil service and government offices to women on the same terms as men.

What gains in status did women make under Nyerere?

KEY TERM

Patriarchal Male-dominated.

According to Source U, how hard is life for women in the villages?

?

Examine Source V. What information does the photo provide regarding the role of women in Tanzanian village life?

SOURCE V

A woman carrying water from a well.

It was in the freer atmosphere encouraged by such measures that TANU'S National Organization of Women (UWT), successfully pressed for:

- women workers to be granted paid maternity leave
- the provision of state-financed day-care centres
- the adjustment of university entrance requirements to make allowance for the special difficulties women faced in society.

As a result of the last initiative, the number of women attending university rose from 8.6 per cent of the student body in 1975 to 25 per cent in 1984.

These were major achievements on the legal front but they did not in themselves mean a major social shift had occurred. Traditional male dominance was so ingrained in east African society that the chances were that it would take generations to alter. Nevertheless, the lead from the top in Nyerere's time helped stimulate an awareness of the inequalities to which women were subject (see Source W).

SOURCE W

?

According to Nyerere in Source W, why is the continued inequality of women in Tanzania unacceptable?

Excerpt from *Freedom and Socialism* by Julius K. Nyerere, published by OUP, 1968, Oxford, UK, p. 339.

There was in most parts of Tanzania, an acceptance of one human inequality. Although we try to hide the fact … it is true that the women in traditional society were regarded as having a place in the community which was not only different, but was also to some extent inferior. This is certainly inconsistent with our socialist conception of the equality of all human beings … If we want our country to make full and quick progress now, it is essential that our women live in terms of full equality.

Treatment of minorities

Ethnic minorities

Did minorities gain or lose in Nyerere's Tanzania?

A problem for many African states after gaining independence was tension between the indigenous population and the settler groups who had usually held power and privilege in the colonial period. Tanzania largely escaped this problem, the main explanation being the relatively small size of the settler groups. Nyerere cited this as the reason for the relatively painless way in which his country had made the transition from colony to independent state (see Source X).

SOURCE X

Excerpt from an interview given by Nyerere in March 1961, quoted in _Two African Statesmen_ by John Hatch, published by Secker & Warburg, London, UK, 1976, p. 143.

Many things have combined to give us in Tanganyika the success we have achieved. One is the fact that being a Trust Territory, we did not attract large numbers of settlers; and so, although we are classified among the so-called multi-racial societies, the settlers did not have actual power. Thus when we began organizing for independence, we could direct our struggle against the colonial powers as such and not against a European minority in Tanganyika.

According to Source X, what is the connection between Tanganyika's racial make-up and the achievement of independence?

Asian-Indians

In 1961, European and Asian settlers made up barely 1 per cent of the Tanzanian population of 10.5 million. Their low numbers encouraged the new government to offer them citizenship provided they were prepared to accept it on Tanzanian terms; they would have to forego their former political privileges, but they would not suffer discrimination. The great majority of the 77,000 Asian-Indians, whose occupations were mainly in shop-keeping and small-scale commerce in the urban areas, chose to stay. Even though some 30 per cent of Asian-owned businesses were taken over during Nyerere's nationalization programme, this did not result in significant migration from Tanzania; the Asians who were affected judged that it was better to adapt to the change, since no other African country offered better prospects.

Europeans

The majority of European settlers, who were mainly British also stayed. Their motive was economic. They calculated correctly that the new nation needed their continuing contribution. Many of them were large farmers and businessmen, whose skills and experience Nyerere and TANU were eager to use. Such was the confidence of the Europeans that they would flourish in Nyerere's new nation that their numbers increased from 10,000 to 22,000 between 1958 and 1968 as new settlers arrived attracted by the economic opportunities. Villagization did present some difficulties for the settlers when and distribution in the 1960s involved encroachment on European-owned farms. But the issues were resolved relatively amicably and there was little lasting settler resentment. There was certainly no sustained government effort to interfere with European interests. Nyerere had always said that he would not allow racism to operate in independent Tanzania. He kept his word. There was no overt ethnic discrimination.

Homosexuals

Nyerere was not always progressive in his social views. He declined to support the advancement of homosexual rights. While it was not a major issue in his time, homosexual relations were forbidden under Tanzanian law, as they had been under British colonial rule. Nyerere saw no reason to change this and he let it be known that he disapproved of the practice for cultural rather than moral reasons. In an interview with a German newspaper in 1974 he remarked: 'Homosexuality is a phenomenon alien to Africa, and in Africa, therefore, there are no grounds for homosexuals and lesbians to be defended against discrimination.'

Yet disapproval did not mean persecution. Notwithstanding the existing laws, prosecutions were rare; there was never an active campaign against homosexuals.

How were the media treated in Nyerere's time?

→ # The media

Frequently unhappy with the criticism which he received in the Tanzanian press, Nyerere took steps to control the media. What had moved him to act was his anger at the suggestion in one journal that his notion of democracy under *Ujamaa* was really a cover for the abolition of free speech (see Source Y).

?

According to Source Y, what threat to democracy does the removal of the two-party system represent?

SOURCE Y

Excerpt from an editorial by Frene Ginwala, in *Spearhead*, February, 1963, quoted in *Africa: a Modern History* by Guy Arnold, published by Atlantic Books, London, UK, 2005, pp. 133–34.

President Nyerere emphasizes the need for discussion as a fundamental characteristic of democracy. He implies that with the removal of two-party disciplines there will be an immediate sprouting of self-criticism and discussion. This may be true in so far as parliament and its members are concerned, but what of the rest of society? Can one believe there will be an atmosphere conducive to the expression of dissent from the norm?

President Nyerere himself says that opposition parties 'tend to be regarded as traitors to the majority of our people'. Might this not also apply to those who in any way differ from official policy? There is in fact an unfortunate tendency, especially among TANU officials, to regard any criticism of the Party, especially from a non-official, as tantamount to treason.

The editor of the journal in question, *Spearhead*, which was published in Dar es Salaam, the Tanzanian capital, was Frene Ginwala, an Asian South African. The journal represented her strong libertarian views. As an ANC member, she had already gained a reputation for her stern criticisms of the leaders of other African states who had adopted authoritarian methods. Nyerere considered her dangerous and ordered that she be treated as a 'prohibited immigrant'. Three months after her editorial had appeared, she was formally deported from Tanzania. The ANC in South Africa complained strongly about her arbitrary treatment, but the reaction in Nyerere's own country was muted and journalists declined to give her sustained support.

Unwilling to be subjected to attacks from the national or foreign press, the government took further steps to limit its freedom. Rather than attack the press after it had made its criticism, the method employed was to restrict what was written before it appeared. This was done by requiring that all journalists were licensed by the government before they were allowed to work. This gave government officials the power to censor copy of which they disapproved.

Newspapers

As part of the programme to bring the media under closer control, newspapers were closed down or amalgamated. At the end of the colonial period in 1961 there had been a number of foreign-owned independent English and Swahili daily papers in circulation. Within three years of Tanganyika's becoming independent, these had closed or had been merged, leaving only one major national daily paper, *The Daily News*, which was owned and operated by TANU. Published in an English and a Swahili version, it became a propaganda mouthpiece for Nyerere and the government.

Radio

Lacking a major news outlet, opposition voices found it very hard to make themselves heard. This was equally the case in relation to radio. There was only one national station, Radio Tanzania, which by 1975 was broadcasting to the million people who had access to radio sets. All programmes were subject to censorship before they were cleared to go on air. Television did not come to Tanzania until the mid-1980s, and so played little part in Nyerere's rule.

The arts

Nyerere wrote and produced theatre plays and translated a number of Shakespeare's plays into Swahili. As a man of artistic talent, he was naturally eager to encourage an appreciation of the arts among his people although financial restraints prevented the investment in them he would have liked. He declared that he wanted Tanzanians to rediscover and cherish their native culture, while at the same time learning to appreciate the culture of the wider world. His personal interest was influential in establishing a Ministry of Culture and Youth and in prompting it to undertake a range of projects.

> ← **How were the arts developed under Nyerere?**

A major development was the formation of National Art Groups (NAGs). Their activities included:

- setting up dance and theatre companies which performed in the cities and toured the rural areas
- using state subsidies to keep ticket prices at a minimum
- selecting promising youngsters and providing them with financial grants to attend art colleges and drama schools.

The arts as politics

Nyerere was prepared to use the arts for directly political purposes. Indeed, he argued that, given Tanzania's colonial past, the arts could not avoid being political. To serve the interests of the nation, the arts had to throw off the legacy of the cultural imperialism to which they had been subjected before independence. Preferment was given to those painters, playwrights, poets, film-makers and theatre directors whose works were directly political, dealing with the problems created by colonialism. Teams of actors went into schools and performed plays and staged readings which praised the efforts being made by the nation to adopt and live up to the *Ujamaa* principles enunciated by Julius Nyerere, the great leader.

Popular music

In order to stimulate indigenous Tanzanian music and dance Nyerere's government placed a ban on foreign music, which was condemned as 'neo-colonialist'. Records of popular Western music could not be imported or played in public. It proved a difficult ban to enforce and it had the effect of encouraging a form of underground musical resistance. By the 1980s, young people in the urban areas had developed a form known as 'hip-hop', a blending of traditional tribal drum rhythms and African-American be-bop. The authorities occasionally arrested defiant hip-hop performers, such as Berry White (named after the American artist Barry White), but by the time of Nyerere's retirement it was clear that the attempt to suppress this musical form had failed. One of the freedoms allowed by the governments after Nyerere was the right to play and perform hip-hop.

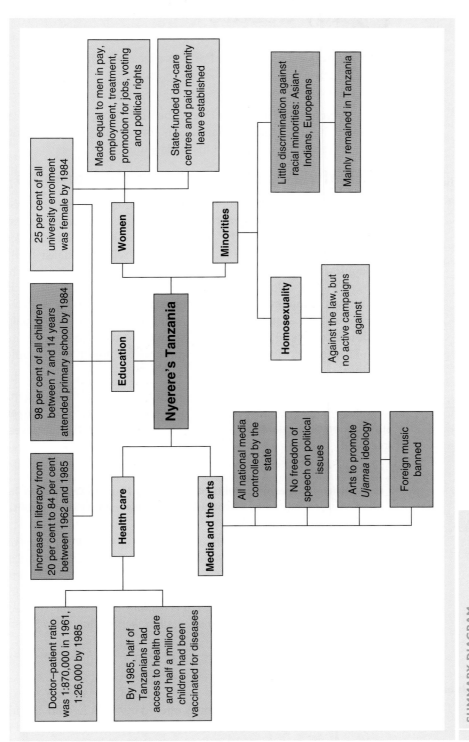

> ▶ **Key question:** How positive in its effects was Nyerere's leadership of Tanzania?

Given Nyerere's importance as one of the major post-colonial African statesmen, it is unsurprising that there is considerable disagreement among historians regarding the level of his achievement.

Critical views of Nyerere's achievements

> **On what grounds has Nyerere been criticized?**

James Robbins, a British observer, draws attention to the gap between Nyerere's aims and achievements. Robbins suggested that Nyerere tried without success to achieve the goal he had set out in the Arusha Declaration of 1967: the development of Tanzania as a self-reliant, socialist state. The Declaration was one of the most significant political statements to have emerged in post-colonial Africa. However, the policy of Ujamaa, with its aim of creating community-based communes, proved a disaster. The idealism on which it rested was undermined by the failure to provide individuals with genuine incentives. It was this failure that damaged Nyerere's reputation as one of the few African leaders at this time who represented principle and integrity.

An Arab writer who takes a similarly critical line is Haroub Othman, who defines Nyerere's chief weakness as a failure to grasp that the Tanzanian state had to be fundamentally reformed if was to serve the purposes he intended:

SOURCE Z

> According to Source Z, what was Nyerere's basic mistake in his leadership of Tanzania?

Excerpt from 'Nyerere's Political Legacy' by Haroub Othman in *Tanzania After Nyerere*, edited by Michael Dodd, published by Pinter Publishers, London, UK, 1988, p. 163.

Nyerere failed to address himself to the question of the state. Tanganyika at the time of independence inherited a colonial state and its institutions and what Nyerere tried to do was to give the state the national colours. But he never considered seriously dismantling the state or how the forces that emerged at independence could effectively use it. It is baffling that, after the 1967 Arusha Declaration, it was thought that a colonially-inherited state could be a vehicle for socialist transformation.

A sympathetic view

> **On what grounds has Nyerere been defended?**

A more sympathetic interpretation is offered by Colin Legum, a British analyst, whose emphasis is on the remarkable success Nyerere had in overcoming Tanzania's very threatening initial problems:

SOURCE AA

Excerpt from 'The Nyerere Years' by Colin Legum, in *Tanzania After Nyerere*, edited by Michael Dodd, published by Pinter Publishers, London, UK, 1988, p. 11.

At independence, Tanzania had all the potential for tribal conflicts as were manifested for example in its two neighbours, Kenya and Uganda; it had people with markedly different cultures and religions, with an almost equal number of Christians and Muslims; and it had small but non-indigenous minority communities, the Asians and Europeans. If for nothing else, Nyerere deserves to be honoured for his personal example and leadership in turning 123 tribes, Catholics, Protestants and Muslims into a fledgling nation.

> According to Source AA, what had Nyerere's leadership achieved in Tanzania?

Legum was writing in 1988, only three years after Nyerere's retirement. With the virtue of twenty years' more reflection, Guy Arnold, a modern authority on Africa, while basically sympathetic, makes this sober assessment of how far Nyerere moved from his original ideals:

SOURCE BB

Excerpt from *Africa: A Modern History* by Guy Arnold, published by Atlantic Books, UK, 2005, pp. 762 and 934.

In Tanzania the collapse of Nyerere's Ujamaa experiment, the [African] continent's most famous attempt at home grown socialism, signalled one more defeat for African self-reliance …

When an African state relies upon aid rather than its own resources it becomes an adjunct, a form of local government, in the global, Western-controlled economic order. Nyerere had warned against this in his Arusha Declaration but his warning had been largely ignored, including in the end by Tanzania itself.

> According Source BB, what had led to the failure of Nyerere's *Ujamaa* experiment in Tanzania?

A Western Left-wing view

Nyerere's rise to the leadership of Tanzania had been highly popular with liberal thinkers in the West who looked upon him as the leader most capable of showing how truly civilized and progressive emergent Africa could be. Of the ex-colonial nations, Tanzania was thought the most likely to prove successful. Such liberals acknowledged he had made mistakes but emphasized that his moral standing was a more important consideration.

> **Why did Nyerere prove popular with Western liberal thinkers?**

A Western Right-wing view

Challenging such liberal notions are those harsher critics who hold that Nyerere's image as a wise leader who understood the people's needs has been tarnished, if not destroyed, by his social policies. The sternest critics suggest that the suffering of the people under *Ujamaa* hangs over Nyerere's reputation and defines the character of his authoritarian regime.

> **On what grounds has the Western liberal view of Nyerere been challenged from the Right?**

Excerpt from *Who's Who in Africa* by Alan Rake, published by Scarecrow Press, Lanham, USA, 1992, p. 366.

He ruled his country for 25 years and tried to involve all his people in his homespun brand of socialism. Though his economic policies were not successful, he did create a moral and social climate superior to most of the rest of Africa and he gave his people good educational standards and a strong belief in his philosophies and themselves.

According to Source CC, what was Nyerere's greatest contribution as an African statesman?

SOURCE DD

Excerpt from *The Shackled Continent* by Robert Guest, published by Macmillan, London, UK, 2003, pp. 46–47.

Nyerere nationalized local industry, expropriated foreign businesses, shut down Indian and Arab traders, and tried to replace them all with bureaucrats … Nyerere favoured price controls. Peasants were obliged to sell grain to the government for as little as a fifth of its value, which was like a supertax on Tanzania's poorest citizens. Nyerere also forced two thirds of the rural population into collective farms. This was a policy that had caused millions of people to starve to death in China.

According to Source DD, what risks did Nyerere's policies involve for Tanzania?

Why have African nationalist views been so favourable towards Nyerere?

African nationalist views

Most African nationalists would regard such views as hopelessly mistaken. They venerate Nyerere as the greatest African leader in the post-colonial era, arguing that the *Ujamaa* policies were hard but necessary in the creation of Tanzania as a sovereign state. Above all, they suggest, Nyerere was the inspiration to all the independent states in Africa struggling to establish themselves as viable nations.

SOURCE EE

Excerpt from 'Mwalimu Nyerere and the Challenge of Human Rights' by Helen Kijo-Bisimba, in *Africa's Liberation: The Legacy of Nyerere*, edited by Chambi Chachage, published by Fountain Publishers, Kampala, Uganda, 2010, p. 156.

Two issues are important. First, appreciating Mwalimu's [Nyerere's] strong and unwavering position on the equality of all human beings as his guiding principle, second, the clear distinction between the individual and the community.

Mwalimu loved the community – the general as opposed to the individual. Whatever Mwalimu did that could be interpreted as violating human rights can always be explained in the wider benefits to the community. Also gratifying later in life Mwalimu was honest in conceding and acknowledging mistakes and making good on them. Few human beings are capable of doing that.

According to Source EE, why, when assessing Nyerere's achievements, does a distinction need to be drawn between the individual and the community?

TOK
Nyerere was one of the first native African leaders of a modern African state. Is it important to be ruled by people like yourself? (History, Emotion, Reason, Ethics)

Chapter summary

Tanzania under Julius Nyerere, 1961–85

As a young man, Julius Nyerere quickly became involved in the anti-British independence movement that developed in Tanganyika after the Second World War. His diplomatic and political gifts soon established him as the undoubted leader of the movement and he was the key player in the negotiations that climaxed with the British withdrawal in 1961. Within three years Tanganyika and Zanzibar had merged and Nyerere became leader of the sovereign state of Tanzania.

The son of a tribal chief, Nyerere retained his love of tribal tradition, which he wished to integrate with socialism as the basis on which Tanzania was to be developed. Believing that firm control and direction were necessary in the building of the new nation, he introduced and maintained a series of repressive measures to crush opposition.

With the aim of implementing practical socialism and increasing food production, Nyerere attempted to transform agriculture through villagization, a vast scheme for the collectivization of the land and the peasants. His other major economic programme was the adoption of a series of Five-Year Plans intended to modernize Tanzania industrially and commercially. Few of his economic targets were met, a failure explained both by his own mistakes in planning and the harmful impact of the international recession of the 1970s which hurt Tanzania particularly badly.

Nyerere retired from office in 1985, disappointed that he had not been able to modernize his nation in the way he had hoped. Yet among his major domestic achievements were the marked improvements in the health and education of Tanzanians and the recognition of the importance of raising the status of women. Moreover, his personal contribution to the emergence and consolidation of Tanzania as a sovereign African state had been immense.

Furthermore, his involvement in the anti-colonial movement made him the outstanding African leader of his time. His reputation as a statesman was secure.

Examination practice

Below are a number of different questions for you to practise. For guidance on how to answer exam-style questions, see Chapter 10.

1. Assess the importance of Nyerere in Tanganyika's achieving independence from Britain by 1961.

2. To what extent did opposition against Nyerere form within Tanzania by 1985?

3. In what ways and for what reasons did Nyerere introduce his policy of Ujamaa?

4. How did Nyerere's rule affect Tanzania's citizens of European descent?

5. Explain the importance of the military in Nyerere's Tanzania.

6. Assess the impact of Nyerere's economic policies on Tanzania by 1985.

7. What was the impact of Nyerere's rule on the arts in Tanzania?

8. To what extent were women affected by Nyerere's rule?

9. Why did Nyerere not continue as Tanzania's ruler after 1985?

10. To what extent was Nyerere a totalitarian ruler?

 # Activities

1. Nyerere attempted to forge a national identity for all people in the country of Tanzania, although there is no language, culture or tribe called Tanzanian. Discuss with your class the meaning and basis of nationalism and whether it is truly possible for a multi-ethnic, multi-national, multi-religious state to be completely successful. This discussion should include references to your TOK about language, history, and so forth.

2. Nyerere held strong views on education, some of which can be found at: www.ibe.unesco.org/fileadmin/user_upload/archive/publications/ThinkersPdf/nyereree.pdf. Read about Nyerere's thoughts on the nature of education and discuss to what extent you agree with him.

3. Tanganyika was part of Britain's colonial empire and Britain delayed granting it independence for many decades. With reference to TOK, is it ever defensible for one people to rule another?

CHAPTER 10

Examination guidance

IB History Paper 2 requires you to write two essays, each from a different topic. Now that you have studied Topic 3: Origins and development of authoritarian and single-party states, you have the knowledge to address several of the questions on the examination. This chapter is designed to help you:

✪ understand the different types of questions

✪ select an appropriate question

✪ make a historical argument using evidence

✪ outline and write your essay

✪ involve historiography appropriately.

① Preparing for Paper 2 examination questions

It is important that you understand the structure and demands of the Paper 2 examination. This section specifically focuses on Topic 3: Origins and development of authoritarian and single-party states.

Types of questions

There will be a choice of six questions for each topic. You should answer only one of these questions for Topic 3 and a second question for the other topic you have studied.

Questions for Topic 3 may address the rise and rule of:

- one or two specifically named leaders of single-party states
- an authoritarian leader of your choice
- unspecified authoritarian leaders from different regions
- unspecified authoritarian leaders from the same or opposite ends of the political spectrum (i.e. Right-wing, Left-wing)
- or the effects of either one or more leaders on a specific theme such as women, minorities, education, culture, etc.

Command terms

A key to success is understanding the demands of the question. IB History questions use key terms and phrases known as command terms. The more common command terms are listed in the table on page 324, with a brief definition of each. More are listed in the appendix of the IB History Guide. Examples of questions using some of the more common command terms are included at the end of each of Chapters 2–9.

Command term	Description	Where found in this book
Analyse	Examine the basic structure or issues.	pages 60, 108, 150, 163, 203, 241, 280
Assess	Analyse the strengths and weakness of various arguments with a concluding opinion.	pages 203, 241, 280, 322, 333
Compare and contrast	Discuss the similarities and differences of leaders, referring to both throughout your answer and not treating each separately. You should not give an overview of each leader but should focus on the most important similarities and differences, rather than every tiny detail.	pages 60, 108, 150, 163, 241, 326, 333
Define	Give the meaning of the concept or term, with examples.	page 163
Describe	Give a detailed overview of some aspect of a leader's rule.	pages 215, 276, 333
Discuss	Review various arguments regarding a leader or leaders and conclude with an argument supported by evidence.	pages 60, 108, 150, 163, 203, 241, 280, 322, 333
Evaluate/Examine	Analyse the strengths and weaknesses of various arguments with a concluding opinion.	pages 282, 289, 333
Explain	Give a thorough overview which includes reasons for developments occuring.	pages 60, 108, 150, 163, 203, 241, 280, 322, 333
For what reasons and with what results	Explain the causes and determine the results of a particular event or events.	pages 163, 203, 280, 333
In what ways, and for what reasons	Analyse various methods or changes to a system or event and their causes.	page 322
Justify	Give legitimate, evidence-supported reasons for a specific conclusion.	pages 276, 333
To what extent	Determine the extent to which something is true or false, with answers usually being 'to no extent', 'to some extent', or 'to a great extent'.	pages 60, 108, 150, 163, 203, 241, 280, 322, 333, 351, 352

Answering questions

You will have five minutes of reading time at the start of your examination. It is during this time that you should review the questions in the two or more topics you have studied, including Topic 3. You will not be able to answer all the questions and this is normal. You should, however, be able to answer two to four questions. Once you have identified which ones you are able to address, choose the question for which you have the most knowledge and whose demands you fully understand. Many students may have great knowledge regarding one or more single-party states, but they may not understand fully what the question wants them to do. If you find the wording of a question confusing, consider addressing another question if you feel more comfortable doing so. Once you have chosen your question for Topic 3, you should look at your other topic(s) of study and repeat this exercise. Once you have made a decision on your second question for Paper 2, return to your Topic 3 question and begin to think about how you will address it, waiting for the end of the reading time.

Marks

All questions on Paper 2 are worth 20 points each for a total of 40 possible points for this paper. Your goal is to achieve marks in the upper mark bands, or range of grades. In order to attain the highest mark band (16–20), your essays should include:

- answers that very clearly address the demands of the question and are well structured and clear
- correct, relevant historical knowledge used appropriately to support your argument
- evidence that is critically analysed
- historical events that are placed in their context
- evidence that you understand there are different historical interpretations.

Timing your writing

You will have 1 hour and 30 minutes to complete both Paper 2 essays. This breaks down to 45 minutes per essay on average.

Part of your writing time, however, should be spent preparing a basic outline which will help you keep your answer structured and focused. You should spend perhaps five minutes on this. An example of a good outline to a question is shown on page 327.

Defining your terms

It is important that you define the terms you are using in the introduction of your essay. For example, if the question asks you:

about some political philosophy, be sure to explain what that philosophy means

- to discuss two rulers, each from a different region, be sure to state clearly the region the rulers are from
- to discuss propaganda, be sure to explain what propaganda is and what formats you will address, such as radio, posters, cinema, or perhaps even education policy.

Making an argument

Your essays should make an argument, not just repeat details of a conflict or issue.

Your argument should be stated explicitly in your essay's introduction and conclusion with the supportive evidence discussed in the body of the essay. To strengthen your argument, you may wish to acknowledge historians whom you agree with, preferably by naming them and either summarizing their remarks or quoting them. You may even have enough knowledge on the issue being examined to be able to discuss opposing historians' viewpoints and why you disagree with their conclusions. This historical debate in which evidence is interpreted differently is called historiography and, if it is used wisely and correctly, it can help you achieve marks in the upper mark band. An example of a historiographical debate could be the extent to which a leader was fully in control of his state.

 # Examination answer

This section gives a high-level sample answer with examination advice and comments. You can apply this guidance when answering different questions on this topic.

> **With reference to two leaders of single-party states, each from a different region, compare and contrast how they maintained their authority.**

Outlining

First you will need to decide which two leaders you wish to address, making sure they are from two different regions. The various regions are found on the front cover of your examination paper. For example, you might decide to focus on Hitler in the Europe and the Middle East region and Mao from the Asia and Oceania region.

At the end of the five-minute reading time you should outline your essay. A example is given opposite.

Paragraph 1:

Defining Hitler and Mao: dates, states. Hypothesis: mostly similar, but with some notable differences

Paragraph 2: Controlling their political parties

- *Hitler:*
  - *Nazi Party*
  - *Executed party rivals, 1934*
- *Mao:*
  - *Purges, executions, imprisonment, exile*
  - *Peng Dehuai example, Great Leap Forward*
  - *Party control = government control, merging party and government*

Paragraph 3: Propaganda

- *Media*
  - *Film, radio, public speeches, posters*
    - *Leni Riefenstahl*
  - *Mein Kampf*
  - *Little Red Book*
- *All reinforces cult of personality which reinforces authority*

Paragraph 4: Similar ways of ending opposition

- *Prisons*
  - *Concentration camps, laogai*
  - *Millions removed/destroyed*
- *Prisons worked with secret police*
  - *Culture of spying created*
    - *Prevents opposition forming*

Paragraph 5: Differences: Hitler steadily increases authority

- *Maintains, builds, consolidates*
  - *Chancellor, 1933*
  - *Enabling Act, 1933*
  - *Führer, 1934*
  - *Army control, 1938*

Paragraphs 6 and 7: Differences: Mao deals with challenges from within CCP

- *100 Flowers campaign*
- *Lushan Conference, 1959*
  - *Peng Dehuai*
  - *Deng Xiaoping*
  - *Liu Shaoqi*
- *Cultural Revolution*

Paragraph 8: Differences: size
- Of country
- Of bureaucracy

Paragraph 9: Conclusion
- Similarities:
  - Party control
  - Propaganda
  - Police/prisons
- Differences:
  - Hitler continues to consolidate authority
  - Mao has to reassert himself at least twice to maintain control

Then write your answer to the question. A sample answer is given below.

> The introduction states clearly that the argument will focus on Hitler and Mao, defines their periods of rule and their states, explains briefly that they shared similarities, yet suggests there were differences.

Hitler and Mao were two authoritarian leaders of single-party states. Adolf Hitler was the leader of Germany from 1933 to 1945, Mao was Chairman of the Chinese Communist Party (CCP) and therefore leader of the People's Republic of China (PRC) from 1949 to 1976. While their methods of maintaining or reasserting their authority were similar, there were notable differences. Both Hitler and Mao were their party's leaders and once their parties controlled the state, the rule of each was consolidated. By controlling their parties, they were necessarily their state's rulers. Propaganda, in its various forms, reinforced this authority and built cults of personality around both men, making them less vulnerable to criticism or challenge, especially from the masses. Hitler expanded his authority over time and was never seriously challenged within or from without the Nazi Party until 1944, but Mao faced some opposition within the CCP itself, if not from the Chinese people themselves.

Most importantly, both Hitler and Mao were able to dominate their respective states because they dominated their political parties. Hitler was leader of the National Socialist, or Nazi, Party of Germany and Mao was the highest ranking leader of the CCP. They both consolidated their power over their political parties by eliminating rivals. In the Night of the Long Knives in 1934, Hitler purged the more socialist and radical elements of the Nazi Party, some of whom challenged his leadership, resulting in the execution of his party rivals. Similarly, Mao removed those in the CCP who opposed him, such as those who wanted Soviet-style urban-based revolution rather than Mao's rural-based, peasant revolution, or those who questioned his authority, such as the Minister of Defence, Peng Dehuai, regarding the failure of the Great Leap Forward. Mao's rivals were eliminated, just as Hitler's had been, through executions, internal exile and imprisonment. Party control meant state control since both parties merged with the government, becoming practically indistinguishable.

Once control over the party was established and the party and government were successfully merged, propaganda was of great importance in maintaining and expanding authority. In both Germany and the People's Republic of China, leaders used mass media to broadcast their messages and appeal to the masses. Hitler made bombastic public speeches, broadcast by radio and prominently used in pro-Nazi films, such as those by Leni Riefenstahl. Mao did much the same thing, speaking in Tiananmen Square in the PRC capital Beijing, for example, to declare the creation of the new communist state. Hitler's book, 'Mein Kampf', which explained his views on the world, the relationship between the people and their state, race and other issues, has some similarities with the 'Little Red Book', a collection of Mao's various statements and writings that were compiled by the PRC's Minister of Defence Lin Biao and widely distributed. Posters were used by both regimes to spread propaganda to motivate the people for a common good, against perceived enemies and to reinforce support for the leader by invoking nationalism and other concepts, including a cult of personality which elevated Hitler and Mao to god-like status.

Finally, both leaders dealt with non-party opposition in similar ways. Under both Hitler and Mao, extensive prison networks were established. In Germany, communists, leading Jews, homosexuals and others were sent to concentration camps, such as Dachau, before the Second World War. This camp system was later vastly expanded to deal with millions, including prisoners of war, racial enemies (such as Jews and Roma), as well as religious and political dissidents. In China, the laogai prison system functioned in a similar way. Millions of prisoners were held in the laogai during Mao's rule. According to historian Philip Short in 'Mao: A Life', Mao saw the killing of his enemies as necessary politics. These prison systems operated in

Uses the phrases 'Most importantly' and of 'great importance' to help indicate that the factors regarding maintenance of authority are being evaluated in terms of their relative significance.

Supportive evidence in the form of events and individuals is presented with dates, helping indicate chronology and therefore cause and effect.

conjunction with various state security police, in both Germany and the PRC, who spied on their people and encouraged them to incriminate others to avoid the possibility of being imprisoned themselves. This prevented opposition within the state from being able to organize and challenge Hitler's and Mao's individual authority.

Links between paragraphs help construct the argument more clearly.

While it is clear that Hitler and Mao had similar ways of maintaining their authority, there are notable, if subtle, differences as well. Hitler did not just maintain his authority from 1933 onwards, but increased and consolidated it between that date and 1938. Hitler not only maintained his authority within the state, but perhaps more importantly, within the Nazi Party which controlled the state. When Hitler was first named Chancellor, his authority was limited in theory by the need to consult Germany's President, von Hindenburg, and parliament, the Reichstag. The Enabling Act of 1933 allowed him to govern as Chancellor without having to consult the Reichstag. His authority was further expanded by his assumption of presidential powers upon Hindenburg's death in 1934 whereupon he was entitled Führer. Finally, in 1938, Hitler assumed full control over the army, the last sector of the government not under his full authority. This was reinforced by the oath of loyalty to Hitler personally that the army had taken earlier.

Specific focus on each leader in terms of maintenance of authority provides opportunity to discuss differences in authority and any limitations.

Mao, however, was clearly seen by the people of the People's Republic of China as the PRC's leader, but may have struggled within the CCP itself. He was the CCP Chairman, his 'Little Red Book' and various speeches were read by practically everyone and he was constantly promoted in the media, by the CCP, and the army, reinforcing the cult of personality that surrounded him. Unlike Hitler, however, he possibly faced some challenge within the CCP itself on at least two occasions. Historians continue to debate whether the challenge to Mao was a result of his paranoia or because there was an actual challenge by those wishing to follow a different line of communism. As the Chinese writer Jung Chang sees it, the 100 Flowers campaign was part of the movement towards a controlled society in which all expression of opinion had to meet the criteria of political correctness as defined by Mao. The way in which 'the anti-rightist' campaign purged the government and Party of his critics

Appropriate, supportive use of historians' views to demonstrate knowledge and understanding.

was of a scale and ruthlessness that anticipated the upheavals of the Cultural Revolution a decade later.

Mao was also challenged within the CCP by Minister of Defence, Peng Dehuai, at the Lushan Conference in 1959 about the Great Leap Forward, although the significance of this challenge is debated. The fact that Peng felt he was able to write about Mao and criticize his policies indicates that Mao had not suppressed all opposition to his programme as had Hitler in Germany. Some historians see as evidence of Mao's limitations within the party the fact that Deng Xiaoping and Liu Shaoqi, two prominent CCP members, took control of the economy at this point. However, other historians stress that it was Mao himself who specifically asked them to take control and then only for a temporary period, which suggests, therefore, that his authority was not under threat. Having first imposed it on the Central Committee and having set up the Central Cultural Revolution Group in May 1966, Mao publicly launched the Cultural Revolution at a great rally in Tiananmen Square in August. The Cultural Revolution attacked Deng and Liu and their policies, and reinstituted Maoism as the state's guiding philosophy.

Historiographical debate about different interpretations of Mao's rule reinforces the argument by indicating understanding of different approaches to historical issues.

The difficulty of dominating a country the great size of China presented Mao with difficulties that did not confront Hitler in Germany. While Germany was one of the most populated states in Europe, it still had only a few tens of millions of inhabitants. While Hitler did not overthrow the existing social and political order, this was certainly what Mao's government did. This was in addition to the sheer scale of the bureaucracy and numbers of political Party officials that Maoism required, which meant that Mao could not personally know and supervise every major political appointment.

Hitler and Mao maintained their authority in similar ways for the most part. Both controlled their political parties and then merged them with the state. Control of their respective parties entailed the elimination of rivals. Hitler was more successful than Mao in this respect after executing his rivals in 1934; Mao had to reassert himself and his political agenda at least twice from within the CCP. Both authoritarian leaders used police networks to spy on their citizens and remove those who were considered threats to the state. These police networks prevented groups from organising, divided

Conclusion summarizes main arguments and makes a definitive statement regarding their maintenance of power.

populations by fear and therefore helped maintain the leader's authority. Propaganda broadcast both parties' messages and reinforced the authority of the leader in various ways. Propaganda took the form of speeches, posters, films and radio broadcasts. While Hitler was able to consolidate and add to his authority after 1933, Mao was ostensibly the ultimate authority as Chairman of the CCP, yet had to reassert himself at least twice by appealing to the Chinese masses, specifically during the 100 Flowers campaign and the Cultural Revolution. In conclusion, both Hitler and Mao kept their political power by utilizing similar methods.

 # Examination practice

Below are a series of exam-style questions for Topic 3: Origins and development of authoritarian and single-party states that are on more than one leader or cover more than one region. Questions on individual leaders can be found at the end of Chapters 2–4 and 6–9 in this book.

1   Evaluate the reasons for a lack of effective opposition to both Stalin and Nasser.

2   For what reasons, and with what results, did both Mao and Nyerere attempt to transform their countries economically?

3   Discuss the impact on education of two authoritarian leaders, each from a different region.

4   Justify the view advanced by some historians that all authoritarian leaders ruled similarly.

5   In what ways did the lives of women improve in both Stalin's Soviet Union and Mao's People's Republic of China?

6   To what extent did both Perón and Nyerere encounter resistance to their rule from the military within their states?

7   Examine the role of nationalism in the policies of Nasser and one other ruler of a single-party state.

8   Compare and contrast the rise to power of Nasser and Castro.

9   Assess the importance of economic success for the rules of Hitler and Castro.

10   Explain the impact of Mao's and Stalin's rule on art in their respective states.

11   With reference to two leaders of authoritarian states, each from a different region, describe their impact on agriculture.

12   'There were benefits arising from authoritarian rule during the twentieth century.' With reference to two leaders, each from a different region, examine the extent to which this statement is true.

13   Compare and contrast the ways in which Castro and Nyerere maintained power.

14   Assess the importance of youth movements in maintaining the authority of two twentieth-century leaders.

15   What was the importance of totalitarian regimes during the twentieth century?

Glossary

26 July Movement   Castro's name for his revolutionary movement, chosen in commemoration of the Moncada Barracks attack, which had taken place on that date in 1953.

The 28 Bolsheviks   A particular set of communists who had been trained in Moscow and came back to China with instructions to make the CCP conform to Soviet concepts of revolution.

5:1 destruction ratio   Perónist policy of killing five opponents in retaliation for every one of their own number killed.

A priori   Latin for 'from the first', a term in philosophy to describe the type of reasoning which assumes an assertion to be true before it has been proven so.

Absolutism   A governmental system in which the levers of power are exclusively in the hands of a group or an individual.

Adult literacy rate   The percentage of the adult population with basic reading and writing skills.

Agit-prop   'Agitation propaganda', the inculcating of political ideas through entertainment.

Agricultural co-operatives   The pooling of local resources and farming for shared profits.

Alfred Rosenberg   The Nazi Party's leading race theorist.

Allies   In the First World War, principally France, Britain, Russia (1914–17), Italy (1915–18) and the USA (1917–18). In the Second World War, principally Britain, France (1939–40 and 1944–45), USSR (1941–5), and the USA (1941–45).

Amnesty International   A charity created in 1961 to call attention to the plight or fate of prisoners of conscience and to apply moral pressure to regimes which transgressed legal and ethical codes.

ANC   The African National Congress, originally formed in 1923 as a political party to press for black rights in South Africa, it reformed in 1961 as a militant force to fight against apartheid and white rule.

Annihilation policies   The programme introduced by Lenin and continued by Stalin for destroying the Soviet Union's internal class enemies, beginning with the Kulaks, the rich peasants.

Anschluss   The re-incorporation of Austria into the Third Reich in 1938.

Anti-movements   The targeting of those in the PRC accused of such crimes as waste, corruption and tax evasion.

Apartheid   A system formally adopted by the white South African government for the 'separate but equal' political and economic development of the different races. In practice it was a method for maintaining white minority rule.

Arab League   Formed in 1945 with six member states – Egypt, Transjordan (Jordan after 1949), Iraq, Lebanon, Saudi Arabia and Yemen – it stood for collaboration between the members on 'the affairs and interests of the Arab countries'. From the beginning, Egypt was the strongest member.

Arab Socialist Union (ASU)   The new name given in 1962 to the National Union, the sole party allowed to function legally in Egypt.

Armistice   An agreement between warring sides to cease fighting in order to prepare the way for a formal peace treaty.

Aryan   A person of Caucasian race; as understood by Hitler, the ideal racial type that was superior to all others.

The Aswan High Dam   A vast construction intended to modernize Egypt by preventing the recurrent, destructive Nile floods and by providing a limitless supply of hydro-electric power.

Auschwitz   The Nazis' main death camp in occupied Poland.

Autarky   An economically self-sufficient nation.

Axis forces   Drawn principally from Germany, Italy, and Vichy (unoccupied but pro-German) France.

The axis of evil   Originally used by US President George W. Bush to refer to those countries which he regarded as supporting terrorism or developing weapons of mass destruction – Iran, Iraq and North Korea.

Baathists   Members of a Pan-Arab socialist party which was particularly strong in Syria and Iraq.

Battle of Stalingrad   A savage six-month battle on the Eastern Front in the winter of 1942–43, which ended with a humiliating defeat for the German armies at the hands of the Soviet forces.

Bi-polar   Divided between the two power blocs, the USA and its allies and the USSR and its allies.

Black Germans There were some 25,000 people of African origin living in the Third Reich, descendants of those whose who had come from the German colonies before 1918.

Bolshevik The dominant branch of Russian communism, led by V.I. Lenin, which claimed to be the true interpreter of Marxism and which took power in Russia in the October Revolution of 1917.

Bolshevik Party The Russian Communist Party which had taken power in 1917.

Bourgeois The Marxist term for the controlling middle class who suppress the workers.

Bourgeois stage The period of history when the middle class, having undermined the previous feudal system, dominate society until the working-class revolution occurs.

British Commonwealth In a process that began in 1931, most of the countries of Britain's former empire, on becoming independent, joined together freely as an informal association of sovereign states under the patronage of the British Crown.

Cadres Dedicated Communist Party workers trained to take over as officials in the event of a revolution.

Canonization The conferring of sainthood by the Catholic Church.

Capitalist methods of finance The system in which the owners of private capital (money) increase their wealth by making loans on which they later receive interest.

Cash crop economy Arable farming for financial profit rather than for mere subsistence.

Caudillos Political military leaders, such as Perón.

CCRG A sub-committee of the Politburo which Mao appointed in May 1965 to direct the Cultural Revolution.

CDC (Commonwealth Development Corporation) Created by Britain in 1948 with the aim of financing self-sufficient agriculture and industry in the poorer countries of the Commonwealth.

Central Powers In the First World War, principally Germany, Austria–Hungary and the Ottoman Empire.

Chauvinist Militant ultra-nationalist.

Cheka The All-Russian Extraordinary Commission for Combating Counter-Revolution, later known by such acronyms as OGPU and KGB.

Chiang Kaishek Became leader of the Nationalists on Sun Yatsen's death in 1925; throughout his career Chiang remained resolutely anti-communist.

Church hierarchy Argentina's Catholic bishops who had authority over the clergy and laity.

CIA Central Intelligence Agency – the USA's espionage and counter-espionage organization.

Civil rights movement A powerful movement in the USA in the 1960s and 1970s, which campaigned for full political and economic equality for the country's ethnic minorities.

Cleansing the class ranks A terror campaign to exterminate all those whose social background made them potential enemies of Mao and the communist state.

Cold War The period of political and diplomatic tension, 1945–91, between the capitalist USA and its allies and the communist USSR and its allies.

Collective farms Farms run as co-operatives in which the peasants shared the labour and the wages.

Collective state The nation conceived of as a single social unit rather than a set of individuals.

Collectivism A system based on the idea that individuals must subordinate their private interests to those of society as a whole.

Collectivization Depriving the peasants of their land and requiring them to live and work in communes.

Colonial Secretary The British minister principally responsible for negotiating with Tanganyika over independence.

Colonialism The takeover by European powers of territories whose people were too weak militarily to prevent their political and economic subjugation.

Columbia One of the most northerly of the South American countries, the Colombian Republic underwent a period of bloody political conflict in the 1940s and 1950s, known as 'the Violence'.

Comintern The Communist International, formed in 1919 in Moscow to organize worldwide revolution. The Comintern took a particular interest in China, believing that it could impose itself on the young CCI

Commercial agreement Signed between the USSR and Cuba in February 1960, according to which the Soviet Union was to buy the bulk of the island's sugar crop in return for selling oil and industrial machinery to Cuba.

Communalism A form of society based on common ownership of property and sharing of resources.

Communes Collective farms.

Communism The revolutionary theories advanced by Karl Marx, who interpreted history as class struggle and called upon the working classes to overthrow their oppressors and create a workers' state.

Concentration camps Originally detention centres where anti-Nazis were held, they developed into a widespread prison network which became notorious for the barbarity with which inmates were treated.

Concordat An agreement between the Papacy and Nazi government signed in July 1933.

Confessional Church Established by Martin Niemöller in 1934 as a protest against the Nazi takeover of the Lutheran Church.

Confucianism A system of ethics, based on the teachings of Confucius (551–479 BC), which emphasized the need for people to be obedient to higher authority in order to preserve social harmony.

Congress The US parliament, made up of the Senate and the House of Representatives.

Conjugal visits Visiting time set aside in Chinese communes for couples to have sex.

Conservatoire A specialist music college.

Constitutional monarchy A system in which a monarch, though formally head of state, has no personal power or authority except that consented to by parliament.

Cordobazo A violent rising in the Argentinian city of Cordoba in May 1969.

Corporate state A society whose various economic and social elements are integrated and controlled by the central government.

Corrective labour A euphemism for enforced work in harsh conditions to oblige the victim to acknowledge his former mistakes.

Council of Ministers A governing Cabinet.

CPSU Communist Party of the Soviet Union.

Criminal libel Publishing false and seditious statements against the authorities.

Cuban *émigrés* Anti-Castro elements who had fled the island after the 1959 revolution.

Cult of personality A consistent use of mass propaganda to promote the idea of the leader as an ideal, heroic figure; elevated above ordinary people and politics.

Cult status A position that entitles the holder to a special veneration among the people and puts him or her beyond criticism.

Dachau Germany's first concentration camp, opened in 1933.

Death's Head Division An SS unit which took its name from the skull and crossbones emblem its members wore on their caps.

Decree Against Terrorist Acts An order giving the NKVD limitless powers in pursuing the enemies of the Soviet state and the Communist Party.

Defectives The Nazi term for those regarded as suffering from incapacitating physical or mental disorders.

Democratic centralism The notion, first advanced by Lenin, that true democracy lies in party members' obedience to enlightened leadership.

Desacato Contempt – a legal restriction which was placed on opinions of which Perón's government disapproved.

Descamisados 'The shirtless ones', a term first used pejoratively by the upper class to describe Argentina's manual workers. Eva Perón's application of the word to the workers and the poor of Argentina, turned it into a term of respect rather than abuse.

Developing world (sometimes 'Third World') Nations with limited financial resources, low industrial growth rates and poor living standards.

DGI Dirección General de Inteligencia (General Directorate of Intelligence) – an internal security agency, concerned with enforcing conformity within Cuba. It was especially active as an anti-US spy network.

Diktat An imposed settlement.

The dialectic The dynamic force that drives history along a predestined path.

'Disappeared' A term that came into common use to describe how authoritarian regimes simply removed people they disapproved of without leaving any trace or offering any explanation. The logical deduction was that the 'disappeared' were killed by the regime.

DNB *Deutsches Nachrichtenbüro* – German newspaper bureau.

Dominican Republic The Dominican Republic in the Caribbean had been led for two decades up to

1952 by Trujillo, who gained a fearsome name for the ferocity with which he suppressed political opposition.

DORA The British Defence of the Realm Act, which restricted civil freedoms by suspending traditional legal procedures and granted the government a range of powers over its citizens, including direction of labour.

Eastern bloc The countries of central and eastern Europe which were dominated by the Soviet Union between the late 1940s and late 1980s.

Eher Verlag A publishing house named after its founder Franz Eher, which the Nazis had bought in the 1920s.

Emperor Hirohito Reigned in Japan 1926–89, considered by some historians to be the driving force behind Japanese imperialism.

Enabling Bill A measure which granted the German Chancellor the power to govern by personal decree without reference to the Reichstag.

Enlightenment A flowering in the eighteenth century of new political, philosophical and social ideas about the nature of society and the individual. Key elements were the promotion of the rights of the individual and emphasis on the power of applied reason to solve society's problems.

Escambray A mountain range in central Cuba.

Estancieros Owners of the *estancias,* the great landed estates in Argentina.

Estates-General A French Assembly made up of 'the three orders' – aristocracy, clergy and commons – which gathered in 1789. The assertion by the commons that they alone were the sovereign authority was a critical stage in the development of the French Revolution.

Eton One of Britain's most exclusive schools, renowned for the number of politicians and statesmen it produced.

Eugenics The science of breeding human beings for their fitness and intelligence.

Excommunicated Formally dismissed from membership of the Catholic Church.

Extended family Parents, children and relatives, including in-laws.

Fabianism A form of socialism which believed that the institutions of society had to be radically altered, not through revolution but by a more gradual approach involving the education of people to accept the principles of social justice.

Factionalism Open criticism within the CPSU of central orders.

Fascism The ultra-nationalist movement that operated in Italy under Mussolini between 1922 and 1943. The term came generally to be used to describe extreme Right-wing regimes and ideas.

Fascist In strict terms, the word applies specifically to Italy's ultra-nationalist Fascist Party whose symbol was a bundle of rods (*fasces* in Latin), representing power and authority, but the term became used generally to describe Right-wing regimes of the twentieth century.

Faute de mieux In the absence of a better alternative.

Fedayeen The term referred to Egyptian civilians who in the 1940s volunteered to fight against the British occupation of the Suez Canal Zone.

Feddans A traditional measure of approximately one acre or half a hectare of land.

Feminists Supporters of the principle of full female equality with men.

Feudal A hierarchical system in which power is in the hands of an absolute ruler who distributes land and positions in return for obligatory civil or military duties being performed.

Feudalism A system in which privileged landowners oblige the landless to work for them.

Final Solution The Nazi euphemism for the extermination of the Jews.

First World War (1914–18) Fought mainly between the Central Powers (Germany and Austria–Hungary) and the Entente Powers (France, Britain and Russia).

Five-Year Plan A programme for industrial development based on a set of production quotas.

Freikorps German paramilitary units of demobbed soldiers.

FRELIMO 'Liberation Front of Mozambique', a guerrilla movement made up of a number of anti-Portuguese resistance groupings.

French Algeria Algeria, part of the French empire, had a large Muslim population, most of whom supported the Algerian independence movement. French forces became involved in a bitter struggle against Algerian nationalists (1954–62).

Führer The 'leader', used informally from 1924 to refer to Hitler and adopted in 1934 as his formal title.

Führer **memorandum**   A document written or authorized by Hitler personally.

Führer **principle**   The notion of Hitler as the faultless leader to whom all Germans owed obedience.

Gang of Four   A group of extreme hardliners drawn from the Chinese Communist Party's Shanghai faction and led by Mao's wife, Jiang Qing.

GATT   General Agreement on Tariffs and Trade, an international body established in 1947 with the aim of making world commerce fairer and more profitable for all concerned by reducing tariffs and removing trade barriers.

Gauleiters   Local Nazi Party secretaries who played a vital role in enforcing Nazi rule in the regions.

GDP   Gross Domestic Product, the annual total value of goods produced and services provided, the standard way of measuring a country's economic strength.

General Confederation of Labour (CGT)   An alliance of Argentinian trade unions, collectively numbering over a third of a million members.

Gestapo   *Geheime Staatspolizei*, special state police in Germany and German-occupied Europe.

Gleichschaltung   Consolidation of authority.

GMD   The Guomindang (People's Party), also known as the Nationalists, a revolutionary party formed in 1905 under Sun Yatsen.

GNP   Gross National Product, the annual total value of goods and services produced by a country at home, added to the profits from its export trade.

Gosplan   The Soviet state economic planning agency.

Governor-General   The official representative of the British government in Tanganyika, who held executive powers.

Great Depression   The international economic recession that started in the USA in 1929 and led to a rapid fall in demand for manufactured goods in all industrial countries, a situation which created high levels of unemployment in the 1930s.

The Great Fatherland War   The term adopted in the Soviet Union to describe the ferocious struggle that began with the German invasion of the USSR in 1941 and concluded with Soviet forces smashing their way into Germany in 1945.

The great helmsman   A reference to Mao's wisdom in guiding the ship of state.

Guatemala   A central American state bordered by Mexico and Belize.

Guerrilla   A style of warfare in which mobile troops, who live off the land, harass the enemy with surprise attacks while avoiding pitched battles.

Gulag   An extensive system of penal colonies spread across the USSR.

Heavy engineering   Large-scale manufactures based on the use of iron and steel.

Heresy   Rejection of the basic political belief on which the movement depends, analogous to the rejection of a basic religious belief.

Hermann Goering   A member of the Nazi Party since its earliest days, he was one of Hitler's most important ministers. At the time of the army scandals in 1938, Goering was chief of the *Luftwaffe* (German air force) and responsible for the Third Reich's economic programme.

Holocaust   The systematic killing by Nazi Germany of 6 million European Jews between 1942 and 1945.

Homo Sovieticus   Perfect proletarian, Soviet man.

Hukou   Internal PRC passport or visa.

Human Rights Watch (HRW)   An international non-governmental organization which monitors and reports on countries which breach human rights.

The Hungarian Uprising   An attempt, in October to November 1956, by the Hungarian communist government to break free of the Soviet Union's control; it was crushed by invading Soviet forces.

Hyper-inflation   Very rapid and destructive fall in the purchasing value of money, causing a rapid drop in the value of the currency and a sharp rise in prices.

Icons   Paintings of Christ and the saints; icons were one of the great achievements of Russian culture.

IMF   International Monetary Fund – a scheme which began operating in 1947 with the aim of preventing nations from becoming insolvent. Member states made deposits into a central fund from which they could draw in time of need.

Imperial powers   Those countries that had developed as colony-owning empires; principally, Russia, Britain, France, Germany, Austria–Hungary and Turkey.

Industrialization   The process of creating a factory-based manufacturing economy.

Infant mortality rate   The number of children who die within eighteen months of birth.

Institute for the Promotion of Argentine Commerce (IAPI)   A state-controlled organization empowered to use government funds to promote Argentina's trade.

Intellectuals   A term stretched in the PRC to encompass all those whose way of life or work was judged to have given them privileges denied to the people.

Intelligentsia   Persons of influence in the intellectual world; for example, academics and writers.

International Development Association (IDA)   Created in 1960 and funded by the USA, it aimed to reduce poverty in the poorest countries by providing them with grants to stimulate economic growth.

Ipso facto   By that very fact.

ISI   Import Substituting Industrialization – replacing imported goods with home-produced commodities in Argentina.

Jahiliyya   A state that has rejected Allah.

Jehovah's Witnesses   A Christian religious sect whose beliefs included the notion that, since the secular state was corrupt, its laws did not need to be obeyed, a view that offended the authorities.

Jihad   An Islamic term meaning a committed struggle of believers against unbelievers.

Junta   Government by military generals.

Justicialismo   A Perónist system said to rest on three fundamental principles: social justice, autarky and national sovereignty.

Konsomol   The Soviet Communist Union of Youth.

KPD   *Kommunistische Partei Deutschlands* (German Communist Party).

Kraft durch Freude **(KDF)**   The Nazi 'Strength through Joy' movement.

Kremlin   A commonly used term referring to the Soviet government, which was located in the Kremlin fortress in Moscow, the USSR's capital.

Kristallnacht   The Night of [Breaking] Glass.

kWh   Kilowatt hours, the main measurement of electrical output.

La Prensa   'The Press' – a widely circulating newspaper that claimed to represent ordinary Argentinians.

La Semana Trágica   The 'week of tragedy' in January 1919 when nationalist gangs roamed the streets of Buenos Aires, beating up foreigners, the main targets being Jews and communists.

Labour camps   Prisons and detention centres in which the inmates are required to perform heavy work in the toughest conditions.

Labour unions   Organized bodies representing such groups as the sugar and tobacco workers in Cuba.

Laogai   The term, which means 're-education through labour', came to be used to describe the extensive prison-camp system which operated under Mao.

Latifundias   The Cuban landowners' great estates.

Latin America   South American countries which historically had been settled or controlled by Spain or Portugal.

League of Nations   The international body created in 1919 with the aim of peacefully resolving disputes between nations.

Leftists   Bolshevik Party members who wanted NEP abandoned.

Legislative Council   Established in Tanganyika in 1926 as a supposedly national representative body but, by 1958, containing only European and Asian members.

Liberal-based programmes   In the UK, between 1945 and 1951, the Labour government implemented a welfare-state programme based on ideas originally advanced by the Liberals.

Liberal-democracy   Descriptive of states which function according to the principles of individual freedom and equality and operate systems under which governments can be removed at elections.

Liberated   The CCP's term for the areas brought under their control and from which they drove out the landlords.

Libertarian   Belief in the need to guard individuals and institutions from excessive government control.

Life expectancy   The age to which an individual was likely to live from birth or a given age.

Light engineering   Skilled, specialized activities such as precision tool-making.

Loess   A type of soil that can be dug into easily and shaped but still remains firm.

Lower middle class   Shopkeepers, traders, professional people, etc.

Lusaka Manifesto   A communiqué condemning racism, presented by Kaunda and Nyerere at the

Conference of East and Central African States in April 1969, and signed by all the heads of state attending.

Mafia An underworld crime syndicate, particularly strong in Florida.

Majority rule The right of the largest group to have the largest representation in government.

Mandate An authority granted by the League of Nations to certain countries to monitor and protect the interests of particular states and regions created at the end of the First World War.

Maoism The identification of Chinese communism with Mao personally.

Marshall Plan A plan adopted by the USA in 1947 under which it offered to provide substantial amounts of dollars to any country willing to grant trade concessions to the United States in return.

Marshals of the Soviet Union Highest ranking military officers.

Martin Bormann Nazi Party Secretary.

Marxism/Marxist Relating to the ideas of Karl Marx, a German revolutionary, who had advanced the notion that human society developed historically as a continuous series of class struggles between those who possessed economic and political power and those who did not. He taught that the culmination of this dialectical process would be the crushing victory of the proletariat over the bourgeoisie.

Marxism–Leninism The revolutionary theories of class war as advanced by Karl Marx and later developed by Lenin.

May Day Or 'Labour Day' – 1 May, traditionally regarded as a special day for honouring the workers and the achievements of socialism.

Metaphysical union A bond between leader and people that goes beyond mere political considerations and suggests an affinity of feeling and respect.

Middle East Never an exact term, it includes such countries as Libya, Egypt, Turkey, Israel, Palestine, Syria, Jordan, Saudi Arabia, Iraq and Iran. Objections are sometimes raised to the use of the term on the grounds that it perpetuates the language of colonialism.

Missionaries Usually religious orders of priests and nuns who sought to spread their Christian message by founding and running schools and hospitals.

Mixed-race persons Those with one black and one white parent.

Modernization The movement of a nation from a rural, agricultural society to an urban, industrial one.

Monopoly capitalism A system in which the state interferes with the working of the economy in order to protect large commercial and industrial interests from competition from smaller concerns.

Monroe Doctrine A warning given by President Monroe in 1823 that the USA would not allow other powers to colonize or interfere in any part of the Americas, and would regard itself as the protector of the region.

Montoneros Formed in 1970 in the wake of the *cordobazo*, they were an extreme Left-wing Perónist group who believed in waging urban guerrilla warfare; arson and assassination were among their preferred methods.

National Assembly The Cuban National Assembly of People's Power, a parliament of 614 members elected every five years.

National People's Congress The elected body drawn from members of the CCP and from which members of the Politiburo and State Council were appointed.

National service A period of compulsory military training.

National Union A title deliberately chosen by the RCC as representing Egypt itself. To oppose it, therefore, was to be anti-Egyptian. It had originally been called Liberation Rally.

Nationalism A devotion to the interests and culture of one's nation, often leading to the belief that certain nationalities are superior to others.

Nazism The National Socialist movement that dominated Germany between 1933 and 1945.

Nazi–Soviet Pact A ten-year non-aggression agreement signed in 1939 between the Third Reich and the USSR.

Nehru The first leader (1947–64) of independent India after Britain's withdrawal.

Neo-colonialism An attempt by the former colonial powers to re-impose their control on their previous possessions.

Neopatriarchal A new form of male domination.

NEP The New Economic Policy, which permitted the Soviet peasants to return to farming for private profit.

Nepmen A derisive term for the profiteers who had supposedly exploited the commercial freedoms allowed under NEP in order to enrich themselves.

Nepotism The granting of positions and privileges to family members or close associates.

New Deal A set of programmes introduced by President Franklin D. Roosevelt's administration to tackle the economic depression which afflicted the USA in the 1930s.

NKVD The People's Commissariat of Internal Affairs, the Soviet secret police.

Nomenklatura The Soviet 'establishment' – privileged officials who ran the Party and government.

Non-aligned movement (NAM) An organization started in 1953, composed of countries which did not wish to support either of the Cold War blocs.

NSDAP National Socialist German Workers' Party (Nazi Party).

Nubians A group of people living in southern Egypt and northern Sudan with a distinct culture, language and history.

Nuclear family Two parents and their children, considered as a unit.

OAU The Organization of African Unity, founded in 1963, with essentially the same objectives as PAC.

Occupied Europe The areas overrun by German forces between 1939 and 1942 which were then placed under German administration and control.

October Revolution The seizure by the Bolsheviks of power in October 1917 from the interim Provisional Government that had led Russia since the abdication of the monarchy in February 1917.

OGPU Succeeded the *Cheka* as the Soviet state security force. In turn it became the NKVD and then the KGB.

Orgburo The Soviet Organizational Bureau of the Secretariat responsible for turning the government's executive decisions and policies into practice.

PAC Pan-African Congress, founded in 1900 to campaign for African freedom from colonial rule.

Packets Special benefits, such as villas and cars.

Pan-Arabism A trans-national movement for the unification of the Arab peoples in order to pursue their common interests and improve their conditions.

Paramount chief The formal title given by British administrators to an African tribal leader who was recognized and respected by the tribe's members as having legitimate authority over them.

Paris Peace Conference The gathering which drew up the Treaty of Versailles, 1919, which, with other peace treaties after the First World War, reshaped much of the post-war world.

Partido Ortodoxo Literally 'Orthodox Party', better translated as 'People's Party', which Castro joined in the late 1940s.

Party card The official CPSU warrant granting membership and privileges to the holder. It was a prized possession in the Soviet Union.

Pastoral letters Formal addresses from the bishops read out to the people attending Sunday mass.

Patriarchal Male-dominated.

Patriotic League An Argentinian nationalist group created to fight the immigrant organizations responsible, so the League claimed, for the strikes and industrial unrest and for bringing communism into the country.

Patronage Providing government approval and support and extending privileges to selected individuals and groups.

Perónists Supporters of Perón and Perónism.

Pharaoh The absolute ruler in ancient Egypt.

PLA China's People's Liberation Army, formerly the Red Army.

Platt Amendments Named after Senator Orville Platt, who introduced them into the US Congress in 1901, the amendments became the basis of what was, in effect, a binding treaty between Cuba and the USA.

PLO Palestinian Liberation Organization, formed in 1964 under Egyptian auspices and pledged to 'prohibit the existence of Zionism' through the use of terror tactics against Israeli targets.

Polaris A nuclear-armed missile.

Politburo An inner core of some twenty leading members of the Communist Party.

Populist A form of politics that seeks to create a direct relationship between the leader and the people, based on the idea that the leader has a special understanding of the people's needs.

PR Proportional representation, the allocation of seats according to the number of votes cast for each party.

Premier Soviet Chairman of the Council of Commissars.

Presumption of guilt A reversal of the principle common in most legal systems that the accused is innocent until proved guilty.

Proletariat The revolutionary working class destined, in Marxist revolutionary theory, to achieve ultimate triumph in the class war.

Prophets Individuals endowed with divine insight, as honoured in the three main monotheistic (belief in one God) religions: Judaism, Christianity and Islam.

Protectorate An area not formally taken over as a colony but still under protective jurisdiction.

Providence The notion that fate is predetermined by the force of history.

Purges A system of terror used by Lenin and Stalin in the USSR and Mao in China for removing anyone regarded as a threat to their authority.

Putschista Someone willing to engage in violent struggle but lacking a true understanding of the revolutionary process.

Qur'an (also Koran) The holy book of Islam, believed by Muslims to be the word of Allah as revealed to the Prophet Muhammad.

Radical Change at the very roots.

Radical Civic Union A conservative group, to which many businessmen belonged, formed in opposition to Perón.

Reactionaries CCP members who had lost faith in the revolution.

Reactionary Fiercely resistant to change.

Reactive pragmatism Responding to events as they occur rather than working to a prescribed plan.

Real wages Earnings measured not by their nominal value but by their purchasing power.

Rectification A revitalizing of the Cuban revolution by the correction of past errors.

Red Army The Bolshevik defence forces; the title was also adopted by the Chinese Communist forces.

Red Guards Units of young people, specially trained by Kang Sheng, the head of Mao's secret police, to act as terror squads.

Reich The German word for 'empire'. There were three Germanic empires, the First (962–1806), the Second (1871–1918) and the Third (1933–45).

Reichsbank The German state bank.

'Reunification' campaigns The Chinese government's euphemism for forcibly bringing the invaded provinces into line in 1950.

Revelation The disclosing of eternal truths.

Revisionism Departure from true communism, a blanket term applied to any idea of which Mao disapproved.

Revisionist Reactionary, anti-Party thinking.

Revolutionary correctness The idea that Chinese communism (Maoism) was a body of political, social and economic truth, as defined by Mao, which all CCP members had to accept.

Rightists Bolshevik Party and CCP members who argued for a slower, less violent development of revolution and for the continuation of the NEP.

Robert Ley Director of the Nazi German Labour Front.

Roca-Runciman Agreement Agreement between Britain and Argentina in 1933 under which Britain gave preferential treatment to Argentina's meat exports in return for Argentina's increasing its imports of British products.

Rogers Plan A proposal put forward in December 1969 by William Rogers, the US Secretary of State, for an Arab–Israeli cease-fire.

Routinization of Fidel Castro's charisma A process which, by constant emphasis, created a common outlook among the Cuban people that Castro's gifts as leader were the standard by which to judge all other politicians.

SA *Sturmabteilung* ('storm troopers'): Hitler's paramilitary force.

Sacrilege Degrading of something sacred.

Scapegoat A sacrificial victim on whom blame for misfortune is placed.

Schwartz Kapelle The 'Black Organization', a Gestapo designation for those on the political Right who were suspected of being anti-Hitler.

The scramble for Africa During the period 1870–1914, the major European powers vied with each other in colonizing various parts of Africa.

Second World War Fought between the Allies (principally Britain, China, USSR and the USA) and the Axis powers (principally Germany, Italy and Japan) 1939–45.

Secular state A nation that does not allow religion a defining or central place in its structure.

Self-determination The right of peoples to be free of domination by an outside power and to form a nation and government of their own choice.

Seminaries Training colleges for priests.

Show trials Special public court hearings, meant as propaganda exercises, in which the accused were paraded as enemies of the people.

Siegfried A legendary knight, regarded as representing the Germanic ideal.

Sierra Cristal A mountain range in northern Cuba.

Sierra Maestra A mountain range running across the province of Oriente in eastern Cuba.

Sino A prefix meaning Chinese.

Sisal A fibre that can be cultivated and processed into rope and twine.

Social justice A system in which the law operates to create equal rights for all and prevent exploitation of the weak by the powerful.

Social realism Representational work which related directly to the lives of the people.

Socialism Capable of taking many forms, it is essentially concerned with the structuring of society and the economy through government action to meet the needs of the people.

Southern Rhodesia A British colony 1923–64, became Rhodesia in 1964, and Zimbabwe in 1980.

Soviet Bolshevik/Communist-dominated worker–soldier local councils. In China, the term described a communist community dedicated to the practical application of Marxist egalitarian principles.

Soviet bloc The USSR and the countries of eastern Europe which it dominated, 1945–49.

Soviet Union of Writers The body which had authority over all published writers and had the right to ban any work of which it disapproved.

SRs Socialist Revolutionaries, the largest of the revolutionary parties in Russia until outlawed by the Bolsheviks after 1917.

SS Nazi *Schutzstaffeln* (protective squads).

Staple Basic crop or commodity on which an economy relies.

State Department The USA's foreign ministry.

State procurements Enforced collections of grain from the peasants in the USSR.

Straits of Tiran The narrow seven-mile (11 km) sea passage between the Sinai and Arabian peninsulas.

Struggle sessions A method for breaking victims' resistance by forcing them to engage in intense self-criticism until they confessed their guilt.

Subsidiary companies Businesses that operate separately in particular areas, often under a different name, but ultimately under the control of a parent company.

Sudan Since 1899, Sudan had been jointly governed by Britain and Egypt as the Anglo-Egyptian Sudan. Nasser regarded Egypt's losing Sudan to be the necessary price for both countries' becoming independent from Britain.

Suez Canal The vital waterway linking the Mediterranean and the Red Sea, thus shortening the distance between Britain and its colonies and trading centres in Asia, east and southern Africa, and Oceania.

Suffrage The right to vote.

Sun Yatsen (1866–1925) The Chinese revolutionary who founded the Chinese Republic in the early twentieth century.

Syndicates State-controlled worker organizations in Argentina.

Tanganyika The large mainland area of what became Tanzania, when the neighbouring island of Zanzibar was incorporated in 1964.

Tango A traditional, stylized, erotic Argentinian dance, said to be the vertical expression of a horizontal desire.

TANZAM Tanzania–Zambia railway.

Teutonic Relating to peoples of Germanic origin, interchangeable as a term with Aryan.

The Whites Tsarists and anti-Bolsheviks.

Third Way An approach that avoids the extremes of communism and capitalism.

Tito The communist leader of Yugoslavia who successfully defied Soviet control.

Total theatre An approach which sought to break down the barriers between actors and audience by novel use of lighting, sound and stage settings.

Triple A The Argentine Anti-communist Alliance.

Triptych A painting made up of three separate panels, hinged together.

Triumvirate A ruling or influential bloc of three persons.

Trusteeship The new United Nations organization which took over from the old League of Nations body which had administered the mandates (renamed trusts

Tsarist Russia   A centuries-old autocratic state, lacking genuinely democratic institutions.

Tsars   The traditional absolute rulers of imperial Russia.

Uighur, Kazakh, Hui and Kirghiz peoples   Ethnic groups, which in regard to race, culture, language and religion were markedly distinct from the Han people who made up over 80 per cent of China's population.

Ujamaa   The word in Swahili, Tanzania's national language, for 'familyhood' or community.

UN forces   Military units brought into being by a formal UN Resolution and composed of troops from a number of member states.

UN Security Council   The body established to resolve international disputes and empowered to use force, its permanent members being the USSR, the USA, Britain, France and Nationalist China.

UN's Human Development Index   A system operated by the United Nations from 1990 for measuring the relative economic and social development of individual states.

United Nations   The organization that superseded the League of Nations in 1945, committed to maintaining international security and promoting human rights. It began with 51 member states and was initially dominated by the USA upon whose financial support it depended.

USSR   Union of Soviet Socialist Republics, the name given to communist Russia and states under its control from 1922, also known as the Soviet Union.

Usury   Charging exorbitant interest on money loans.

Varela Project   A Catholic organization calling for political and religious freedom in Cuba.

Vatican The administrative centre of the Roman Catholic Church in Rome.

Veto   Each individual permanent member of the UN Security Council had the right to block the collective or majority decision of the others.

Vietnam War   The USA's failed attempt (1965–73) to defeat the communists in Vietnam, a venture that caused deep divisions at home and damaged the USA's international reputation.

Villagization   The collectivization of the peasantry, based on the programme adopted by Mao Zedong in the PRC, which Nyerere had observed at first hand on his visits to China.

Volk   The nation as a community of racially pure Germans.

Vozhd   Russian for a supreme leader, equivalent to the *Führer* in German.

Wabenzi   The 'Benz people', a pejorative term used to describe Tanzanian officials in mocking reference to their buying luxurious Mercedes-Benz cars.

Wafd   Arabic for 'delegation', suggesting the Party's claim to represent the people.

War Commissars   Soviet ministers responsible for military organization.

Washington   A term commonly used to refer to the US government, which is located in that city.

Wehrmacht (previously the *Reichswehr*)   The German armed services, comprising the army, navy and air force, though the term was often used simply to describe the army.

Weimar   A country town chosen as the new capital and seat of government of Germany in 1919 instead of troubled Berlin.

White *émigrés*   Tsarist supporters who had fled to Germany from Russia after the Russian Revolution.

White Rose   A group opposed to the Nazis, named after the flower as a symbol of peace.

Wilhelmine Germany   The German state during the reigns of Kaiser William I (1871–88) and William II (1888–1918).

Zambia   Formerly Northern Rhodesia.

Zionism   The movement for the creation of a Jewish state; the term is often used to denote Israeli expansionism.

Further reading

Stalin

Books

Sheila Fitzpatrick (ed.), *Stalinism: New Directions*, Routledge, London, 2000
An outstanding modern analyst's collection of key contributions to the debate on Stalinism.

Barry McLoughlin and Kevin McDermott, *Stalin's Terror: High Politics and Mass Repression in the Soviet Union*, Palgrave, London, 2003
A detailed study of the Stalinist purges, the motives behind them and those involved in implementing them.

Simon Sebag Montefiore, *Stalin: The Court of the Red Tsar*, Weidenfeld & Nicolson, London, 2004
A fascinating account of how Stalin ran his government, dominating his ministers and officials and reducing them to frightened sycophants eager to carry out his will.

Robert Service, *Stalin: A Biography*, Macmillan, London, 2004
A lively analysis of Stalin's character and actions by a leading Western authority on Soviet history.

Robert Tucker, *Stalinism: Essays in Historical Interpretation*, Norton, New York, 1999
A particularly valuable analysis of the Stalinist system and how it has been interpreted by Russian and Western scholars.

Dmitri Volkogonov, *Stalin: Triumph and Tragedy*, Weidenfeld & Nicholson, London 1991
Special insights provided by a Soviet scholar, who lived and worked in the USSR under Stalin.

Websites

www.marxists.org/history/ussr/text-index.htm
Soviet History Archive: a rich set of sources covering politics, economics, foreign affairs and culture. 177 pieces of documentary footage of the Soviet Union under Stalin.

Hitler

Books

Michael Burleigh, *The Third Reich: A New History*, Macmillan, London, 2000
Taking as its theme the notion of National Socialism as a secular religion, the book is particularly impressive in its treatment of Nazi propaganda and the Hitler cult.

Joachim Fest, *Hitler*, Penguin, London, 1977
An important biography by a German writer concerned to place Hitler in his historical context as a particular product of German history.

Robert Gellately, *Lenin, Stalin and Hitler: The Age of Social Catastrophe*, Jonathan Cape, London, 2007
An especially helpful study that puts Hitler's dictatorship in context by comparing him with his great Soviet rivals.

Ian Kershaw, *Hitler 1889–1936: Hubris* and *Hitler 1936–45: Nemesis*, Allen Lane, London, 1998 and 2000
A vast two-volume study, but well worth dipping into since it is written by a scholar acknowledged as the world's greatest authority on Hitler.

Michael Lynch, *Hitler*, Routledge, London, 2013
An up-to-date biography that incorporates many of the latest findings on Hitler and Nazi Germany.

Richard Overy, *The Dictators: Hitler's Germany and Stalin's Russia*, Allen Lane, London, 2004
An important book that analyses the character of Hitler's regime by comparing it with Stalin's.

DVD

BBC TV series, 1997: *The Nazis: A Warning from History*

Website

www.hitler.org
Hitler Historical Museum: contains a large selection of writings, speeches, images and posters.

Mao

Books

Gregor Benton and Lin Chun (eds) *Was Mao Really a Monster?*, Routledge, London, 2010
An important collection of articles which, by mounting a strong critique of Jung Chang's methodology, seeks to present a balanced assessment of Mao's impact on China.

Jung Chang and Jon Halliday, *Mao: The Unknown Story*, Jonathan Cape, London, 2005
A strongly committed and very readable account of Mao's policies, but criticized by other historians for its heavy bias against Mao.

Timothy Cheek (ed.) *A Critical Introduction to Mao*, Cambridge University Press, Cambridge, 2010
Fourteen of the world's leading authorities on Mao contribute to a set of essays, covering his ideas, policies and legacy and examining the historiography that has developed around him.

Frank Dikötter, *Mao's Great Famine: The History of China's Most Devastating Catastrophe, 1958–62*, Bloomsbury, London, 2010
A harrowing account of the disastrous results of Mao's Great Leap Forward.

Michael Lynch, *Mao*, Routledge, London, 2004
A combination of narrative and analysis, written with students in mind.

Roderick MacFarquhar and Michael Schoenhals, *Mao's Last Revolution*, Belknap Press, 2006
An important book that traces the origins, course and consequences of Mao's extraordinary attempt to leave his permanent mark on the revolutionary China he had created.

Jonathan Spence, *The Search for Modern China*, Norton, New York, USA, 1990
The classic account of Mao and his times by the leading Western authority on China's modern history.

Websites
www.youtube.com/watch?v=TfJy_wduFy4
BBC 20th Century History File: *Mao's China – One Man's Revolution.*

http://chineseposters.net/themes/mao-cult.php
Collection of propaganda posters in Mao's PRC.

Nasser

Books
Saïd K. Aburish, *Nasser: The Last Arab*, Duckworth, London, 2005
An Arab scholar's sympathetic treatment of Egypt's great modernizer.

Guy Arnold, *Africa: A Modern History*, Atlantic Books, London, 2005
A major study which sets Nasser's Egypt in the context of African development.

Steven A. Cook, *The Struggle for Egypt: From Nasser to Tahrir Square*, Oxford University Press, Oxford, 2012
An up-to-date account of Nasser's achievements and his lasting influence on Egypt.

Jean Lacouture, *Nasser*, Secker & Warburg, London, 1973
A compelling biography by a French writer who was eyewitness to much of what he describes.

Anthony Nutting, *Nasser*, Constable, London, 1972
An interesting mixture of criticism and praise of Nasser's regime by someone who knew Nasser personally.

Abdel Magid Farid, *Nasser: The Final Years*, Ithaca Press, Reading, 1994
Thought-provoking reflections on the legacy left by Nasser to Egypt and the Arab world.

DVD
Feature film, 2007: *Six Days in June: The War that Redefined the Middle East.*

Websites
http://avalon.law.yale.edu/subject_menus/mideast.asp
The Middle East 1916–2001: A Documentary Record. Contains the key documents dealing with Egypt, Palestine and Israel.

www.youtube.com/watch?v=LqG6UyTsEOI
The Life and Death of Gamal Abdel Nasser. A documentary film made in 1971.

Castro

Books

Leycester Coltman and Julia Sweig, *The Real Fidel*, Yale University Press, New Haven, 2003
A rounded and balanced study of Castro's leadership of the Cubans, written by a British diplomat who knew Castro personally.

Jorge Dominguez, *Cuba: Order and Revolution*, Belknap Press, Harvard, 1978
A very useful reference book with graphs and tables illustrating the narrative that deals with the early years of Castro's regime.

Clive Foss, *Fidel Castro*, Sutton Publishing, Stroud, 2000
An excellent short introduction to the main features of Castro's career and achievements.

Richard Gott, *Cuba: A New History*, Yale University Press, New Haven, 2004
A sympathetic and stimulating study of Castro by a committed Left-wing British writer.

Robert E. Quirk, *Fidel Castro*, Norton, New York, 1993
A detailed study of Castro that pays particular attention to his relations with the USA and the Soviet Union.

Simon Reid-Henry, *Fidel and Che: A Revolutionary Friendship*, Sceptre Books, London, 2009
A long but highly readable account of one of the great formative relationships in Castro's career as a revolutionary.

Websites

www.fordham.edu/halsalt/mod/modsbook.asp
Fordham University's Internet Modern History Sourcebook. A very valuable source having sections devoted to Castro's Cuba (and all the regimes covered in this book).

www.marxists.org/history/cuba/archive/index.htm
Cuba government documents: contains important documents on Castro and Guevara.

http://mssa.library.yale.edu/findaids
Guide to the Cuban Revolution Collection, Manuscripts and Archives, Yale University Library: an important set of documents on Castro and the Cuban Revolution.

Perón

Books

Robert D. Crassweller, *Perón and the Enigma of Argentina*, Norton, New York, 1988
Examines both Perón as a leader and Perónism as a movement that existed independently of Perón.

Clive Foss, *Juan and Eva Perón*, Sutton, Stroud, 2006
A short but very readable analysis of the importance of Eva Perón to the Perónist regime.

Jill Hedges, *Argentina: A Modern History*, I.B. Tauris, New York, 2011
An up-to-date work that traces Argentina's development since the 1850s, paying particular attention to the Perón period.

Douglas Madsen and Peter G. Snow, *The Charismatic Bond: Political Behaviour in Time of Crisis*, Harvard University Press, Cambridge, Mass.,1996
Examines Perónism as a cult and analyses the character of Perón's popularity as leader of Argentina.

Joseph Page, *Perón, a Biography*, Random House, New York, 1983
This long biography takes a sympathetic view of its subject and, while not always an easy read, provides many striking insights into Perón's leadership.

Robert A. Potash, *The Army and Politics in Argentina, 1945–1962*, Athlone Press, London, 1980
A study of Argentina under Perón, focusing on the vital relationship between him and the armed services.

David Rock, *Authoritarian Argentina*, University of California Press, Berkeley, 1993
A work that places Perón and Perónism in the context of Argentinian nationalism.

Websites

www.casahistoria.net/peron.htm
Argentina and the Peróns: a wide range of documents covering all the main features of Perón's regime.

www.marxists.org/history/argentina.htm
History of the Left in Argentina: a wide selection of documents illustrating the Left-wing movements in Perón's time.

Nyerere

Books

Guy Arnold, *Africa: A Modern History*, Atlantic Books, London, 2005
A large and very reliable study of Africa, containing many informative sections on Nyerere and Tanzania.

Chambi Chachage and Annar Cassam, *Africa's Liberation: The Legacy of Nyerere*, Pambazuka Press, Kampala, Uganda, 2010
A collection of seventeen short essays by a range of African scholars dealing sympathetically with all the major aspects of Nyerere's leadership of Tanzania.

John Hatch, *Two African Statesmen*, Secker & Warburg, London, 1976
A comparative study of the leadership styles and achievements of Nyerere and Kenneth Kaunda, President of Zambia.

Michael Hodd (ed.) *Tanzania After Nyerere*, Pinter Publishers, London, 1988
Twenty studies by Western and African contributors, dealing with the political, economic and social issues that confronted Nyerere.

Godfrey Mwakikagile, *Nyerere and Africa: End of an Era. Biography of Julius Kambarage Nyerere (1922–1999) President of Tanzania*, Protea Publishing, Atlanta, Georgia, 2002
A basically sympathetic study of Nyerere and his policies.

Ludovik S. Mwijage, *Julius K Nyerere: Servant of God or Untarnished Tyrant?*, Wisdom House Books, Chapel Hill, North Carolina, 1994
Written by a Tanzanian dissident who was imprisoned by Nyerere's government, this book concentrates on the repressive aspects of the regime that Nyerere operated.

Websites

www.juliusnyerere.info/index.php/media/videos
Audio and video recordings of Nyerere during his time as leader.

www.juliusnyerere.info/index.php/resources
A collection of Nyerere's speeches and writings.

Internal assessment

The internal assessment is a historical investigation on a historical topic. Below is a list of possible topics that could warrant further investigation. They have been organized by theme.

Stalin

1. To what extent did Stalin control the Soviet Union's government by 1928?
2. How different were Stalin's views on international communism from Trotsky's views?
3. For what reasons and with what results did the Russian Orthodox Church endure persecution during Stalin's rule up to 1941?
4. How did communist rule affect Russia's Hermitage Palace in Leningrad between 1917 and 1941?
5. To what extent did the university curriculum change within the Soviet Union from 1924 to 1941?

Hitler

1. What was the importance of *Mein Kampf* for Hitler's foreign policy according to historian Richard Overy?
2. How were female teachers affected by the government's education policies between 1933 and 1939 in Germany?
3. To what extent did *Gleischaltung* merge provincial and national governments?
4. How did the US government's foreign policy alter towards Germany from 1933 to 1939?
5. How did the German government's use of propaganda differ from its use by the French government between 1933 and 1939?

Mao

1. What was the importance of the Soviet Union for the People's Republic of China during the Korean War, 1950 to 1953?
2. To what extent were Muslims treated differently to Tibetan Buddhists in the People's Republic of China during the Cultural Revolution?
3. To what extent did the Great Leap Forward affect the north and south of the People's Republic of China differently?
4. What was the role of government corruption in causing the Cultural Revolution?
5. For what reasons and with what results did the People's Republic of China and India battle over their mutual borders before 1976?

Nasser

1. How consistent was Nasser's foreign policy towards Britain between 1954 and 1970?
2. What was the significance of the Aswan High Dam for Egypt up to 1970?
3. To what extent were Egyptian Greeks affected by Nasser's economic policies?
4. Why did Nasser involve Egypt in Yemen in the 1960s?
5. How were the arts in Egypt affected by the military-established government between 1952 and 1980?

Castro

1. How did Castro's foreign policy towards France differ from his foreign policy towards Italy between 1962 and 2000?
2. What was the effect of the US economic embargo on Cuba's tourist industry between 1962 and 2000?
3. To what extent did school curricula change in Cuba from Batista's overthrow until 1980?
4. Why did Cuba become involved in the conflict in Angola between 1975 and 1991?
5. How successful was Castro in creating a communist society in Cuba by 1970?

Perón

1. To what extent were the visual arts affected by Perón's rule?
2. How did Perón's policies affect European immigration to Argentina between 1946 and 1955?
3. Did Perón's foreign policies towards other South American states differ from those of earlier Argentinian governments?
4. What was the economic effect of Perón's rule on Argentina's beef industry?
5. Why was Perón unable to remove opposition to his rule from Argentina's armed forces?

Nyerere

. How did Tanzania's villagization programme affect neighbouring states?
. To what extent was the standard of living of people living in Zanzibar different from those living on Tanzania's mainland during Nyerere's rule?
. For what reasons and with what results did Tanzania become involved in a conflict with Uganda in 1978 and 1979?
. How was the city of Dar es Salam affected architecturally by Nyerere's rule?
. To what extent was tribal cohesion affected by Nyerere's political policies?

Index